Praise for

SUPERGODS

"*Supergods* is a maniacally enthusiastic stream-of-consciousness narrative, seventy years of superhero history with erudite analysis and autobiography thrown in—an account of what it's like to plunge your brain into these fictional universes for decades, refusing to come up for air." —*Rolling Stone*

"The perfect textbook for fanboys and the mainstream alike." —*USA Today*

"An analysis of what superheroes, caped crusaders, and masked men can tell us about ourselves and our culture . . . fascinating." —*Entertainment Weekly*

"A personal and erudite history of the medium by one of its most intelligent and articulate practitioners . . . Morrison lays out the history of comics with infectious passion and amusement." —*Financial Times*

"*Supergods* is an enjoyable read for both rabid comic book fans who want to take a trip down memory lane and casual readers who want to understand how these colorful, sometimes crude books offer us a glimpse at how far we've come as a society." —*BookPage*

"Morrison provides an examination of the superhero phenomenon that is at once a well-researched history, an entertaining memoir, intriguing cosmological analysis, and a surprising personal revelation that will challenge readers to reevaluate everything they've thought about the writer and his work." —*Memphis Flyer*

"*Supergods* is not just an insider's dissection of American comic books—specifically, the one particular genre that's influenced popular culture for more than seven decades. . . . Morrison has more in mind: Midway through the book, he begins to weave in unexpected memoir passages, and that's precisely when it gets really interesting. . . . The more personal he gets, the more thrilling the book becomes." —*Time Out Chicago*

"Morrison possesses that trick of the best teachers—he shows you how and why he is excited about these ideas, so you get excited by them as well. . . . *Supergods* is a blast, a pure hit of hero worship and deep understanding of comics."

—Statesman

"[Readers] can't help but be charmed by the author's passion for a genre that confronts the bewildering complexities of modern culture by reaching for a pure vision of right and wrong." —*The Arizona Republic*

SPIEGEL & GRAU

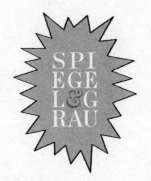

SUPERGODS

SUPERGODS

WHAT MASKED VIGILANTES, MIRACULOUS MUTANTS,
AND A SUN GOD FROM SMALLVILLE CAN
TEACH US ABOUT BEING HUMAN

GRANT MORRISON

SPIEGEL & GRAU
NEW YORK
2012

2012 Spiegel & Grau Trade Paperback Edition

Published in the United States by Spiegel & Grau, an imprint of The Random House Publishing Group, a division of Random House, Inc., New York.

Spiegel & Grau and Design is a registered trademark of Random House, Inc.

Originally published in hardcover in the United States by Spiegel & Grau, an imprint of The Random House Publishing Group, a division of Random House, Inc., in 2011.

ISBN 978-0-8129-8138-4
eBook ISBN 978-0-679-60346-7

Printed in the United States of America

www.spiegelandgrau.com

6 8 9 7

Book design by Christopher M. Zucker

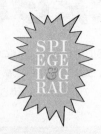

For Kristan, supergoddess

Behold, I teach you the superman: He is this lightning, he is this madness!

—Friedrich Nietzsche, *Thus Spake Zarathustra*

CONTENTS

INTRODUCTION

FOUR MILES ACROSS a placid stretch of water from where I live in Scotland is RNAD Coulport, home of the UK's Trident-missile-armed nuclear submarine force. Here, I've been told, enough firepower is stored in underground bunkers to annihilate the human population of our planet fifty times over. One day, when Earth is ambushed in Hyperspace by fifty Evil Duplicate Earths, this megadestructive capability may, ironically, save us all—but until then, it seems extravagant, somehow emblematic of the accelerated, digital hypersimulation we've all come to inhabit.

At night, the inverted reflection of the submarine dockyards looks like a red, mailed fist, rippling on a flag made of waves. A couple of miles of winding road from here is where my dad was arrested during the antinuclear protest marches of the sixties. He was a working-class World War II veteran who'd swapped his bayonet for a Campaign for Nuclear Disarmament badge and became a pacifist "Spy for Peace" in the Committee of 100. Already the world of my childhood was one of proliferating Cold War acronyms and code names.

And the Bomb, always the Bomb, a grim and looming, raincoated lodger, liable to go off at any minute, killing everybody and everything.

His bastard minstrels were gloomy existentialist folkies whining horn-rimmed dirges about the "Hard Rain" and the "All on That Day" while I trembled in the corner, awaiting bony-fingered judgment and the extinction of all terrestrial life. Accompanying imagery was provided by the radical antiwar samizdat zines my dad brought home from political bookstores on High Street. Typically, the passionate pacifist manifestoes within were illustrated with gruesome hand-drawn images of how the world might look after a spirited thermonuclear missile exchange. The creators of these enthusiastically rendered carrion landscapes never overlooked any opportunity to depict shattered, obliterated skeletons contorted against blazing horizons of nuked and blackened urban devastation. If the artist could find space in his composition for a macabre, eight-hundred-foot-tall Grim Reaper astride a flayed horror horse, sowing missiles like grain across the snaggle-toothed, half-melted skyline, *all* the better.

Like visions of Heaven and Hell on a medieval triptych, the postatomic wastelands of my dad's mags sat side by side with the exotic, triple-sunned vistas that graced the covers of my mum's beloved science fiction paperbacks. Digest-sized windows onto shiny futurity, they offered android amazons in chrome monokinis chasing marooned spacemen beneath the pearlescent skies of impossible alien worlds. Robots burdened with souls lurched through Day-Glo jungles or strode the moving steel walkways of cities designed by Le Corbusier, Frank Lloyd Wright, and LSD. The titles evoked Surrealist poetry: *The Day It Rained Forever, The Man Who Fell to Earth, The Silver Locusts, Flowers for Algernon*, "A Rose for Ecclesiastes," *Barefoot in the Head.*

On television, images of pioneering astronauts vied with bleak scenes from Hiroshima and Vietnam: It was an all-or-nothing choice between the A-Bomb and the Spaceship. I had already picked sides, but the Cold War tension between Apocalypse and Utopia was becoming almost unbearable. And then the superheroes rained down across the Atlantic, in a dazzling prism-light of heraldic jumpsuits, bringing new ways to see and hear and think about everything.

The first comic shop in the UK—The Yankee Book Store—opened in Paisley, home of the pattern, just outside Glasgow in the years after the war. With a keen sense of ironic symmetry, the comics arrived as ballast alongside the US service personnel whose missiles threatened my very existence. As early R&B and rock 'n' roll records sailed into Liverpool to inspire the Mersey generation of musicians, so American comics hit in the west of Scotland, courtesy of the military-industrial complex, to inflame the imaginations and change the lives of kids like me.

The superheroes laughed at the Atom Bomb. Superman could walk on the surface of the sun and barely register a tan. The Hulk's adventures were only just beginning in those fragile hours after a Gamma Bomb test went wrong in the face of his alter ego, Bruce Banner. In the shadow of cosmic destroyers like Anti-Matter Man or Galactus, the all-powerful Bomb seemed provincial in scale. I'd found my way into a separate universe tucked inside our own, a place where dramas spanning decades and galaxies were played out across the second dimension of newsprint pages. Here men, women, and noble monsters dressed in flags and struck from shadows to make the world a better place. My own world felt better already. I was beginning to understand something that gave me power over my fears.

Before it was a Bomb, the Bomb was an Idea.

Superman, however, was a Faster, Stronger, Better Idea.

It's not that I needed Superman to be "real," I just needed him to be more real than the Idea of the Bomb that ravaged my dreams. I needn't have worried; Superman is so indefatigable a product of the human imagination, such a perfectly designed emblem of our highest, kindest, wisest, toughest selves, that my Idea of the Bomb had no defense against him. In Superman and his fellow superheroes, modern human beings had brought into being ideas that were invulnerable to all harm, immune to deconstruction, built to outsmart diabolical masterminds, made to confront pure Evil and, somehow, against the odds, to always win.

I entered the US comics field as a professional writer in the mideighties at a time of radical innovation and technical advance, when the acknowledged landmarks of superhero fiction like *The Dark Knight Returns* and *Watchmen* were being published and the possibilities seemed limitless, along with the opportunities for creative freedom. I joined a generation of writers and artists, mostly from a UK working-class background, who saw in the moribund hero universes the potential to create expressive, adult, challenging work that could recharge the dry husk of the superhero concept with a new relevance and vitality. As a result, stories got smarter, artwork became more sophisticated, and the superhero began a new lease on life in books that were philosophical, postmodern, and wildly ambitious. The last twenty years have seen startling, innovative work from dozens of distinctive and flamboyant talents in the field. The low production costs (pen and ink can conjure scenes that would cost millions of dollars of computer time to re-create onscreen) and rapid publication frequency mean that in comic books, almost anything goes. No idea is too bizarre, no twist too fanciful, no storytelling technique too experimental. I've been aware of comic books' range, and of the big ideas and emotions they can communicate, for a long time now, so it's with amazement and a little pride that I've watched the ongoing, bloodless surrender of mainstream culture to relentless colonization from the geek hinterlands. Names that once were arcane outsider shibboleths now front global marketing campaigns.

Batman, Spider-Man, X-Men, Green Lantern, Iron Man. Why have superheroes become so popular? Why now?

On one level, it's simple: Someone, somewhere figured out that, like chimpanzees, superheroes make everything more entertaining. Boring tea party? Add a few chimps and it's unforgettable comedy mayhem. Conventional murder mystery? Add superheroes and a startling and provocative new genre springs to life. Urban crime thriller? Seen it all before . . . until Batman gets involved. Superheroes can spice up any dish.

But there's even more going on beneath the surface of our appetite for the antics of outlandishly dressed characters who will never let us down. Look away from the page or the screen and you'd be forgiven for thinking they've arrived into mass consciousness, as they tend to arrive everywhere else, in response to a desperate SOS from a world in crisis.

We've come to accept that most of our politicians will be exposed, in the end, as sex-mad liars or imbeciles, just as we've come to expect gorgeous supermodels to be bulimic, neurotic wretches. We've seen through the illusions that once sustained our fantasies and know from bitter experience that beloved comedians will stand unmasked, sooner or later, as alcoholic perverts or suicidal depressives. We tell our children they're trapped like rats on a doomed, bankrupt, gangster-haunted planet with dwindling resources, with nothing to look forward to but rising sea levels and imminent mass extinctions, then raise a disapproving eyebrow when, in response, they dress in black, cut themselves with razors, starve themselves, gorge themselves, or kill one another.

Traumatized by war footage and disaster clips, spied upon by ubiquitous surveillance cams, threatened by exotic villains who plot from their caverns and subterranean lairs, preyed upon by dark and monumental Gods of Fear, we are being sucked inexorably into Comic Book Reality, with only moments to save the world, as usual. Towering, cadaverous Death-Angels, like the ones on the covers of Dad's antinuke rags, seem to overshadow the gleaming spires of our collective imagination.

Could it be that a culture starved of optimistic images of its own future has turned to the primary source in search of utopian role models? Could the superhero in his cape and skintight suit be the best current representation of something we all might become, if we allow ourselves to feel worthy of a tomorrow where our best qualities are strong enough to overcome the destructive impulses that seek to undo the human project?

We live in the stories we tell ourselves. In a secular, scientific rational culture lacking in any convincing spiritual leadership, superhero stories speak loudly and boldly to our greatest fears, deepest longings, and highest aspirations. They're not afraid to be hopeful, not embarrassed to be optimistic, and utterly fearless in the dark. They're about as far from social realism as you can get, but the best superhero stories deal directly with mythic elements of human experience that we can all relate to, in ways that are imaginative, profound, funny, and provocative. They exist to solve problems of all kinds and can always be counted on to find a way to save the day. At their best, they help us to confront and resolve even the deepest existential crises. We should listen to what they have to tell us.

Supergods is your definitive guide to the world of the superheroes— what they are, where they came from, and how they can help us change the way we think about ourselves, our environment, and the multiverse of possibilities that surrounds us. Get ready to take off your disguise, prepare to whisper your magic word of transformation, and summon the lightning. It's time to save the world.

PART 1

THE GOLDEN AGE

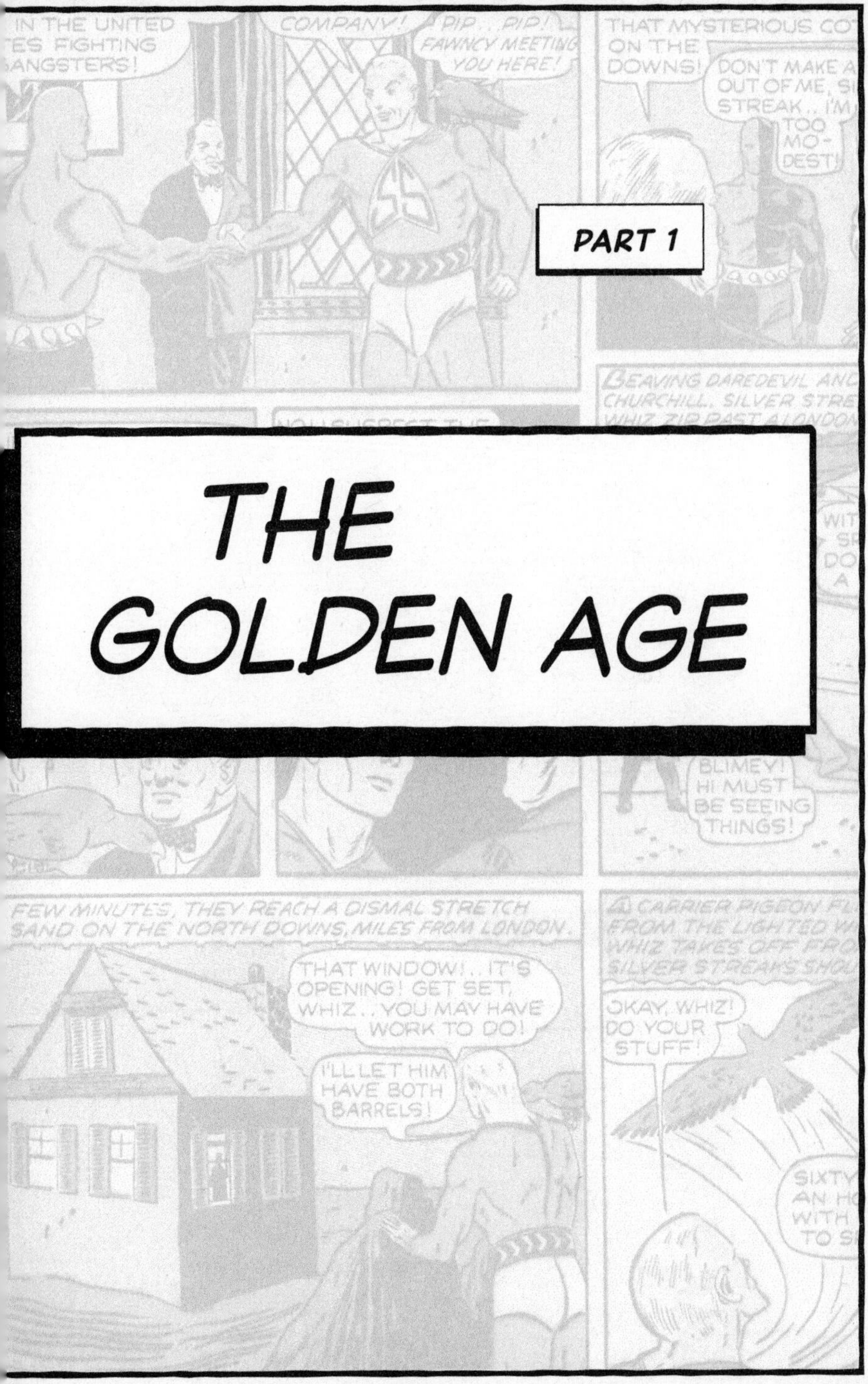
IN THE UNITED
TES FIGHTING
ANGSTERS!
COMPANY!
PIP...PIP! FAWNCY MEETING YOU HERE!
THAT MYSTERIOUS CO
ON THE DOWNS!
DON'T MAKE A
OUT OF ME, S
STREAK.. I'M
TOO MO-DEST!
LEAVING DAREDEVIL AND
CHURCHILL, SILVER STRE
WHIZ ZIP PAST A LONDON
BLIMEY! HI MUST BE SEEING THINGS!
FEW MINUTES, THEY REACH A DISMAL STRETCH
SAND ON THE NORTH DOWNS, MILES FROM LONDON.
THAT WINDOW!.. IT'S OPENING! GET SET, WHIZ.. YOU MAY HAVE WORK TO DO!
I'LL LET HIM HAVE BOTH BARRELS!
A CARRIER PIGEON FL
FROM THE LIGHTED W
WHIZ TAKES OFF FRO
SILVER STREAK'S SHOU
OKAY, WHIZ! DO YOUR STUFF!

CHAPTER 1

THE SUN GOD AND THE DARK KNIGHT

CALLING ALL RED-BLOODED YOUNG AMERICANS!

> This certifies that: (your name and address here) has been duly elected a MEMBER of this organization upon the pledge to do everything possible to increase his or her STRENGTH and COURAGE, to aid the cause of JUSTICE, to keep absolutely SECRET the SUPERMAN CODE, and to adhere to all the principles of good citizenship.

IT MAY NOT be the Ten Commandments, but as a set of moral guidelines for the secular children of an age of reason, the Supermen of America creed was a start. This is the story of the founding of a new belief and its conquest of the world: With a stroke of lightning, the spark of divine inspiration ignited cheap newsprint and the superhero was born in an explosion of color and action. From the beginning, the ur-god and his dark twin presented the world with a frame through which our own best and worst impulses could be personified in an epic struggle across a larger-than-life, two-dimensional canvas upon which our outer and inner worlds, our present and future, could be laid out and explored. They came to save us from the existential abyss, but first they had to find a way into our collective imagination.

Superman was the first of the new creatures to arrive, summoned into print in 1938—nine years after the Wall Street crash triggered a catastrophic worldwide depression. In America, banks were toppled, people lost jobs and homes, and, in extreme cases, relocated to hastily convened shanty-towns. There were rumblings too from Europe, where the ambitious Chancellor Adolf Hitler had declared himself dictator of Germany following a triumphant election to power five years earlier. With the arrival of the first real-life global supervillain, the stage was set for the Free World's imaginative response. When the retort came, it was from the ranks of the underdogs; two shy, bespectacled, and imaginative young science fiction fans from Cleveland, who were revving up typewriter and bristol board to unleash a power greater than bombs, giving form to an ideal that would effortlessly outlast Hitler and his dreams of a Thousand Year Reich.

Jerry Siegel and Joseph Shuster spent seven years tinkering with their Superman idea before it was ready to take on the world. Their first attempt at a comic strip resulted in a dystopian sci-fi story based around the idea of an evil psychic despot. The second pass featured a big, tough, but very much human good guy righting wrongs on the mean streets. Neither showed the spark of originality that publishers were seeking. Four years later, after many fruitless attempts to sell *Superman* as a newspaper strip, Siegel and Shuster finally figured out how to adapt the pacing and construction of their stories to take full advantage of the possibilities of the new comic-book format, and suddenly this fledgling form had found its defining content.

The Superman who made his debut on the cover of *Action Comics* no. 1 was just a demigod, not yet the pop deity he would become. The 1938 model had the power to "LEAP ⅛th OF A MILE; HURDLE A TWENTY STORY BUILDING...RAISE TREMENDOUS WEIGHTS...RUN FASTER THAN AN EXPRESS TRAIN...NOTHING LESS THAN A BURSTING SHELL COULD PENETRATE HIS SKIN!" Although "A GENIUS IN INTELLECT. A HERCULES IN STRENGTH. A NEMESIS TO WRONG-DOERS," this Superman was unable to fly, resorting instead to tremendous single bounds. He could neither orbit the world at the speed of light nor stop the flow of time. That would come later. In his youth, he was almost believable. Siegel and Shuster were careful to ground his adventures in a contemporary city, much like New York, in a fictional world haunted by the all-too-familiar injustices of the real one.

The cover image that introduced the world to this remarkable character had a particular unrepeatable virtue: It showed something no one had ever seen before. It looked like a cave painting waiting to be discovered on a subway wall ten thousand years from now—a powerful, at once futuristic and primitive image of a hunter killing a rogue car.

The vivid yellow background with a jagged corona of red—Superman's colors—suggested some explosive detonation of raw power illuminating the sky. Aside from the bold Deco *whoosh* of the *Action Comics* logo, the date (June 1938), the issue (no. 1), and the price (10 cents), there is no copy and not a single mention of the name *Superman*. Additional words would have been superfluous. The message was succinct: Action was what

mattered. What a hero did counted far more than the things he said, and from the beginning, Superman was in constant motion.

Back to the cover: Look at the black-haired man dressed in a tight-fitting blue and red outfit with a cape trailing behind him as he moves left to right across the drawing's equator line. The bright shield design on his chest contained an *S* (gules on a field or, as they say down at the heraldry society). The man is captured in motion, poised on the toes of his left foot, almost taking flight as he weightlessly hefts an olive green car above his head. Using both hands, he hammers the vehicle to fragments against a conveniently placed rocky outcrop in what appears to be a desert landscape. In the bottom left corner, a man with a blue business suit runs off the frame, clutching his head like Edvard Munch's *Screamer*, his face a cartoon of gibbering existential terror, like a man driven to the city limits of sanity by what he has just witnessed. Above his head, another man, wearing a conservative brown two-piece, can be seen racing north to the first man's west. A third, equally terrified, character crouches on his hands and knees, jacketless, gaping at the feet of the superhuman vandal. His abject posture displays his whimpering submission to the ultimate alpha male. There is no fourth man: His place in the lower right corner is taken by a bouncing whitewall tire torn loose from its axle. Like the bug-eyed bad guys, it too is trying its best to get away from the destructive muscleman.

In any other hands but Superman's, the green sedan on that inaugural cover would boast proudly of America's technological superiority and the wonders of mass manufacturing. Imagine the oozing ad copy: "luxurious whitewall tire trim makes it seem like you're driving on whipped cream," and black-and-white newsreel cars in mind-boggling procession, rolling off the automated belts at Ford. But this was August 1938. Production lines were making laborers redundant across the entire developed world while Charlie Chaplin's poignant film masterpiece *Modern Times* articulated in pantomime the silent cry of the little fellow, the authentic man, not to be forgotten above the relentless din of the factory floor.

Superman made his position plain: He was a hero of the people. The original Superman was a bold humanist response to Depression-era fears of runaway scientific advance and soulless industrialism. We would see this early incarnation wrestling giant trains to a standstill, overturning tanks, or bench-pressing construction cranes. Superman rewrote folk hero John Henry's brave, futile battle with the steam hammer to have a happy ending. He made explicit the fantasies of power and agency that kept the little fellow trudging along toward another sunset fade-out. He was Charlie's tramp character, with the same burning hatred of injustice and bullies, but instead of guile and charm, Superman had the strength of fifty men, and nothing could hurt him. If the dystopian nightmare visions of the age foresaw a dehumanized, mechanized world, Superman offered another possibility: an image of a fiercely human tomorrow that delivered the spectacle of triumphant individualism exercising its sovereignty over the implacable forces of industrial oppression. It's no surprise that he was a big hit with the oppressed. He was as resolutely lowbrow, as pro-poor, as any savior born in a pigsty.

Returning to the cover again, notice how the composition is based around a barely hidden X shape, which gives the drawing its solid framework and graphic appeal. This subliminal X suggests the intriguing unknown, and that's exactly what Superman was when *Action Comics* no. 1 was published: the caped enigma at the eye of a Pop Art storm. He stands at the center of the compass, master of the four elements and the cardinal directions. In Haitian voodoo, the crossroads is the gateway of the *loa* (or spirit) Legba, another manifestation of the "god" known variously as Mercury, Thoth, Ganesh, Odin, or Ogma. Like these others, Legba is a gatekeeper and guards the boundary where the human and divine worlds make contact. It makes perfect sense for Superman to inhabit the same nexus.

As a compositional crossbar, the X allowed Shuster to set a number of elements in a spinning motion that highlighted his central figure. There are moving people with expressions on their faces, car parts, and very bright colors, but layered over the firm brace of the X, they form a second, spiral arrangement that drags our eye up and around on a perceptual Ferris wheel, eliciting frantic questions as it compels our minds to motion:

> Why is this running man so scared?
> What's this car doing up here?
> Why is it being smashed against a rock?
> What is the man on his knees looking at?

Knowing what we do of Superman today, we can assume that the fleeing, frightened men are lawbreakers of some kind. Readers in 1938 simply had no idea what was going on. Undoubtedly, action would be involved, but the first glimpse of Superman was deliberately ambiguous. The men we've taken for granted as fleeing gangsters could as easily be ordinary passersby running from a grimacing power thug in some kind of Russian ballet dancer kit. There's no stolen loot spilling from swag bags, no blue five o'clock shadows, cheap suits, or even weapons to identify the fleeing men as anything other than innocent onlookers. Based on first appearances alone, this gaudy muscleman could be friend or foe, and the only way to answer a multitude of questions is to read on.

But there's a further innovation to notice, another clever trick to lure us inside. The cover image is a snapshot from the *climax* of a story we've yet to see. By the time the world catches up to Superman, he's concluding an adventure we've already missed! Only by reading the story inside can we put the image in context.

That first, untitled Superman adventure opened explosively on a freeze-frame of frantic action. Siegel dumped conventional story setups and cut literally to the chase in a bravura first panel that rearranged the conventional action-story arc in a startling way. The caption box read, "A TIRELESS FIGURE RACES THRU THE NIGHT. SECONDS COUNT . . . DELAY MEANS FORFEIT FOR AN INNOCENT LIFE," to accompany a Joe Shuster image of Superman leaping through the air with a tied and gagged blond woman under his arm. The image is as confident, muscular, and redolent of threat as Superman himself.

By the second panel, we've reached "the Governor's estate," and Superman is already sprinting across the lawn, calling back over his shoulder to the bondaged blonde in the foreground, whom he's dumped by a tree. "MAKE YOURSELF COMFORTABLE! I HAVEN'T TIME TO ATTEND TO IT." We don't know who this girl is, although Superman's gruff demeanor implies that she must be a bad egg—unless, as the cover is willing to imply, *the star of the strip* is the villain.

Already we are compelled through the narrative at Superman's speed and required to focus on the most significant, most intense elements of every scene as if with supersenses. The only solution is to be swept up in the high-velocity slipstream of his streaming red cape, one breathless step behind him.

THE SUN GOD AND THE DARK KNIGHT

When the governor's dressing-gowned butler refused to open the door to the well-built stranger in the skintight suit, Superman smashed it down, sprinted up the stairs with the butler held screaming above his head, then tore a locked steel door off its hinges to reach the terrified (and clearly security-conscious) official within. The butler, in the meantime, had recovered his wits enough to seize a pistol. "PUT THAT TOY AWAY," Superman warned, advancing with a clenched fist. The butler fired, only to discover the muscular hero's immunity to bullets, which bounced harmlessly off his brawny, monogrammed chest.

This virtuoso kinetic overture alone would be worth ten cents from the pocket of any fantasy-starved reader of the Depression. But Siegel and Shuster were not yet done. They still had a masterstroke to play. Just when we think we have this incredible Superman concept figured out, after witnessing the Man of Steel's prodigious strength and determination, we are treated to Clark Kent—the man behind the S—a man with a job, a boss, and girl trouble. Clark the nerd, the nebbish, the bespectacled, mild-mannered shadow self of the confident Man of Steel. The boys had struck a primal mother lode.

Hercules was always Hercules. Agamemnon and Perseus were heroes from the moment they leapt out of bed in the morning until the end of a long battle-crazed day, but Superman was secretly someone else. Clark was the soul, the transcendent element in the Superman equation. Clark Kent is what made him endure. In Clark, Siegel had created the ultimate reader identification figure: misunderstood, put-upon, denied respect in spite of his obvious talents as a newspaperman at Metropolis's *Daily Planet*. As both Siegel and Shuster had learned, to their cost, some girls preferred bounding heroic warriors to skinny men who wrote or drew pretty pictures. But Clark Kent was more than the ultimate nerd fantasy; *everyone* could identify with him. We've all felt clumsy and misunderstood, once or twice, or more often, in our lives. Just as everyone suspects the existence of an inner Superman— an angelic, perfect self who personifies only our best moods and deeds— there is something of Clark in all of us.

Page 3 introduced *Daily Star* reporter Kent on his way to work, where a phone tip sent him in pursuit of an alleged wife beater, but it was Superman who arrived on the scene. He found the bully threatening his victim with a belt looped in his meaty fist. He smacked the brute against the wall, cracking the plaster, and yelled, "YOU'RE NOT FIGHTING A WOMAN NOW!" whereupon the bully fainted, allowing Superman to switch back to his Kent identity in time for the police to arrive.

There was still one more foundation stone to lay in the Superman template. Page 5 now, and the pivotal player in an absorbing ménage à trois that would fascinate readers for decades arrived in an oddly understated introductory panel. Back at the office, Kent introduced us to cool, dismissive Lois Lane, his rival on the news beat, with the words "W-WHAT DO YOU SAY TO A—ER—DATE TONIGHT, LOIS?" Her first words defined her for the ages: "I SUPPOSE I'LL GIVE YOU A BREAK . . . FOR A CHANGE." On the date, Kent managed half a lopsided dance, but before long he and Lois were menaced by Butch Matson, a gorilla-like mobster. Clark quivered and quavered, but Lois, without hesitation, slapped Matson a hard one, and warned him to back off. As her taxi pulled away, she turned her withering scorn on the meek, undeserving Kent, there on the sidewalk. "YOU ASKED ME EARLIER IN THE EVENING WHY I AVOID YOU. I'LL TELL YOU WHY NOW: YOU'RE A SPINELESS, UNBEARABLE COWARD."

Considering that Clark was an ace crime reporter for a respected newspaper and with a good apartment in the city, it was hard to believe Lois would hold him in such low regard, but the stories made it hard to disagree with her as Kent fabricated excuse after elaborate excuse to conceal his true identity. Clark complained of nausea or headaches every time his sensitive ears picked up a police alert and Superman was needed. As a justification for this subterfuge, he made constant dark references to underworld enemies who would be able to strike at him through his loved ones if they knew who he was. He had created a total disguise, a persona so much the reverse of his true Superman self, it would throw off any snoop and allow him a taste of normal life.

By the time the first Superman story concluded, thirteen pages after its breathtaking opening scene, our hero had apprehended no fewer than five lawbreakers *and* taken a moment to root out corruption in the US Senate. Every new reveal made both the individual story and the overall concept seem even more exciting. It gave the medium a character innovation to call its own. He gave the world the first superhero. Thirteen pages—unlucky for the enemies of the oppressed.

The superhero concept caught on immediately with the public. The Superman Fan Club soon had hundreds of thousands of members, like some benign *Hitlerjugend* or sci-fi Scout movement. By 1941, he was the star of *Action Comics*; had his own *Superman* title; was in *World's Finest Comics*; and was popping in and out of *All Star Comics,* another series. At the same time, he was making the mighty leap to other media, which helped to spread his fame and provided what would become a vital life for him beyond the comic page. He embedded Superman in the consciousness of the whole country—the whole world: he was on the radio, syndicated across the funny pages of every major US newspaper, and selling stamps, greetings cards, coloring books, bubble gum, board games, and war bonds.

Early comic books used a four-color printing process in which alchemic, elemental red, yellow, blue, and black were combined to create a processed spectrum. Superman, of course, was the first character to take full advantage of the new technology, and these fundamental building blocks of the comic-book universe gave superhero comics a luminous, spectral radiance that had never been seen before in a democratic, popular form. For readers accustomed to the black-and-white images of cinema, newspaper photographs, and pulp illustrations, the comics must have seemed hallucinatory, as potent as dreams. That Siegel and his fellows borrowed an earnest sheen of naturalism from movies and newsreel footage made the candid surrealism of the superhero books even more alluring. They were folk art for the restless new century, a genuine American magic realism forty years before that term set literary circles alight.

The innovative rapid-editing style of Siegel and Shuster stories brought new speed and life to the form. It meant that the space between a country mansion and a city block could disappear into the white gutter between panels. A journey of miles, sliced to nothing by Superman's leap. To follow the hero across the frames was to experience a dislocation in time that suggested both superhuman perception and impossible velocity. Unlike the composed and formal newspaper strips, which were comics' only rival as imaginative color entertainment, the early superhero comics had a driving left-to-right forward momentum, the work of young pioneers defining the form. It was a kind of animation but slowed down into a sequence of freeze-frames that required the reader to fill in the gaps between pictures.

Shuster's artwork was basic. Those sturdy black-and-white ink lines of the early comics were there to ensure that nothing was lost in the crude reproduction process. Any kind of fine detail, shading, and nuance would simply vanish in the finished printed edition. Drawing was also streamlined to a shorthand in order to meet punishing delivery dates.

But it's still possible to find depths in Shuster's drawing. I can't help but see in these handmade fantasies the poignant products of young minds dreaming better tomorrows. The depth of engaged meditation, the focus that goes into writing and drawing even the crudest of the comics, emerges through the least-assured line. The pages are the result of human hours, and the glory and confusion of what it means to *be here now*—on a coffee and pills jag at four in the morning with a story to hand in by lunchtime—shines from between the lines of the lowliest eight-pager.

After all those years, the frustrated false starts and countless rejections, Siegel and Shuster had struck gold. Naturally, the obvious thing to do would be to sell all the rights to National Comics (later to become DC) for the sum of $130. Yes. Stop for a moment and consider that sum in light of the mega-fortune that Superman has made for his corporate masters since then.

If you listen to the right voices, you'll hear and believe what I heard and believed growing up in this business, and it won't be long before a dark and evil fairy tale unfolds: the grim cautionary fable of two innocent seventeen-year-old boys seduced by the forked tongues of cartoon fat-cat capitalists and top-hatted bloodsuckers. In this Hollywood tragedy, Jerry Siegel and Joe Shuster are depicted as doe-eyed ingénues in a world of razor-toothed predators.

The truth, as ever, is less dramatic. The deal was done in 1938, before Superman boomed. Siegel and Shuster were both twenty-three when they sold the copyright to Superman. They had worked together for several years in the cutthroat world of pulp periodical publishing, and, like so many artists, musicians, and entertainers, they were creating a product to sell. Superman was a foot in the door, a potential break that might put them in demand as big-time pop content providers. Superman was a sacrifice to the gods of commercial success. If my own understanding of the creative mind carries any weight, I'd suspect that both Siegel and Shuster imagined they'd create other, better characters.

But by 1946, they realized how much money their creation was raking in. They sued National, unsuccessfully, and then tried to repeat Superman's success with the unendearing, short-lived *Funnyman* (a crime-fighting clown). Siegel was also responsible for the gruesomely vindictive avenging superghost the Spectre and cyborg hero Robotman. He would even write that quintessential British antihero strip *The Spider,* but the relative obscurity of those perfectly well-conceived characters tells its own story. Jerry Siegel failed to create any more features with the primal impact of Superman, but he and Joe Shuster had done something spectacular— established the rules and foundations upon which new universes could be built.

(In 1975, in the face of mounting bad publicity, Warner Bros. [DC's parent company] finally awarded Siegel and Shuster each a $20,000 per year compensation along with an assured creator credit on every subsequent Superman comic, TV show, movie, or game. I'm sure it helped, but as an example of how far the business has come, today a prolific and popular comics writer could make the same amount in a week. Legal battles between the Siegel estate and DC over the ownership of Superman continue to this day.)

And of course, once they had sold the rights and Superman started to thrive in other media, Siegel and Shuster were no longer sole arbiters of their brainchild's destiny. The radio writers had added new essential elements to the lore, such as the killer space mineral kryptonite. On the comics side a team of studio assistants helped keep the furnace fed. Superman needed the power of ten men, and more, to supply the demand for his incredible feats. Set free of his creators, he was to change radically and constantly over the next seven decades, to keep up with—or, in some cases predict—seismic shifts in fashion, politics, and audience demographics. Superman now had a metamorphic, elastic quality that would allow him to survive. Forty years later, with a big-budget Superman movie on the way in 1978, Siegel was employed as a clerk and Shuster was partially blind in a California nursing home. As for Superman, he hadn't aged a single day. Whatever those boys made, it was made to last: stronger, faster, fitter, and more durable than any human being.

Actually, it's as if he's more real than we are. We writers come and go, generations of artists leave their interpretations, and yet something persists, something that is always Superman. We have to adapt to his rules if we enter his world. We can never change him too much, or we lose what he is. There is a persistent set of characteristics that define Superman through decades of creative voices and it's that essential, unshakeable quality of Superman-ness the character possesses in every incarnation, which is divinity by any other name.

But never mind all that, you say; there's really only one question everyone wants to ask when the subject of Superman comes up: If he's so goddamn super, why does he wear his underpants outside his tights?

Growing up with Superman, I accepted his "action suit" as part of the package. It was common for the advanced races in pulp illustrations to sport capes, tights, and exterior underpants, as if foremost among the natural consequences of millennia of peace, progress, and one-world government would be a vogue for knee-length boots on men. For me, the real insight into Superman's distinctive look arrived much later, when I discovered some photographs of circus strongmen in the 1930s. There among the taut tent guy ropes and painted caravans at the country fair was the familiar, faintly disturbing overpants-belt combo, here worn by men with handlebar mustaches, pumping dumbbells in their meaty fists and staring bullishly at the camera. Finally it made perfect sense. The solution to the riddle of the ages was here all along in the boring old past, where no one had bothered to look. Underpants on tights were signifiers of extramasculine strength and endurance in 1938. The cape, showman-like boots, belt, and skintight spandex were all derived from circus outfits and helped to emphasize the performative, even freak-show-esque, aspect of Superman's adventures. Lifting bridges, stopping trains with his bare hands, wrestling elephants: These were superstrongman feats that benefited from the carnival flair implied by skintight spandex. Shuster had dressed the first superhero as his culture's most prominent exemplar of the strongman ideal, unwittingly setting him up as the butt of ten thousand jokes.

With its most obvious feature out of the way, the Superman costume has more to reveal about our hero and his appeal. From his creation,

Superman was as recognizable as Mickey Mouse, Charlie Chaplin, or Santa Claus. He was immediately intriguing, immediately marketable. Aggressively branding the lead with his own initial had never been done before and was a masterstroke of marketing know-how. Superman wore his own logo. He was his own T-shirt. His emblem was the flag of a personal country, and, like the Red Cross, he was welcome anywhere.

The red and blue contrast added a patriotic touch of Stars and Stripes Americana to the character, and in a series where the scale of Superman's activities tended to profit from the panoramic long shot, the primary colors of his constantly mobile form helped to identify the hero even when he was little more than a distant speck against the skyline of Metropolis. The trailing cape also had practical uses, giving the illusion of movement and speed to static images—the sharp, modern editing techniques of the Siegel and Shuster narrative style did the rest.

Back to that chest emblem. Superman—so unashamedly special, so absolutely individual that he wore his own initial as a badge—reaffirmed human dignity by looking ahead to another time. Shuster and Siegel had envisaged a future when we'd all wear our own proud emblems of revealed, recognized greatness, when technology would simply be a tool to help us express the creativity and connectedness that was the birthright of our golden superselves.

In Superman, some of the loftiest aspirations of our species came hurtling down from imagination's bright heaven to collide with the lowest form of entertainment, and from their union something powerful and resonant was born, albeit in its underwear. He was brave. He was clever. He never gave up and he never let anyone down. He stood up for the weak and knew how to see off bullies of all kinds. He couldn't be hurt or killed by the bad guys, hard as they might try. He didn't get sick. He was fiercely loyal to his friends and to his adopted world. He was Apollo, the sun god, the unbeatable supreme self, the personal greatness of which we all know we're capable. He was the righteous inner authority and lover of justice that blazed behind the starched-shirt front of hierarchical conformity.

In other words, then, Superman was the rebirth of our oldest idea: He was a god. His throne topped the peaks of an emergent dime-store Olympus, and, like Zeus, he would disguise himself as a mortal to walk among the common people and stay in touch with their dramas and passions. The parallels continued: His S is a stylized lighting stroke—the weapon of Zeus, motivating bolt of stern authority and just retribution. And, as the opening caption of the Superman "origin" story from 1939 suggested—"AS A DISTANT PLANET WAS DESTROYED BY OLD AGE, A SCIENTIST PLACED HIS INFANT SON WITHIN A HASTILY-DEVISED SPACE-SHIP, LAUNCHING IT TOWARD EARTH"—he was like the baby Moses or the Hindu Karna, set adrift in a "basket" on the river of destiny. And then there was the Western deity he best resembled: Superman was Christ, an unkillable champion sent down by his heavenly father (Jor-El) to redeem us by example and teach us how to solve our problems without killing one another. In his shameless Technicolor dream suit, he was a pop star, too, a machine-age messiah, a sci-fi redeemer. He seemed designed to press as many buttons as you had.

But if the story of Jesus has a central theme, it's surely this: When a god elects to come to Earth, he has to make a few sacrifices. In order to be born, Superman was called upon to surrender a few of his principles. As the price of incarnation, the son of Jor-El of Krypton was compelled to make a terrible bargain with the complex, twisty forces of this material world. That S is a serpent, too, and carries its own curse.

Irony, the cosmic "stuff" of which it often seems our lives are secretly woven, had the perfect man in its sights all along. And so it came to pass that our socialist, utopian, humanist hero was slowly transformed into a marketing tool, a patriotic stooge, and, worse: the betrayer of his own creators. Leaving his fathers far behind on the doomed planet Poverty, the Superman, with his immediate need to be real, flew into the hands of anyone who could afford to hire him.

Superman's image and name, his significance, spread in wider and wider ripples at the speed of newsprint, the speed of radio. He had managed to plant the standard of Krypton in the soil of Kansas and Metropolis. A strong, elegant, and handsome alien had arrived to set a precedent that rang a bell with audiences. Where would the next hit superhero come from? How to follow up Superman without copying him—which many tried—and triggering a lawsuit? It seems obvious now. The answer was to reverse the polarity. Superman was a hero of the day, bright and gaudy and ultimately optimistic. What about a hero of the night?

Enter Batman.

It all began in 1938 on a dark and stormy night in New York's midtown, when editor Vin Sullivan at *Detective Comics* was instructed by his boss to whip up a new hero in the Superman mold, one that could capitalize on this new fad for "long underwear characters," as the superheroes were becoming known. They imagined that Superman's muscular extroversion might find a suitable counterpart in the introversion of the detective genre. Just as the "action" in *Action Comics* had proved to be the perfect springboard for Superman, this new character would complement *Detective Comics'* primary diet of mystery, crime, and horror.

Bob Kane, born Robert Kahn, was twenty-three in 1939 when Batman made his debut. His collaborator on the new strip was Bill Finger, two years older than Kane. They called Finger the finest comics writer of his generation and always described him as the dreamer of the team. Kane the artist, by contrast, had a head for business. It's easy to see where this melodrama is headed, and it may help explain why you will certainly have seen Bob Kane's name in association with any and all Batman products, but not Bill Finger's.

Kane's cold, commercial intelligence was all over Batman from the start. Where Superman felt like the happy result of trial, error, and patient refinement, Batman was clearly the product of applied craft, cleverly but rapidly assembled from an assortment of pop culture debris that together transcended the sum of its parts. His appearance was based on a number of sources, including the lead character from a 1930 silent film entitled *The Bat Whispers* (the resemblance is slight, but the idea of the bestial alter ego is there); Leonardo da Vinci's sketches for an "ornithopter" flying machine, its design based on the wings of a bat; and 1920's *The Mark of Zorro*, starring Douglas Fairbanks. Bill Finger saw Batman as combining the athleticism of D'Artagnan from the novel *The Three Musketeers* with the deductive skills of Sherlock Holmes. But the strip also showed the undeniable influence of the 1934 pulp character the Bat, a hooded crime fighter who paralyzed villains with a gas gun—like Batman, he was motivated to choose his particular crime-fighting guise when a bat flew in his window during one particularly intense and pivotal brooding session. Another bat character, the Black Bat—a district attorney scarred in an acid attack—appeared almost simultaneously in his own scalloped cape and black mask. The two coexisted until the early 1950s: the Black Bat in the fading pulps, and Batman in the comics. There was very little about Batman that could not be traced directly back to some recent predecessor, but what he had was soul and staying power.

His villainous opponents, who would proliferate during the life of the strip, were, if anything, even less original; introduced in the first issue of Batman's own title in spring 1940, the Joker's appearance was a straight lift from Conrad Veidt's 1928 silent film *The Man Who Laughs*—to see the famous pictures of Veidt in the role is to wonder how they got away with it. The character also incorporated influences from the Coney Island mascot, and, of course, the playing card itself. Nineteen forty-two's Two-Face, his features half-erased by an acid attack (sound familiar?), literalized the symbolic image of warring personalities on the movie poster for *Doctor Jekyll and Mr. Hyde*, in which Spencer Tracy's 1941 Oscar-winning mug was split into two halves—one handsome, the other demonic and deformed.

Bob Kane and his studio opted for a heavy, Gothic woodcut effect and weirdly distorted anatomy in their artwork, cheerfully improvising impossible contortions of the human frame in order to make a particular sequence work. He repeated poses he liked over and over again in story after story, making Kane's Batman an oddly posed, self-conscious figure whose cape often appeared to have been carved from solid mahogany. Set design was perfunctory—the police commissioner's office suggested by two chairs, a telephone, and a gruesome table lamp—but it was as much as the young, raw Bruce Wayne needed to frame his simple desire for vengeance. The best of Kane's ghost artists, like the gifted Jerry Robinson, who drew the first Joker story, brought a shadow-drenched atmosphere of dread and mystery to Batman's world of paneled mansions, urban alleyways, and deserted chemical factories, setting him apart from his competitors.

Batman's first appearance on the cover of *Detective Comics* no. 27 in May 1939 was more orthodox than Superman's. A circular balloon promised "64 Pages of Action," while a banner stripe reads, "STARTING THIS ISSUE: THE AMAZING AND UNIQUE ADVENTURES OF THE BAT-MAN!" The word *adventures* suggested a hero, at least, and mitigated the sinister vampiric aspect of Batman's appearance.

This image, even cruder than Shuster's *Action Comics* cover, shows two men in hats on a rooftop overlooking an urban skyline and gawking at an eerie spectacle unfolding in the sky. One man holds a tiny, ladylike gun, marking him as some delicate variety of crook. Batman swings in from the right, with his Bat line disappearing off the top right-hand corner, attached to nothing. He's a dramatic figure with the outstretched scalloped wings of a giant bat. He has a third man in a grip that leaves the unfortunate victim's legs kicking and dangling over the streets of the city far below. Although it is meant to be night, the sky is a searing acidic yellow, perhaps to suggest the intense reflection onto low cloud of the teeming city below. The effect is of a Magritte painting, where it's day and night, impossibly, at the same time.

All in all, it lacks the powerful composition of Superman's debut. Kane was simply not as good an artist as Shuster, and it showed, but the deeply spooky nature of this hero was expressed in no uncertain terms. The six-page introductory story opened with the same striking, spiky silhouette, posed this time against a full moon rising over the city. What Bob Kane lacked in draftsmanship, his chunky potato print lines made up for with atmosphere and a style that was somehow suggestive of European Expressionist cinema.

Where Superman had broken and established rules and catapulted his readers into the middle of a new kind of action, Batman played it safe with an opening caption that told readers everything they needed to know:

"THE 'BAT-MAN,' A MYSTERIOUS AND ADVENTUROUS FIGURE FIGHTING FOR RIGHTEOUSNESS AND APPREHENDING THE WRONG DOER IN HIS LONE BATTLE AGAINST THE EVIL FORCES OF SOCIETY—HIS IDENTITY REMAINS UNKNOWN!"

A hand-drawn logo read "The 'Bat-Man,' " while a red box below carried the byline Bob Kane. There was no mention of Bill Finger, even though he wrote "The Case of the Chemical Syndicate" along with hundreds more of the best Batman stories until his last in 1964.

The opening story frame brought us into the home of Commissioner Gordon, currently entertaining his "YOUNG SOCIALITE FRIEND, BRUCE WAYNE," a bored young man who puffs heroically on a pipe while asking the question "WELL, COMMISSIONER, ANYTHING EXCITING HAPPENING THESE DAYS?" The middle-aged police chief was a keen smoker too, igniting a cigar that sent a miniature mushroom cloud into the air between the two.

"NO-O-," Gordon began tentatively. Then, as if the most intriguing element of the story were a mere afterthought: "EXCEPT THIS FELLOW THEY CALL THE 'BAT-MAN' PUZZLES ME." When Gordon was summoned to the scene of a brutal murder at a nearby mansion, Wayne tagged along, as if there was nothing at all odd about a member of the public who treated deathly serious police investigations as sightseeing trips.

Bat-Man appeared on the third page, standing on the roof in the moonlight. His stance displayed confidence; his arms were folded, and he seemed unafraid, almost laconic. The crooks recognized him, cuing readers that this adventure was not the first night out for our hero. As with Superman, we arrived after the story had already begun, groping for our seats in the dark. Almost immediately, Batman erupted into violence against the men in a rapid sequence of action panels.

In his first outing, he broke up the bizarrely complex plot of a chemical syndicate involving several murders and some money. It's not a great story, and no matter how often I read it, I'm still left slightly in the dark as to what it was about, but the striking appearance of the hero made it unforgettable. It also established an important trend in the early Batman stories. From the very beginning, Batman habitually found himself dealing with crimes involving chemicals and crazy people, and over the years he would take on innumerable villains armed with lethal Laughing Gas, mind-control lipstick, Fear Dust, toxic aerosols, and "artificial phobia" pills. Indeed, his career had barely begun before he was heroically inhaling countless bizarre chemical concoctions cooked up by mad black-market alchemists. Superman might have faced a few psychic attacks, but, even if it was against his will every time, Batman was hip to serious mind-bending drugs. Batman knew what it was like to trip balls without seriously losing his shit, and that savoir faire added another layer to his outlaw sexiness and alluring aura of decadence and wealth.

In July 1939's *Detective Comics* no. 29, he faced another drug-dispensing no-gooder in "The Batman Meets Doctor Death." Doctor Death was Karl Hellfern, a seriously disgruntled middle-aged chemist and obviously a devious bastard, as indicated by the presence of a monocle. Unable to rustle up even the simplest of hair-restoring formulas, he was seriously balding but sported a devilish goatee and pointed ears, which may or may not have been hereditary. In this adventure, Batman was shot and wounded, showing that, unlike Superman, he was as mortal as the rest of us, only much more tenacious.

The ending to the story found a new note of hysteria that would enliven the best Batman adventures: trapped in his laboratory, Doctor Death fought back by inadvertently setting the whole place alight. As he realized what he'd done and was consumed by flames, the doctor lost it completely, screaming, "**HA! HA!** OH—HA-HA-HA—YOU—YOU **FOOL!**" To which Batman, pausing a moment to watch the spreading inferno, replied grimly, "YOU ARE THE POOR FOOL! HE HAS GONE MAD! DEATH . . . TO DOCTOR DEATH!"

The introduction of the secret identity, given away so generously as just one more brilliant idea halfway through the first *Superman* story, was saved for the twist ending of the third Batman story, which kept it in line with the mystery and detective aspects of the Batman strip. The last two panels showed a door, creaking open from its curious position ajar until the "Bat-Man" stood revealed in full costume. There's something genuinely strange about this dreamlike conclusion to the story, this weird emergence from the closet into the half-light. It seemed a miracle that Wayne, our chain-smoking pipe abuser, could wheeze his way out of the cupboard and down the hall, let alone spring and glide across the rooftops of Gotham, but the distinctive visual of Batman was so arresting, so visceral, he caught on with the reading public as rapidly as Superman had.

Where *Superman* strove for modernity in everything from the image of its hero to the kinetic editing of its torn-from-the-headlines narrative, the *Batman* strip reveled in the trashy aesthetic of the mystery pulps and the penny dreadfuls. Crime, madness, and the supernatural defined Batman's theater of operations and allowed him to mine a rich seam of blood and thunder sensationalism stretching back a couple of centuries to the Gothic horror novels of Horace Walpole and "Monk" Lewis. Indeed, the eerie and atmospheric story of one of Batman's earliest supernatural opponents, the vampire Monk, seemed to directly reference the Gothic classics, with evocations of "The Lost Mountains of Cathala by the Turbulent River Dess" sounding like the copy in a *Rough Guide to Mysterious Romania* guidebook. The cover showed a vast, hunched Batman figure looming across the horizon to overlook a castle cresting a Romantic peak sampled from a Caspar David Friedrich painting. It was Batman as Dracula, the vampire as hero, preying on the even more unwholesome creatures of the night.

Convention has it that Batman's adventures work best when they're rooted in a basically realistic world of gritty crime violence and backstreet reprisals, but from the very start of his career, he was drawn into demented episodes of the supernatural, uncanny and inexplicable. His was the territory of the dark unconscious, after all, and writer Finger wasn't afraid to try Batman in any kind of story that played with elements of the grotesque. For instance, another story, indebted to the Decadent and Symbolist authors of the late nineteenth century, was set in Paris and featured a man whose face had been wiped blank for reasons never adequately explained. "ASK CHARLES HERE," the swooning heroine pleaded with Bruce Wayne, "HE WHO OWNS NO FACE. HE CAN

TELL YOU. HE IS NOT AFRAID TO DIE." Even without a mouth, the afflicted Charles was somehow able to explain himself perfectly, and he quickly identified the source of his unlikely troubles as a Duc D'Orterre, who sounded like an escapee from a bound volume of the Marquis de Sade or Comte de Lautréamont.

A confrontation with the diabolical Duc ended when Batman was hurled from a giant spinning wheel through a trapdoor in the ceiling, only to land in an upstairs garden where the giant flowers all came complete with life-sized, female, and exquisitely made-up faces at the heart of their petals. During a brief, matter-of-fact conversation with the head of a blond girl on a giant green stalk, it was requested of Batman that he "release" the girls. This baffling episode was never mentioned again or resolved in any way, and its conclusion staunchly offered no explanation for the chatty flowers. As for the evil Duc D'Orterre, he perished obliquely without revealing the lucrative secret of how to genetically splice giant crocuses with Parisian showgirls.

Superman would have seemed pompous and preposterous in Gotham, but Batman pioneered and owned his twilight territory with the swiftness of an alpha predator. The hard-boiled noir, the supernatural, the high-tech, the superrich, the fetishistic—all combined in *Batman*. He was the Rolling Stones to Superman's Beatles, the Oasis to his Blur. Immediately and without question or competition, Batman became the coolest superhero of them all.

The stories in the Superman strips dealt with politics and injustice on the daylight stage of jobs, media, and government, but Batman took the fight to the shadows: the grimy derelict warehouses and dive bars where criminal scum plied their trade beyond the reach of the law but not beyond the range of a batarang or a leathery fist. Batman was out there nightclubbing in his crackling black leathers and battling almost supernatural villains, chemically deranged, archetypal bad-trip fairy-tale nightmares who would never feature in Superman's world.

As everybody knows, the Joker was Batman's most enduring, accommodating, and iconic nemesis. Foreshadowing David Bowie, Madonna, and Lady Gaga, he shared Batman's chameleonic ability to adapt his routine to suit the tastes of the day. In his first appearance (*Batman* no. 1, 1940), the "Grim Jester" was a sour-faced homicidal maniac who left chilling clues for the police. Ten years later, he'd become a chortling crime clown robbing banks in his Jokermobile. In the eighties, he was a gender-bending serial killer, and in actor Heath Ledger's 2008 film portrayal, he appeared as a punk-influenced agent of performance-art-inspired chaos. The Joker's ruined mug was the face at the end of it all, the makeup melting on the funeral mask of Von Aschenbach in Visconti's *Death in Venice*, the grinning skull caked under troweled layers of cosmetics. Corrupt and unhealthy, protopunk, proto-Goth, he was skinny, pale, hunched, and psychopathic. He was Johnny Rotten, Steerpike, Bowie strung out in Berlin, or Joel Grey in *Cabaret*. The Joker was the perfect dissolute European response to Batman's essentially can-do New World determination, toned physique, and outrageous wealth. While Batman cut a swath through blackened streets and leapt between skyscrapers, the Joker had to hunch beneath bare bulbs like a heroin addict facing a nightmare comedown with an acid tongue and a graveyard wit. He dressed like a riverboat gambler, his face composed to suggest some unhallowed marriage of showbiz, drag culture, and the art of the mortician. If Batman was cool, the Joker was cooler. The pair shared the perfect symmetry of Jesus and the Devil, Holmes and Moriarty, Tom and Jerry.

Bill Finger wrote the Joker with relish, finding, as he did with Batman, fresh and unremittingly inventive ways to reintroduce the villain. His narrative captions took on a deliciously creepy-crawly tenor any time the Clown Prince of Crime made an entrance:

> THE JOKER—GRIM JESTER, ARCH-CRIMINAL, MASTER-FIEND . . . AN EMBER OF LIFE GLOWS WITHIN THAT GHASTLY SHELL OF HUMAN CLAY . . . AND THE ICY CLAWS OF FEAR AND APPREHENSION CLUTCH TIGHTER ABOUT THE HEARTS OF THE DENIZENS OF THE WORLD!! ONLY THREE DARE TO PLAY THE GAME OF CARDS WITH THIS MAD, EVIL GENIUS—THE FEARLESS **BATMAN**, THE **HEROIC** ROBIN, AND THE BEAUTIFUL, LITHE CAT-WOMAN . . . TO THE WINNER BELONG THE PHARAOH'S GEMS . . . THE LOSER—GETS DEATH!!

The rest of Batman's rogues' gallery personified various psychiatric disorders to great effect: Two-Face was schizophrenia. Catwoman was kleptomania. The Scarecrow was phobias of all kinds. By psychoanalyzing his

enemies with his fists, Batman may have hoped to escape the probing gaze
of the analyst himself, but it was not to be. There was, after all, something
deeply mad about Batman. Superman made a kind of sense in a hopeful,
science fiction way: a do-gooding orphan from another world who decided
to use his special alien powers to help the people of his adopted world
achieve their greatness. The decision of the rich but otherwise powerless
Bruce Wayne to fight crime dressed as a bat took a bit more swallowing.
After witnessing the senseless murder of his parents (a story revealed in
Batman no. 1), the young Bruce would have been forgiven for spending his
inheritance on drink, drugs, hookers, and therapy, but instead he chose to
fight crime on his own somewhat unconventional terms. Madness haunted
Batman from the start.

And then there were the ladies. The essentially monogamous Superman
would never dare to indulge enemies like the Catwoman (also from
Batman no. 1), Poison Ivy (1966), or Talia (1971's "Daughter of the
Demon"—and eventually mother of Batman's son Damian), but these
were exactly the kind of damaged sex kittens who prowled regularly into
playboy Bruce Wayne's anything-goes world. The bad girls in *Batman*
were all deranged fetish queens who loved and hated the hero in equal,
exquisite measure. These were tough, glamorous dames, always happy to
engage in full contact, to-the-death rooftop bouts with the world's greatest martial artist when the hypno-lipstick failed to do its job.

Batman, then, may have been a construct, but he was an immaculate
construct, precision engineered to endure. Batman was born of the deliberate reversal of everything in the Superman dynamic: Superman was an
alien with incredible powers; Batman was a human being with no superhuman abilities. Superman's costume was brightly colored; Batman's was
grayscale and somber with mocking flashes of yellow. In his secret Clark
Kent identity, Superman was a hardworking farmer's son who grew up in
small-town Kansas, while Batman's Bruce Wayne enjoyed life as a wealthy
playboy—an East Coast sophisticate descended from old money. Clark
had a boss; Bruce had a butler. Clark pined after Lois; Bruce burned
through a string of debutantes and leading ladies. Superman worked
alone; Batman had a boy partner, Robin, who wore green briefs, a black
mask, and a yellow cape. Superman was of the day; Batman was of the
night and the shadows. Superman was rational, Apollonian; Batman was

Dionysian. Superman's mission was the measured allotment of justice; Batman's, an emotive two-fisted ask-questions-later vendetta.

Superman began as a socialist, but Batman was the ultimate capitalist hero, which may help explain his current popularity and Superman's relative loss of significance. Batman was a wish-fulfillment figure as both filthy-rich Bruce Wayne *and* his swashbuckling alter ego. He was a millionaire who vented his childlike fury on the criminal classes of the lower orders. He was the defender of privilege and hierarchy. In a world where wealth and celebrity are the measures of accomplishment, it's no surprise that the most popular superhero characters today—Batman and Iron Man—are both handsome tycoons. The socialist and the socialite, the only thing Superman and Batman could agree on was that killing is wrong.

This fascinating new hero was horned like the Devil and most at home in darkness; a terrifying, demonic presence who worked on the side of the angels. Whatever the reasons, these carefully calculated tensions and contradictions ensured Batman's cyclically renewed popularity, while Superman's appeal would eventually blur into something tackier as his fierce humanism became reconfigured as nostalgic self-delusion. Superman's brand of essentially optimistic problem solving found its cynical counterpart in Batman's obsessive, impossible quest to punch crime into extinction, one bastard at a time.

As distinct as they were, Superman and Batman would eventually become friends. This future meeting would inaugurate the dawn of the shared DC Comics universe—an immense virtual reality inhabited by fictional characters, spanning decades and hundreds of thousands of pages, with its own rules, laws of physics, and alternative forms of time. The first emergent comic-book universe began with this grand separation of light from dark, is from isn't, this from that, up from down, in a kabbalistic, Hermetic symmetry. The first light had cast the first shadow.

A kind of alchemy was under way.

CHAPTER 2

LIGHTNING'S CHILD

ONCE THE FORMULA was established, dozens, hundreds, of variations and combinations of the hero type could be run. Some had special powers, but most were otherwise ordinary men and women who gave themselves names like the Mighty Atom (1940), Phantom Lady (1941), or Black Canary (1947) and dressed in flamboyant disguises to fight crime, armed only with their wits and a seemingly insatiable appetite for violent street justice. Many superhero strips were based around a single gimmick: the Sandman (1939) sent his crooked victims to sleep with a gas gun, while Madame Fatal (1940) was secretly retired actor Richard Stanton, who fought crime dressed as an old lady—making him the first transvestite superhero, although certainly not the last.

The rapid growth of superhero titles in the wake of *Superman* and *Batman* and the devouring demand for fresh material encouraged young writers and artists to pursue increasingly surreal pixie paths to inspiration. Superheroes were driven to specialize in a savage Darwinian search for new, evolutionary niches.

The most successful of these specialists were two early entries from one of National Comics' biggest rivals. A publisher called Timely Comics sprang up to take advantage of the superhero fad and launched its first title, *Marvel Comics*, in October 1939, with two new characters: the Human Torch and Prince Namor the Sub-Mariner. Batman and Superman were the pillars of what would come to be known as the DC universe; the Sub-Mariner and the Human Torch were the first residents of what would one day be the Marvel Comics universe.

Timely's big innovation, which was to serve the embryonic Marvel well and help to distinguish it from DC, was to come down from Olympus and give voice to the elements themselves by personifying the forces of nature as heroes.

Prince Namor (*Roman* spelled backward) of Atlantis, the Sub-Mariner, was the creation of seventeen-year-old Bill Everett. In photographs, the handsome Everett has a shock of hair like Rimbaud, geek glasses, a pipe clenched between his teeth, and a demonic glint in his eye. Superman sometimes flouted the law, but decent people had nothing to fear from the essentially upstanding Man of Steel. Prince Namor was different: This half-human terrorist was prepared to inundate the just and unjust alike as he rode on whaleback at the foaming apocalyptic crest of the devastating mega-tsunami that he unleashed on New York in his first adventure. Everett's version of the crude, comic pulp style was edgier, more angular, and more fantastic than anything seen previously.

With his jet-black widow's peak, piercing eyes, pointed ears, bladelike cheekbones, and winged feet, the otherwise naked prince of the deep wore only a pair of scaly green briefs as the badge of his nobility. Namor was the face of JD insolence, awaiting rock 'n' roll, Marlon Brando, and James Dean to ratify his power. Driven by passions and brief allegiances, Namor faced the entire world with a fuck-you snarl, committing acts of high anarchy on a scale undreamed of by terrorists in the real world.

There was no shortage of sea stories, tales of Atlantis, storms, piracy, dynastic succession, and imperial vengeance from which to draw inspiration for Namor's fertile new fantasy playground.

His inevitable counterpart and opposite, the Human Torch, was less of a success. An intelligent artificial man with a serious design flaw that made him combustible in air, this do-gooding mechanical man was less easy to relate to than the impulsive Namor, and interest in the Torch declined steadily. (When Stan Lee revived the concept for *The Fantastic*

Four, he wisely made sure the new Torch was a human being; a literally hotheaded teenage hipster.)

The elements of water and fire were soon joined by a reborn pantheon of gods and figures from legend and myth. Hawkman, for example, resembled a hieroglyphic god from an Egyptian frieze, an avatar of hawk-headed Horus, the lord of force and fire, the son of the ancient dying god Osiris. When he spread his wings in comic form, it was as Khufu, an Egyptian prince resurrected conveniently in the manner to which he was accustomed as millionaire Carter Hall.

Green Lantern, who first appeared in 1940 in *All American Comics* no. 16, weighed in with an updated Aladdin story in which railwayman Alan Scott discovered a mysterious railroad lamp with equally mysterious powers. To make his inspiration even more explicit, the lead was to have been called Alan Ladd, but that name had already been taken by a popular screen star, and so Ladd became Scott. Leaving behind his ruggedly blue-collar life as a railwayman, Alan Scott chose to fight crime wearing a green, red, and yellow trapeze artist outfit that far outshone Superman's and anticipated the excesses of glam rock by thirty years. If Liberace had arrived at a Bel Air pool party dressed as the immaculate collision of circus aerialist with Christmas tree, the Green Lantern would still make him look drab by comparison—as well as thoroughly butch. With the sexy villainess Harlequin vying for his attention and comedy foil Doiby Dickles by his side, Alan Scott was secure in his masculinity, and there was something challenging about his "costume" that deferred mockery. Not one criminal commented on the Green Lantern's elaborate departure from any form of sartorial normality or functionality. He was also the first superhero influenced by the esoteric culture of the East: His wish-fulfilling gem recalled the language of *The Tibetan Book of the Dead*, while the Lantern was Arabic, Islamic, and exotic. Echoes of the Green Lantern's eccentric costume—the high collar or the billowing sleeves— would appear in later "mystical" superheroes such as Doctor Strange as visual shorthand for the same Eastern influence.

The Flash (1940) was the first of the accidental supermen, prefiguring the heroes of the future Marvel universe: all victims of science, motivated by sheer altruism to use their great powers in the service of their communities. Jay Garrick, a research chemist who inadvertently inhaled "heavy water" fumes that gave him his power, wasn't strong or invulnerable or immortal, but he could run fast, and what kid hadn't dreamed of running faster and faster until the whole world accelerated into a blur and hurricane? In his crime-fighting guise as the Flash, Jay Garrick wore a tin-winged helmet, a red shirt with a lighting bolt motif, blue slacks, and boots with wings. In this way, he personified comic books' debts to one of their secret patron gods.

We've all seen the logo of the Interflora chain of florists. We may be familiar with Greek statues depicting a gracefully gliding youth in a tin helmet. This hat and the Flash's winged heels belong to the Greek god Hermes and his Roman counterpart, Mercury. He is the messenger of the gods, and he represents, quite simply, language itself. Like language, he is swift, inventive, tricky, slippery, and elusive.

In India, he is personified as elephant-headed Ganesh, who writes the story of existence with his own broken-off tusk. In Egypt, he was Thoth, the ibis-headed scribe. The earliest Babylonian cultures portrayed him as Nabu. In the voodoo pantheon, he is Legba; to the Celts, he was Ogma; and Viking mythology knew him as Odin, the one-eyed god, from whose shoulders the magical ravens—thought and memory—fly hither and yon to bring the god instant knowledge from all corners of the cosmos. In 1940 Hermes just couldn't resist showing up in person to join in all the fun as his fellow gods were reborn on paper.

He washed up with the rest of the trash in the swill of twentieth-century gutter culture but was given a new vitality down there where no one but children and illiterates were looking. No longer a god, but still a popular representation of a god, he was that bridge between man and the divine now known as the superhero. And the wing-festooned Flash was only one manifestation: Those were Hermes' fledged heels on Prince Namor, too, and the swift god's lightning brand would be worn by generations of superheroes. But he would find his truest expression, perhaps, in the form of Captain Marvel, the *bishonen*, the condemned young man who became the most serious threat to Superman's sales domination.

Today every comics company has at least one, and sometimes several, characters who are direct analogues of Superman: Mr. Majestic, Supreme, Samaritan, Sentry, Hyperion, Omega, the High, Apollo, Gladiator, Omniman, Optiman, the Public Spirit, Atoman the Homelander, Superior the Plutonian, Alpha One—the list unfurls like a toilet roll. All of these characters are thinly disguised copies of Superman published by companies other than DC, or in some cases by DC itself, as if one Superman was too few.

Things were different in 1940. A lucrative trademark was a jealously guarded intellectual property. National had their socialist strongman in fetters, milking his uniqueness for every dime and dollar. The last thing anyone there wanted was another Superman, let alone a potentially more charming and profitable one.

While National's legal team would eventually contrive to prove otherwise, Captain Marvel wasn't much like Superman at all. Superman celebrated the power of the individual in settings drawn to look as true to life as possible. Captain Marvel's stories offered a world that slid and slipped and became unreal, a world where the *word* took center stage. He embraced the interior world of dream logic, fairy-tale time, and toys that come to life. If Superman was Science Fiction, and Batman was Crime, Captain Marvel planted his flag in the wider territory of pure Fantasy.

His origin story detailed an out-and-out shamanic experience of a kind familiar to any witch doctor, ritual magician, anthropologist, or alien abductee.

Young Billy Batson's journey begins in a typically mundane setting. Here on a city street corner at night, the reader is introduced to an orphan boy, a victim of the Depression, selling newspapers outside the subway station where he sleeps rough. When Billy is approached by an odd character in a slouch hat and trench coat, he seems to take it all in stride. The stranger's face is hidden in the shadows beneath his hat brim, and Billy shows a level of trust that would seem unfeasible in our pedophile-haunted twenty-first-century world when he agrees to follow the dodgy figure into the station.

A train arrives in the otherwise deserted station, and it can only be a train from another reality, with modernist motifs daubed across its side like graffiti painted by Joan Miró. Resembling the streamlined Platonic prototype for Harry Potter's Hogwarts Express, the train carries Billy into a deep, dark tunnel that leads from this world to an elevated, magical plane where words are superspells that change the nature of reality.

Billy's psychedelic tunnel voyage culminates in another empty train station. Entering, the boy finds himself in a threatening archway of flaring shadows. At the end of the corridor, Billy stands face-to-face with a long-bearded "wizard" who outlines the boy's new and unexpected duties and abilities. All the while, a monstrous, trembling cube of granite hangs suspended by a splintering thread above the wise man's venerable skull. Everything is heightened, torch lit, and feverishly real as higher powers explain to Billy their plan.

Billy Batson, good and true, has been selected to take the place of the retiring wizard, who has used his powers to protect humankind for the last three thousand years and wants a break. The transfer of power is accomplished when Billy speaks the wizard's name—"Shazam!"— triggering a thunderclap and flash of lightning. In the swirling smoke of the ultimate conjuring trick stands a tall man in a cape. He wears a red military-style tunic with a chunky yellow lightning bolt on the chest. His cape is white with a high collar and braided yellow trim. He has a yellow sash around his waist, red tights, and yellow boots. (He wisely steers clear of the underpants-on-the-outside look.) With his slicked-back brilliantined hair, he looks like the boy Billy grown up, perfected. He looks, in actual fact, almost exactly like the actor Fred McMurray, upon whose features Charles Clarence Beck based those of his hero. His final task complete, the wizard slumps back in his throne, and the immense block of stone drops to smash his body flat. His spirit form haunts the panel like Obi-Wan Kenobi dispensing postmortem advice to the fledgling superhero.

It's a heady brew and it extends the potential of the superhero in the way that "Lucy in the Sky with Diamonds" pushed the prevailing idea of popular music into something unforeseen.

The magic word was a concept that connected the hero to the basis of human speech; language, storytelling. Captain Marvel's power came not from years in the gym or from his alien biology or his royal blood. His power came from a spell. He was a magician.

I remember walking alone as a child, chanting every word in the dictionary in the hope of finding my own *Shazam!* Eventually, everybody searches for his or her own magic word: the diet, the relationship, the wisdom that might liberate us from the conventional into the extraordinary. That eternal human hope for transcendence gave the Captain Marvel strip rocket fuel.

Shazam! has entered the culture as an *Abracadabra* or *Hey Presto!*—an all-purpose magical incantation. It was a word of enlightenment and personal transformation that accomplished, in a white-hot instant, what decades of Buddhist meditation could only point toward. His powers were the *siddhis* claimed by ultimate yogins. In the language of ceremonial magic, *Shazam!* summoned the holy guardian angel—the exalted future self—to come to one's aid. When Billy's natural curiosity got him into trouble, the word could summon Captain Marvel to deal with any and all consequences.

In fact, *Shazam* was an acronym. Captain Marvel's powers were derived from six gods and heroes of legend. He was endowed with the wisdom of Solomon, the strength of Hercules, the stamina of Atlas, the power of Zeus, the courage of Achilles, and the speed of Mercury. Mercury was all over the concept, from the bright yellow thunderbolt motif on the captain's scarlet tunic, to the word games and the presence of the old wizard who gave Billy his word. Billy worked as a roving boy reporter for WHIZ radio, going one step beyond newspaperman Clark Kent in scoring such a prestigious adult job. The tower atop the WHIZ building crackled like the RKO Pictures logo with graphic zigzags. A boy radio announcer seems so perfect a job for a modern Hermes that it's barely remarkable.

All of this made Marvel the first occult—or, perhaps more accurately, *Hermetic*—superhero; Marvel was the magus in tights, empowered by angels and the divine. Where Superman's strength relied on pseudoscientific explanations, Marvel's adventures opened doors to a world of magical self-belief and transformation. Where Superman tightened his jaw and tackled the ills of the real world, Marvel smiled a lot and had room for whimsy, warmth, and a well-developed personality. Where Superman's cape was plain, adorned with only his *S* brand, Marvel's was flamboyantly decorated with gold trim and fleur-de-lys; the military dress uniform of a regiment of future men and women.

Marvel heralded another innovation. Superheroes had so far been loners. In 1940 Batman had only just hooked up with Robin, and the era of boy sidekicks was yet to kick off in earnest, but Captain Marvel had family. A superhero family! In 1942, he was joined by his cousin Mary Batson, who only had to speak the name of her hero, "Captain Marvel," to transform from wise and good Mary Batson into the wise and good Mary Marvel, who could punch a building to dust. The third member of their team was the magnificent Captain Marvel Jr., from *Whiz Comics* no. 25, 1941.

In an era when so much of the artwork could at best be described as robust *primitif*, the work of Mac Raboy on these strips had an illustrative delicacy and a grasp of anatomy and movement that made it unique. His Captain Marvel Jr. was a lithe Ariel, effortlessly capturing the blue-sky freedom and potential of youth better than any other superhero. With such accomplished competition as Raboy in the studio, Beck's polished professional line work also developed a new gloss that propelled Captain Marvel's sales beyond those of even the mighty Superman. Backgrounds seemed more solid in Marvel Family stories, the shadows were blacker and more distinct, the focus and depth of field somehow sharper, and the comics developed a deluxe look that recalled Disney animation and the best of the newspaper strips.

In his turn, Captain Marvel spawned his own imitator, the British Marvelman—a character who provided my own first exposure to superheroes, when I was three years old and picking my way through a bizarre "Marvelman Meets Baron Munchausen" adventure. Marvelman was a child of necessity rather than inspiration. When DC successfully sued Fawcett Comics, Captain Marvel's publisher, in 1952 and new Captain Marvel comics ceased to appear, a hasty substitute strip was assembled to fill the pages of his ongoing British reprint title. Editor Mick Anglo reconfigured the basic Marvel Family setup and remade the character as a blond hero in a streamlined jet-age blue costume with no cape and no exterior underpants. Billy and Mary were replaced by Young Marvelman and Kid Marvelman. And yet, as if litigation was somehow built into the concept's atomic structure, Marvelman himself became the subject of a bitter court wrangle that continued for decades and involved major comic-book industry players like Alan Moore, Neil Gaiman, and Todd McFarlane. Captain Marvel and his cloned offspring found themselves tangled in statutes as if the law had enacted its judgment on Prometheus. Exile would follow. DC would go on to completely destroy Fawcett in court, but the word *Marvel* would return to haunt DC Comics.

Despite the legal wrangling, the exile and disempowerment of the original Captain Marvel, he and his family had made their mark on the culture. Elvis Presley's first single appeared three years after DC filed the lawsuit that brought down the entire Marvel Family universe, but the king of rock 'n' roll identified so strongly with Mac Raboy's lithe superboy that by the time his own physique was somewhat less than slender, he had his costumes designed to recall Captain Marvel Jr.'s boyish, cavalier spirit. Take a look at the short capes and high collars Presley wore in his later years and note how Captain Marvel Jr.'s tousled, jet-blue cut was re-created on Elvis's troubled head. Even the lightning bolt *TCB* logo on the tail of his private jet derived from Captain Marvel's chest emblem, marking the beginning of a continuing cross-pollination between comics and popular music, two equally despised and scapegoated midcentury art forms.

It is hardly any surprise that Captain Marvel was Ken Kesey's favorite superhero as well. In 1959 Kesey had volunteered to take part in a series of clinical LSD trials, which inspired him to write *One Flew Over the Cuckoo's Nest*. Kesey and some young followers painted a school bus with Day-Glo colors, wrote *Furthur* on the destination board, and set out to recruit an army of rebels—an alternative society of liberated superhuman beings.

The story of Kesey and his Pranksters with their superhero alter egos—Mountain Girl, Cool Breeze, Black Maria, Doris Delay—and dreams of a new society was transformed into myth by Tom Wolfe in *The Electric Kool-Aid Acid Test*, which talks of Kesey's trips into the mountains to summon down lightning from the Rock of Eternity and release a thunderbolt pure enough to blind the squares and deafen the bigots and change the world forever.

The spirit of Marvel lived on.

CHAPTER 3

THE SUPERWARRIOR AND THE AMAZON PRINCESS

TWO MONTHS BEFORE the December 7, 1941, Japanese attack on Pearl Harbor, the story "How Superman Would End the War" appeared in *Look* magazine. It showed Superman breaking into the führer's bunker, lifting the whimpering dictator by the throat, thus acting out the wishes of so many of his readers:

"I'D LIKE TO LAND A STRICTLY NON-ARYAN SOCK ON YOUR JAW, BUT THERE'S NO TIME FOR THAT! YOU'RE COMING WITH ME WHILE I VISIT A CERTAIN PAL OF YOURS."

The "pal" turned out to be Joseph Stalin. Superman whisked both men to the League of Nations headquarters in Geneva where, as the scowling despots sulked like scolded children, a headmasterly man with a gavel delivered his verdict:

"ADOLF HITLER AND JOSEPH STALIN—WE PRONOUNCE YOU GUILTY OF MODERN HISTORY'S GREATEST CRIME—UNPROVOKED AGGRESSION AGAINST DEFENSELESS COUNTRIES."

And that was how Superman would end the war. The Superman who slung wife beaters out of windows or threatened elected officials—the outlaw reformer of 1938—had somehow survived into a very different world from the world of his creation. In 1941 the idea of the revolutionary working-class hero was already suspect. Rough-and-ready toughs who took the law into their own hands were potentially traitorous revolutionaries. In a time of war, patriots were heroes and so the ultimate hero became a superpatriot. The man from Krypton was now a Good American, a staunch and enthusiastic defender of the status quo. There could be no such thing as a crooked president or corrupt cops in the world of forties Superman. It was a hostile makeover no less thorough than the one that sublimated the oily haired, transgressive libido of Elvis Presley into a US Army uniform and regulation buzz cut in 1958. Sample covers show the Man of Steel riding a phallic missile rodeo-style through the sky, twenty years before *Dr. Strangelove*. This newly domesticated Superman posed with an American Eagle perched on his arm, and in one memorably tasteless episode, he encouraged his readers to "Slap a Jap!" as an aid to the war effort.

Then in 1941, Marvel's *Captain America Comics* no. 1 pioneered a new superhero who made it his mission to strike back against the "Japanazi" menace with no holds barred. Captain America, the ultimate patriotic superhero, was the brainchild of another of comics' great creative double acts: Joe Simon and Jack Kirby.

Jack "King" Kirby was the most influential superhero artist of them all, with an imagination and range that sat comfortably inside a visionary tradition running all the way from Hebrew scriptures and epic mythology through William Blake and Allen Ginsberg. Born Jakob Kurtzberg in August 1917—Jack Kirby was the one of his many pennames that stuck—Kirby grew up in a tenement on Manhattan's Lower East Side. As a member of the Suffolk Street Gang, he was familiar with the thrill of full-on physical conflict in a way that many of his bookish young contemporaries were not. Indeed, unlike Joe Shuster or Bob Kane, who drew fights at a sniffy remove, Kirby dragged his readers directly into the wild flail of fists and boots that typified the real combat he'd experienced. His figures captured how it *felt* to somersault through a crowd of antagonists. His heroes and villains clashed in bony, meaty brawls that could sprawl across page after page. Superman might wrestle a giant ape for a panel or two, but in Kirby's hands, the fight scenes were a thrilling end in themselves.

Kirby served in World War II as a private first class in Company F of the Eleventh Infantry. He landed on Omaha Beach at Normandy two months after D-day in 1944 and proceeded with his unit into occupied France. There he saw action at the battle for Bastogne, Belgium, enduring frostbite so severe that Kirby almost lost both feet and was finally mustered out with a combat infantry badge and Bronze Star for his trouble. His memories of the war informed his work for the rest of his life, but nonetheless, Kirby portrayed violence as a joyous expression of natural masculine exuberance. When American Nazis marched into the building where Simon and Kirby had their studio, demanding the blood of the *Captain America* creative team, it was Jack who rolled up his sleeves and went to sort them out.

As for Captain America himself, he was Steve Rogers, a skinny 4-F who volunteered for a military experiment designed to turn an ordinary man into a superwarrior. Like my dad, or Jack Kirby, Steve just wanted a crack at Hitler. And, like many men in the populations of the Allied nations, he reckoned he could take the scrawny little paperhanger if only there weren't thousands of miles of occupied territory, barbed wire, soldiers, tanks, and minefields between the sniveling Adolf and the proud fist of retribution.

Unlike Superman or Batman, Captain America was a soldier with permission to kill. Until this point, the superheroes operated on the fringes of the law, but Captain America's violent work was endorsed by the Constitution itself! Turned down for the military, Steve applied for an experimental treatment of Super Soldier Serum and Vita-Rays. Before the formula could be mass-produced, its creator was murdered by Nazi agents, leaving a newly brawny and supercharged Steve Rogers as Uncle Sam's one and only supersoldier.

Each issue of *Captain America* was kinetic, brutally overwrought, and sensationalistic. Every cover featured a brand-new tableau of imminent superatrocity: A girl, her blouse ripped to ribbons, writhes on a medieval torture rack while a leering hunchback, preferably sporting swastika tattoos, threatens her cleavage with a glowing poker; Captain America launches himself through a wall on a motorcycle, destroying a portrait of Hitler on the way and simultaneously repelling a hail of bullets with his Stars and Stripes shield, while his faithful teen partner, Bucky, mows down Ratzis with the feral glee of a William S. Burroughs wild boy. There would invariably be some combination of boiling oil, rabid gorillas, vampires, or fiendish snake-fanged Japanese involved. Every square inch of illustration contained a frozen moment of grotesque threat or swashbuckling derring-do.

Kirby relied on his remarkable drawing skills to provide a living for his family and was serious about selling his books in an overcrowded market. Where Superman had flown the Axis leaders to an international court of law, Captain America took the fantasy to its far more satisfying next level. Kirby knew that wish-fulfillment pictures of American superheroes punching out Hitler's teeth would sell magazines in a fearful world, and his instincts were right. In Captain America, Simon and Kirby gave America's troops, in the field or at home, a hero they could call their own.

Superhero stories were written to be universal and inclusive, but often they've been aimed, it must be said, at boys and young men. Perhaps that's why a mainstream myth has developed in which comic-book superheroines are all big-breasted *Playboy* girls with impossibly nipped waists and legs like jointed stilts in six-inch heels. But while it's true that superhero costumes allow artists to draw what is effectively the nude figure in motion, there have in fact been more female superhero body types than male.

The first superheroine, you may be surprised to learn, was not a voluptuous cutie in thigh boots but a raw-faced middle-aged housewife called Ma Hunkel, who wore a blanket cape and a pan on her head in her debut appearance, *All-American* no. 20, 1940. A harridan with the build of a brick shithouse she was the first "real-world" superhero—with no powers, a DIY outfit, and a strictly local beat—and the first parody of the superhero genre all in one. Ma Hunkel, aka the Red Tornado, was a Lower East Side lampoon of Siegel and Shuster's lofty idealism. The mainstream has forgotten Ma Hunkel, although, like all the rest, she's still a part of the DC universe and now has a granddaughter named Maxine Hunkel, a talkative, realistically proportioned, and likeable teenage girl who also challenges the superbimbo stereotype.

But, of course, the comic-book industry in the throes of the war machine did churn out its fair share of pinup bombshells and no-nonsense dames with names like Spitfire and Miss Victory, or the strangely comforting Pat Parker, War Nurse. With no particular ax to grind against the Axis forces, Pat Parker was driven only by her desire to dress up like a showgirl and take to the battlefields of Western Europe on life-threatening missions of mercy. She was prepared to take on entire tank divisions with a refugee quivering under each arm. What made her tank-battling activities especially brave was the fact that this war nurse had no special powers and wore a costume so insubstantial, there could be nothing secret about her lunch, let alone her identity. But, absurd as she may seem, she did her best to exemplify the can-do, Rosie the Riveter spirit of those women who were "manning" the home front.

And then there was the most famous superheroine of them all. Wonder Woman was the creation of William Moulton Marston, the man who, not incidentally, invented the controversial polygraph test apparatus, or lie detector, that is still in use today. Marston was a professor at Columbia and Tufts universities, and Radcliffe College—and a good one, according to accounts of the time—and the author of several respected works of popular psychology. Like other forward thinkers, Marston saw in comics the potential to convey complex ideas in the form of exciting and violent symbolic dramas. He described the great educational potential of the comics in an article titled "Don't Laugh at the Comics," which appeared in the popular women's magazine *Family Circle* in 1940 and led to his getting hired as an educational consultant at DC-National.

Marston coupled his ideas with an unorthodox lifestyle: his wife, Elizabeth, was also a psychologist, and is credited with having suggested a superheroine character. Both were enthusiastic proponents of a progressive attitude toward sex and relationships. They shared a mutual lover, a student of Marston's named Olive Byrne, said to be the physical model for the original Harry Peter drawings of Wonder Woman. Together, Marston and Peter (with indispensable input from Elizabeth and Olive) developed a fantasy world of staggering richness. For sheer invention, for relentless dedication to the core concept, the Wonder Woman strip far surpassed its competitors.

But unlike traditional pinups, the girls of *Wonder Woman* were athletic and forceful. They wore tiaras and togas while they engaged in violent gladiatorial contests on the backs of giant, genetically engineered monster kangaroos. Wonder Woman was traditionally sexy—there were pinup shots—but in most panels, she yomped and stomped like some martial arts majorette, outracing automobiles for fun.

1941's "Introducing Wonder Woman" began when an air force plane crashed on an uncharted island inhabited exclusively by beautiful scantily clad women capable of carrying the full-grown air force pilot "as if he were a child." The man, Captain Steve Trevor of US Army Intelligence, was the first to ever set foot on Paradise Island, and within moments, the queen's daughter, Princess Diana, had fallen in love.

A two-page illustrated-text section revealed the history of the Amazons since their slavery at the hands of Hercules. Encouraged by their patron goddess Aphrodite, they liberated themselves and set sail for a magical island where they could establish a new civilization of women, far from the cruelty, greed, and violence that typified "man's world." On Paradise Island, the immortal women set about fashioning their fabulous alternative to patriarchal, heliocentric society.

In this first issue, Hippolyta, the queen of the Amazons, consulted apparitions of Aphrodite and Athena, who clarified that Trevor had been sent deliberately by the gods. It was time, apparently, for the Amazons to emerge from seclusion and join the worldwide struggle against Axis tyranny. Trevor had to be sent home to complete his mission against the enemy—but he was not to return alone.

"YOU MUST SEND WITH HIM THE STRONGEST OF YOUR WONDER WOMEN!—FOR AMERICA, THE LAST CITADEL OF DEMOCRACY, AND OF EQUAL RIGHTS FOR WOMEN, NEEDS YOUR HELP!"

A contest was declared to identify the most appropriate candidate. Tests included outrunning a deer and culminated in the favorite sport of these immortal ladettes: bullets and bracelets. A kind of Russian roulette, the game saw the final contenders facing one another with loaded revolvers (where the staunchly antiwar Amazons managed to get hold of working firearms remains a mystery). Bullets were fired at the opponent, who was obliged to deflect them with her bracelets in order to win the game. The loser took a flesh wound to the shoulder. In the end one champion remained: a masked brunette, revealed in a not entirely unexpected twist to be Princess Diana herself.

"AND SO DIANA, THE WONDER WOMAN, GIVING UP HER HERITAGE AND HER RIGHT TO ETERNAL LIFE, LEAVES PARADISE ISLAND TO TAKE THE MAN SHE LOVES BACK TO

AMERICA—THE LAND SHE LEARNS TO LOVE AND PROTECT, AND ADOPTS AS HER OWN!"

However, within this world—and supplying it with depth and enticing richness—lurked barely hidden libidinal elements. To begin with, it has to be said that these Amazons were drawn to be sexy. Whereas Siegel rendered Superman in dynamic futurist lines and Bob Kane gave Batman the look of a Prague potato print, Peter brought a flowing, scrolling quality to his drawings of superwomen in action and at play. Everything was curved and calligraphic. The lips of his women were modishly bee stung and glossy, as if to suggest that Hollywood-style glamour makeup never went out of vogue among the warrior women and philosopher princesses of Paradise Island.

However, as you may expect in a society of immortal women cut off from the rest of the world since classical antiquity, the diversions of the Amazons turned out to be somewhat specialized, to say the least. As the strips developed, Marston's prose swooned over detailed accounts of Amazonian chase and capture rituals in which some girls were "eaten" by others.

Moreover thousands of years of sophisticated living without men had bled the phallic thrust out of sexuality, leaving the peculiar, ritualistic eroticism of leash and lock. Marston and Peter built slavery and shackles into "Meet Wonder Woman," and as the strip progressed, the bondage elements became more overt, increasing sales. For instance, chief among Wonder Woman's weapons of peace was a magic lasso, which compelled anyone bound in its coils to tell the absolute truth and only the truth—shades of Marston's polygraph. It wasn't long before she was breathlessly demonstrating the joys of submission to "loving authority": A Nazi villain's slave girls were released in one story, with no idea what to do with their lives out of captivity. Wonder Woman's solution was to allow them to continue to express their nature as born slaves by relocating to Paradise Island, where they could enjoy bondage under the loving gaze of a kind mistress instead of the crop-cracking Hitler-loving Paula von Gunther.

The flipside of the Amazons' essentially benign and formalized endorsement of healthy S/M was the dungeon world of sadistic bondage, humiliation, and mind control that existed in the world beyond Paradise Island. These were crystallized in the form of Doctor Poison, a twisted dwarf in a rubber coat. Wielding a dripping syringe, Poison hated women and loved to humiliate them. In a surprising twist, "he" was revealed to be a mentally ill woman acting out of her frustrations.

The women of Paradise Island embodied an enticing blend of the politically right-on and the libidinous. As such, they were exemplars of a newfangled twentieth-century creed that was the same old bohemian "free love" with a new lexicon culled from psychoanalytical theory and the pink and squeezy world of dreams and desire. Theirs was a kind of radical Second Wave separatist feminism where men were forbidden and things could only get better as a result.

Indeed, in Marston's feminine paradise, happiness and security were in far greater supply than elsewhere in the superworld. In looking at other superhero comics he had noted, "it seemed from a psychological angle that the comics' worst offence was their blood-curdling masculinity. A male hero, at best, lacks the qualities of maternal love and tenderness which are as essential to the child as the breath of life."

And so, while Batman was a brooding orphan, and the destruction of Superman's Krypton had robbed him of his birth parents, the magnificent scientists Jor-El and Lara, Wonder Woman could ride her invisible plane down the rainbow runway to Paradise Island and check in with Mom any time she wanted. Queen Hippolyta even had a magic mirror that allowed her to observe her daughter at any location on Earth. It was closed-circuit television by any other name, but in late 1941, Hippolyta's magic mirror could only be a product of imaginary feminist superscience.

There were some similarities with Wonder Woman's male predecessors. Like Superman, in his way, Wonder Woman fearlessly championed alternative culture and a powerful vision of outsider politics. And, like Batman, she was thoroughly the progressive sort of aristocrat. She preached peace in a time of war, although she was as eager as any other superhero to tackle her fair share of Nazis. Unlike the essentially solitary Batman and Superman, Wonder Woman had a huge cast of friends. Her allies, the Holliday Girls of Beta Lamda, were a rambunctious group of sorority sisters fronted by the immense, freckled redhead Etta Candy. As the gorgeous Wonder Woman's inevitable fat pal, Etta's positive energy and physicality added an earthiness and humor that complemented Diana's cool grace and perfect poise.

When Marston died of cancer in 1947, the erotic charge left the *Wonder Woman* strip, and sales declined, never to recover. Without the originality and energy that Marston's obsessions brought to the stories, Wonder Woman was an exotic bloom starved of rare nutrients. Once the lush, pervy undercurrents were purged, the character foundered. The island of Themiscyra was scraped clean of any hint of impropriety, and all girl-chasing rituals ceased, along with reader commitment to the character. It wasn't long before Wonder Woman was coming across as an odd maiden aunt—a disturbing cross between the Virgin Mary and Mary Tyler Moore; but Elizabeth and Olive, her inspirations, continued to live together. The unconventional, liberated Elizabeth was one hundred years old when she died in 1993, the true Wonder Woman of this story.

CHAPTER 4

THE EXPLOSION AND THE EXTINCTION

WITH THE WORLD on the verge of war, readers couldn't get enough of the superheroes, especially in the comic books. Superheroes flowed into every free and available conceptual niche and found publishers eager to mass-produce the color fantasies of a generation of children, servicemen, and science fiction fans. If one short-lived company was having brief success with a bird-winged star, another would inevitably try out a guy with a tail. There were superhero cowboys (the Vigilante), superhero knights (the Shining Knight), superhero cops (the Guardian), and then there was the Gay Ghost, a sixteenth-century Cavalier. What had been one superhero tentatively testing the possibilities of the market became two, then too many to count. This grand condensation from nothing into storms and rainbows brought forth a florid array of extraordinary, archetypal, and outright weird mystery men and women.

The race to create superheroes with fresh gimmicks crashed headlong into one spectacular dead end with the Red Bee, the crime-fighting persona of a man named Rick Raleigh. Rick took to the streets wearing a costume that would result in immediate arrest if worn anywhere outside of Studio 54 in 1978. But whereas the Green Lantern was able to defend himself with a magic ring that could do virtually anything, the Red Bee had chosen a more specialized weapon.

Raleigh was clever enough to have invented his own "sting gun," which shot effective knockout darts. He could have simply loaded up his sting gun, stopped right there, and still made a perfectly serviceable Golden Age mystery man called the Red Bee. But for Rick Raleigh, only one thing guaranteed his crucial edge over the violent underbelly of society: the hive of trained crime-fighting bees he kept confined in the *buckle of his belt*—a space no bigger than a pack of ten cigarettes—until crime reared its snout. Ever eager to be set free in the cause of justice, the lead bee and chief offensive weapon in Raleigh's apian arsenal was somewhat endearingly named Michael. However, as the writer of the Red Bee's Wikipedia article cruelly observes, male bees *do not sting*, calling into question Michael's effectiveness in any potential struggle against armed thugs or machete-wielding Triad enforcers.

If it seems ridiculous, it's because it is. But there was something else going on here: a radical enchantment of the mundane. As the creators of the superheroes pitched their nets ever wider in search of fresh and original gimmicks, they touched more and more of the everyday world with childlike wonder dust. Bees could be special, just as they were in medieval illuminated texts and mysteries. Boring gym equipment could become the lethal arsenal of the criminal known as Sportsmaster. A discarded railroad lantern could be a mystic artifact capable of bestowing immense power. In the world of the superheroes, everything had value, potential, mystery. Any person, thing, or object could be drafted into service in the struggle against darkness and evil—remade as a weapon or a warrior or a superhero. Even a little bee named Michael—after God's own avenging angel—could pitch in to win the battle against wickedness.

There was a superhero or villain for every profession, every class, every walk of life. Need a superhero lawyer? Call Native American Jeff Dixon, the Bronze Terror. Navy lieutenant Peter Noble kept the oceans safe as the Fin. Ted Knight, aka Starman, was an astronomer. Duke O'Dowd, the Human Meteor, drove a taxi. The blind doctor Charles McNider, whose particular condition enabled him to see in the dark, cleverly assumed that no one in his right mind would see any connection between handsome six-foot-two Doctor McNider and handsome six-foot-two Doctor Mid-Nite. Dinah Drake, the Black Canary, ran a small flower shop when she wasn't rough-riding her motorcycle into the face of urban crime. This was the first explosion of the rainbow, the Precambrian abundance of memes before the imminent mass extinction.

Like jazz and rock 'n' roll, the superhero is a uniquely American creation. This glorification of strength, health, and simple morality seems born of a corn-fed, plain-talking, fair-minded midwestern sensibility. But superheroes were nothing if not adaptable, and as they grew and multiplied across the comic-book pages of the Free World, they happily took on the flavor of their surroundings, like milk left in a fridge with onions, or bananas.

British superheroes were a rum bunch, beginning with odd cargo cult creations like 1944's the Amazing Mr. X from *The Dandy*, the first home-grown Superman rip-off. Clad in a black cape and cowl, with black tights and a white vest on which a red *X* was marked, this abject knockoff was saved from being completely derivative only by his utter rejection of Superman's professionalism. X was Len Manners, whose superstrength was the result of nothing more than vigorous exercise. He looked like a man who'd tried enthusiastically to copy a description of Superman supplied to him by another man with early-onset Alzheimer's. The design was simple and graphic, but the character had about him—like almost all UK superheroes—the stink of the bargain bin, the jumble sale, and the Sunday flea market. He left behind the stale odor of rationing and austerity, in a costume that may as well have been assembled from oddments found at a Salvation Army thrift store.

Then there were Ace Hart, Atoman, Captain Magnet, and the questionable Electroman, who was archcriminal Dan Watkins endowed with the powers of the electric chair when his planned execution went wrong, resulting in a change of heart and a vow to fight evil wherever he found it. Like their American cousins, British heroes dressed in what were intended to be tight-fitting jumpsuits, but somehow they contrived to look rumpled, wrinkled, and ill fitting. The strongmen of Blighty eschewed the Charles Atlas method and nurtured their doughy, unimpressive muscles on a diet of porridge and corned beef.

Elsewhere abroad, there were further mutations. In Japan, there was Astro Boy (1951), with his odd hieratic gestures and staccato cries. He was a robot boy, a techno-Pinocchio in a story that was updated and subjected to ruthless real-world logic and drama in Naoki Urasawa's 2007 *Pluto*. *Gigantor* (1964) spoke directly to my own childhood dream of owning a remote control box that put me in charge of a thirty-foot-tall mechanical man. I imagined sitting on his back, manipulating the joysticks to make him demolish the walls and roof of my school. Later there was 1967's Marine Boy, who chewed "oxy-gum" so that he could breathe underwater. Japan's Superman was Ultraman—a towering alien/human hybrid with the soul of a hero.

France had *Le Chat*, *Fantax*, *Satanax*, and several other Scrabble high-score hits. These heroes, you may not be surprised to learn, were racy and often unscrupulous heirs to the tradition of Fantômas, the Parisian superthief created by Pierre Souvestre and Marcel Allain and beloved by surrealists. Their heroines, like Jean-Claude Forest's space girl Barbarella, based on Brigitte Bardot, were leggy practitioners of free love, capable of extending their amorous intent toward robots or even monsters. Barbarella would fuck her way across the cosmos with the untroubled gaze of a wide-eyed debutante. She was played by Jane Fonda in Roger Vadim's camp 1968 movie version, a film that was, I have to admit, responsible for my own feverish sexual awakening and retains a fond place in my imagination.

Italy had all the sexy, violent antiheroes. In 1962 the sisters Angela and Luciana Giussani would create Diabolik, a kind of Batman in reverse, who dressed in white leather. He was the hero Batman would be if he'd chosen to really fuck with the law. Diabolik was yet another chic Fantômas reworking: a master thief, handsome, intelligent, and immensely wealthy. He drove an E-type Jag, and his constant companion was the drop-dead-brilliant überwoman Eva Kant. The characters were played to beautiful, deadpan perfection by John Phillip Law and Marisa Mell in the 1968 film *Danger: Diabolik*. This character's success would inspire a rash of copy-cat antiheroes and the rise of Italy's controversial *fumetti neri* or "black comic books." Characters like Kriminal, Satanik, and Sadistik developed Diabolik's Nietzschean amorality through new extremes of sadism and sexual violence that eventually led to the banning of the *fumetti neri* in the mid-1960s. Even the monstrous Kriminal was castrated and forced to re-emerge as a debonair gentleman thief with, it must be said, no particular appeal for readers (his strip was subsequently canceled in 1974).

The unconscious ease with which the superheroes of each country cheerfully embodied the stereotypical qualities of their homelands was almost embarrassing. As in music, they all played their own version of the US sound, but only America had the real deal—Boy Scouts with explosive fight scenes, dazzling costumes, and soap opera. When Brits played the superhero song, it came with an indie drone; a nasal whine perfected in the sniveling rain. European heroes played it like Gains-bourg, with a roguish, cynical, and antiestablishment sexuality. The Japanese sound was a futurist electro din of machine men and monsters, echoes of the Bomb.

When American comics became more inclusive and began to introduce their own versions of foreign characters, it was in the vein of the International Club of Heroes (1955), a group of Batman counterparts from different countries. There were the figures of national stereotype: the Legionary dressed like a Roman soldier to fight crime, for instance. The Musketeer wore D'Artagnan drag to battle the Parisian underworld. The Knight and the Squire were an aristocratic father-and-son duo who donned suits of armor and raced onto the cobbled streets of Merrie England on motorcycles done up to look like medieval warhorses whenever the rectory bell summoned them to action.

The Brits would generally have origin stories rooted in legend or history. When Marvel dipped its toes in the British weekly market by launching *Captain Britain* as a weekly comic in 1976, the assignment was handed to American Anglophile Chris Claremont on the grounds that he'd visited the place once or twice and had a fondness for TV shows like *The Avengers*. He went directly to the stone circles of pseudo-Arthurian legend where the captain received his powers and his fighting staff as a result of some mystic glowing folderol among the menhirs. Merlin, naturally, was implicated.

As *Captain Britain* demonstrated, local legend could always be relied upon to produce superheroes from whole cloth, so we also had the Beef-eater, Godiva—with her living hair—Union Jack, Spitfire, the Black Knight, Jack O'Lantern, and many others.

The simplest option was to base the character's look on a national flag, like the Canadian superhero Weapon Alpha, whose otherwise elegant one-piece costume was built around a giant red maple leaf motif. His teammate, Wolverine, started life as a result of that same shorthand approach to national disposition, but he was able to struggle free of his origins to develop a more rounded character that made him one of the most successful creations in comics.

During the years of the Second World War, the superhero concept spread like wildfire, but then died as rapidly and mysteriously as it had begun. Mass popular interest dwindled sharply after 1945, and superhero titles disappeared to be replaced by genre books that tripled the overall sales of the comics business between 1945 and 1954. Horror, Western, humor, romance, and war titles proliferated and made the kind of money that superheroes couldn't match. With no more heroes left to hold back the tide, the streets of the American popular imagination filled with zombies, junkies, radioactive monsters, and sweating gunmen.

What had made the superheroes so resonant and then so equally ir-relevant? Was it only World War II that gave the supermen their urgent significance? The end of the war tipped Americans into a new age of plenty and paranoia. The United States had everything, but it shared with its enemies a superweapon capable of reducing even the sunniest suburban garden party to a fleshless, howling wasteland. Is it any won-der that gloomy existentialism captured so many imaginations in the 1950s? In the postwar West, having X-ray eyes would henceforth be a horror movie curse.

We end the Golden Age as it began, with Superman—one of the last survi-vors of the initial brief expansion and rapid contraction of the DC universe. It had been too much too soon for the superheroes, but although many of them would lie dormant for decades, no potential trademark truly dies. The superheroes, like cockroaches or Terminators, are impossible to kill. But in 1954 a sinister scientist straight from the pages of the comics tried to wipe them all out and came close to succeeding.

As the lights went out on the Golden Age, characters such as Superman, Batman, and Wonder Woman, who'd achieved a wider recognition thanks to serials and merchandising, survived the cull. Because of their status as backup strips in *Adventure Comics*, second stringers like Green Arrow and Aquaman weathered the storm—perhaps undeservedly—but the survivors did not always flourish.

For instance, a popular TV series (1953's *The Adventures of Superman*) had cemented Superman's status as an American icon, but budgetary restrictions meant that its star, the likeable but ultimately troubled George Reeves, was rarely seen in the air. At best, he might jump in through a window at an angle that suggested methods of entry other than flight, possibly involving trampolines. The stories revolved around low-level criminal activity in Metropolis and ended when Superman burst through another flimsy wall to apprehend another gang of bank robbers or spies. Bullets would bounce from his monochrome chest (the series was shot and transmitted before color TV, so Reeves's costume was actually rendered in grayscale, not red and blue, which wouldn't have contrasted so well in black and white.)

Reeves, at nearly forty, was a patrician Superman with a touch of gray around the temples and a physique that suggested middle-aged spread rather than six-pack, but he fit the mold of the fifties establishment figure: fatherly, conservative, and trustworthy. The problem with Superman was more obvious in the comic books. By aping the kitchen-sink scale of the Reeves show, Superman's writers and artists squandered his epic potential on a parade of gangsters, pranksters, and thieves. The character born in a futurist blaze of color and motion had washed up on a black-and-white stage set, grounded by the turgid rules of a real world that kept his wings clipped and his rebel spirit chained. Superman was now locked into a death trap more devious than anything Lex Luthor could have devised. Here was Superman—even *Superman*—tamed and domesticated in a world where the ceiling, not the sky, was the limit.

Fifties comics had taken a turn toward the dark, lurid, and horrific. The story of EC Comics, which replaced the popularity of the hero titles and brought about a nationwide moral panic, is a fascinating one and has been covered in depth elsewhere—David Hajdu's *The Ten-Cent Plague: The Great Comic-Book Scare and How It Changed America* has a chilling fifteen-page roll call of artists and writers, many young and promising, who never worked again after the comic-book purges of the fifties. But this book is about superheroes, and for superheroes, times were especially tough.

Imagine the response at a dinner party this evening if you whipped out your rouged nipples and proudly announced a passion for hard-core kiddie porn. As difficult as it may be to believe today, in 1955 the kind of outrage that would reasonably greet your twisted confession was directed toward artists, writers, editors, and anyone else involved in the business of comic books. Comic books and their creators were painted as cunning corrupters of children, as monstrous artifacts crafted by experts to twist young and impressionable minds in the direction of crime, drug addiction, and debauch.

At the heart of this attempt to annihilate an art form was an elderly psychiatrist named Fredric Wertham who would throw his considerable weight and expertise behind a sustained hate campaign aimed at comic books. His 1954 best-seller *Seduction of the Innocent* blamed the comics and their creators for every social ill to afflict America's children.

However, it wasn't just EC's often tasteless horror stories that fired Dr. Wertham's rage; almost inexplicably, it was the innocent, floundering superhero titles that really got him foaming. Like any good predator, he could sense their weakness and knew that no articulate voice was likely to speak up as comic books' advocate. If an "expert" like Wertham said they were pornography, then they were pornography. With little to offend anyone in the content of these comics, Wertham was forced to dig deep into an ever-fertile loam of subtext in order to justify a fevered one-handed attack that was conducted with the same brutish, ignorant disregard for the truth that was said to characterize America's enemies.

For example, in Batman's living arrangements with ward Dick Grayson (Robin) and Alfred the butler, the good doctor was certain that he discerned the "wish-dream of two homosexuals living together." Perhaps it *was* the wish-dream of two homosexuals. Only those particular two homosexuals could tell us for certain.

Yes, it's all too easy from a knowing adult perspective to infer Bruce Wayne's epicene qualities. It wouldn't take much pressure to gently dial up all the familiar elements of a Batman story until the fetishistic homosexual undercurrent implicit in the basic scenario of three generations of men living together in luxury and lawlessness stood revealed in all its black rubber glory. Director Joel Schumacher walked some way down that road in his universally reviled 1997 film *Batman and Robin*, with George Clooney, Chris O'Donnell, and Michael Gough occupying the central roles. There's a case to be made for the satanic and even sexually transgressive appeal of Batman to adults: wealthy, literally Plutonian, and of the underworld, Batman inhabits a subterranean secret lair, dresses in badass black leather, enjoys the company of a small boy in tights, and has no steady girlfriend. Perhaps there remains to be written the great gay Batman story where he and Robin, and potentially Alfred too, are going at it like trip hammers between Batmobile cruising scenes, but the hollow specter of Dr. Wertham can take it from me that the young readers of Batman saw only a wish-dream of freedom and high adventure. It is Wertham whose name belongs in the annals of perversity, not Batman's.

Unsurprisingly, Wertham's blue-movie take on *Wonder Woman* cast her as an outrageous lesbian, representing an island of perverse militant dykes with a taste for ritual bondage and domination. Astonishingly, he seemed almost oblivious to the more candid kinks of his rival pop psychologist Marston's lifestyle, gnawing instead at the blatant lesbian shout-out in Wonder Woman's oft-repeated oath, "*SUFFERING SAPPHO!*" which no doubt conjured predictable images in the good doctor's strobe-lit imagination.

But it was Superman—benign Superman—who bore the brunt of Wertham's hatred. Describing the Man of Steel as a fascistic distortion of truth designed to make children feel inadequate and inclined toward delinquency, he opined obliquely:

> How can they respect the hard-working mother, father, or teacher who is so pedestrian, trying to teach the common rules of conduct, wanting you to keep your feet on the ground and unable even figuratively speaking to fly through the air? Psychologically Superman undermines the authority and dignity of the ordinary man and woman in the minds of children.

In Wertham's diagnosis, then, children were too underdeveloped to separate the outlandish fantasy in their comic books from everyday reality, and this made them vulnerable to barely concealed homosexual and antisocial content.

I tend to believe the reverse is true: that it's adults who have the most trouble separating fact from fiction. A child knows that real crabs on the beach do not sing or talk like the cartoon crabs in *The Little Mermaid*. A child can accept all kinds of weird-looking creatures and bizarre occurrences in a story because the child understands that stories have different rules that allow for pretty much anything to happen.

Adults, on the other hand, struggle desperately with fiction, demanding constantly that it conform to the rules of everyday life. Adults foolishly demand to know *how* Superman can possibly fly, or *how* Batman can possibly run a multibillion-dollar business empire during the day and fight crime at night, when the answer is obvious even to the smallest child: because it's not real.

Wertham's assault made comics the focus of a nationwide hate campaign. Good Americans who had grown up with the inoffensive adventures of Superman and Batman gathered in howling mobs to burn superhero comics in mountainous heaps upon which the colorful, optimistic dream-people were turned to flame and ash, smoke and soot. (Within ten years, packs of goons just like these would be hurling Beatles albums on similar bonfires with equal brainless fervor.)

In 1954 congressional hearings left horror publisher EC Comics wounded beyond repair. Purged of outlaw content, the remaining publishers banded together for survival and drafted a draconian Comics Code that would ensure child-friendly content. In its mean-spirited, machinelike thoroughness, its precise articulation of dos and don'ts, it was almost— to use the language of the day—*Soviet* in tone. In many ways, born from similar circumstances, the Comics Code mirrored the Hays Motion Picture Production Code of 1930, which aimed to transform the racy, intoxicated Hollywood movies of the day into inoffensive, sexless fairy tales. The Thought Police were marching proudly in the Land of the Free:

- Policemen, judges, government officials, and respected institutions shall never be presented in such a way as to create disrespect for established authority.
- Scenes dealing with, or instruments associated with, walking dead, torture, vampires and vampirism, ghouls, cannibalism, and werewolfism are prohibited.

- Respect for parents, the moral code, and for honorable behavior shall be fostered.

And so on. Comics that conformed to code standards were published with a little "Approved by the Comics Code Authority" stamp in the top right corner. Comic books that didn't carry the code were unlikely to be distributed or given space on newsstands and therefore faced extinction, so it was in the interests of publishers to comply. It seemed now that even the form that had conceived the superheroes, the 2-D universe in which they lived, was in peril.

The Golden Age was over. But the world in which the heroes were dying was a world that needed them like never before. Fifties America was a land of edginess and prowling paranoia hovering as it did on the verge of thermonuclear annihilation. Alone at night, in the midst of unprecedented luxury after a successfully won world war, Americans were more frightened than ever before; there was fear of the Bomb, the Communist, the Homo, the Negro, the Teenager, the Id, the Flying Saucers, the Existential Void. There was the space race, with its launch into the limitless unknown, and Kinsey's groundbreaking surveys into the sexual habits of Americans, opening the dripping treasure chest of a buttoned-up country's inner life, revealing a sleep world of polychromatic polymorphous perversity acted out behind a camouflage of pipe-smoking patriarchs and Stepford wives. There were as many different kinds of fear as there were brands of gum.

And as America turned its gaze inward in search of solutions to its sunlit terrors, it found the Shadow, and the multiheaded thing in the cellar emerged blinking in the light: Survival cultists, split personalities, UFO contactees like George Adamski were all admitted to the discourse, and people were willing to listen. The Dharma Bums and the beatniks had begun to crystallize from the margins into a movement. The queer, the criminal, the deranged, and the inspired emerged like Morlocks from subterranean nightclub cellars spitting poetry. The spread of psychedelics and marijuana through the jazz underground into the arts schools and the emergent culture of rock 'n' roll hastened the rise of this fringe. The urge to control and tame the American subconscious was now spawning new things to attempt to control, newer and weirder ideas to understand and explain away.

By the middle of the twentieth century, then, history was happening too fast, at an increasingly heightened pitch, and the tide of futurity seemed unstoppable. Nothing was stable after all. Not the war, not the peace, not the Self. Perhaps only the superheroes could have made sense of an accelerated, mediated world like this, but to a man, to a woman, they were gone, banished beyond the outer dark by their fearful adversaries.

Soon, though, they would return to soar higher, faster, and farther than ever before. So high, so far, and so fast, in fact, that they had to start up a whole new age just to contain them.

PART 2

The SILVER AGE

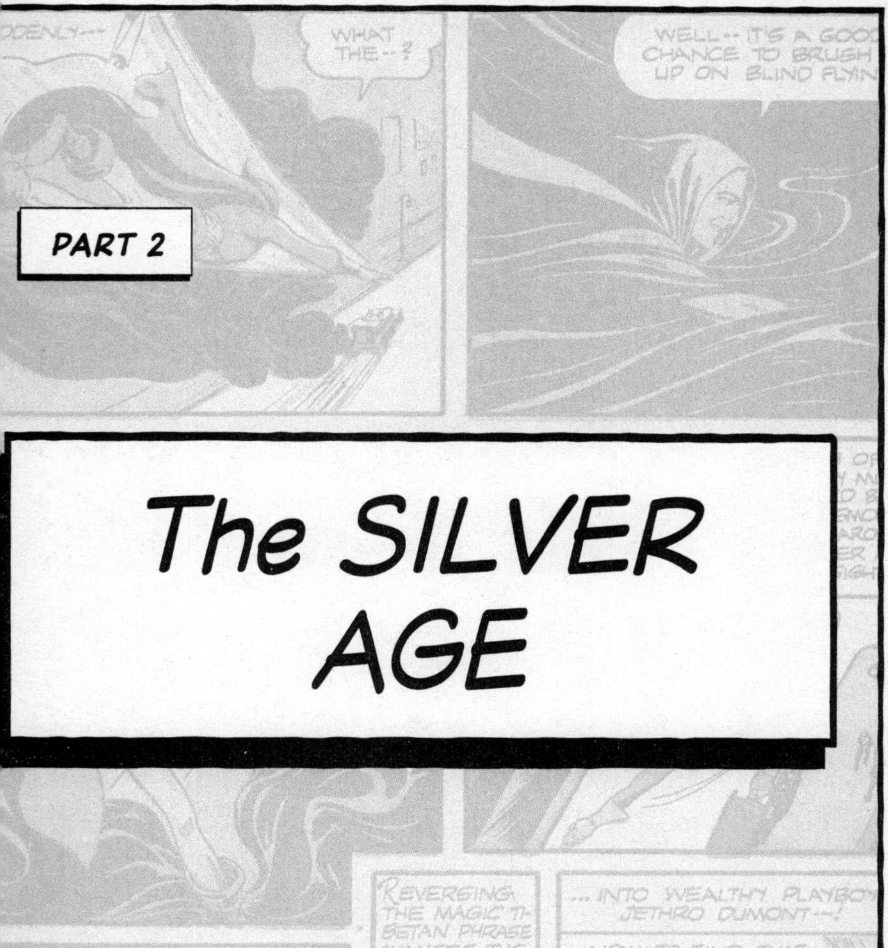
WHAT THE--?
I'LL HAVE TO FIND OUT WHY THE TOY WAS SO VALUABLE! BUT FIRST--HUM PADME MANI OM!
REVERSING THE MAGIC TIBETAN PHRASE CHANGES THE MIGHTY GREEN LAMA...
...INTO WEALTHY PLAYBOY JETHRO DUMONT--!
NOW TO FIND THAT KID AND GET TO THE BOTTOM OF THIS MYSTERY!

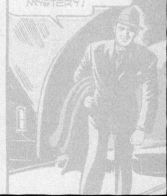

CHAPTER 5

SUPERMAN ON THE COUCH

IN 1958 SUPERMAN comics were still big sellers, having weathered the storms of the witch-hunt years by adhering closely to the central tenets of the Comics Code and aping the formula of the popular TV show. After Mortimer Weisinger occupied the editorial chair that year, Superman sales overtook even the Disney titles, making him the most popular comic character in the world.

Famously described by comics writer Roy Thomas as "a malevolent toad," Mort Weisinger had worked as a story editor on TV's *Adventures of Superman* before returning to New York to revamp the comic book. While other comics strove to connect with an older audience, Weisinger aimed his books at the gigantic audience of children from the postwar population boom. To keep the bright, active kids of the 1950s engaged, Weisinger and his writers exchanged the pedestrian realism of the TV series and the comic stories it had inspired for the kind of science-fantasy spectacle that couldn't be duplicated on film or TV. No other popular form existed where spectacular scenes of men tossing planets at one another could be created with any degree of believability. Under Weisinger, a sci-fi fan, Superman reached levels of power previously enjoyed only by Hindu gods.

Even the covers became more exciting, transformed into compelling poster-like advertisements for the stories within. In the forties and early fifties, a typical Superman cover portrayed him in iconic pose: lifting a car, towing a liner, or waving the Stars and Stripes. But Weisinger favored sensational "situation" covers with word balloons and unlikely setups that could only be resolved by purchasing the issue. Oddly, while this cosmic inflation was taking place, Superman stories were becoming more intimate and more universal in their appeal. In tune with the psychoanalytic movement (and to evade the code), Weisinger developed an uncanny ability to transform every dirty nugget from the collective unconscious into curiously compelling narratives for kids.

Superman was now a grown-up, a mature patriarch, drawn in the clean fifties lines of an artist with the unfortunate name of Wayne Boring.

Boring brought us classic Superman. Static. Conservative. Reserved. Gone was the restless, antiestablishment futurist; Boring's drawings shared the airless qualities of Roman frescoes. Where Joe Shuster had tried to capture the velocity of passing time, Boring slowed it all down, crystallizing single moments into myth. There was a weird formal remove, a proscenium arch, that maintained an even distance between the reader and the action. Wayne Boring's entire cosmos could be reduced to a two-by-two-inch square. His smooth, polished little planets floated like billiard balls in a compressed, flattened universe where outer space was neither vast nor intimidating but enclosed and teeming with life and color. Using the same, endlessly repeated, running-on-air pose, Boring's Man of Steel casually jogged across light-years of unfathomable distance in the space between one picture and the next, with the same stoic absence of expression. Centuries of epic time could pass in a single caption. Dynasties fell between balloons, and the sun could grow old and die on the turn of a page.

It was a toy world, too, observed through the wrong end of a telescope. Boring made eternity tiny, capable of being held in two small hands. He reduced the infinite to fit in a cameo, and he did this in service to the great insight of the Weisinger era: that human emotions can grow to overwhelm the vastnesses of space and endless time. Wayne Boring's tight, repressed lines were necessary to contain and shape the thunderous outpouring of Dionysian Sturm und Drang that animated the pages.

These stories were all about emotion. Fifties Superman plunged into great surging tides of feelings so big and unashamed that they could break a young heart or blind the stars. The socialist power fantasies, the jingoistic propaganda and gimmick adventures that had defined the previous twenty years of *Superman* adventures, gave way to cataclysmic tales of love and loss, guilt, grief, friendship, judgment, terror, and redemption, biblical in their scale and primal purity. And always, Weisinger's godlike Superman became more like us than ever before. He was fifties America with its atom-powered fist, its deadly archenemy, its brave allies. Like America, he was a flawed colossus, protector of Earth from the iron-walled forces of tyranny and yet, somehow, riven from within by a gnawing guilt, a growing uncertainty, a fear of change, and a terror of conformity.

Weisinger was in therapy, and he used the material from his sessions as raw plot ore for his writers to process into story material. The editor's entire psychology was stretched naked on the dissecting table via some of the most outlandish and unashamed deployments of pure symbolic content that the comics had ever seen. Its like would not be truly viewed again, in fact, until the drug-inspired cosmic comics of the early seventies.

For example, there was the bottle city of Kandor. Kandor had been the capital city of Superman's home world Krypton, thought destroyed. Shrunken and preserved by the villain Brainiac, Kandor was now a tiny city in a bell jar. This living diorama, this ant colony of real people, had great appeal for children, adding to the childlike nature of this era's Superman. In Kandor, lost memories were preserved under glass, and Superman could go there, in private, to experience a world he left behind. Kandor was every snow globe and music box that stood for every bittersweet memory in every movie there would ever be. Kandor was the tinkling voice of a lost world, a past that might have been, unreachable. Kandor was survivor's guilt endowed with new meaning.

Fifties Superman found himself domesticated at the heart of a strange nuclear family of friends, foes, and relatives. Weisinger had taken his lessons from Captain Marvel and his Family. Many of his favorite writers, like Otto Binder and Edmond Hamilton, had contributed to the Captain Marvel mythos and were able to adapt that style to suit a new kind of dream world that was more pointed, angular, and paranoid. This was the nuclear family glowing in the dark. No longer the last survivor of a lost alien civilization, Superman was joined by an entire photo album's worth of new supercompanions. He'd already gained his own superdog, named Krypto, and now discovered that he had a pretty blond cousin named Kara Zor-El, who'd also managed to survive the destruction of Krypton, along with a supermonkey, Beppo. There were stories of Superman as a boy (Superboy) and as a comically superpowered infant (Superbaby). Lois Lane was popular enough to graduate to her own monthly comic book. So too did Superman's Pal, Jimmy Olsen.

The young Olsen had no sooner installed himself within the pages of his own title than he began to experience a series of fantastic physical contortions typical of the Silver Age. A sampling of stories from Olsen's solo title showed the results as he metamorphosed into a porcupine boy, a giant turtle, a wolfman, Elastic Lad, and a "human skyscraper," with no pause for reflection. These transformations never produced any lasting ill effects or neuroses.

So great was the intrusion of the fantastic into the everyday that even Superboy's small-town sweetheart, red-haired Lana Lang, the home-town girl deluxe, began her own dual career as Insect Lass, using an "alien ring" to reorganize the slim-legged, petite figure of a Kansas homecoming queen into the bulbous abdomen and crawling feelers of a giant wasp or monster moth, complete with a shapely human torso and head that made it ten times more disturbing. Like Jimmy, Lana experienced no body horror or psychological trauma when she inflated her trim teenage stomach into a monstrous spider belly, clacked her chitinous forelegs together, and played out superhard silk from spinnerets where her normal midwestern buttocks should be. Had Franz Kafka's mild-mannered accountant Gregor Samsa been born to the sunshine of the emergent DC universe, he might have pressed his incredible new cock-roach powers into action in the fight against crime and injustice. Before too long, he would have been invited to join the Justice League. Kafka never once paused to consider that his outcasts could be heroic like the X-Men, freakishly glamorous like Jimmy Olsen, or as gorgeous as trend-setting Pulitzer Prize winner Lois Lane.

When not under alien influence, Jimmy Olsen could barely stand to be himself for more than five pages and maintained a much-resorted-to "disguise kit" in times of emergency. Prefiguring David Bowie, Madonna, or Lady Gaga, his life became a shifting parade of costume changes and reinventions of identity. And long before those performers were challenging the boundaries of masculine and feminine, Olsen was deconstructing the macho stereotype in a sequence of softcore gender-blending adventures for children that beggar belief when read today.

The three unforgettable transvestite Olsen tales, including "Miss Jimmy Olsen," can be summed up by the following heart-fluttering caption that opens the lead story in *Jimmy Olsen* no. 95:

> IF YOU EVER WONDERED TO WHAT EXTREME LENGTHS **JIMMY OLSEN** WOULD GO TO GET A NEWSPAPER SCOOP, WAIT TILL YOU SEE JIMMY IN OPERATION AS A MEMBER OF THE FAIR SEX! YES, READERS. **SUPERMAN'S** YOUNG PAL UNDERGOES A DRASTIC CHANGE OF IDENTITY AND PUTS HIS HIGH-HEELED FEET INTO A HUGE MESS OF TROUBLE WHEN HE BECOMES THE SWEETHEART OF GANGLAND.

These words accompany a picture of Jimmy mincing past a mailbox in a green dress while a group of admiring men whoop and check out his ass.

"HA! HA! THOSE WOLVES WOULD DROP DEAD IF THEY KNEW THAT UNDER THIS FEMALE DISGUISE BEATS THE **VERY** MASCULINE HEART OF **PLANET** REPORTER **JIMMY OLSEN!**" read the smirking, transvestite Olsen's thought balloon.

The salacious, winking quality of the phrasing suggested an immaculate deconstruction of the masculine adventure genre into the arena of showbiz, shifting identities, and anything-goes sexuality.

Jimmy became a mobster's moll, even joining a chorus line and proving that he could high-kick with the best of the showgirls. Bestiality reared its shaggy head when Jimmy was forced to substitute the lips of a slobbering pet chimp named Dora for his own during a tense romantic moment in a dimly lit apartment. Believing the mouth of the ape in question to be the fragrant glossy red lips of Jimmy Olsen, racketeer Big Monte

McGraw melted into the simian's lewd embrace while Jimmy made a hasty getaway. The level of derangement was high. These were stories that could *never* happen in the real world, even if there was a Superman. This was now a world all its own, living inside our own, growing, getting smarter and more elaborate.

Artist Curt Swan drew the cub reporter as outrageously attractive in his makeup and a red wig. In heels and stockings, Olsen looked like he'd wandered in off a Pussycat Dolls video shoot. And there were a few gloriously disorienting panels where, sans wig, he was seen talking to Superman while still casually dressed in a pink dressing gown, fluffy slippers, and movie star makeup.

And yet, if it was okay for Olsen, wasn't it okay? I grew up with this idea of the disguise kit and the performance, the idea of both body and identity as canvas. When I adopted as a youthful role model the shape-shifting, bisexual assassin Jerry Cornelius from Michael Moorcock's novels, I was following in the footsteps of Jimmy Olsen. Olsen played in bands, and so did I. Olsen was freewheeling and nonjudgmental, even in the fifties, and so was I. If it was cool with Superman's pal, it was A-OK with me. Clearly these stories were written by perverts with an intent to pervert the young that was entirely successful.

The transvestite Olsen stories seem deeply rooted in the underground world of mimeographed porn mags and the bondage comics of Eric Stanton, whose studio also employed a certain Joe Shuster, Superman creator. The language used recalls stories like *Panty Raid* (discussed at length by Robert J. Stoller, M.D., in his 1985 book *Observing the Erotic Imagination*) and other 1950s transgender tales in which hunky young jocks got more than they bargained for when a trip to the sorority house turned into a forced initiation into the pleasures of female underwear and makeup. The difference being that Olsen was fully in control of his transformations and could hardly wait more than a couple of pages to get them under way.

At the same time, Superman's treatment of Lois became more cruel and misogynistic, while she became more shrewish and snoopy. It was hard to match this often boorish, devious brute of a man to any popular conception of Superman, and yet here he was lying, deceiving, and thwarting her dreams of matrimony over and over again while Lois fumed and plotted.

Superman's fear of commitment was a significant, perhaps dominant, feature of his Silver Age adventures. It was as if all the sublimated resentment of fifties men, home from the excitement of the war to the nine-to-five and to ticky-tacky houses in suburbia, seethed between the covers.

Those echoes were never louder than in *Superman's Girl Friend, Lois Lane* no. 73, which allowed into this fragile world of sanity an image so peculiar that words alone are not capable of doing justice to it. The story inside was tame fare by comparison, but Weisinger's trademark self-searching ability to transform every dirty subconscious coal into the gem of an idea was never more evident than here. This was a Jungian bowel movement rendered as a story for children. The kind of behavior this primed young boys to expect from their own future girlfriends was more obscene than the blow jobs, boob jobs, and anal entry they now expect as a result of boring old Internet porn. Superman was educating a genera-tion of sadomasochistic swingers with tastes trending beyond the outré.

As we look again in disbelief or amusement at this outlandish image, stop to consider how ten years previously, the portrayal of Lois Lane had been one of a fairly convincing hard-nosed lady reporter in a man's world, while Jimmy Olsen had been portrayed as a somewhat believable cub photographer making his way on a big-city paper. In that context these images ripped bleeding from the fantastic nightside of the American imagination become even more provocative and outrageous.

Was the hostility Weisinger's or that of his writers? He was, after all, a notoriously mean-spirited man. Was fifties Superman a product of his age, a backlash against emancipation and a postwar desire to get the working gals of WWII back into the kitchen and the bedroom before they got too serious about building aircraft, voting, or even making comics?

Or was this less an adult approach to sexual politics than an attempt to depict Superman's attitude toward women in ways—"Ugh! Girls!"—a ten-year-old boy might relate to? Superman and his cast could be all of these. They were in flux, slippery and eager to adapt in order to ensure their own continued survival. As ideas they could change shape to speak to the fears and fantasies of a postwar generation and its armies of children.

There is, of course, a third reason for the viciousness of male-female power relationships in fifties superhero comics. As the Comics Code explicitly states:

- Passion or romantic interest shall never be treated in such a way as to stimulate the lower and base emotions.
- The treatment of love-romance stories shall emphasize the value of the home and the sanctity of marriage.

The young men and women who wrote and drew these stories were no fools—they were artists on the fringes, marginalized and despised. Perhaps the rejected outsiders who created these comics were taking their revenge on society by exposing the curdled power politics that lay beneath the clipped lawns, starched shirts, and baking aprons of 1950s America. Maybe the distorted lives of Silver Age superheroes were a deliberate, scabrous attempt to sneak social commentary and satire under the noses of the censors. The creators of post–Comics Code superhero comics followed the diktat of the CMA to the letter, while at the same time exposing postwar relationships as hotbeds of abnormality, where women were ring-chasing harridans and men were quivering *puer aeternae* terrified of responsibility.

On a particular favorite cover of mine, Superman watched, helplessly emasculated, as his girlfriends Lois and Lana paraded past him, each with a different historical strongman on her arm.

"LOIS! LANA!" Superman exclaimed meekly. "WHAT ARE YOU DOING WITH HERCULES AND SAMSON?"

"WE'RE ON THE WAY TO THE MARRIAGE LICENSE BUREAU!" Lois chirped proudly. "I'M GOING TO BE MRS. HERCULES!" "AND I'M GOING TO BE MRS. SAMSON!" tittered Lana. It was a bold and unforgettable lesson for young male readers: This was what happened when you couldn't make decisions or offer any lasting commitment. Samson pounced on your best girl. And for Superman, it was a horrific challenge to his modernity. Was he really no better than these archaic toughs? Or could he prove himself stronger, faster than any previous man-god?

As a further irony, girls still read these comics too; for all the stories' undercurrents of fear of commitment, and of women as predators intent on robbing men of their independence, the energy that drives them can also be read as essentially "feminine," favoring stories about relationships and strong emotions. This made them popular with children of both sexes. These stories liquefied the armored hard body of the wartime supersoldiers and patriotic strongmen. This was Superman on the analyst's couch after almost twenty years of unconscious adventuring, finally letting the freakishness, the alien-ness, all hang out. America was in therapy too, and along with all the insights and the wonders of the interior, poison was being squeezed out. Fears were being lanced like boils, expressed in the art, music, and popular culture of the time.

Outsider culture, in the form of Lenny Bruce, the Beats, and the bohos, was developing a new bardic language to express things that had until now haunted the echoing four-in-the-morning thoughts of men and women in a world they could barely make sense of from cradle to grave. They said things everyone had felt but never dared articulate because it was forbidden by consensus. A new willingness—an especially American willingness—not to mock but to learn from the fringes was opening up the country to its sexuality, its fears and fantasies of freedom and slavery, emancipation and mind control, man and machine. It was time for new dreams to replace the derelict, bombed-out, and vacant shells of the old. The future would not be denied.

Fifties Superman cheerfully embodied every human terror on our behalf: In a succession of early Silver Age adventures, he became monstrously obese, insect headed, a Frankenstein's monster, a lion-faced outcast, a dome-headed, emotionless "future man," and a senile, doddering granddad flying with the aid of a knobbly cane.

In each case, the perfect man was made finally to experience all the horrors of being different, growing old, or mutating into any of the many ugly distortions of normality that haunted buttoned-down Normalville, USA, in those days of monster films and fears of mutation. It often seemed as though the most awful thing one could be in Superman's world was not a monster or an evil genius but, as writer Mark Waid observed, old, fat, and bald. Each new transformation inflicted on him some fundamental human suffering. The strongman went soft at the edge and could no longer contain his own shape. To survive, he had to endure, wait for the story's inevitable cycle to return him to normality within the new hierarchical structure of the *Daily Planet* office and Superman's superlife of pets and fortresses, time machines and alien relatives.

And it wasn't only Superman: His entire supporting cast of reporters and grocery store owners was subject to inhuman forces of transformation on a monthly basis. Lois Lane became Lois Lane the Witch of Metropolis—a hag on a broomstick casting ghastly vaporous spells in Superman's direction—or Phantom Lois, Baby Lois, even Super Lois. The familiar faces of *Superman* cast stalwarts became grotesque, unloved, undergoing cyclical trials that tested their foundational concepts to the outermost limits, in the way that children would stretch an elastic band: so far, not too far, but nearly. The heroes learned their lessons and forgot them in time for the next issue, in order to present those lessons in a new form. This was the world of dreams, complexes, the twilight territory of Dr. Freud's unconscious, where the body was formless and metamorphic. Adolescent themes prevailed and formed the basis for perfect superhero stories.

Weisinger-era *Superman* was a remarkable feat of imagination and reinvention. Jerry Siegel himself rose to the challenge, taking his original concept further than ever before. In beautiful stories such as "Superman's Return to Krypton," he reached a stylistic peak he would find hard to surpass. As the title suggested, time travel allowed Superman to return to the world of his birth before its destruction. There, powerless under the red sun of Krypton, he met his own parents as a young couple and found his eternal soul mate in the ravishing Lyla Lerrol, a Kryptonian actress whose life was ultimately as doomed as all the others on that ill-starred orb.

"BUT THE FLAMES WITHIN THE PLANET ARE LIKE COLD GLA-CIERS COMPARED TO THE MIGHTY LOVE BLAZING BETWEEN **SUPERMAN** OF EARTH AND **LYLA LERROL OF KRYPTON**."

The scenes of young Jor-El, Lara, Lyla, and Kal-El toasting the future, "NO MATTER WHAT TOMORROW BRINGS!" had the genuine bittersweetness of school photographs discovered in middle age. When Superman was forced to leave a weeping Lyla behind to die and return to his own time, a new kind of Superman story had been born. These were no longer political fantasies or propaganda, and they were not, as later superhero comic books would become, scoreboards of cross-referenced continuities. These stories had the simple universal appeal of folktales. They never talked down to their intended audience of children or pulled punches on dark matters of mortality, grief, jealousy, and love.

Then there were the so-called imaginary stories that deviated from the official *Superman* canon (described as "real life" by the comics themselves). In imaginary stories, intriguing what-if? scenarios could play out to comic or tragic effect: What if Superman married Lana Lang? What if Luthor had raised Superboy as his own son? What if Superman had been raised by Batman's parents and Bruce Wayne was Clark Kent's adopted brother? Happy endings were rarely guaranteed, which made many of these speculative tragedies more powerful and memorable than the "real" adventures.

The superhero had turned to face the interior with spectacularly inventive results. By turning his back on the political or social realities of the material world, by stealing where it counted from *Captain Marvel* (both in content and in talent), Weisinger and his team had opened the doors onto a new frontier where the superheroes could soar free. No longer shackled to the rules of social realism, the stories themselves were liberated to become what a generation of young readers demanded: allegorical super–science fiction about how it felt to be twelve. Fifties Superman proudly inhabited and brought order, humor, and meaning to the primary-colored, Jackson Pollock–spattered protocontinent of the great American unconscious.

Weisinger had admitted a protean, Dionysian spirit into Superman's world, and he left that world supercharged, reinvigorated with new ideas and fresh spins on old ones, wide open and reborn into the lysergic dawn of the 1960s.

Before moving on, I have a pet story from this period that I'd like to share, on the grounds that it perfectly sums up this era and Weisinger's approach to the American drama. The title is "Superman's New Power." You might presume the promised new power will fit within the basically scientific range of Superman's abilities. Maybe he could develop electrical powers or telepathy. No. Writer Jerry Coleman, operating under Weisinger's instruction, and artist Curt Swan had something quite different in mind.

Superman's new power was this: He found he could manifest from the palm of his right hand a mute, six-inch-high Superman duplicate, in full costume. Emerging without explanation from Superman's hand, the mini-Superman rocketed off to thwart injustice and save innocent lives in Superman's stead. Of course, it did its job even better than Superman could do it, in its weird, mini-me way. What's worse, when the imp set forth, Superman lost all his powers and was left impotent, only able to watch as his palmtop doppelgänger saved the day again and again and was rewarded with all the kudos and love that Superman thought he deserved.

Feel free to analyze.

Samson's hair. Achilles' heel. The oddly elaborate gymnastic contortions that exposed the vulnerable spots of Celtic superwarriors. Even the greatest heroes needed a weakness, or there would be no drama, no fall or redemption.

If nothing could hurt Superman, what could hurt him?

In fact, Weisinger and his writers understood the most important thing about Superman: that his heart was vulnerable, and his self-esteem could be fragile. The Super was the icing on the cake, the sugar coating: These were stories about Man and his role in a new world.

But now that the Man of Tomorrow had achieved near-divine heights of omnipotence, the need for some kind of convincing physical vulnerability was becoming greater. Or so goes the prevailing opinion. The glowing green killer mineral kryptonite had been introduced in the 1943 Superman radio series. The contaminated remains of Superman's home planet fell to Earth in meteor form—much more often than the debris of a distant world might reasonably be expected to fall, and in sufficient quantities to threaten Superman's life on a regular basis. As a weapon, it had a certain symbolic resonance: The notion that radioactive fragments of Superman's birth world had become toxic to him spoke of the old country, the old ways, the threat of the failure to assimilate. Superman was a naturalized American. The last thing he needed were these lethal reminders of where he'd come from; that he, the son of lordly scientists, had been reduced to toiling in a farmer's field or minding the general store.

Weisinger knew how his young readers' minds worked and stretched the idea a little further: If there was *green* kryptonite, couldn't there be other colors too? The prismatic splintering began with the invention of Red K, the cool kryptonite, possibly because it made literal the master Silver Age theme of bodily transformation. It was mineral LSD for Superman, affecting not just his mind but also reshaping his body into a playground of fleshly hallucination.

No two trips on Red K were the same, in-story logic promised. Red K would affect Superman in a different way every time and theoretically might never become boring. So, under its influence, Superman might develop the head of an ant, scaling the *Daily Planet* building as the commander of a nightmarish army of giant insects—"BZZ-BZZZ . . . WE MUST CAPTURE LOIS LANE . . . SHE WILL BE OUR QUEEN!"—or split into good Clark, bad Superman, or even become goofy for forty-eight hours.

Red K and the Silver Age are inextricable. Red K was LSD for superheroes, and under its influence Superman could unclench his entire being and walk the razor's edge of joyous self-abandonment and ego-annihilating terror—an American pioneer. Red K served equally as a handy metaphor for the adolescent hormonal shifts, physical changes, and weird moods of elation and despair that were being experienced by its readers.

Other kryptonite variants were created as plot mechanics demanded rather than with any eye to longevity. That's why gold kryptonite removes Superman's powers permanently, blue kryptonite affects only Bizarros, and white kryptonite is deadly to plants, which makes it about as interesting as matches, DDT, or a stout spade.

But, of course, Superman's ultimate weakness was his secret identity. Why wouldn't shy Clark Kent choose to tear open his shirt and reveal to his unrequited love the potent god-man behind the buttons? Instead he hid the truth from Lois Lane, devising deceptions that became so elaborate as to be cruel: the ghastly tricks of semantics a man-boy might play on a child-woman, all in the guise of "teaching her a lesson."

A story like "The Two Faces of Superman" showed the hero promising to marry Lois Lane but only if she met him at a particular time outside the church. When she met his conditions, he contrived to seal her car door with his heat vision so that she couldn't get out. Unable to marry him at precisely the correct hour meant that Lois forfeited her chance. A relieved, chortling Superman took to the skies, having hoodwinked the predator once more.

Like Rumpelstiltskin, Tom Tit Tot, and the other creatures of folklore who knew that names held power and kept theirs secret, Superman maintained his distance from Clark and vice versa. Their paths rarely crossed. He hid his heart in a plain suit, behind glasses. For Lois, *a girl*, to know who he was would be the end. She'd only pressure him into exchanging his gaudy suit and life of adventure for something less embarrassing, more domestic. She would expect him to be home for dinner, when there were stricken ocean liners to rescue. In the end, his self-deceiving fantasies of one day carrying Lois up the aisle were just that, and if he married Lois, he'd be Clark forever. It wouldn't matter how strong or fast he was, he'd be Clark racing around the globe to pick up groceries.

Robin the Boy Wonder first appeared in Detective Comics in 1940. Introduced as "*THE LAUGHING YOUNG DAREDEVIL . . .*" and "*THE CHARACTER FIND OF 1940,*" he burst through a circus ringmaster's hoop held by a grinning Batman. It was an explosion of exuberance that signaled the arrival of a plucky can-do spirit to comics born of the Depression.

Dick Grayson was introduced to readers as a typical *Boys Town* character; a feisty urchin scrapper; the orphaned son of murdered circus aerialists. Robin was a carny kid, as far from Batman's class and social milieu as one could get, but he had a stout heart and was as brave as any boy Batman had ever met. So it made sense to team up and share the crime-fighting life.

Robin's upbeat, enthusiastic charisma obliged the uptight, millionaire Protestant Wayne to loosen up a little. The kid brought a big-top splash of joie de vivre to the mean streets of the urban avenger. The introduction of Robin turned Batman's story from a shady crime-and-revenge narrative into the thrilling adventures of two swashbuckling friends who were so rich that they could do anything.

After 1940, the formerly dour Batman rarely lost his smile. The Batcave filled with trophies, as outlandish mementoes of his adventures with Robin began to accumulate; there was a Lincoln penny as big as a Ferris wheel, a robot tyrannosaur, several deadly umbrellas from the arsenal of the Penguin, and a collection of remarkable Bat vehicles. The cave became part museum, part mega toy box, part theme park. Seen through Robin's eyes, the Batman's harsh, lawless world of shadows, blood, and poisonous chemicals became a Disneyland of crime. Even the attitude of the law changed toward the crime fighters: The Bat-Man of 1939 was a fearsome vigilante, hunted across rooftops by the Gotham City Police Department, but Batman and Robin were proud citizens and sworn GCPD deputies who worked alongside their uniformed, sanctioned counterparts to protect the city they loved.

There was the sense that the young Bruce Wayne, who died emotionally along with his parents in Crime Alley, had finally met a friend with whom to share his strange, exciting secret life. The emotionally stunted Batman found a perfect pal in the ten-year-old orphaned acrobat. Batman was forced to grow up and develop responsibility as soon as Robin came on the scene, and the savage young Dark Knight of the original pulp-tinged adventures was replaced by a very different kind of hero: a dashing big brother, the best friend any kid could have. The outlaw gangbuster became a detective, a man we could trust, even with our children.

Then came the insinuations of Wertham in an atmosphere of paranoia and self-analysis. Only a few superheroes remained in the darkness that had fallen over the face of DC Comics during the era of congressional hearings and public denunciations, turning freakish with the lights out. And it was as if their skeletons had begun to glow sickly green right through their flesh, as radioactive nightside selves came out to play. Not even Robin was immune to the scalding return of the repressed. All the creepiness, the curdled ink, the whispered innuendo floated to the surface as the Boy Wonder gave in, emasculated by the judgment of the sinister Doctor W.

Robin began to show evidence of a fundamental lack of confidence about his permanent role in Batman's life. In stories such as "Batman's New Partner," the Boy Wonder skulked, sulked, and sweated nervously as suspicions grew that he was being phased out in favor of Wingman, an adult who dressed like a pigeon spray-painted by hippies. As this primary threat of being relegated to the sidelines became more frequent, Robin's reactions became increasingly flustered and teary.

Lacking music and sound effects to punch up emotional scenes, comic books relied on pouring tears and melodrama. Characters really had to blubber to get the point that they were *quite upset* across to young readers.

Expecting these masklike, often masked faces to convey understatement was like expecting stained glass to act. Emotions were broadcast at maximum volume. With a ban on crime, no room for good old-fashioned brawling, and a desperate need to survive, the superheroes surrendered their dignity to the zeitgeist and began to talk about their needs, their fears, and their [*choke!*] hopes.

And so, in the fifties, the Boy Wonder transformed from a bounding paragon of vigilante boy justice to a weeping, petulant nervous wreck who lived in fear of losing his beloved Batman to fresher, more accomplished boy partners—or, worse, to the charms of Batwoman. With lower lip set in a permanent sullen pout courtesy of artist Sheldon Moldoff, his world became a schizoid cold war hell where Batman was secretly conniving to betray and dump him any time his guard was down. If he found the Caped Crusader drinking tea, Robin would instantly assume the flask was next in line to replace him at Batman's side, then burst into tears. Covers show the boy reaching the church only to find Batman and Batwoman exchanging vows at the altar, in full costume, with the dreamlike touch of veil and tux to intensify the surreal indecency of the image. He was shown over and over opening a door only to find Batman and Batwoman with patronizing looks on their faces that suggested he was interrupting something only grown-ups could hope to understand.

"Choke!" was usually all he could manage before hanging on for dear life until the story resolved itself in the usual welter of misconceptions and misread scenarios.

This new image of the crying boy haunted the fascinating and demented stories of this period. Wertham had made innocent comic superheroes aware of their own sexual potential, and like Adam and Eve blinking in the garden, there was embarrassment, denial, and overwhelming eruptions of feelings so new they could only be represented by outlandish monstrosities of a kind that were entirely original. Space aliens, with designs and planetary environments inspired by the spiky murals on the walls of futurist jazz clubs or Village beatnik cellars, began to outnumber the criminals in Gotham City. Robin was besieged by a delirium of fractured shapes and grotesque creatures. The code ruled out realistic depictions of crime, so Batman was maneuvered awkwardly into ever more outlandish confrontations with monsters, spacemen, and . . . women. With Doc Wertham's seedy denunciations still ringing in their ears, DC's editors were keen to validate Batman's hetero credentials with an injection of estrogen into the book; elderly Aunt Harriet soon replaced the ever-attentive Alfred, but the biggest feminine intrusion came with the arrival of the shapely Batwoman and her partner, Batgirl.

Kathy Kane, Batwoman, made her debut as a plainly obvious beard for a Batman who had (let's remind ourselves) no real need to prove his heterosexuality, on the grounds that he was a creation of pen and ink made to entertain children and had no sex life on the page or off it. What made this era of kissy-kissy Batman-and-Batwoman-at-the-altar story lines even more bizarre than the alien worlds and jagged modernist design aesthetic was Kathy Kane's mannish civilian identity as a circus-owning daredevil who wore jodhpurs and rode a motorcycle. Kathy Kane was Marlon Brando in drag, Honor Blackman's Pussy Galore from *Goldfinger* ten years before the movie. And just like Pussy and James Bond, Kathy had fallen head over heels for Batman.

Smitten or not, Kathy was hard as nails. Batwoman *detourned* the image of the atom age housewife by packing her handbag with laser lipsticks and dainty cologne sprays that could chemically castrate you there on the spot. Kathy Kane was the weaponization of the Stepford Wife, the Avon lady as a Special Forces commando: pixie boots, fringed leather gloves, high-gloss lipstick so red it was jet black and reflective. If Bettie Page were the scourge of the underworld, she would look a little like this. No wonder Batman fell in love and the Boy Wonder's stuttering tongue kept snagging on the same expletive:

[*Choke!*]

Kathy's niece was a fluffy blonde named Betty Kane, who later gave up crime fighting to become a tennis pro, and yes, it's easy to imagine Wertham's inventive neurons hastily reconfiguring to provide this new and potentially more perverse tangle of relationships with a thrilling porno twist. Far from replacing the troubling Bruce-Dick-Alfred bachelor three-way with a respectable family unit, including Mom, Dad, Sis, Junior, and Dog (a resourceful and masked German shepherd named Ace joined the cast around this time), the Wayne-Kane era comes across in a welter of mind-warping, emotionally charged psychosexual hysteria. The two adults' cruel treatment and emotional manipulation of a clearly distressed Robin in "Bat-Mite Meets Bat-Girl" motivated Les Daniels to observe in his book *Batman: The Complete History*: "If a comic book could actually turn people gay as Doctor Wertham had suggested . . . this one might have had the power to do it."

If rebellion against the Comics Code took the form of these devastating, coded analyses of America's psychosexual temperature, it was only to be expected. Squeezed down and controlled by conformity cops, comic-book creators chose the Hermetic route. Transforming their insights and rage into fables for children, the debts to the queer underground and the echoes of the narcotic, psychedelic visions of Ginsberg and Burroughs are still hard to miss.

Imagine the tight-lipped, plausible Batman played by Christian Bale in Christopher Nolan's twenty-first-century movie series facing some of the adversaries encountered by fifties Batman: a Rainbow Batman, a Zebra Batman, a Creature from Dimension X that resembled a one-eyed testicle on stalk-like legs. With titles including "The Jungle Batman," "The Merman Batman" ("YES, ROBIN. I'VE BECOME A HUMAN FISH"), "The Valley of Giant Bees" ("ROBIN! HE'S BEEN CAPTURED AND MADE A JESTER IN THE COURT OF THE QUEEN BEE!"), and "Batman Becomes Bat-Baby," it was an anything-goes atmosphere. And there's more where they came from: a whole decade's worth of unfiltered madness as DC writers used every trick in the book to keep Batman away from the crime-haunted streets where he belonged.

Weisinger's fluid bodies, his foregrounding of intense emotions, laid the groundwork for the Silver Age of comics and the arrival of a jet-powered, supersonic LSD consciousness that would turn the world's largest-ever collection of young people into self-proclaimed superhumans overnight.

But before that, and for the therapy to be successful, the process of miniaturization, compression, and self-annihilation had to be completed. A collapsing star, a black hole, was created, from which only a god could escape, or an idea. Not even light can escape from a black hole. The event horizon marks the limit of human science, not human imagination.

Along came the Flash, who could run faster than the speed of light.

Things began to melt.

Things began to stream.

CHAPTER 6

CHEMICALS AND LIGHTNING

ACCORDING TO *The Comic Book Heroes*, Gerard Jones and Will Jacobs's seminal overview of the Silver Age, the purveyors of children's mass entertainment were requested by representatives of the US State Department to cultivate in their readers an interest in science and technology, in an effort to breed a generation of boffins capable of realizing their president's cosmic dreams.

And so, Kennedy Man: the astronaut, the handsome scientist, the confident, pioneering go-getter with the beautiful wife or girlfriend and an eye on the stars and the shining future. The mad scientist villains of the past were being replaced by the sanest of scientist heroes. As the anxieties of Sputnik and Yuri Gagarin yielded to the heroism of John Glenn and the Mercury spacemen by the mid-1960s, a new confidence was shaping the American heroes of the Silver Age. These men and women were already the winners of the Cold War, and their great armies of children were growing up in a world that could promise them the Earth.

DC Comics editor Julius Schwartz was a survivor of the pulps and the early fan scene. A longtime colleague of Weisinger's, he'd also been a literary agent for cult authors such as H. P. Lovecraft and Ray Bradbury. He brought to comics a calm and sunlit rationality and a love of perfectly constructed sci-fi puzzles often crafted around solutions to chemistry or physics problems. He favored an untroubling style that was neither dark nor goofy.

Schwartz built his team around artist Carmine Infantino and two writers, Gardner Fox and John Broome. Another of their set, Gil Kane, was a rakish wit and dandy with a drawing style that seemed to define a middle ground between Mac Raboy and Jack Kirby. Kane relied on stock poses a little too often, but his work was otherwise clean, fresh, and dynamic. His heroes were built like ballet dancers rather than wrestlers or strongmen, a new feminine grace that Infantino also brought to his American superpioneers. This was the team that relaunched the Flash.

You may remember the Golden Age Flash as Jay Garrick, who inhaled heavy water fumes, blah blah blah. When it was suggested to Schwartz that he bring the character back with new stories as a way of testing the market response to superheroes, he agreed—but on the condition that he was allowed to rebuild the series from the ground up, keeping only the name and the superspeed powers. When he launched the new Flash in the pages of *Showcase* no. 4, at the end of 1956, it was an instant hit, a lightning stroke that lit the touchpaper on the Silver Age.

Barry Allen was the fastest man alive. He could run faster than the fastest car, faster than the fastest jet. He could run so fast that he skipped across oceans like a stone or a rocket-powered Jesus. At top speed, he could race around Earth seven times in a single second, hitting the speed of light, and "vibrating" his atoms through solid objects. With the aid of his wondrous, preposterous "Cosmic Treadmill," a super running machine, he could break the time barrier itself. Dressed in the red, frictionless bodysuit of the Flash, he used these fantastic powers to protect the citizens of Central City and beyond.

Androgynous, mercurial, sleek, and intelligent, the Flash was appropriately blessed with the coolest costume in comics. A design classic, the Flash costume was a head-to-toe sheath of clinging Ferrari-red frictionless material. His cowl featured decorative "earphones" with little golden Hermes wings that resembled the hood ornaments of some incredible concept car. On his chest was a yellow lightning bolt graphic that split a circle descending right to left in the manner of the kabbalistic lightning flash of magical illumination. The Flash's one-piece ski jump suit had the effect of spotlighting and outlining the hero-runner's perfect buttocks. His bright yellow boots had chunky inch-thick ridged treads and little streamlined wings at the ankles. For sheer gee-whiz modernity and graphic beauty, the Flash costume was exceeded only by that of his side-kick, nephew Wally West, alias Kid Flash.

Barry's own dream suit was compressed into his ring and spat forth when he needed it, clinging like a second skin to his lean musculature. Carmine Infantino drew the Flash as a runner, not a wrestler or muscle-man. Infantino broke free of the static, pressurized fifties style with a jazzy, expressive brushstroke, and a battery of new visual effects to suggest the strobing blur of a superfast man in motion. Taking tips from Marcel Duchamp's *Nude Descending a Staircase* and the Futurist canvases of Umberto Boccioni, Infantino's Flash could become a multilimbed composite image of a body in motion through time. His cityscapes, though, were always poised on two-dimensional, stage-backdrop planes—like cardboard cutouts of modernist skyscrapers, silhouettes, always on the horizon, like jazz-era prints on the walls of young urban professionals.

Barry Allen was an affable, crew-cut forensic scientist working late one night at the lab when a chance combination of lightning striking a rack of chemicals endowed him with superspeed. His villains were rogue person-ifications of scientific principles: thermodynamic (Heat Wave, Captain Cold), optical (Mirror Master), meteorological (Weather Wizard), sonic (the Pied Piper), gyroscopic (the Top), chemical (Mr. Element). Stories often turned around some simple fact of physics. Yet there was rarely the feeling of being lectured to. These science facts were exactly what boys of the Silver Age wanted to learn about, and what better way to learn than with this new avatar of one of our oldest gods? Chemical reactions were acted out as drama, while physics lessons could become dreams of velocity and romance.

This is where I joined the continuity: born at one in the morning on the last, bitter cold January day of 1960. The Flash was always my favorite superhero. Even now, if I could have any superpower, I'd choose his.

The Flash stories I loved most were drawn by Infantino and written by the aforementioned John Broome, who saw where the Kennedy hero was headed. The pioneering spirit that was urging America's youth into outer space would fuel a corresponding drive toward inner space. Ten years before Stanley Kubrick rocketed Keir Dullea through the celestial kaleidoscope for the final act of *2001: A Space Odyssey*, Broome, the elegant stoner, was creating connections that would link John Glenn with *2001*'s Dave Bowman, and sending clean-cut heroes like Barry Allen and Hal Jordan (the new Green Lantern) across event horizons of total derangement that young readers had never witnessed before. As Broome, the jazz-loving hipster, typed in a sparkling haze in upstate New York or in Paris, how could his test pilots, cops, and spacemen fail to get high on the fumes?

For crew-cut Barry Allen, the outer reaches of psychedelia were occupational hazards. Like the astronauts he resembled, Barry could be relied upon to travel beyond the frontiers of the reasonable without losing his mind or soiling his scarlet speed suit. Batman might have faced intricate death traps, Superman might have dealt with alien conquerors, but Barry Allen, forensic scientist, could spend whole issues trapped in what amounted to a *Salvia divinorum* hallucination. In one series of stories, he was transformed into a wooden mannequin stumbling clumsily in his strings, dehumanized. Other episodes brought a curse that left him unable to see any color but green or saw him flattened underfoot to become a living paving stone crying out for help while an oblivious crowd hurried all over him. But the pièce de résistance came with "The Flash Stakes His Life on—You!" in August 1966. It's one of the first stories I remember as having a profound impact on my young mind. I can trace many of my own obsessions and concerns as a writer back to this particular root.

The cover showed a close-up shot of the Flash. The background was black, without feature or detail. He was holding up his hand into the foreground as if he were standing only feet away from us, almost life sized, addressing us directly. His expression was frenzied. His eyes were those of a saint eyeballing the infinite. His palm extended, almost life sized, to bring us to a halt. He was the Flash—the Fastest Man Alive. The bold red title perfectly placed in the black space above his head told us so.

"*STOP!*" he cried in inch-high letters. "DON'T PASS UP THIS ISSUE! MY **LIFE** DEPENDS ON IT!"

The Fastest Man Alive was ordering us to *stop* and breaking the fourth wall of the second dimension to deliver his plea. This was the first time a superhero looked out from the flat picture plane into a theoretical higher dimensional space he could not see, only intuit, to ask his readers for help. He even seemed to know that he was in a comic-book publication. His world was not our own, and we were separated by a membrane as hard and permeable as Alice's mirror. This was genuine Pop Art in its natural mass-produced Platonic form. This was art as product in a way that the gallery works of Roy Lichtenstein could only aspire to, and Infantino's design would look spectacular in the Museum of Modern Art or the Tate, twenty feet tall.

Inside the story began. One day the Flash fell afoul of a bad bastard who'd invented a new weapon that caused people to forget about anyone caught in the path of its ray. He tested the device by turning it on his pet cat Jessica, whom everyone promptly forgot, causing the animal to vanish forever like a tree not falling in a nonexistent forest. Giving the cat a name, even though it appeared in only two panels before being banished to forgetfulness, was a typical Broome detail. We, as readers, would remember Jessica forever. It wasn't long before the weapon was turned on the Flash himself. With no one to remember or recognize him, he began to dissolve like a smoke ring.

"SINCE OUR OWN BELIEF IN OURSELVES IS BASED ON HOW OTHERS FEEL ABOUT US—YOU BEGAN AT ONCE TO *LOSE YOUR IDENTITY!*" the villain explained to the dwindling superhero.

I could feel the horror. I knew those dreams where I was dragging a leaden unresponsive body in slow motion through air like Gloy gum, and could imagine a weightless, gaseous body being an even worse torment.

So here was the Flash spaced out, vaporized but still barely aware, on the edge of disintegration, a personality attenuated into bodiless abstraction. He could no longer function in the material world, and Infantino drew him as drifting red smoke in the vague form of a man, buffeted and disorganized by the breeze of passing pedestrians. Like an egoless Buddhist, he haunted the streets of Central City as a smear of living disintegrating consciousness. Infantino contrived to make it look how Alzheimer's might feel. How could our hero get out of this ultimate trap? One little girl, whose dolly he'd rescued from the river that day, still somehow remembered the Flash, and through her he began to reassemble his ontological status—just in case you were wondering.

An adult eye may judge the simple morality, the unlikely motivations, and find Broome's story light. It's true that there's all too often an airy, affectless tone to Broome's work, but this one had deep resonance. It showed in precise detail the breakdown of the superheroic hard body that was occurring everywhere during the Silver Age. It depicted the end of the trip, the spacey, terrifying loss of self and volition that would be experienced by so many young people unprepared for the psychoanalytical effects of Albert Hoffman's chemical child in a time of war. And it showed them that the only way back was through kindness, connection, and community.

Flash stories, too, were an entertaining source of so-called Flash Facts: editorial interruptions or features explaining how wind velocity during a hurricane could drive a blade of straw deep into solid wood, or how light took nine minutes to reach us from the sun, so that we wouldn't know that it had gone out until nine minutes after the fact. Flash Facts were perfect for impressing teachers and parents and for proving that comics had something to offer an upstanding young generation of fresh-faced futurians.

Flash stories were the work of well-adjusted grown-ups who really understood children. In contrast to the titanic but all too often cruel and cloying sensuality of the Superman and Batman tales, the female leads in Schwartz books brought a brisk self-assurance to the proceedings. In the graceful hands of Infantino or Kane, women like Iris Allen, Sue Dibny, and Jean Loring were styled in the finest New Look Paris modes. Their hair was cut to keep up with the latest trends. This was partly a result of fallout from the code, which insisted that female characters be realistically proportioned and modestly attired, but it helped turn the Schwartz heroines into hip and pretty exemplars of the Jackie Kennedy style. Out of costume, their men wore slacks, blazers, and trilby hats or sported short-back-and-sides establishment haircuts. An aesthetic that would one day be called metrosexual was born here in full bloom. They all hung out together, these settled young couples with good jobs, positive can-do attitudes, and crime-fighting double lives they still kept secret from their loved ones.

Schwartz was also establishing a shared universe. Flash was friends with Green Lantern, Hal Jordan. He was also friends with Ivy League physics professor Ray Palmer, aka the Atom, and his lawyer girlfriend, Jean Loring. He also hung out with the Elongated Man (the Stretchable Sleuth) Ralph Dibny and his wife, Sue. They didn't meet to fight one another as the later Marvel heroes would do. They didn't overemote. They enjoyed picnics, which were routinely disrupted by oddly small-scale, almost polite, alien invasions—the kind easily repelled by the deployment of some quirky science fact that rendered the invaders vulnerable to common table salt or H_2O. Their sexuality was never dubious or in doubt. Relaxed, cosmopolitan, they represented the epitome of our Kennedy Man, our postwar Madison Avenue pioneer astronaut American role model. Hopeful in the clear light of the morning of the Sun King. Poignant in their certainty.

And then the president was dead. The golden walls of Camelot collapsed, flimsy as any stage set, to reveal the bloody screaming mires of

Vietnam beyond, where two million potential astronauts, artists, poets, musicians, and scientists were being lined up to die in the sacrifice of an American generation.

And with that came the new turn of the wheel, the biggest revolution of all.

The Marvel superheroes had arrived.

CHAPTER 7

THE FAB FOUR AND THE BIRTH OF THE MARVELOUS

AS IF SOMEONE had planned it all along, the new era of superheroes began with these words:

"WITH THE SUDDEN FURY OF A THUNDERBOLT . . ."

The Promethean age had been announced; the time of men as gods who bore fire in the palms of their hands had come. And with that recognition of the superhero's Promethean dimension came the acknowledgment of punishment, Fall, retribution, and guilt—themes that would resonate through the experience of a very unusual generation of children. From now on, having superpowers would come at the very least with great responsibility and, at worst, would be regarded as a horrific curse.

Stan Lee had been writing comic-book stories for twenty years and was ready to quit. The business was dead in the water after the Wertham years, latching on to one brief fad after another in an attempt to attract readers. Lee had written Westerns, romances, monster stories, and crime comics until his wife, Joan, suggested he give it one last go, one last all-or-nothing demonstration of the kind of books he wanted to read rather than the kind his publishers compelled him to write.

Superheroes were on the way back, thanks to the Silver Age innovations over at DC and the success of their *Justice League of America*. This prompted publisher Martin Goodman to throw Lee a new challenge when he asked him to create a team of superheroes like Schwartz's JLA but modern, fresh, and relevant.

And so Lee, with nothing to lose, gave it a go and in the process founded an empire. He was fortunate to have on his team the finest, most imaginative artists in the field: Jack Kirby and Steve Ditko. Marvel saw Julius Schwartz's connected world and built its own, almost overnight; a whole universe that would be a stronger, faster, and smarter evolutionary improvement.

Fantastic Four no. 1 arrived in late 1961, two years before the real Fab Four would arrive from Liverpool. Flaunting tradition from the beginning, the Fantastic Four wore civilian clothes. When finally pressured to give them more recognizably superheroic costumes, Jack Kirby responded with functional blue jumpsuits that owed more to the Mercury astronauts than to circus acrobats and established the FF as a new breed of space-age superheroes with their feet on the ground. Marvel was going back to Jerry Siegel's original idea. What if superheroes were real? What if they weren't just fairy tales for kiddies? What if superheroes appeared here and now, among us, like the Martians—or the Reds, who'd threatened the previous decade? That was the premise.

They were also a family, but unlike the Marvel Family, where everyone was everyone's friend, or the Superman family, where every day was an epic emotional doomsday, the Fantastic Four quarreled and hugged and stood together like a real family.

The first *Fantastic Four* cover quoted the cover of *Justice League of America* no. 1, which depicted the heroes dwarfed by a monster. The Justice League had found themselves up against a giant alien starfish, but here the threat was one of Kirby's rocky underworld titans.

"I CAN'T TURN INVISIBLE FAST ENOUGH!" came the poignant cry of the postwar independent woman.

"IT'LL TAKE MORE THAN *ROPES* TO KEEP MISTER FANTASTIC OUT OF ACTION!" boasted a man with weird attenuated limbs who was stretching his way free of a coil of rope. There was no explanation as to how he'd wound up in this embarrassing tangle. The other two characters were a fiery flying man who looked a little like the 1940s Human Torch and an orange-skinned walking pile of rocks named the Thing.

Of the four leads, only two were even faced in our direction. These new Marvel heroes were small; they dressed like us even though they had fantastic physical abilities. They worked on the street, not in the sky.

The whole thing took place on a street corner, a set constructed in the void of the empty background. The creature appeared to be emerging through the page surface itself, uttering the last roar of the dying monster comics of the fifties. It was all mouth, all devouring, and there was no Superman here to lock it up in his interplanetary zoo, no Flash to analyze it out of existence. The heroes of *Fantastic Four* were barely distinguishable at first from the screaming passersby, or the useless cop on the sidewalk, quailing at the sight of a green arm as big as a container truck shattering the concrete and clawing its way into the daylight world.

Yet there was a new confidence here: Comic-book covers of the fifties had shown ordinary people running from symbolic monsters of the id. Now four people were fighting back. Superman stood at the center of the elements on the cover of *Action* no. 1. These new heroes *were* the elements. The Fantastic Four formed a living equation. The exploration of their constantly shifting, always familiar, family dynamic made them a perpetual-motion story engine.

Swooping in a half circle around the Invisible Girl, the blazing cometary figure of the Human Torch brought our gaze with him around the cover and back. The composition made a swirling figure eight that enclosed and trapped the monster. The figure eight was the eternal family braid of the FF, the promise of a saga that might never end, with characters designed to last. The figure eight was also the sign of the cosmic voyager, the astronaut of the infinite, and it looked forward to themes that Jack Kirby would develop in his mature work.

The balloons seemed awkwardly placed, but they too were sited so that our eye was swept around the page in constant motion.

"THE THING! MR. FANTASTIC! HUMAN TORCH! INVISIBLE GIRL! TOGETHER FOR THE FIRST TIME IN ONE MIGHTY MAGAZINE."

Soon Lee would establish a proud banner above the title that read simply, "THE WORLD'S GREATEST COMIC MAGAZINE."

It was no empty boast. In an astonishing 102-issue sustained run with Jack Kirby, *Fantastic Four* rebuilt the superhero concept for the Silver Age and gave readers a monthly ticket to a world of planet-eating gods, undersea kingdoms, alternate dimensions, and ever-changing, ever-returning family dynamics.

That first Fantastic Four adventure began in midflow with a crowd of people pointing to the words *The Fantastic Four*, writ vast on a cloud in the sky. This alarm, outdoing Batman's signal in scale and literalism, and turning the story and series title into active parts of the adventure itself, brought together a group of intriguing freaks, including a misanthropic monster whose every movement or transaction provided a new source of irritation or violent confrontation. Each character was given a few pages to display (or in the Invisible Girl's case, not display) his or her superpower before the first act ended with the promise of a "fearful task" ahead for the quartet.

Keeping readers on their toes, the story backtracked to the fateful day when each of these incredible beings received his or her strange power. Their leader, the smug, pipe-smoking Dr. Reed Richards, was shown deliberately ignoring the warnings of a man named Ben Grimm, who seemed to think that stealing an experimental space rocket and flying it through lethal cosmic rays was a potentially bad idea. Richards left the dirty work to his glamorous blond fiancée, Sue Storm:

"BEN, WE'VE GOT TO TAKE THAT CHANCE UNLESS WE WANT THE COMMIES TO BEAT US TO IT. I NEVER THOUGHT THAT YOU WOULD BE A COWARD."

Sue's passive-aggressive challenge was enough to send Ben off the deep end.

"A COWARD! NOBODY CALLS ME A COWARD!"

And so the rest of the group was able to convince the only level head among them to take part in a harebrained scheme that could only end in disaster. For some reason, Reed and Ben allowed both Sue and her teenage brother Johnny to accompany them on their suicidal mission to stop the Reds from getting there first.

"WE HAD TO DO IT! WE HAD TO BE THE FIRST!" Richards yelled in triumph as the rocket accelerated through the ionosphere. It was the leonine roar of the Kennedy spaceman claiming the vacuum. It was the hubris of the golden young president and the atom-age scientist, and it preceded both Fall and Guilt.

The only sound effect in the story occurred in the panel after Richards's cockcrow and indicated the terrifying presence of cosmic rays—smashing through the unprotected hull to bathe the four rebel astronauts in pure Silver Age radiation.

RAK TAC TAC TAC TAC TAC!

When the stricken spaceship crash-landed, and the four stumbled from the wreckage one by one, we watched the rays wreak upon each a terrible transformation: Sue turned invisible for the first time. Johnny burst into flames and learned he could fly, on fire. Reed's entire body became elastic, and Ben drew the short straw as his reward for trying to prevent this whole insane escapade from ever taking place, when he transformed into the monstrous orange-plated Thing, unable to return to his human form.

Reed, quite rightly, blamed himself for Ben's shocking deformity and loss of a normal life. Sue, meanwhile, had attracted the amorous attentions of a renovated Prince Namor the Sub-Mariner, back from the deep like a horny Peter Pan, and Johnny struggled with youthful impetuousness and a "hotheaded" temper.

The Marvel superhero was born: a hero who tussled not only with monsters and mad scientists but also with relatable personal issues.

Soon the storm-laden atmosphere of the early *Fantastic Four* episodes was replaced by an easy flow that could encompass high drama, science fiction, situation comedy, pathos, and an entirely innovative approach to the superhero concept that aligned it with the pioneering spirit of the astronauts. The fragmenting nuclear family would provide Lee, Kirby, and everyone who followed them on the book with an endless supply of stories that could become myths. Evil uncles, weddings, births, breakups—*Fantastic Four* gave everyone's family album a superhero twist. After the wedding of Mr. and Mrs. Fantastic, a new, more playful dynamic emerged, with Reed and Sue as Mom and Pop, Johnny as the brattish teenage son, and Ben the monstrous nightmare baby.

The Marvel supermen were scientists too. The Fantastic Four were astronauts. The Hulk was Bruce Banner, a physicist. Henry Pym, the shrinking Ant-Man, was a particle physicist. Spider-Man, Peter Parker, was a science major. Thor's Don Blake was a doctor, but Lee and his artists—primarily a reinvigorated Jack Kirby, who was beginning a period that would come to be regarded as his creative peak, and the prickly Steve Ditko—would show a new, darker side to the PhD hero.

Lee and Ditko, on a roll, cocreated the next big Marvel hit: Spider-Man. There was another new wrinkle: a teenage superhero who wasn't a sidekick, who could star in his own book, and who didn't have a name ending in Kid or Lad. Peter Parker was, as Lee wrote at the end of the first adventure, "the hero who could be you," and he brought a new level of realism to superhero strips, creating another revolution in the process. Parker, a bespectacled science nerd, was introduced to the world in Amazing Fantasy no. 15 in August 1962 as "MIDTOWN HIGH'S ONLY PROFESSIONAL WALLFLOWER."

It was unlikely that the young readers of superhero books could identify too closely with the likes of Barry Allen or Hal Jordan—handsome young men with careers and wonderful girlfriends—but Peter Parker brought the specky Clark Kent archetype back and gave readers a teenage hero who felt like a teenager. He couldn't mitigate his geekdom by pointing to a reporting job or a science degree, and with his furtive behavior, gangly awkward posture, and bouts of self-lacerating guilt that alternated with elation, Spider-Man was a million miles away from the clean-limbed, well-mannered, thirtieth-century teens from DC's Legion of Super-Heroes or from the Marvel Family, and a million miles closer to home.

The first time we saw Parker, he wasn't leaping through the air or catching crooks, he was standing isolated from a crowd of mocking teenagers, at a physical and emotional remove that seemed impassable. The bookworm himself, with sunken shoulders, dated clothes, and huge, round spectacles, gazed across what might as well have been an infinite abyss at the popular kids giggling among themselves at the ludicrous notion of inviting Peter to a dance. In one hand he carried his textbooks. It was a scene from every high school yard, and many of Spider-Man's young readers must have projected themselves immediately onto the quiet, self-effacing Peter Parker. We could be in Riverdale High except that there was something extra, something strange and wonderful about Peter. Unlike Peter Pan, Peter Parker had a shadow.

In fact, in the cover illustration he seemed to cast a three-part shadow: There was a proud muscular man with hands on hips standing at the center of a spiderweb with the black outline of a huge spider poised above his head. Clearly there was more to the shy wallflower than met the eye. The picture was already evocative, but Lee had only begun.

Lee's conversational narrative captions dropped all pretense of a dispassionate authorial voice in favor of a chummy camaraderie that made it feel as if he were there with you, reading the same comic and cringing at the same "corny" moments. The comic itself became a buddy. Lee interjected his own persona into little editor's footnotes that provided links between stories or reminded readers of salient facts, all in Stan's wink-wink "How's-it-goin'-pal?" style. Then came "Stan's Soapbox," a regular bulletin column in which Lee could sound off about whatever was on his mind. Mostly he was promoting new Marvel books with a knowing hyperbole that could do the huckster's job while maintaining an ironic distance, but often he'd lay on the line his feelings about civil rights or world peace.

Sometimes he'd even talk about visits to the Marvel offices by luminaries of the nouvelle vague such as film directors Federico Fellini, Alain Resnais, and Jean-Luc Godard. Mostly they were "funky Frenchmen," as Lee might put it, who had accepted the fantasy comics into the mainstream of their culture long ago in the form of expensively bound *bandes dessinées* or *fumetti*. Clever and innovative comic-book artists like Stan's crew didn't have to prove themselves to the Euro auteurs, but the American mainstream rarely took seriously the artwork or the language or the radical new storytelling structures of the work. They seemed barely aware that a new underground mythology was circulating. Within ten years, the Marvel universe would supplant DC's as the most successful in both sales and fan approval.

By 1965, with a successful stable of new and offbeat superheroes, including the Hulk, Daredevil, Iron Man, Thor, and Giant Man, Lee was bannering each new issue "A MARVEL POP ART PRODUCTION." The new banner allowed Stan Lee to both distance himself from his staid competitors at DC (whom Stan was to charitably rename "Brand Ecch") and also to ally himself with the wider currents of popular culture. Stan used his columns and other means to whip up a fierce rivalry between Marvel and DC, while the giant paid him no heed, at least not in public.

But the new Marvel heroes were so radioactive with rough-hewn novelty and pure personality, they made DC's product seem like juvenilia, forcing DC to change in order to keep up.

The very first words in the Spider-Man strips signaled the new compact between reader and creator that was the hallmark of the Marvel style. "LIKE COSTUMED HEROES?" Lee asked, knowing that we must if we'd bought the book. It was rare for readers to be asked such direct questions about the object in their hands. Then he opened up with a few trade secrets to gain our trust:

"CONFIDENTIALLY, WE IN THE COMIC MAG BUSINESS REFER TO THEM AS 'LONG UNDERWEAR CHARACTERS'! AND, AS YOU KNOW, THEY'RE A DIME A DOZEN! BUT, WE THINK YOU MAY FIND OUR **SPIDERMAN** JUST A BIT . . . DIFFERENT!"

With one caption, Lee became our friend, our confidant. He reminded us up front that we were reading a made-up story, then created with Ditko a story and characters so compelling, we were drawn in, despite its avowed fictional nature, in a display of showmanship. It was perfectly composed in just eleven pages. (When writer Brian Michael Bendis was called on to update and retell the Spider-Man origin for a new generation of readers in 2000, it took six twenty-two-page issues to tell the same story in the "decompressed" screenplay style of twenty-first-century comics.)

Doted upon by his elderly guardians, Aunt May and Uncle Ben, Peter was nevertheless rejected by every girl he met.

"SOME DAY I'LL SHOW THEM! [*Sob*] SOME DAY THEY'LL BE SORRY—SORRY THAT THEY LAUGHED AT ME."

Fortunately for our hero, "some day" turned up a few minutes later when Peter was bitten by a spider that had inadvertently absorbed an unusually high dose of radiation during a science demonstration. In the real world, Peter would have succumbed to radiation poisoning and died in confused agony with no hair and no teeth several weeks later, but this was the Marvel universe establishing its own rules of engagement. In the Marvel U, radiation was a kind of pixie dust: sprinkle it on a scientist, and voilà! A superhero was born. Radiation was responsible for the origins of the Fantastic Four, Spider-Man, the Hulk, the X-Men, Daredevil, and several other early Marvel superheroes, transforming the isotopes of fear into fuel rods of wonder and possibility. Lee stole back the annihilating radiation of the Bomb, and for children like me—raised in its icy shadow—he peopled the glowing darkness with extraordinary heroes.

It was traditional for superhero characters to opt for a crime-fighting life-style as quickly as they could design an embarrassing costume and give themselves a ridiculous name. The Golden Age mystery men fought crime because that was what you did. DC's Silver Age science heroes did it because they read about it in Golden Age comics. They didn't need to see their worlds destroyed or their parents killed; they used their new abilities to fight crime because that was the community-minded thing to do. Stan Lee went back to first principles. In the Marvel universe, heroes needed reasons, motivations.

On gaining his powers, Peter's first choice was not to fight criminals but to make money, using his newfound "spider strength" in a wrestling match. This brought him to the attention of a TV promoter who offered him a wad of cash to appear on *The Ed Sullivan Show*. Peter accepted and designed his Spider-Man costume not to frighten criminals or to repre-sent his totem animal but to look good on TV.

This was very new in 1962. Here was a hero who anticipated celebrity culture. Within days, Spider-Man was "THE SENSATION OF THE NA-TION," but Lee and Ditko were not finished with us. They still needed to turn this slightly unlikeable power-tripping nerd into a superhero, and they accomplished this in a classic sequence. Spider-Man had just shaken off an adoring media crowd and was about to slip away quietly when a policeman called for his help in apprehending a fleeing crook.

As Spider-Man selfishly ignored the cop's yells, the thief darted into the elevator and made his escape. "LUCKY THAT GOON IN THE COS-TUME DIDN'T STOP ME!" he cackled, rubbing it in.

When the cop admonished Spider-Man, the not-quite-a-hero-yet had his dismissive reply ready:

"SORRY, PAL! THAT'S YOUR JOB! I'M THRU BEING PUSHED AROUND—BY ANYONE! FROM NOW ON I JUST LOOK OUT FOR NUMBER ONE—THAT MEANS—ME!"

It was easy to see, when a doting Uncle Ben and Aunt May bought Peter the microscope he'd always wanted, that the stage was set for tragedy.

Peter returned from another TV performance to find police lights around his house. A burglar had shot and killed Uncle Ben, and when an enraged Spider-Man tracked the killer to his lair, he recognized the man as the thief he'd ignored three pages earlier. It was Peter's fault that Uncle Ben was dead. At least Batman could blame someone else for his parents' deaths. It was at this point that Spider-Man the entertainer was replaced by Spider-Man the crime fighter, driven to expiate his own awful guilt.

As Ditko's tiny, lonely silhouette walked into the darkness under the moon in a blacked-out city, Lee closed off his first sobering adventure with these immortal words:

"WITH GREAT POWER THERE MUST ALSO COME—GREAT RESPONSIBILITY!"

The final caption, like the first, led us out of this intense, emotionally charged situation with an oddly phrased reminder that none of this is real:

"AND SO A LEGEND IS BORN AND A NEW NAME IS ADDED TO THE ROSTER OF THOSE WHO MAKE THE WORLD OF FANTASY THE MOST EXCITING REALM OF ALL."

Spotty, hormonal outsiders had a new hero in Peter. Clark Kent had his own apartment and a steady job, but Peter was a genuine loser. Peter revealed the truth behind the sugared lies of Barry Allen and Ray Palmer: No good-looking girl ever fancied a scientist. Peter fucked up, got the flu, ran out of money and hope. Peter would sit hand sewing his damaged Spider-Man costume in his tiny room at Aunt May's in Queens while newspapers condemned his crime-fighting alter ego as a menace to society.

Straight out of the oven, Marvel Comics had delivered two hit series that completely reinvented the superhero paradigm. As new troubled heroes were added to the mix, the stories began to build on one another, cross-referencing various titles to develop an engrossing mosaic of a whole new world. At DC, an earth-shaking event could happen in one issue and be forgotten by the next. Batman might be nursing a broken leg in his own title while bouncing across the rooftops in *World's Finest, Detective*, or *Justice League*, but the Marvel universe was laying down more solid foundations. Thus, if Peter Parker had a bruise at the end of one story, he'd still have it at the beginning of the next, which made the entire Marvel line one huge and interwoven saga.

Fantastic Four had turned familiar family dramas into superhuman epics. Now *Spider-Man* transformed ordinary teenage life into a weird symbolic soap opera. Spindly and angular, Spider-Man was as creepy as his namesake, and Ditko made a point of posing him in twisted, unnatural attitudes. He had no face. In the Golden Age, his faceless mask design would have suited a spooky and taciturn avenger of evil, but Lee's genius was to turn Spider-Man into comics' most talkative hero. Spider-Man never shut up! He mocked his enemies, cracked gags, and kept up a running commentary on his every movement, every feeling. It was as if shy Peter came alive only when he hid his face behind a mask. As Spider-Man, he spun and tumbled weightlessly down the avenues of Manhattan, spurting sticky web fluid in ecstatic abandon.

Between them, Kirby and Ditko overhauled the look of American comics and established the general tenor of two interdependent strands of expression. On one side, you had superhero books, as represented by the bluff, physical war veteran Kirby—the Picasso, or perhaps more plausibly, the William Blake, of the superheroes, who set the ground rules for manipulating and distorting perspective. On the other side, the reclusive, bespectacled Ditko was preparing the way for elements of the underground alternative comics style, with a measured pace and thematic concerns that led all the way to the politics and formalism of later works like *Watchmen* and beyond.

Ditko's tense, regular panel grids were like tenement windows that could sometimes open onto bizarre wonders. Where Kirby sought to explode, Ditko sought to contain; to stratify and regulate his world on the page with a metronomic, repetitive rhythm over which he could maintain complete control. Committed to conveying the ordinariness and truth of real life, Ditko made his characters thin, hunched, withdrawn, and plain. He drew them sweating, sobbing, and cowering, which only made it more moving when they overcame insurmountable odds to do the right thing.

Ditko became a devotee of Ayn Rand's philosophy of objectivism, then a popular response to the disenchantment of the psychoanalyzed soul and the collapse of "values" into relativistic chaos. The bold, simple, and aggressive distinctions of objectivism appealed to Ditko's analytical mind and gave him a new vocabulary around which to organize his world even more efficiently. More and more, his comics tended toward baffling, overheated polemic, like the hellfire tracts handed out by some dull, hectoring monochrome sect.

It was inevitable that his uncompromising worldview would collide with Lee's liberal, *Playboy* "Why can't we all just make up and get along?" philosophies, and the two eventually parted company. This left Spider-Man in the hands of Lee and new artist John Romita, who made Peter handsome and gave him a choice of two drop-dead-gorgeous girlfriends (one of whom, Gwen Stacy, *did* literally drop dead). Even Aunt May got a makeover that chucked the death's-door frailty and replaced it with robust actressy look that undercut her original role and purged the strip of the last echoes of Ditko's run-down, mundane authenticity.

Unlike the DC heroes, with their totemistic weaknesses to wood or fire (or the color yellow, as in the new Schwartz version of Green Lantern), every Marvel hero had to have a psychological Achilles' heel. If they didn't harbor a deadly personal secret capable of destroying careers and marriages, they weren't good Marvel heroes. And they fought constantly. Superheroes had battled against injustice in the 1930s and fought Hitler in the 1940s, while the 1950s superhumans had tackled monsters and aliens. The Marvel heroes of the 1960s fought one another in between epic clashes with memorably operatic villains such as Doctor Doom, Magneto, Galactus, Doctor Octopus, and the Green Goblin, all of whom had personalities and extra dimensions that elevated them beyond the traditional despots, hoodlums, and madmen of the Golden Age. An emboldened Lee aimed for the heightened rhythms of iambic pentameter and found a way to re-create a pseudo-Shakespearean voice via Brooklyn so that Peter Parker could be riven by a guilt that made Hamlet look like an underachiever.

Here from my own school jotter, detailing a fine day out for a seven-year-old in the Summer of Love, is my first recorded impression of a Marvel Comic:

> I got a kite and a magnet, I got thick comics too. I have got one with two people. One is called Wonderful Wasp and one is called Giant Man. They were fighting someone called the Human Top.

And yet there was something I didn't like about the Marvel superheroes. Those characters seemed constantly angry and weird, and I found stories of conflict between heroes exhausting. Spider-Man's stressy life was a bit too grown-up, it seemed.

After World War II, my dad had declared himself a pacifist. Both he and my mother agreed that I should be raised according to "nonviolent principles," which meant that guns and military toys or uniforms were frowned upon. I didn't miss them, and I actually liked being able to describe myself as a pacifist, because I thought it made me different and more interesting. When the Boy Scouts turned up at our school in search of new recruits, I stood up proudly, fixed the scoutmaster with a glare, and announced, "I refuse to be part of any paramilitary organization, and that includes the Boy Scouts."

I liked my heroes to come in and fix things effortlessly and hated even the slightest obstacle to be placed in the clear path of their success. I just wanted all the wars to be over so that we could spend the money on starships and Mars colonies.

CHAPTER 8

SUPERPOP

BACK FROM THE brink, it was time for a new superhero proliferation. Other companies joined in now that the pioneers had taken the lead and tested the waters. The superheroes caught the mood of the times—like the spies and spacemen, they offered a passport to sleek adventure.

Wally Wood, an accomplished artist, writer, editor, and alcoholic, identified a waiting ecological niche, and combined the sixties spy fiction craze with superheroes to create *T.H.U.N.D.E.R. Agents* (The Higher United Nations Defense Enforcement Reserves) for Tower Comics in 1967. Wood was a veteran of EC whose perfectly lit and composed panels showed a higher degree of skill than that of many of his contemporaries. Yet even they looked stiff and mannered next to Kirby's Heavy Metal.

His T.H.U.N.D.E.R. Agents were another disturbing bunch. As I've explained, I preferred my heroes straight jawed and uncomplicated. The T.H.U.N.D.E.R. Agents were miserable men inhabiting a grim world of Cold War corridors, aircraft hangars, and concrete bunkers. NoMan, one of the central characters whose name suggested some existential afterthought, was an interesting concept, but his adventures were so pedestrian, he could have been a British superhero.

Prefiguring the superheroes of the George W. Bush era, the T.H.U.N.D.E.R. Agents' powers came from gadgets provided by government sponsors. T.H.U.N.D.E.R. Agents gave me a very specific, unpleasant tingle that I find hard to articulate. Perhaps the paramilitary flavor was too troubling for a child from a pacifist household. Wood's art for all its elegant precision seemed posed, always at a distance.

I felt the same about Harvey Comics: the Fly, the Hangman, Bee-Man. An uninspired bunch of lifeless knockoffs, they lacked some solid foundation that DC and Marvel characters had. Gold Key Comics offered the aggressively dull Doctor Solar, Man of the Atom. Attractive painted covers in the pulp style and the lead character's sleekly designed and attractive costume barely distracted from the desperate tedium of repetitive story lines. DC's patchwork universe had been assembled into a comforting quilt over decades, Marvel's was a fashionable mod suit woven from whole cloth by genuinely talented innovators and craftsmen. All the other comic-book universes seemed ill-tailored afterthoughts, cheesy attempts to cash in on something they barely understood. Even as a very young boy, I could sense the difference. I could taste the authenticity and missed it when it wasn't there.

They all wanted to channel the new energy that made young people feel like mutants and superheroes on the verge of a utopian future in space. Driven by sheer youth, the human race managed to send its little feelers to the moon and back, and left footprints where No Man Had Gone Before. Anything seemed possible, and the superheroes were exemplars of this horizonless possibility. They were what we all might become.

Even the Archie Comics characters got in on the act when Archie Andrews became Pureheart the Powerful, and his rival Reggie Mantle transformed into the scheming Evilheart. Disney, too, was touched by the lightning, so that Goofy had only to swallow a few of his special power peanuts to summon his Super Goof alter ego, dressed in red long johns and a blue blanket cape. I took them all equally seriously, as happy to play at being Pureheart or Super Goof as Batman.

The comics were once again exploding off the page and into electronic life. But with a twist. The *Batman* TV show of 1966–68 can be seen as a pure Pop Art creation: It borrows from a previous source—the *Batman* serials of the forties—but reframes its subject in a way that causes us to challenge all the preconceptions of the source material and makes someone rich.

According to the best version of the story, Hugh Hefner had a few pals over to the Playboy Mansion, including Bob Kane and NBC producer Bill Dozier. I like to imagine that in between sessions of swinging Bunny humping in the grotto, they found time to screen the *Batman* serials. Like me, these imagined sophisticates saw in the serials an opportunity for cheap laughs and easy mockery. The serials intended to entertain children and idiots had, in short, become "camp."

Another version of the story has Dozier reading *Batman* no. 171, one of the early New Look books. He picked up immediately on the Pop Art influence and on Infantino's bold new addition to Batman's graphic appeal. By highlighting the bat silhouette with a yellow oval that recalled the Bat signal the police projected onto the clouds whenever they needed to summon the hero to action, Infantino had turned the chest emblem into a logo and a marketing tool.

Perhaps the truth lay in some combination of influences. The New Look provided a visual template, and there was an undeniable influence from the UK TV show *The Avengers*.

Dozier saw a way to make a Pop Art series that would appeal not only to kids but to hip teens and grown-ups as well. A hero pitched directly at the psychedelic youth who were recapitulating vaudeville, gramophones, and granny glasses. This Batman could play to fans of Beatles movies like *Help!* Dozier even provided a portentous voiceover narration that aped the style of the serials. What's more, the story structure—two thirty-minute episodes stretched across consecutive nights with a cliff-hanger ending in between—was another nod in the direction of the serial format. Each half-hour episode had its own title.

Upon its debut in January 1966, *Batman* became the biggest show on TV, triggering a "Batmania" that for a short, intense period rivaled the Beatlemania that had greeted John, Paul, George, and Ringo upon their arrival in the States two years earlier. Played strictly for irony, *Batman* the TV series had a simple gimmick: The ludicrously earnest dialogue was delivered absolutely straight by Adam West and Burt Ward. In this bright iteration, there were no shadows, no mention of why Batman did what he did, no flashbacks to his parents dying of gunshot wounds in a grimy alley. Adam West's Batman was Batman because being Batman made perfect sense to him. His flat, earnest delivery may have amused the chortling *Playboy* set, but every child knew that was exactly how a superhero would talk.

Matinee heartthrob Cesar Romero refused to shave his trademark mustache for his role as the Joker, so it was slathered over with white greasepaint, clearly visible in every shot. Watching *Batman* on a tiny black-and-white screen with such poor resolution that it mimicked the eyesight of a myopic man attempting to peer through time itself, I was oblivious to Romero's whitewashed facial hair. It was the Joker on-screen, pure and simple. A leering, manic, evil clown. I didn't see Burt Ward's tights and would have sworn he was bare legged, like Robin in the comics. There was nothing funny, ironic, or camp about Batman for me. It was thrilling, scary, and completely addictive. It was an absolute guarantee of a good time.

If Batman in the sixties seems ridiculous, consider 1967's James Bond movie, a free-form adaptation of Ian Fleming's first Bond novel, *Casino Royale*. The same story was remade in 2006 as a violent, "naturalistic" thriller with Daniel Craig in the Bond role. But in the Summer of Love, *Casino Royale* became a psychedelic, absurdist, virtually plot-free romp.

The 1967 Bond, like Batman, was an outmoded Establishment stooge, played strictly for laughs. What was camp ultimately but the serious attitudes of a previous generation as seen through the rose-colored lenses of hash and LSD? Even the story logic crumbles as the characters stumble across a film set where they are revealed as mere players, encountering cowboys and Indians who have thundered in from another movie, another soundstage, or another parallel universe. It's a flower-power Bond; druggy, fashion conscious, tongue in cheek. It's a film that would be inconceivable in the ruthless world of today's rigorously constructed three-act screenplays.

Everything was up for grabs. The establishment heroes of an earlier age were being lined up as the targets of lampoon. If recipients of LSD and mescaline could scarcely sit through Holocaust footage without laughing, what chance did the earnest, square-jawed heroes of the past have, now exposed to the harsh scrutiny of the young as hysterically deluded dupes of conformity and reaction? *Mr. Terrific* was a TV show about a nerd in a silver flying suit, while *Captain Nice* brought the weekly adventures of a bespectacled half-wit into homes across America. The superhero was one more clown on the bus, one more Haight-Ashbury spook with fire in his eyes and tinfoil on his head, and even kids knew that "funny" superheroes didn't work.

But for me, shows like *Mr. Terrific* were the real thing—as close as TV could come to making my beloved comics move, and therefore serious by their very nature. I was so hungry for any sight of superhero activity that I was willing to overlook the obvious stupidity of these characters and tried to take them seriously.

In 1990 I stood in line at the Virgin Megastore to have my videocassette copy of *Batman: The Movie* signed by Adam West. As he scribbled his spoor, I told him I'd just had my own Batman book, *Arkham Asylum*, published to some acclaim. He looked at me the way you'd look at a floater drifting across the viscera of your eye and grunted.

That was good enough for me.

In 1966 my family had moved a few miles south from Govan to a working-class residential development known as Corkerhill. It was a pretty model-railway village of Victorian red sandstone cottage-style houses—which would be devastated by planners and replaced with concrete crack houses several years later. The lovely station, whose stationmaster won awards every year for his spectacular floral displays, became a frightening dead zone strung with lethal power cables for electric trains. Shorn of its personality, electro-shocked and lobotomized, Corkerhill Rail Station was dressed like a Maoist Chinese worker in regulation council orange and plastic, with chipped Formica and graffiti where once flourished overstuffed bouquets and pride. The romance of the train line was brutalized into hard facts made of wire and cable and grilles by people who knew nothing of romance, only function.

I had a sister now. She enjoyed reading *Lois Lane, Jimmy Olsen*, and any story with Superbaby or Bizarro in it. Then there was the Legion of Super-Heroes, written by a precocious and—based on his adult height of seven-foot plus—presumably gigantic thirteen-year-old named Jim Shooter. He would go on to become a feared editor at Marvel Comics in the eighties. But the young Shooter's stories were fast paced, punchy, and filled with genuine teen earnestness, humor, and romance. With a cast of convincingly drawn and individual characters, the sprawling Legion roster of up to thirty superheroes never seemed enough, let alone too much. Shooter introduced Marvel-style high-tension situations and terrifying, seemingly unstoppable villains into the now predictable world of Superman and his extended cast. He lacked the arch sophistication of the middle-aged Stan Lee but more than made up for it with verve, invention, and a deft talent for creating situations of escalating jeopardy.

I liked those stories, and *The Flash* and *Justice League of America*. I knew American comics as "thick comics." Otherwise I had cheaper, flimsier British weekly comics competing for my attention. There were funny ones like the *Beezer* and action-adventure titles like *Valiant* or *Lion*. The latter type tended to feature World War II adventures, which I read dutifully, sensing in them the deadening weight of a history I'd narrowly avoided. The Second World War was now entering its fourth decade in comics, and the plucky chaps of the boys' papers could be relied on to continue the relentless killing well into the eighties. The German death toll in British comics surpassed by several factors the actual casualty statistics of both world wars.

"HE MAY WEAR SPECS BUT HE'S A CRACKING GOOD SHOT!" came the approving cry as bespectacled conscientious objector "Four-Eyes" Foster admitted the error of his ways and rose to the challenge of murdering Germans with a glee and vigor his previous life as an accountant had denied him.

Comics were only a part of it. There were a lot of children around and lots of space for playing for long hours without adult supervision.

I was obsessed with space, astronauts, constellations, UFOs—anything in the sky. My mum enrolled us both in astronomy classes to feed my need for knowledge, and there I sat diligently, converting dry lectures about magnitude and albedo into science fiction vistas in my head. I was only there for the telescope and for the sense all this gave me of being special and a little otherworldly. Jupiter. The rings of Saturn. Passing comets. I saw them all. I saw a V-shaped flock of geese that I was certain were cruising saucers. I saw a group of what I was assured were urban Satanist swingers dressed in hooded robes and carrying candles up the back stairs of the big house across the road. Or maybe they were penitent monks. All that mattered was the story potential in everything.

In the same year, my eighth, Mum took me to see *2001: A Space Odyssey* three times in fairly rapid succession, which was certainly enough to create a powerful imprint and to reinforce the sense of a cosmic dimension to my own life. I began to look for the same feeling in comics and eventually found it in Jack Kirby's work at Marvel. The Bomb became less important. By the time I was five years old, I'd decided I wanted to be a writer. It was that, astronaut, or cowboy.

But things changed all the time. President Kennedy had already been shot dead out there somewhere on the threshold of my awareness, and now it was his brother Bobby's turn, in June 1968. My mum cried that day, as she had two months earlier when Martin Luther King was gunned down in Memphis. It was getting dark outside, and the flower children had begun to notice how creepy the woods were at the end of Penny Lane.

My dad was unemployed again. I didn't know what to write when my teacher asked me what he did for a living. He wasn't doing terrazzo flooring anymore, and he'd been kicked out of his shop steward position at the Factory for Peace, a workers-run collective, after triggering all-out war between the shop floor and "management."

Soon I was making regular appearances in the papers, waving a picket sign outside one or the other of my dad's former places of employment. There would be my mum, my sister, and me, immaculately dressed and waving placards condemning the sacking of our family breadwinner from yet another utopian socialist cooperative. My mum kept up her part-time job as a shorthand typist, supporting everything Dad did until he made the mistake of having an affair with a teenage Ban the Bomber, and the fallout slowly blew the family apart.

Entering adolescence, as if overdosed on the illusory, I began to find myself slipping into a disassociated state in which the world seemed flat and unreal; as if I were seeing through to a cardboard world lacking in significance, painted on screens I could no longer touch. Even comics seemed dead to me, stripped of their magic and emptied of color. I was acutely aware of the exact moment when my toys ceased to be alive and when the play environment lost its potential to be anything I wanted it to be and became only a room.

I could feel time setting in around me like a jelly. When I uncovered some old comics, lost for maybe two or three years at the bottom of a box in the linen cupboard, they felt haunted. Those few years had painted them with a weird gloss, imposing an extra layer of memory and meaning on their pages. I felt like a hunter who had stumbled upon his own tracks in the forest and realized for the first time how long he'd been doing this without thinking.

Those closets at Dad's place remained that way until he moved out; time machines freighted with the plunder of the ages. There were piled issues of the London *Observer* and London *Sunday Times* magazines dating back to the dawn of the sixties with model Jean Shrimpton and actor Terence Stamp on the covers, or girls in Paco Rabanne and Courrèges, dressed for a future that would resolutely refuse to arrive. They inspired the clothes I chose to wear when I was creating my own identity as a teenager. This lost vision of the sixties would become part of my own private world of obsession and symbol.

I couldn't stop thinking about time travel, either, gripped with the idea of drawing an object from the fifth dimension and bending my way out of school through the walls. I'd begin with a point, then rule a line, then build a square and construct a perspective cube, and then my head would expand and pop with frustration, leaving the taste of a higher dimension on the tip of my tongue.

I should have paid more attention to my comics.

CHAPTER 9

INFINITE EARTHS

IN 1961 JULIUS Schwartz hit upon a way of resurrecting the old DC trademarks that his new generation of heroes had supplanted. Editorial offices at the publishing giant were all rivals, which is why their universe came together more by accident than design, unlike Marvel's meticulously constructed interconnected world. While the other DC editors held on to their trademark characters, Julie's office specialized in assembling the streamlined beginnings of a shared universe where all the DC superheroes were friends and partners.

By spreading a given brand across multiple versions of a character designed to appeal to different sections of his audience, Julie had invented a trick that would be adopted as the industry standard. Schwartz was a world builder, and, under his guidance, the DC universe became part of a "multiverse," in which an infinite number of alternate Earths occupied the same space as our own, each vibrating out of phase with the others so that they could never meet. The idea of infinite worlds, each with its own history and its own superheroes, was intoxicating and gave DC an even more expansive canvas.

In the story "Flash of Two Worlds," police scientist Barry Allen was shown reading an old comic about the Flash adventures of Jay Garrick. In Allen's world (soon to be known as Earth-1), Garrick was a fictional comics character who inspired Allen's choice of a superhero identity when he too became the Flash, the Fastest Man Alive. Not only did this confirm that Barry was a comics fan like his readers, it enmeshed the character and his audience in a complex meta-story that would eerily mimic the large-scale structures of our universe, as they're currently being debated by cosmologists.

By spinning fast enough to alter the pitch at which his molecules vibrated, Barry Allen discovered he could cross over to a second Earth. Here twenty years had passed for the wartime champions of the Justice Society, so that Jay Garrick was middle aged and married to his Golden Age sweetheart, Joan. It took the arrival of Barry Allen and the machinations of a trio of Golden Age criminals to bring Jay out of retirement. The way was paved for the return of Doctors Fate and Mid-Nite, Wildcat, Sandman, and Hourman. The vanished heroes of the Golden Age were duly resurrected as denizens of the newly christened Earth-2, but there were even more Earths—as many as imagination could conceive. On some of these worlds, the familiar superheroes had evil counterparts like the Crime Syndicate of America. On Earth-X lived DC's recently acquired stable of Quality Comics characters locked in a decades-long battle with an unbeatable mechanized Hitler.

As a child, I loved to angle two bathroom mirrors so that I could look down a virtual corridor into the infinity of reflections that lay in either direction. I imagined that those distant versions of myself, glimpsed at the far end of the receding stack, were inhabitants of parallel worlds, peering back down the hall of faces at me. Alternate realities were as easy as that; they were waiting for us in our bathrooms.

There were inevitably philosophical ramifications for the reader. If Barry lived on a world where Jay was fictional, and we lived in a world where Barry was fictional, did that mean we, as readers, were also part of Schwartz's elegant multiversal architecture? It did indeed, and it was soon revealed that we all lived on Earth-Prime. Julius Schwartz even met the Flash on several occasions in print, and in one story, two young writers named Cary Bates and Elliot Maggin wrote themselves into a Justice

League adventure involving Earth-Prime. Bates became an insane villain and immediately donned a garish costume with cape, boots, and overpants, while adding a new twist to the standard superhero look with his long hair, beard, and glasses. When the clean-cut Maggin joined the Justice League in a search for the rogue Bates, this Schwartz-edited adventure pushed the Earth-Prime idea as far as it could go. Or so it seemed.

By the 1980s, as comics became more realistic, or at least more like Hollywood's version of realism, the idea of parallel worlds was declared too outlandish and prepubescent—as well as too forgiving of any ludicrous story turn. Batman could be shot dead, only for a last page to reveal that he was really the middle-aged Earth-2 Batman or even the evil Earth-3 Batman/Owlman, and it's true that many writers used the parallel Earths not to create a sense of wonder and possibility but to justify some overcooked twist in an undercooked story.

Then, in the intervening years, something became apparent to our cosmologists.

The multiverse was real.

Flash Fact: Our universe is one of many, grown inside some unimaginable amniotic hypertime. It may even all be hologram, projected onto a flat mega-membrane, which is, in turn, embedded, along with many others like it, within a higher dimensional space some scientists have dubbed "the bulk." In the brane model of the multiverse, all history is spread as thin as emulsion on a celestial tissue that floats in some immense, Brahmanic ocean of . . . meta-stuff. Got all that?

If cosmologists are right about this (and I'd dearly love to hope they are), the superheroes, as usual, have been here already.

It will take a long time for these new maps of existence to instill themselves in the culture at large, but it will happen. It's fun to imagine what our world might be like when theories of simultaneous time, parallel worlds, and holographic branes in hyperspace are taught to schoolchildren as the accepted facts of nature they will be.

I've always imagined that the structure and underlying patterns of the universe would most likely be repeated across every aspect of its disposition, including the lowliest superhero comic books. If our universe is some kind of hologram, it would make sense for the same patterns to turn up on all scales, from the infinitesimal to the unimaginably vast, like the spirals that coil through our DNA and our galaxies, and track the vast Coriolis of some Prime Movement.

If a comic-book universe were a scaled-down representation of the kind of reality we all inhabit, we might expect it to behave in certain ways. It would have a beginning and an end: a big bang and a heat death. It would be populated with life-forms capable of replicating themselves through time.

And in place of time, comic-book universes offer something called "continuity."

Continuity is an emergent phenomenon, at first recognized by Gardner Fox, Julius Schwartz, and Stan Lee as a kind of imaginative real estate that would turn mere comic books into chronicles of alternate histories. DC's incoherent origins formed an archipelago of island concepts that were slowly bolted together to create a mega-continuity involving multiple parallel worlds that could not only make sense of pre–Silver Age versions of characters like the Flash, but also fit new acquisitions from defunct companies into a framework that made Marvel's universe look provincial. Marvel improved on the formula by taking us on human journeys that could last as long as our own lives—eternally recurring soap operas—where everything changed but always wound up in the same place; where Aunt May was always on the verge of another heart attack, and Peter Parker couldn't get a break from J. Jonah Jameson, his editor at the New York newspaper the *Daily Bugle*.

"IT IS NOT TOO FAR-FETCHED TO PREDICT THAT SOME DAY OUR VERY OWN PLANET MAY BE PEOPLED ENTIRELY BY SUPERMEN!" Joe Shuster assured us back in 1938, but comic-book reality predicts developments in our own in many other ways.

What we construct in our imaginations, we have a knack of building or discovering. We may not have flying men or invulnerable women racing among us, but we now have access to supertechnologies that once existed only in comic-book stories.

"Mother Boxes," empathic personal computers like the ones in Jack Kirby's *Fourth World* story cycle, are already here in embryonic form. Is the soothing contact offered by the Mother Box so different from the instant connection that a cell phone provides? Twenty-four-hour access to friends, family, and the buzz of constant social exchange can make us feel cocooned and safe in a reportedly hostile world. In many cases, Mother herself can be summoned on the Box.

Metron was Kirby's avatar of ruthless, questing intellect, whose Mobius Chair twisted through time and space to make him the god of couch potatoes, surfing channels, gathering information, without ever leaving the comfort of his armchair. Metron's magic furniture seems less a wonder of supertechnology than a fact of daily life. As Kirby tried to tell us in his book of the same name, we are the new gods, just as we are the old ones, too.

There is already technology that allows people to drive remote-controlled cars with their minds. What's to stop someone becoming Auto-Man, the Human Car? Secretly, he sits in his room, munching Maltesers at his computer screen, while he listlessly pilots his incredible RV supercar around town to save lives and fight the crime that ordinary police cars just aren't fast enough to handle.

In so many ways, we're already superhuman. Being extraordinary is so much a part of our heritage as human beings that we often overlook what we've done and how very unique it all is. We have made machines to extend our physical reach and the reach of our senses, allowing us to peer into the depths of space and outer time. Our cameras and receivers allow us to see across the entire electromagnetic spectrum. We can slow down, freeze, and accelerate time on our screens. We can study and manipulate microscopic worlds, print our names on single atoms, analyze soil on Mars, and observe the rings of Saturn at close range. Our voices and our photographic records of everything we've seen are carried at the speed of light on an expanding bubble of radio, into the infinite. Television broadcasts of the first moon landing are still traveling, growing fainter as the waves spread out. If you had a powerful enough receiver and a TV on a planet forty light-years from here, you could watch Neil Armstrong take his first step on mankind's behalf and hear our silly, hopeful summer 1969 songs.

Our space machines are the remote physical tendrils of our species launched across gulfs of nothing to land on other worlds or to travel, gathering data until the signal fades, or until there's no one left to listen. These ultimate extensions of human senses thread our awareness into the absolute freezing dark 10.518 billion miles from where you're sitting. As I write, that's how far Voyager 1, humanity's farthest-reaching finger, has extended. Launched in 1977, it remains connected to its home world by radio and by the silver thread of its passage through time from launchpad to interstellar void. Individual humans may not be super-beings, but the organism of which we are all tiny cellular parts is most certainly that. The life-form that's so big we forget it's there, that turns minerals on its planet into tools to touch the infinite black gap between stars or probe the obliterating pressures at the bottom of oceans. We are already part of a superthing, a monster, a god, a living process that is so all encompassing that it is to an individual life what water is to fish. We are cells in the body of a three-billion-year-old life-form whose roots are in the Precambrian oceans and whose genetic wiring extends through the living structures of everything on the planet, connecting everything that has ever lived in one immense nervous system embedded in time.

The superheroes may have their greatest value in a future where real superhuman beings are searching for role models. When the superhumans of tomorrow step dripping from their tanks, they could do much worse than to look to Superman for guidance. Superhero comics may yet find a purpose all along as the social realist fiction of tomorrow.

Superhero science has taught me this: Entire universes fit comfortably inside our skulls. Not just one or two but endless universes can be packed into that dark, wet, and bony hollow without breaking it open from the inside. The space in our heads will stretch to accommodate them all. The real doorway to the fifth dimension was always right here. *Inside.* That infinite interior space contains all the divine, the alien, and the un-worldly we'll ever need.

To find out what higher dimensions might look like, all we have to do is study the relationship between our 3-D world and the 2-D comics. A 4-D creature could look "down" on us through our walls, our clothes, even our skeletons. Our world would be a Cubist X-ray, and perhaps even our thoughts might be laid bare to their gaze.

As comics readers gazing down from a higher dimension perpendicular to the page surface, we *can* actually peer inside characters' thoughts with balloons or captions that provide running commentary. We can also control time in a comics universe. We can stop on page 12 and look back to page 5 to check a story point we missed. The characters themselves continue to act out their own dramas in the same linear sequence, oblivious to our shifting perspective. They can go back in time only with the help of supermachines, like the Flash's cosmic treadmill, but we can look at 1938 Superman next to 1999 Superman without colliding the two stories anywhere but in our heads.

Stan Lee and Jack Kirby could send drawn versions of themselves into the created world of *Fantastic Four*, and those little drawings of Stan and Jack were like angels, UFOs, avatars from a higher universe, entering a world they'd made to interact with its inhabitants. They created, as I came to call them, "fiction suits," like space suits for sending yourself into stories. The comics page depicted the flow of a different kind of digital time, expressed in discrete images, each of which captured a single visual moment and usually a snippet of audio time in the form of a balloon-dialogue exchange. The comics page, like the movie screen, took us through a story in a straight, linear progression from past read to present reading and future completion, but the comics page was a more personal and intimate interface than the cinema screen. It lacked the intimidating luster of the movies, and the images could be slowed down, rewound, fast-forwarded, and studied in detail. They could even be copied, traced, or improved upon, making this an ideal DIY medium for the imaginative and reasonably gifted. The pace of a film or television show was dictated by its director. The comics allowed its reader to direct his or her own experience of the story.

And now there were *two* healthy universes living and growing inside our own. The DC universe was a series of islands separated for years, suddenly discovering one another and setting up trade routes. And there was Marvel's beautifully orchestrated growth and development. Two living virtual worlds had been grown and nurtured inside conventional space-time. These were not like closed *continua* with beginnings, middles, and ends; the fictional "universe" ran on certain repeating rules but could essentially change and develop beyond the intention of its creators. It was an evolving, learning, cybernetic system that could reproduce itself into the future using new generations of creators who would be attracted like worker bees to serve and renew the universe.

Just as generations of aboriginal artists have taken it upon themselves to repaint the totems, so too does the enchanted environment of the comic-book dreamtime replicate itself through time. A superhero universe will change in order to remain viable and stay alive. As long as the signs stay constant—the trademark *S* shields and spiderweb patterns, and the copyrighted hero names—everything else can bend and adapt to the tune of the times.

These characters were like twelve-bar blues or other chord progressions. Given the basic parameters of Batman, different creators could play very different music. This meant interesting work could be done by writers and artists who knew what they were getting into and were happy to add their own little square to a vast patchwork quilt of stories that would outlast their lives. In return for higher page rates and royalties, of course. The parasitic relationship of universe to creator that saw the rebellions of people like Siegel and Shuster or Jack Kirby had become a little more symbiotic; following changes in the business in the eighties, creative people adding to the DC or Marvel universe would be ripped off with a little more reward on the back end.

In this respect, a thriving fictional universe simulates the behavior of a "real" organism, but only as far as you wish to follow me down this path of conjecture.

Nevertheless, human beings had built working parallel realities. Given market value as corporate trademarks, the inhabitants of these functioning microcosms could be self-sustaining and outlast their creators. New trademarks could be grown in the concept farms of fictional universes under the auspices of the corporate concerns that kept them under control, maintaining, trimming, and looking after their burgeoning gardens of newsprint and ink. Most important, they had acolytes: priests in the form of creative types such as artists who would grow up with a strange desire to draw Superman in motion and writers who would form early bonds that encouraged them to devote their talents to putting words in the mouths of characters they'd grown up with. These creative people would sustain the likes of Spider-Man, dripping their blood and sweat into the ink to give their lives to him. Batman could regularly feed on energy that kept him vital for another ten or fifteen years until the next transfusion of meaning.

Emergence is a simple idea. The universe is the way it is because it grew that way. It emerged piece by piece, like a jigsaw solving itself over billions of years of trial and error. When atoms stuck together, they naturally formed molecules. Molecules naturally grouped into compounds. People naturally formed tribal associations that made them look much bigger to predators from a distance, and as a result of clumping together and swapping experiences, they naturally developed specialization and created a shared culture or collective higher intelligence.

Everybody's heard writers talk about a moment in the process of writing a novel or story when "it was as if the characters took over." I can confirm from my own experience that immersion in stories and characters does reach a point where the fiction appears to take on a life of its own. When a character becomes sufficiently fleshed out and complex, he or she can often cause the author to abandon original well-laid plans in favor of new plotlines based on a better understanding of the character's motivations. When I was halfway through the seven-year process of writing *The Invisibles*, I found several characters actively resisting directions I'd planned for them. It was a disorienting, fascinating experience, and I eventually had to give in and let the story lead me to places I might not have chosen to go. How could a story come to life? It seemed ridiculous, but it occurred to me that perhaps, like a beehive or a sponge colony, I'd put enough information into my model world to trigger emergent complexity.

I wondered if ficto-scientists of the future might finally locate this theoretical point where a story becomes sufficiently complex to begin its own form of calculation, and even to become in some way self-aware. Perhaps that had already happened.

If this was true of *The Invisibles*, then might it not apply more so to the truly epic, long-running superhero universes? Marvel and DC have roots that run seventy years deep. Could they actually have a kind of elementary awareness, a set of programs that define their rules and maintain their basic shapes while allowing for development, complexity, and, potentially, some kind of rudimentary consciousness?

I imagined a sentient paper universe and decided I would try to contact it.

CHAPTER 10

SHAMANS OF MADISON AVENUE

NEIL GAIMAN'S DESCRIPTION of Jack Kirby is the best: "Even when he was given someone else's idea, he would build it into something unbelievable and new, like a man who was asked to repair a vacuum cleaner but instead built it into a functioning jet pack."

Jack was a pioneer, a one-man army, the unstoppable cartographer of new territory and new possibilities. Kirby had experimented with the cosmic before on *Thor* and *Fantastic Four* at Marvel, but this project was far more elaborate and he had no time for the past. His definitive statement proved to be contemporary, futuristic, and timeless all at once. He was at least forty years ahead of everyone else in his business at this moment of creative fruition.

The unfinished epic, which came to be known as the *Fourth World* cycle, began in the unlikely pages of *Jimmy Olsen*, where Kirby recast the formerly buffoonish Olsen as a handsome young adventurer caught up in a breakneck thriller plot involving alien intervention, genetic engineering, and media manipulation.

The launch of Kirby's epic would require nothing less than a new creation myth that began with the end of the age of the old gods. A primal

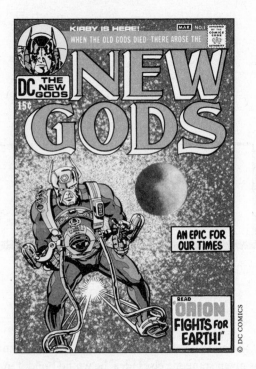

Manichean fracture caused a single world of gods to split into two worlds: sunlit, progressive New Genesis; and, spinning perpetually in its sister world's shadow, Apokolips, the planet of evil and slavery, ruled by the tyrant god Darkseid. Kirby's ambition was clear: He intended to revamp the Bible, the Kirby way.

The Fourth World story was a carefully constructed modern myth that encompassed everything from the gutters of the Lower East Side to transcendent dimensions that only Kirby could articulate in his mind-bending collages. Kirby's new heroes were science fiction gods, machine-age archetypes designed to embody the fears and hopes of a secular world. There was Orion, the god of "techno-cosmic war," and Lightray, the carefree photon-riding prince of Silver Age positivity. And in the black corner: Granny Goodness, the sadistic wire mother; Desaad, the god of torture and interrogation; the bestial Kalibak; and their dark master, Kirby's monolithic personification of the totalitarian will to power, his god of absolute control, Darkseid, the greatest villain in comic-book history.

The cover of the March 1971 *New Gods* no. 1 showed the warrior Orion sailing toward us through space on a contraption that resembled a high-tech walker for seniors. Orion was expressionless. Part god, part astronaut, part soldier. A man with a mission with red, laser-like pupils that burned through us into a higher dimension behind our backs.

The banner read, "Kirby Is Here!" And for the first time on any of the covers we've looked at so far, the creator was the star.

The face of the stern, helmeted warrior was repeated for emphasis in a circle at the top left. Below, a box read, "DC THE NEW GODS," then "WHEN THE OLD GODS DIED—THERE AROSE THE NEW GODS."

"AN EPIC FOR OUR TIMES" only underscored Kirby's ambition and his willingness to back up his grandiose statements with work that left his contemporaries in the dust of another century.

"ORION FIGHTS FOR EARTH!"

Oddly, for a hero, Orion was placed to the left in the image. It was to indicate the canvas, the immensity of the backdrop, that mattered now.

Kirby was refining his comics into emblematic gestures, outstripping his competitors effortlessly and leaving his audience behind him too. Like the fifties teenagers left speechless and motionless when time-traveling Marty McFly plays Jimi Hendrix guitar in *Back to the Future*, they had no reference point for this.

New Gods' principal story line began on the eve of war. A pact of non-aggression had been in place since the devastating god wars, ratified by an exchange of sons between the rulers of New Genesis and Apokolips. Darkseid's bestial brat, Orion, was raised on pacifist, creative New Genesis, while Scott Free, the gentle son of New Genesis, went to Hell. Darkseid had broken the rules in his search for the ultimate weapon, the Anti-Life Equation, an ultimate mind control formula, "THE OUTSIDE CONTROL OF THOUGHT," which could enslave all living things to a dark mathematician's will.

The elements of the equation were hidden within the minds of human beings on an otherwise insignificant planet called Earth. When Darkseid's intervention in human affairs revealed his intent, it triggered absolute war between New Genesis and Apokolips. Freedom versus repression, to the death.

As the monster-child, Orion, grew to manhood on New Genesis, his life dramatized debates of nature versus nurture, good versus evil, youth versus age, tyranny versus freedom. Kirby was dealing with the big dualities and had assembled his own gleaming pantheon to help him articulate the questions of the age.

Kirby told us that humanity's better nature would inevitably prevail. That was the story, and we all knew it deep in our hearts. Kindness and understanding could turn even a demon into a holy warrior, but an angel could never be broken to the Devil's service and would always find ways to soar and to be free. The war would never end, but the outcome was never in any doubt.

He has been criticized since the publication of the Fourth World books for being a ham-fisted writer who should have left the words to a professional like Stan Lee. His dialogue was and still is mocked for its lack of naturalness and conversational flow, as if those dull virtues could ever produce anything as expressive or powerful as Kirby's creativity in full spate. To dismiss his voice is to miss out on the pounding heavy metal that is the true music of Jack Kirby unleashed. Don't think of the streets: Think of Ginsberg when you read Kirby. Listen to the lofty Hebraic cadence, as shown here from the remarkable antiwar story "The Glory Boat":

> AS IF IN **ANSWER** TO ITS **ATTACKER**, THE WOODEN SHIP BLASTS **OPEN!** AND **SOMETHING** INSIDE **RUSHES** OUT INTO THE CALAMITOUS NIGHT—SINGING AND SHINING AND SLEEK AND DEADLY!!! WHAT LIGHTRAY HAS **"IMPRINTED"** ON THE **"LIFE CUBE"** IS NOW FULLY **"GROWN,"** AND IT CARRIES ON ITS **GLISTENING** WARHEAD, THE **LIVING**— THE **DEAD**—AND THE FIERY TRUMPETS OF THE SOURCE!!!

Or listen to the voice of Darkseid himself, talking to his propagandist Glorious Godfrey, Kirby's golden-coiffed, silver-tongued amalgam of Joseph Goebbels and Billy Graham:

> I LIKE YOU, *GLORIOUS GODFREY!* YOU'RE A SHALLOW, PRECIOUS CHILD—THE *REVELATIONIST*—HAPPY WITH THE SWEEPING SOUND OF WORDS!

BUT **I AM THE REVELATION!** THE **TIGER-FORCE** AT
THE CORE OF ALL THINGS! WHEN YOU CRY OUT IN YOUR
DREAMS—IT IS **DARKSEID** THAT YOU SEE!

And understand how perfectly these simple but sonorous declamations
complement their accompanying monumental, eerily crackling drawings
of gods.

When I read Kirby's tales of shining contemporary gods walking the
streets of Manhattan, I can even see beyond the Beats to Ginsberg's solar
sunflower muse, William Blake, whose titanic primal figures Orc and
Urthona are given new dress as Kirby's Mister Miracle and Mantis. The
dark fires of Urizen burn again in the firepits of Darkseid's death planet,
Apokolips. In Blake and Kirby both, we see the play of immense revolutionary forces that will not be chained or fettered, the Romantic revolution of the 1800s and the hip sixties.

And like Blake, who harnessed the new technology of the printing
press to mass-produce his visions, Kirby manipulated the four-color
press and extended his art to the limits of the four-color reproduction
process to deliver the incandescent harvest of a restless imagination
in florid full pages and spreads. This artist of the interior had eschewed realism, creating monumental heroic figures to carry the
energetic charge of his visions. He drew the infinite space inside his
head, and, in his world, everything looked like it had been designed
by Jack Kirby. Kirby machines operated in accordance with no known
laws but sported Aztec zigzags and go-faster stripes. They look the
way engines might dream of themselves. He created vivid and surreal
collages that stressed the limits of the printing process but appeared
to be actual blurred photographs from the depths of his numinous
otherworlds.

And the profusion of ideas! Kirby could throw away in one single panel
a high concept that would keep others busy for years: Crippled Vietnam
War veteran Willie Walker became the vessel for the New God of Death—
a black man in full armor hurtling through walls and space on skis. The
Black Racer was a twist on Kirby's original idea for the Silver Surfer, here
as an angel of death, not life. The Mother Box, a living, emotionally nur-
turing, personal computer was the fusion of soul and machine carried by

126 SUPERGODS

all the inhabitants of New Genesis. Metron the amoral science god with his dimension-traveling Mobius chair. The Source was for Kirby the ultimate ground of being, like the Ain Soph Aur of Judaic mysticism, beyond gods, beyond all divisions and definitions. Genetic manipulation, media control, the roots of Fascism—Kirby was on fire and had something new to say about everything under the sun.

The *Fourth World* cycle was to be a great interlocking mechanism of books combining to form a complete modern myth, while, as an afterthought, re-creating the very idea of the superhero from the ground up and infusing it with divinity. It might have run for five more years.

But then the Fourth World spun off its axis. Carmine Infantino, promoted to DC's vice president, allegedly looked at sales figures and canceled the books, which were doing well enough but not as well as had been hoped based on Kirby's name. The king was hit hard, and the world lost the conclusion to a great work. He went on to create more titles, of course. Hundreds more original, quirky stories burst from that relentless mind, but the great mythographer had been thwarted in the midst of his masterpiece, brought down by dark forces and jealous gods. Kirby's personal vision, his avalanche of novelty and energy, was too new for a culture in retreat, looking back to the fifties, dreaming of sock hops and ponytails, in the happy days before 'Nam and Richard Nixon.

When Kirby returned in 1985, older and more wary, to complete his story, he was given only sixty pages to wrap up a saga that warranted thousands more. Imagine God halfway through Exodus having to hurry it up. The result, *The Hunger Dogs* showed the passage of time and the footprints left by the relentless march of cynicism. Still the King delivered. As a dreadful elegy for the hopes of the baby boomers and the stark truth of their lives—growing older, facing Reagan and Thatcher—*The Hunger Dogs* was bleak, unforgettable, and in many ways the only perfect end to the Fourth World saga.

But by the time it was released, Kirby's hand-to-eye coordination had deteriorated significantly, making some pages appear ugly and roughhewn. A more generous approach might imagine the artist embracing a new primitivism, a shorthand in which scale and perspective played second fiddle to the immediate expression of the ideas. But too many of the drawings were doodles that told the story with the barest minimum of effort. And his audience had flown. Fashion had passed him by. He was "Jack the Hack" now, an old man mocked and derided by the same people who had hailed his genius twenty years earlier and would again ten years later.

The epic had stalled and, like the great Aquarian youth revolution that had inspired so much of it, unraveled into world-weary cynicism. The Forever People had all grown up, gone bald, got jobs, and given up the struggle for a future among the stars. But Kirby had one final trick, one last visionary warning to leave his readers: A new superhero saga that would jump so far into the future that it's still reverberating and is more relevant today than it was when it was published to little acclaim in 1974.

OMAC (One Man Army Corps) was a manic update on the Captain America concept. The wealth of new and provocative ideas in *OMAC* would be staggering if this was any artist other than Jack Kirby.

Lila was a Build-a-Friend "synthetic playmate" in kit form. Before the story ended, she and her kind would be turned into walking bombs as part of a plan to assassinate the world's leaders.

The faceless, masked agents of the Global Peace Agency were representative of all nations and none, Kirby explained in captions. The world of OMAC was monitored and policed by Brother Eye, an all-seeing satellite surveillance system.

OMAC presented a near future where gangsters could rent entire cities for weekend parties; an empty world in which "test parents" in the form of lonely old couples were paired up with rootless young superheroes by the state. Office buildings had Silent Rooms for meditation and Destruct Rooms where frustrated white-collar workers could act out their rage by kicking mechanical "pseudo-people."

"THEY'VE MADE A MOCKERY OF THE SPIRIT...OMAC LIVES...SO THAT MAN MAY LIVE!"

Sporting a prepunk Mohican crest as an echo of the plumed helmet of the war god Ares, and a watching-eye motif on his chest that looked forward to TV's *Big Brother*, OMAC embarked on a series of wild science fiction thrillers set in "THE WORLD THAT'S COMING!" Reminiscent of Philip K. Dick, *The Prisoner*, and *1984*, *OMAC* saw Kirby at his

incandescent peak and should be immediately greenlit as a movie by the first DC Entertainment executive to read these words.

Stan Lee and his team had stripped down and rebuilt the superhero concept in a dozen new ways. With minds like Kirby's on overdrive, they'd been able to innovate at a furious rate, throwing out Day-Glo megaconcepts that it would take generations of writers and artists decades to fully mine. They were still creating stories that would be retold again and again, sharpened, freshened, and rebuilt to suit the fashions, technology, and narrative styles of each new age.

Kirby's cosmos was as rugged and warlike as the Norse myths that inspired him, but Lee's own flirtations with the ineffable tended toward a

New Testament sermonizing crossed with existential self-examination among the stars. Together they had created the contentious Silver Surfer character, which would come to embody their growing divisions.

Kirby saw the Surfer as an inscrutable alien intelligence, but for Lee, the character was a personal mouthpiece. His Surfer was the first emo superhero, shackled to Earth by a celestial curse. Forbidden to roam his beloved "spaceways," he sulked around the world, a gleaming target of mankind's hatred and ignorance. Lee's vision of the sentinel of the spaceways was more Suffer than Surfer, and the character was given to endless gnarled-hand outbursts that questioned his very being or expressed his infinite agony in the form of one more claw-fingered gesture in the direction of a mute and merciless firmament. Every issue saw him hurling himself vainly at one insurmountable barrier after another before fizzling back to Earth, limp and futile, but just in time for one more miserable monologue on a lonely mountaintop far from cruel nonsilver bastards. I suspect the yearning warble of Stan Lee's own tortured teenage soul. Somewhere behind the reassuring huckster image of Smilin' Stan lay this sobbing mask of chrome, but readers found the hand-wringing lyricism uncomfortable. The *Silver Surfer* series lasted eighteen issues before it was put to death with the same ruthless efficiency as Jesus himself.

More to my taste was Lee's eventual successor as Marvel's editor in chief, Roy Thomas.

Thomas was twenty-six when he joined the Marvel team in 1965. An erudite, lusciously verbose ex-teacher of English, he'd been instrumental in creating the original Golden Age fan movement when fans of the lost heroes of the first age of supercomics banded together using a pre-Internet web of snail mail and homemade magazines—fanzines, like Thomas's *Alter Ego*—to share their passion. This same network connected him with men like Julius Schwartz and Mort Weisinger, so when Thomas decided to try his luck in the comic-book industry, he first accepted an offer as an editorial assistant in the *Superman* office. The job with Weisinger lasted all of a week before Thomas cut his losses and went to work with Stan Lee at Marvel. It was, without a doubt, the best thing he could have done.

Assigned to write the monthly *Avengers* title, Thomas seized on Lee's self-conscious literary flourishes—the asides to the reader, the Thees and

Thous, the metered rhythms—and cultivated them into a narrative technique that positively bloomed with deadpan self-importance. With Lee's direct-to-reader flourishes of showmanship as his starting point, Thomas evolved a style that took his readers by the hand and welcomed them in, as if to a ballet or musical recital, in the manner of John Lennon's "Let me take you down," or "Picture yourself in a boat on a river."

There was the same Pied Piper–ish invitation to the dance in Thomas's comics: "COME WITH US NOW, GENTLE READER . . ." It's the whispered offer of the pusher, the dream-monger, offering tickets out of consensus reality. In the case of both Lennon and Thomas, the gentle personal invite helps to make us comfortable before the artist leads us through the looking glass into his world of "plasticine porters with looking glass ties," or in Thomas's case, "THE SOUL-SEARING **HOLOCAUST** OF SUPERNOVA SUN AND CASCADING HEAT."

Thomas took the language of semi-ironic bombast and hyperbole that Marvel was becoming famous for, then superinjected it with classical references, knowing pop-culture in-jokes, and bleedingly emotive exchanges that left readers fighting back tears. Thomas's approach to superheroes was different from that of the men who'd created them. Even Stan Lee dreamed of writing the Great American Novel, and for a long time, he tried to pretend that comics were only his day job. For Thomas and the writers and artists who followed him, there was no such stigma. Like the British and American Beat groups who'd taken rock 'n' roll and Tin Pan Alley to the gates of art, Thomas didn't have to fake his love of low culture; he lived and breathed it. Comics were in his blood, and he came to these characters with a genuine reverence and an absolute belief in their ability to be profound. Lee delivered his proclamations with a wink, but Thomas was for real.

Unlike the Justice League's static pantheon of gods, the lineup of Marvel's rival superhero team the Avengers was in constant, and constantly exciting, upheaval, a trick that has helped to keep the comic a bestseller for the last fifty years.

In 1968, Thomas had introduced a troubled android called the Vision, who quietly became the hero of emotionally armored introverts everywhere as he began a long and turbulent journey toward humanity. Thomas even ended one story with an extended sequence that paced out the lines of Percy Shelley's "Ozymandias" across artist John Buscema's panels.

For many of us, this was our first introduction to Romantic poetry. For me it led to a lifelong pleasure and provided some wonderful floppy-cuffed and swooning role models when I needed them most. Roy "the Boy" Thomas, that teacher turned longhair, was far more effective than any of my own teachers when it came to turning me on to the literature and culture of late-eighteenth-century Europe.

Thomas and Buscema's lyricism was nakedly emotive in a way newly empathic, stoned teens could easily relate to, and the stories were well written enough to justify the attention of older hipsters too. Their other-worldly vistas and increasingly sophisticated artwork were a perfect accompaniment for tripping. Their simple archetypal psychodramas, exotic settings, and endlessly morphing plots within plots were far more engrossing than the DC alternative.

Thomas's stylistic advances reached their peak in his masterpiece, 1970's *The Kree-Skrull War*, a typically ambitious multipart story based around a simple, thrilling idea: What if Planet Earth became a cosmic Midway Islands, a strategic outpost trapped in the crossfire between two immensely powerful warring space empires?

On one side were the vile, shape-shifting Skrulls, who wanted to enslave us, prompting McCarthyesque witch hunts and a disbanding of the Avengers. On the other, the fascistic but handsome Kree, who'd visited our planet in prehistory to evolve a strain of humans into the bizarre race of Inhumans (another Kirby concept).

Shot by both sides, the superheroes of the Marvel universe faced their biggest challenge ever as Thomas set about creating the superhero equivalent of *Sgt. Pepper's Lonely Hearts Club Band*. He cranked up the emotion, tension, and trust-no-one paranoia by increasing the bewildering number of interweaving plots. Stories had no real beginning or end. Thomas was plugged into the unfolding continuity, the timestream of the Marvel experience, and it often seemed as if it was all he could do to stop transcribing the rush of images and sounds when he hit the last page of any given issue. If he could have written every *Avengers* script on one continuous, seamless roll of paper, like Kerouac, or Ann-Margret in 1966's *The Swinger*, it would have summed up the energetic fluency, the finger-popping urgency that drove his never-ending hypersoap.

The story opened with a bedraggled, beaten vision pushing two vast doors open and staggering into Avengers Mansion. His fellow Avengers were seen turning, awkward, off balance as they reacted to the super-android's uncommon arrival. They were drawn in foreground from a per-fectly exaggerated angle that put the reader in the position of a child looking up at adults. Scared adults. The image alone, with its startling new level of naturalism, would have been enough to guarantee our im-mersion, but the writer wanted us to *hear* this one, too. The caption was vintage Thomas, with covert Shakespeare references embedded in the writer's willingness to hit the loudest power chords he possibly could:

"SOUNDS: WE LIVE IN A COSMOS OF CACOPHONY AND CA-DENCE. BLEATING CAR-HORNS—BELCHED OBSCENITIES—STACCATO JACK-HAMMERS—A THOUSAND OTHER NOISES THAT CIVILIZED FLESH IS HEIR TO—AND PERHAPS ONCE IN A DOZEN LIFETIMES—A SOUND WHICH RENDS THE FABRIC OF FATE ITSELF—AND TOLLS THE DEATH-KNELL OF AN ERA—!"

After this buildup, the accompanying sound effect THOOOM seems almost tame and unambitious and hardly matches the noise in our heads, of which the final piano chord of the Beatles' "A Day in the Life" is only a faint echo.

That sound, the very crack of doom itself, reverberated through the story and was heard again and again on its multiple scales. Thomas knew he was doing something new and turned the script into a kind of libretto, a Joycean running commentary that was completely new to comic books.

The amnesiac king of the Inhumans was Black Bolt, the ultimate meta-phor, a leader whose spoken voice was literally a devastating weapon of mass destruction. In fact, Black Bolt's least audible whisper could shatter mountains. It was the whole concept of monarchy itself wrapped in a devastatingly pure Kirby design. Black Bolt wore a beautiful black and dark blue costume that appeared to have been designed for a twenty-fifth-century Mayan god. His crown was reduced to a single stylized flourish in the center of his black hood: a tiny tuning fork that carried the note, the voice. It was Roy Thomas reminding us always to *listen*.

The story begins with the jittery stream-of-consciousness narration of Ant-Man lecturing a character directly:

"YES HENRY PYM—TALK TO YOURSELF—LET BIOLOGICAL CHARTS AND MATHEMATICAL FORMULAS RACE THROUGH YOUR TRAINED MIND LIKE WILDFIRE—FOR THEREIN LIES THE

ONLY TRUE SUPERIORITY OF THE EDUCATED MAN—THAT HE
ANALYZES—DISSECTS—PROBES—RECONSTRUCTS."

From there the flow continued into a third-person perspective;
spoken-word balloons merged with flashback captions or thought bubbles depicting inner processes. At any moment, all of these multiple
voices could be gathered up by the soothing, omniscient narrator, who
held the reader's hands through this kaleidoscopic superhero hall of mirrors. There had never been anything like this before for sheer sensory
overload. Thomas was determined to make you hear his comics, and he
was entirely successful. I can still quote passages from memory.

As the Beatles gave sound a visual dimension, Thomas brought sound
to the comic page.

From that first crack of doom on, everything in *The Kree-Skrull War*
was cranked up to near intolerable levels of brittle hyperawareness.
From ants and antibodies to hovering armadas made of a thousand
space warships, the focus could zoom in an instant between the infini-
tesimally micro and the unimaginably macro—from the plastic vein of
an android to the edge of galactic space, in a furiously choreographed
Alice in Wonderland, mescaline-trip collision of scales and multiple
voices in perfect harmony.

"YOU HAVEN'T HEARD AN ANT SCREAM. WELL I HAVE—AND
IT'S A SOUND TO HAUNT A LIFETIME'S WORTH OF DREAMS!
A SOUND LIKE LOST SOULS IN TORMENT OR THE WAILING OF
A FORSAKEN CHILD."

This was up there in the electric blue arc-light mushroom frequencies
where everything glowed in an overlit high-definition so sharp and so
distinct that it hurt. Every sound had a thousand pinpoint echoes, and
even the tiniest cry of an ant was as loud as the death roar of a god.
Thomas gave us an elevated, giddy, 360-degree perspective roller-coaster
vision, a phosphorescent synesthesia that blended his words with the
drawings of Neal Adams at his peak (with that extra polish and glaze that
only inker Tom Palmer ever gave him) into a reverberant whole. It was
the narrative equivalent of Phil Spector's Wall of Sound, but Thomas
never let the feedback become disorienting. There were always touch-
stones, familiar voices, the returning third-person chorus to remind us
this was all a wonderful story told by expert storytellers.

When Black Bolt finally did open his mouth, we heard no words. Thomas and Adams spoke for him:

"AND NOW—THE WORD—THE SINGLE WHISPERED **SYLLA-BLE** WHICH GROWS INTO A **WHINE—A SHOUT**—AN INCESSANT WORLD-SHAKING **ROAR** THAT MAKES THE MOUNTAINS TREMBLE."

Here was the language of the Eddas and the Old Testament, retooled for the baby boom. The high-flown dream *sprech* of bombast with which the archetypes expressed themselves in dreams and stories, according to Carl Jung in his *Memories, Dreams, Reflections*, was given a new gloss. How about this stirring, precise evocation of the bright, righteous spirit that burns best in adolescent hearts:

"NO **TRUMPETS** HAWK THEM FORTH TO BATTLE—NO SLIGHTEST **SOUND** ECHOES IN THE NEAR-VACUUM OF SPACE—YET, TRUE HEROES **NEED** NO ALARUMS, NO PIPING OF PIPES OR ROLLING OF DRUMS—ONLY A **CAUSE** TO BELIEVE IN—SUCH AS **FREEDOM**—NAY, **LIFE** ITSELF—FOR A WORLD STILL YOUNG ENOUGH TO CHERISH **IDEALS**."

Visually, *The Kree-Skrull War* was miles away from the rough-hewn architecture of Kirby. Adams's cosmos was shiny and reflective, his men were impossibly handsome, and his women looked like sixties models. We'd seen alien invasions before, but never like this, not with hundreds of individual spaceships floating in perfect perspective. We'd seen Marvel superheroes but never so real: never with such expressive emotion or dynamic, foreshortened flying poses. They were 3-D Sensurround comic books.

And just as the Beatles, Kinks, Beach Boys, and others had tooled their nostalgia for the Jazz Age, vaudeville, and the British Music Hall tradition into lysergic concept albums, Thomas revealed that Avengers mascot Rick Jones had the power to manifest his thoughts in the form of Golden Age comics characters. As the final curtain fell on the Kree-Skrull war, Rick unleashed a horde of figures from his mind: Timely Comics superheroes of the "Fabulous Forties" like the Patriot, Blazing Skull, and the Angel, who beat the Skrulls senseless, giving the Avengers the time they needed to regroup and save the day. After all the buildup, it was pure dumb imagination that came through in the end. The unexpected, the impossible, the illogical.

Thomas had struck a gong and the reverberations are still being felt. A recent Marvel Comics event series entitled *Secret Invasion* was a direct sequel to *The Kree-Skrull War* but without any of the dazzling narrative tricks that made the original so remarkable.

Central to the Kree-Skrull epic was Captain Marvel, the rebel Kree soldier. Retooled in a striking blue and red uniform, he was awarded his own new series, which is where I discovered him.

After school, I'd wandered into a bookstore on Buchanan Street that had a slightly disreputable air. They kept their comics separate from the porno, at least, in a fat vertical stack on the lowest bookshelf, like discards. I was a DC fan and never picked up Marvel Comics, but there wasn't much else to check out, and one cover in particular caught my eye: *Captain Marvel* no. 29, with its hero in a dramatic red and black costume soaring up against a hyperreal star field, courtesy of Wayne Boring via Steve Ditko.

"DON'T DARE MISS THE BIG CHANGE IN MAR-VELL, IN THE THRILLER WE CALL—METAMORPHOSIS! HE'S COMING YOUR WAY! **THE MOST COSMIC SUPERHERO** OF ALL!"

Many covers of the seventies showed the questing hero in space, the cosmic seeker. No longer on the streets or even in the air between city skyscrapers, superheroes were head-tripping, off on journeys, finding themselves while the world got its own act together.

The writer-artist on *Captain Marvel* was ex–navy photographer Jim Starlin, who was closer to the experiences and temperament of his young audience than Kirby. Like many of his peers, Starlin was an acidhead, and he made it plain in his stories. His mythology was more pop psych than Kirby's, but it synthesized everything about the Marvel style in a new, easy-to-digest package that absorbed the lessons of *New Gods*, flattened out the spiky edges, and made Kirby look as old-fashioned as *Gunsmoke* on black-and-white TV.

Starlin's Freudian universe, which echoed and reversed Kirby's Fourth World, revolved around the power struggles of Thanos of Titan and his family of demigods, including, of course, the libidinous Eros. Starlin recruited the Captain Marvel character to play the Orion war god role, reaffirming the captain's shamanic roots and his appeal to psychedelic voyagers everywhere. Marvel's Captain Marvel had begun as an uninspired attempt to secure the trademark by rustling up a character from whole cloth. The only Captain Marvel allowed to use that name on the cover of his book was Mar-Vell, a dull warrior of the Kree, until Roy Thomas drafted Marvel's ubiquitous sidekick-for-hire, Rick Jones, into the Billy Batson role. Jones was soon slamming his "nega-band" bracelets together to summon the hero in a blast of energy that recalled the original captain's vocal detonation of occult thunder. In one sly scene, the meaning of which passed my young self by, a bored Rick Jones, adrift in the Negative Zone while Captain Marvel went to work, passed the time by dropping acid. Unsurprisingly, this affected the captain's performance, and problems ensued.

If Kirby's Promethean dialectic was informed by his experiences in World War II, Starlin's came courtesy of the post–Vietnam War counterculture. Thanos was Darkseid not as galactic tyrant but as thwarted lover, a gnarled and massive embodiment of the death wish that had overwhelmed so many young Americans in the sixties. To make sure no one missed the point, Thanos even courted Death itself in the alluring form of a robed, hooded, voluptuously breasted female figure that followed him around like some ghostly Benedictine groupie. Kirby's Satan was a monster of tyranny; Starlin's was a frustrated nihilist, wooing Death like a lovesick puppy. Thanos was a Gothic teenage villain who spoke to a generation that couldn't care less about Hitler or the will to power. I was fourteen when I found *Captain Marvel* no. 29, immediately arrested by its front cover. We were punk chrysalids, and Starlin's existential heroes spoke our language, as they overcame foes that we all recognized from our spotty, sleepless nightmares.

In a story portentously entitled "Metamorphosis," Captain Marvel found himself on a distant planet, about to be judged by the godlike Eon. We know Eon is godlike because he resembles an enormous, hovering potato with jelly hands, a stern human face, and a giant staring eye in an acidhead's best approximation of an angel. His opening statement included these words:

"WE ARE EON—HE WHO WAITS! SINCE THE DAWN OF OLYMPUS WE HAVE AWAITED YOUR COMING, AN ARRIVAL FORETOLD BY KRONOS, THE COSMIC BALANCE!"

Starlin's dialogue lacked Kirby's percussive beat poetry but was more naturalistic and much easier for a fourteen-year-old to take seriously. If Kirby was the King James Bible, Starlin was the New English translation. Starlin smoothed Kirby's rough edges into a solid, plastic finish. His figures were as massively proportioned and as given to sudden, violent action as the King's but were drawn with a supple, clean line that gave them the springy believability of plasticine animation. The frenzied expressionist slashes of Kirby's outlines were refined, mellowed out to a 3-D finish. Closer inspection revealed Starlin's greatest innovations as a combination of Ditko and Kirby into one fresh new look. From Ditko he borrowed his mind-bending psychescapes and grubby urban scenes, his abstract concepts rendered into anthropomorphic form, his sliced-time panel grids and formal page compositions. From Kirby it was the relentless action, the epic vision, the massive figures, and the brawling masculinity.

"WHY ARE YOU TORTURING ME SO?" snarled Captain Marvel through gritted enamel as he balled his fists and glanced back over his shoulder at the impassive Eon.

"BECAUSE **KNOWLEDGE** IS **TORTURE** AND THERE MUST BE **AWARENESS** BEFORE THERE IS **CHANGE**."

Before Captain Marvel or we the readers had any chance to ask for evidence to back this up, the booming inhuman voice of Eon continued.

"THIS WE KNOW BECAUSE WE WERE **CREATED** TO **KNOW!"**

Which placed us in no doubt whatsoever.

And so his warrior spirit was subjected to a series of symbolic visions showing the futility of war: a montage of weeping children, limbless veterans, and *sieg heil*ing Nazis. The universe needed a protector, not a warrior, Captain Marvel was informed, and his agonizing shamanic ordeal among the stars was designed to bring about the birth of a new "cosmically aware" superman, a being intimately connected to everything in the cosmos. An out-and-out psychedelic superhero had emerged from the chrysalis of Captain Marvel.

"TO BE TRULY FREE ONE MUST OVERCOME HIS OWN INNER DEMON!" This was the intro to Captain Marvel's two-page fight with a crumbling stone version of himself that was conveyed in dazzling freeze-frame digital panels intercut with wide borderless shots in which two decisive figures clashed against the white space of the page. A series of devastating strikes reduced the inner demon to builders' chips, and Captain Marvel was, at last, ready to move on. I'd never seen anything like it. This comic felt like it had been custom created with my specific needs in mind as a reader. I was transported, hooked on a new drug.

As ever, it's easy to look back and laugh, but to a fourteen-year-old who wished he'd never seen Uncle Jimmy's porn, or squashed dogs called Shep at the side of the road, knowledge was torture. Which meant that maybe there did have to be awareness before there could be change. To an introspective, imaginative, and repressed teenage boy who had timidly rejected the Bible, this cosmic creed was as good as any. The Justice League seemed childish compared to Starlin's beefy Pop Art psycho sci-fi—an increasingly guilty pleasure as the DC universe became stale and conservative, congealing to a set of repeated gestures played out with exhausted emblems, empty signs.

The age-old lessons of psychedelic drug trips, the booming, inevitable voice of the bloody obvious suddenly given godlike status, were passed on to me via these stories as surely as they were through the music of the Beatles or the Doors.

Mar-Vell was now "cosmically aware," which meant that his features would often cloud over with a beautiful graphic representation of starry, unbounded consciousness. His face would plunge into shadows lit with moving star fields and nebulae, with only his two blue eyes gazing out of infinite space at us.

This was how it felt to live inside my head too. These cosmic battles of consciousness were ones I was fighting in my own adolescent soul. Marvel Comics' original conception of Mar-Vell had been too boring to contain the voltage of Captain Marvel, the original super shaman, but here he was finally living up to the promise of his stolen name and the responsibility of his heritage.

Even better was Starlin's masterpiece *Warlock*. An acid-drenched existential journey that began with some of his best work, *Warlock* was another reinvention of a preexisting character, a throwaway Kirby concept given flesh and meaning by more urgent times. Warlock was an artificial Adam stepping from a cocoon created by genetic engineers, a notion Kirby left undeveloped in a half-cooked *Fantastic Four* story.

Starlin conveyed all the backstory in one of his quirky opening monologues, then set the character free, wrapped now in a billowing, red-and-
yellow high-collared cape—the traditional garb of the mystic superhero,
you may recall. Adam Warlock was a psychedelic champion who did
nothing by halves and who had chosen as his enemy not crime, injustice,
or even other superheroes but the Universal Church of Truth, a monolithic star-conquering faith led by a godlike sadist known as the Magus,
who just happened to be Adam Warlock's own corrupted future self!

In "1000 Clowns!" the ever-suffering Adam Warlock was cast adrift on
a planet of clowns, all toiling on a gigantic garbage heap scattered with
diamonds. The head lunatic was Len Teans, a near-anagram of Stan Lee,
while the clown who painted the same smiling face on everyone he met
was Jan Hatroomi, an almost anagram for John Romita, Marvel's art director and the man who enforced the Marvel house style.

The word *cosmic* came to typify these wild forays into the often drug-
illuminated imagination, and there were more to come. These strange
new superhero stories were created by younger writers and artists,
longhairs and weirdos who were pouring into the comics industry, drawn
to Marvel's iconoclastic universe of possibilities.

Urbane, and openly self-aware, writer Steve Englehart plunged *Doctor
Strange* into a series of voyages to the beginning of the universe, beyond
the veil of death, and the hinterlands of his own psyche. Englehart's rush
of pop philosophy came wrapped in the kind of arresting imagery that
looked best when redrawn on the covers of school textbooks: floating,
laughing skulls, bone horses, hooded lepers clanging handbells in dismal,
postmortem cities. Unlike Starlin, who wrote and drew his own stories,
Englehart worked with a series of talented artistic collaborators to bring
a new twist to the superhero landscape. He took Roy Thomas's fascination with continuity to new levels of jaw-dropping ingenuity, and he had
a voice that brought new life to old characters, along with a worldly nonjudgmental counterculture perspective that spoke to an older audience.

His most accomplished collaborator on *Doctor Strange* was artist Frank
Brunner, whose style ran Neal Adams–style naturalism through a European filter of Alphonse Mucha and Aubrey Beardsley. Brunner combined
the Adams aesthetic with the decorative Art Nouveau–inspired touch that
Brit artist Barry Smith was bringing to *Conan the Barbarian*. (Like so

many of his generation, Brunner was able to profit from the growth of specialist comics and fan culture. He went into the lucrative portfolio market with one set of limited-edition, beautifully drawn illustrations depicting Lewis Carroll's Alice wandering around Wonderland with her tits and muff out, which was indicative of where things were at that time, as childhood toys and storybook characters were suddenly sexualized.) Orthodox fans of the Ditko original, like my uncle Billy, had no time for Englehart and Brunner's research-heavy, decadent take on *Doctor Strange*. Their otherworldy dimensions were easily rooted in books they'd read, or aped Gustave Doré's nineteenth-century illustrations of the underworld, and lacked the genuine menace and eerie schizoid originality of Ditko's visionary landscape.

The same sense of liberation that had fueled the hedonism of the sixties and early seventies was turning kids' comics into revolutionary tracts. Freedom. Magic. Rebellion. Even the superheroes were getting in on the act. The patriot days were behind them, and camp was over. Superheroes were Beat hipsters in search of meaning on the Great Road, wherever it led. Their enemies were blind Gnostic Archons, ossified, personified forces of restriction.

The semiunderground hippie superheroes of Englehart, Starlin, and writer Steve Gerber had one thing in common. They could and would fight to defend what had become the Marvel house philosophy: a kind of college-liberal morality that even with a new cynical edge never lost sight of the essential ideals of heroic self-sacrifice that powered the Marvel universe. "We won't get fooled again!" the Who had sung, playing out the end of the sixties hippie dream with a typically bitter working-class pragmatism. The gleaming silver spaceships were rusting in their hangars. For America, there was more torment, more soul-searching, and the heroes were right there suffering with the nation, on the cross, perishing beneath merciless stars.

In cinema, the auteur era had arrived. UCLA film school graduates were bringing to Hollywood rule-breaking influences from the European cinema of the nouvelle vague. Even leading men changed, as a vogue for mournful or manic, rumpled Everyman antiheroes allowed fine but quirky actors like Donald Sutherland, Elliott Gould, and Dustin Hoffman to strut their stuff upon the stage as unlikely heartthrobs. In the era of the disillusioned antihero, even the "*I told you so . . .*" voice of Woody Allen could be sexy. The sixties had feminized men and made gay or dandy styles and haircuts acceptable. As women considered new social possibilities, men chameleoned wildly in response. Some tried to appear unthreatening, others tried to define a new sexuality based around wit or intelligence. The square-jawed cowboy superhero retreated beneath the mocking stings of gay men and women, and intellectuals. It was as if nature was giving everyone a chance to get laid. Even populist Hollywood was wide open to new talent, new voices with a more authentic cadence. For a few years, maybe even less, anything could happen as we watched a young art form grow up and stretch its wings.

At Marvel, the books were going out unedited in an atmosphere of anarchy. The name on the door of Marvel's editor in chief changed five times in 1976 as a succession of writers accepted the job and then just as swiftly pulled out. It was impossible for one mortal to supervise all of Marvel's output, with the result that none of it was supervised. This collapse of the command structure allowed for some of the most subversive superhero stories ever to slip through the net and influence the next generation of creators. Only three years previously, Spider-Man had defied the Comics Code by responsibly tackling the menace of teenage drug taking. Now Rick Jones was tripping in the Negative Zone.

A new current was flowing. A new polarity. Fashion was about to turn on its heels again. The flame of the interior was burning low, like the weakly sparking fused neurons of the burnouts, the casualties who hadn't been able to handle the Nightside, the Negative World when it came knocking, as it always must. The new drugs were cocaine and heroin, offering escape from the visceral soul-wrenching effects of psychedelic drugs into the hard sheen of gleaming self-regard or numb self-obliteration. The impulse was to turn outward again. Like so many young seekers in the chilly, sweaty, shivering comedown mornings, superhero comics were crying out for some input from the real world before they lost touch with the concrete and the clay altogether.

The psychedelic wave shaded into the self-indulgent, self-absorbed musical bywater known as progressive rock, or "prog." It seems hardly surprising that music and comics were on this parallel course at the same time. These were reverberations from an original gong.

And as if summoned by some collective invocation, a new Dark Age came on like a freight train from the shadows under a long tunnel.

PART 3

THE DARK AGE

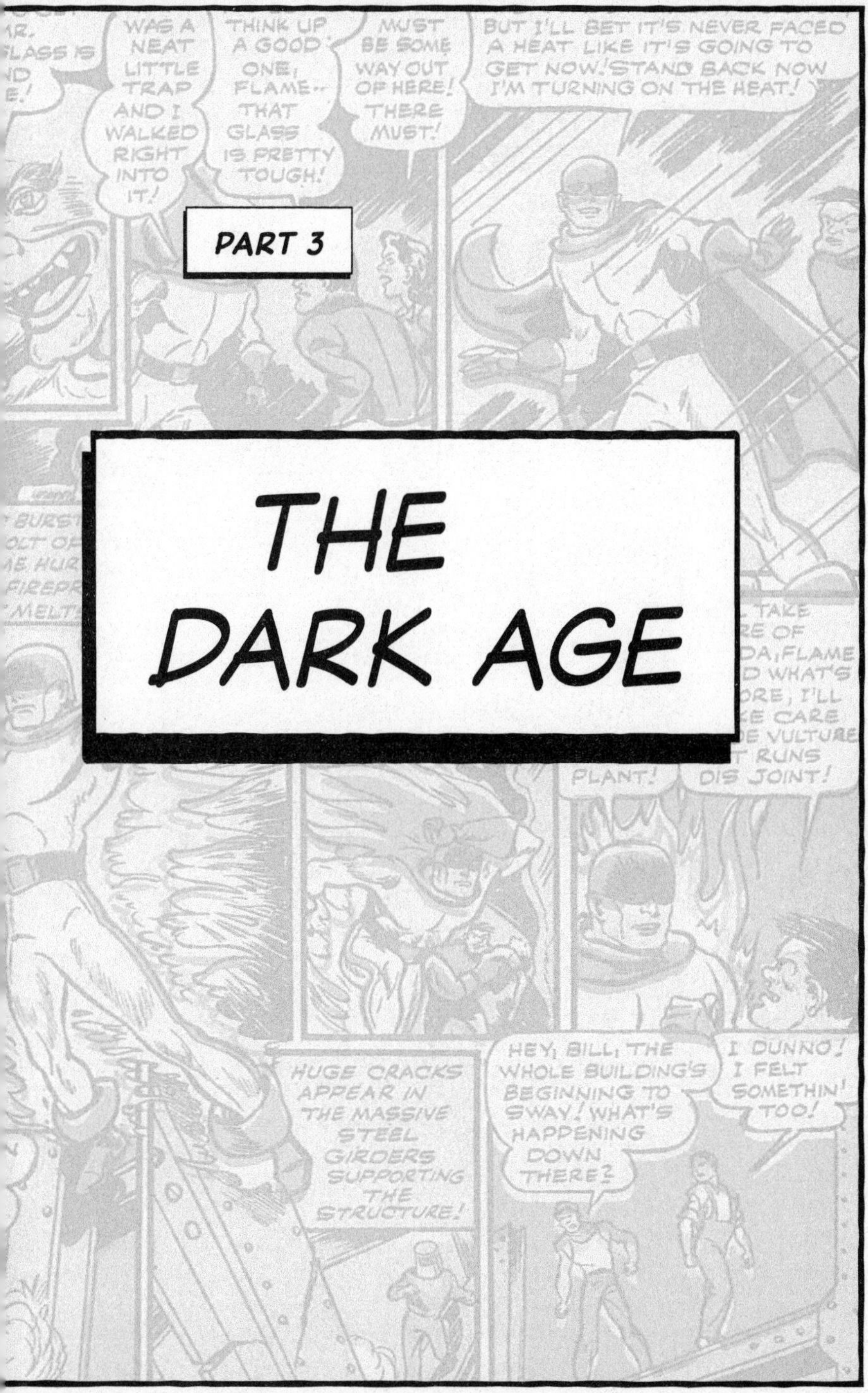

WAS A NEAT LITTLE TRAP AND I WALKED RIGHT INTO IT!
THINK UP A GOOD ONE, FLAME-- THAT GLASS IS PRETTY TOUGH!
MUST BE SOME WAY OUT OF HERE! THERE MUST!
BUT I'LL BET IT'S NEVER FACED A HEAT LIKE IT'S GOING TO GET NOW! STAND BACK NOW I'M TURNING ON THE HEAT!
HUGE CRACKS APPEAR IN THE MASSIVE STEEL GIRDERS SUPPORTING THE STRUCTURE!
HEY, BILL, THE WHOLE BUILDING'S BEGINNING TO SWAY! WHAT'S HAPPENING DOWN THERE?
I DUNNO! I FELT SOMETHIN' TOO!

CHAPTER 11

BRIGHTEST DAY, BLACKEST NIGHT

THE STRANDS OF influence that came together in the Dark Age went back to the dawn of the superhero comics—Batman's dark and violent pulp roots, Superman's social activism, and Wonder Woman's outsider sexuality—but it took a team of ambitious young artists and writers to define a voice and a look for the new direction.

The fathers of the Dark Age were writer Denny O'Neil and artist Neal Adams, who, in 1970, anticipated its themes and concerns in a revolutionary series entitled *Green Lantern/Green Arrow*. O'Neil was of Irish Catholic descent and, as the writer himself later confessed after a successful recovery from alcoholism, reveled in the hard-drinking stereotype that his heritage allowed him to indulge. Intense, opinionated, and unwilling to leave his politics at the door when he started writing superhero stories, O'Neil launched his career as a Missouri newspaper reporter, where he learned his virtues of brevity and clarity of expression. (It was O'Neil who came up with my favorite description of comic-book dialogue and captions: "headlines written by a poet.") A local-boy-does-good piece he penned on Roy Thomas brought O'Neil to the attention of Marvel Comics editorial, which offered him a job.

There he was, uncomfortable among the costumed crusaders but eager to give this new form of self-expression a shot. He came to comics, like so many drifting young intellectuals of the time, as a way of paying the bills. After bailing from Marvel, he became a favorite of Julius Schwartz, who gave the unorthodox writer a chance to shine on some of his biggest titles. Under pressure to modernize in the face of Marvel's unstoppable challenge to DC's sales supremacy, Schwartz had no choice but to break up his old Silver Age stable and retire the men who'd given an audience of mad-eyed kids the kind of well-adjusted, fearless heroes they could look up to. In an emblematic gesture, he replaced DC veteran Gardner Fox after sixty-five issues of inventive work on *Justice League of America* and a clever run on *Batman*. The sixty-year-old Fox pulled out all the stops to impress, but his long tenure as DC's premier writer was suddenly over. John Broome mailed the last of his *Green Lantern* stories from Paris or India and hit the Zen trail. This left the comics to younger, hipper writers who could duplicate the Marvel formula, such as Steve Skeates, Mike Friedrich, and Elliot Maggin, all fresh out of college and eager to enlist the heroes of their childhood as mouthpieces for their politics.

Chief among Schwartz's new breed was O'Neil, who accepted the Justice League assignment on the understanding that he'd be required to "Marvelize" the formula by introducing personality clashes and awkward misunderstandings to the ordered lives of the venerable heroes. It was a mistake, of course: Instead of providing a real alternative to Marvel—a lesson DC would learn a decade later—the company made a fool of itself with a series of weak and ill-at-ease impressions of a narrative style that came naturally to Lee and suited his roster of troubled characters but failed to translate to DC's world of smiling superfriends.

O'Neil's love of the urban, the human, and the ordinary needed a more appropriate outlet than *Justice League* or *Superman* comics. Inspired by the writers of New Journalism, like Tom Wolfe, Norman Mailer, and Jimmy Breslin, O'Neil had a restless desire to wrench the gaze of comics up from the psychic depths and turn it back on the world outside the window. After the cartoon pop of *Batman* and the Monkees and the blissful Summer of Woodstock, the adult world had returned with a vengeance to early seventies America. The fear stalked newly violent

Manhattan streets, and O'Neil wondered if there was a way to combine the gonzo touch with comic-book superheroes.

In artist Neal Adams, he found the perfect collaborator to help him realize his vision of this holy, paradoxical union of opposites: fantasy fiction and journalism.

A whirling tornado in the classical halls of DC Comics, Adams was an outstanding draftsman with a flair for foreshortened hyperdramatic poses and faces contorted by intense emotion. Fingers clawed outward from the panel surface, faces were stressed, agonized, running with tears, or simply chiseled, beautiful, idealized. Trained in advertising illustration and newspaper strip cartooning, Adams combined slick Madison Avenue photo-realism with the power of Jack Kirby in a way that made comic-book characters more convincingly naturalistic than ever before. His innovative layouts broke with convention and enabled his heroes to reach through the panels into a virtual 3-D space, or formed hidden composite images when viewed from a distance. His camera angles, intense character acting, and scene setting borrowed from cinema while marrying those techniques to compositions and poses that were possible only on the comics page.

Adams's work was grown-up and contemporary—a defiantly Romantic and electrifying answer to the traditionalism that was beginning to make DC Comics look stuffy and out of touch. He could even bring new conviction and depth to characters devoid of all charm or originality, such as Green Arrow, so when he tackled a character with real potential like O'Neil's version of Batman, the results were extraordinary. Readers instantly took notice, and the word went out: The Grim Avenger of the Night was back.

When scenes in a script called for Batman to be seen in action around Gotham City during the daytime, Adams simply made it night. He elongated the cape and ears of the "Dark Night Detective," making them more like the devil horns of the Golden Age original. He brought a shadowy, mood-heavy Gothic sensibility back from the 1930s that went well with O'Neil's wild pulp tales of immoral aristocrats, carnival freaks, and ex-Nazis, and he returned the Joker to his homicidal, psychopathic roots. His Batman was believably big but lean and athletic, and he displayed a new mastery of martial arts in extended, choreographed kung fu sequences that were framed and edited like Bruce Lee movies. Together Adams and O'Neil created two classic and abiding Batman antagonists, in the forms of international crime lord Ra's al Ghul and his sexy daughter Talia, who updated the Fu Manchu exotic villain archetype into the fashionably seventies world of ecoterror. Adams's drawings of the impossibly glamorous Talia locked in passionate clinches with a shirtless, hairy-chested Batman brought an electric surge of pure testosterone back to Bruce Wayne that seemed a direct and full-throated riposte to Dr. Wertham's indictment.

The success of the *Batman* TV show had left the mainstream audience with an enduring comedic vision of Batman, but Adams's simple, effective adjustments brought the original Weird Figure of the Night back, establishing a look and a mood that would reconstruct Batman for a generation and finally make it onto the screen thirty years later in Christopher Nolan's *Batman Begins*. That film featured Ra's as its main villain but neglected to feature Talia, alas.

It was Adams who went to war with DC over the ill treatment of the elderly Jerry Siegel and Joe Shuster. It was a time of national audit, another changing of the guard. In 1967 John Broome, Gardner Fox, and several other writers—including the maverick Bob Haney, *Batman* maestro Bill Finger, and *Doom Patrol* creator Arnold Drake—had threatened to form a comics freelancers union, which would allow them some kind of financial stake in their creations for DC and provide long-term security in the form of health coverage. Facing implacable resistance from management and no solidarity from the artists, who earned much more than the writers anyway, that dream miscarried. But in Neal Adams, the revolutionary spirit was reborn. He'd already made intimidating noises about refloating the union idea. The big companies' shoddy treatment of their creative talent *was* deplorable, and the case of Siegel and Shuster made for a perfect rallying point for Adams's reform demands. Thanks to his efforts, both men received at least some extra compensation for their work, and the first steps were taken down a road that would lead to many fundamental changes in DC's relationship with its freelance contributors.

In 1970 Adams depicted himself in self-portraits as an almost archetypal go-getting Mad man, in tie and rolled-up shirt sleeves, and as handsome as any of his heroes. He could have been Ray Palmer or Barry Allen. O'Neil was generally shown chewing on his specs, eyes on the wild blue yonder, hair like Dylan.

Together, as "Denny O'Neal Adams," they forced superheroes into the national discourse and brought the conflicts and complexities of the real world back into the DC universe. The goofy and fantastic stories of the previous decade were seen as glib and uncommitted. It was time for comic-book superheroes to tap into the same self-critical, antiauthoritarian cultural energy source that would drive *The Godfather, Dirty Harry, Death Wish,* and *Midnight Cowboy.*

The O'Neal-Adams collaborations were state-of-the-art for maturing fans who wanted themselves and their passions to be taken seriously. Although a great deal of their "criticism" consisted of little more than sarcastic exposés of the logic flaws in stories, much of it had a learned collegiate twang. Along with acerbic critiques, fans offered the kind of wildly effusive praise and serious engagement with the work that made creative and editorial staff feel elevated and appreciated. These were teenagers who began to insist that comics could and should be for adults, mostly because they didn't want to let go of childhood and had to find a new way to sell its pleasure back to themselves.

These older comic-book hobbyists—often collectors of back issues, compilers of price lists, and publishers of DIY fanzines—favored work that was edgy and defensibly mature, distorting the scale of the adult-oriented superhero's appeal with passionate and clever letters of comment, fan awards, and relentless rubbishing of everything that didn't fit the strict diktat of a culture understandably keen to establish the art credentials of its beloved comics. Anxious to escape the mocking echoes of the *Batman* TV show and the disrepute it had brought upon the "serious" business of collecting and critiquing comics, these adolescent advocates were ready to embrace any development that validated their growing interest in politics, poetry, sex, and expressions of emotional pain. They preferred the artfully stressed and heightened photo-realism of Neal Adams's illustrative technique to the expressionistic gut drawing of Kirby, or the classical power and weight of Curt Swan's increasingly old-fashioned *Superman* work, where the figures had come to seem like waxy statues posed and reposed in a stuffy gallery of recycled, reheated Silver Age attitudes. They called loudly and relentlessly for superhero stories to be "relevant," embrace a new realism, a new vocabulary, and a fresh engagement with the headlines; all of which undermined the success of the comics and drastically limited their mass-market appeal. Nevertheless, it was this retreat from the mainstream that gave the comics some quiet R & D time in which to hone a far greater sophistication and develop a "grounded" approach to superheroes that would make them perfect for Hollywood mass exploitation in the twenty-first century. As Superman himself might say, leading the charge on-screen with 1978's big-budget *Superman*: "IRONIC."

Prickly and unself-confident, the new "fandom" especially liked its stories about powerful men and women in Day-Glo Lycra to come embellished with extended Ernest Hemingway and T. S. Eliot quotes, and so more of these odd adventures began to appear—lumpen children of Roy Thomas's grace notes from Shelley, strange chimeras, that were part cape-and-mask workouts, part campus polemic. At best, there might be a powerful recontextualization of familiar lines played against unfamiliar images. At worst, which was more often, the writers became ventriloquist dummies who relied on the proven excellence of others to elevate their ill-conceived and aimless efforts. Was it a superhero adventure or an English lit student bitching about pollution with Walt Whitman samples running in ironic counterpoint to the action?

Aside from the gift to Hollywood of believable superheroes, perhaps the best that could be said for relevance was the way it eliminated any need to hide a comic book inside a poetry anthology for a sneak read in class; lines from "The Love Song of J. Alfred Prufrock" were just as likely to appear in both. As far as I was concerned, the sincere products of the relevance movement helped me justify the excellence of superhero stories to sneering teachers. Although I was clearly well read and articulate, my ever-encouraging tutors regarded the comics reading habit as a warning sign that I was on a collision course with some catastrophic breakdown of literacy that was almost certain to leave me with a fifteen-word "ZAP! KER-POW!" space monkey vocabulary of neuronal pops and frazzles. So these thoughtful and informed comics were powerful ammunition for me, as they were for all the other earnest teenage fans so captivated by the imaginary universes of Marvel and DC that they'd lingered there past the age of twelve and become trapped like Lost Boys. It was easier to be caught reading comics at school if you could smugly direct an infuriated physics master to the award-winning *Green Lantern/ Green Arrow* no. 86,

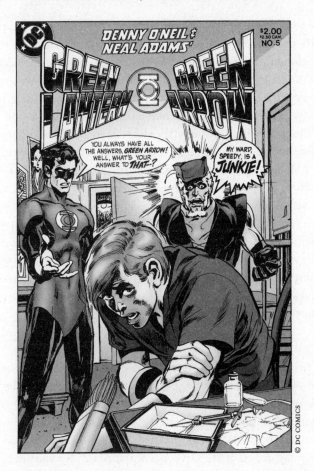

with its letter of thanks from the mayor of New York for helping to dramatize the scourge of drugs.

Thus superhero comics began their slow retreat from the mainstream of popular entertainment to its geek-haunted margins, where their arcane flavors could be distilled and savored by solitary, monkish boys and men—rarely women or teenage girls, who tended to outgrow *Lois Lane* and *Jimmy Olsen*, while their weird brothers were still taking comfort in those pages. (Unsurprisingly, given my profession, I do know a disproportionate number of otherwise reasonable women who grew up reading or still read the better superhero comics as part of a general diet of pop culture adrenaline, but as the scorecard element—the collecting crowd—came in, the demographic skewed heavily toward introverted males in their teens and twenties.) Color TV, too, played its part in the decline of comics sales, but comics still offered the best, most immersive superhero stories available and showcased the work of some genuinely talented artists. By 1970, the field had become flooded with brilliant and restless young innovators like Jim Steranko, Mike Kaluta, Bernie Wrightson, and Barry Smith, and O'Neil opened the door to other "relevant" writers such as Elliot Maggin and Mike Friedrich. Maggin wrote the classic, collegiate "Must There Be a Superman?" in which the Man of Steel's very role was questioned as if he were real, with no clear resolution.

Stories about Indian land rights, pollution, overcrowding, and women's lib proliferated like toxic algae across the willing suspension of disbelief that allowed us to accept the existence of flying, godlike characters in a world not too different from our own. The new anxieties of America and the West at the end of the sixties were stamped directly onto the pages of the comics.

When *Green Lantern/Green Arrow* teamed DC's most prominent green-themed crusaders, the Dark Age crystallized. It was all here: the photo-realistic artwork, the social and political awareness, the superhero divided into agent of the Establishment or rebel anarchist.

Sales had been declining on *Green Lantern* as the square-jawed Kennedy daydreams of the Silver Age degraded into a sequence of daring manned missions to the moon that were each more resolutely ignored by humankind than the last. Julius Schwartz turned O'Neil loose, trusting the young radical to bring a new fire to the book's pages. Pairing Green Lantern with an equally green-themed Justice League colleague seemed like an interesting combination that would draw attention to the new direction, and Green Arrow was a pet character redesign of artist Neal Adams. It's often books like this, on the way out, that become energetic breeding grounds for new ideas and directions. When a title or character is unpopular, it's easier to defend drastic changes.

To make the big concept behind *Green Lantern/Green Arrow* work, unfortunately, O'Neil was required to overlook fifteen years of work on the character of Hal Jordan, the self-assured Green Lantern of Broome and Fox, who began his adventures as a test pilot before giving it all up for life on the road—first as an insurance salesman, then as a traveling rep for the Merlin Toy Company. What may have seemed like erratic character revision made sense as Broome's carefully orchestrated depiction of a man's search for meaning in mundane things after his induction into an extraterrestrial police force. Like the astronauts who'd found God in orbit, Hal had flipped and discovered himself anew. The Hal Jordan of Broome and Fox was a beatific Kerouac Dharma Bum, but in O'Neil's hands, he became a soul-searching, bewildered representative of every dumb-ass cop who ever pounded the beat; the unthinking stooge of geriatric authorities from a galaxy far, far away.

Recruited as a hip foil to Green Lantern's boneheaded knee-jerk conservatism was Green Arrow, stripped of his fortune and his faux Batman trappings and remade as a jive-talking, Douglas Fairbanks–style Lothario with a goatee, a bachelor apartment on the Lower East Side of Star City, and a newfound love of rock 'n' roll. "I USED TO THINK IT ROLLED OUT FROM UNDER A ROCK," quipped the ex–millionaire businessman turned ghetto champion in one wince-inducing scene. The bland, gimmick-driven Green Arrow found a voice at last as the title's fiery liberal conscience, O'Neil's "lusty, hot-tempered anarchist." Oliver Queen—Ollie to his fans—was a man who'd lost his fortune and lived in the ghetto yet still generously donated a dollar to every charity that dropped a flyer in his mailbox.

In retrospect—and as the subject of a sharp and pungent series written by Tom Peyer in 1999—Green Arrow seems the cruel archetype of the born-again midlife man of the sixties. But in 1970 Ollie was the Dude, a long-awaited return to the lost notion of the working-class hero who wasn't afraid to tell the man where to shove it. For thirteen issues that are still regarded as landmarks, he became Virgil to Green Lantern's conflicted Dante, road-tripping through the dark side of the American Dream as a pitch-perfect "buddy" team who argued and fought but learned from each other what each man needed to know. Together these unlikely allies—the Simon and Garfunkel of crime fighting—faced Manson-style death cults, feminist harpies, the menace of overpopulation, the threat of pollution, and two villains drawn to look like President Nixon and Vice President Spiro Agnew.

The ultimate accolades were saved for the two "drug" issues, *Green Lantern/Green Arrow* no. 85 and no. 86, in 1971. On a cover as eye-poppingly melodramatic as any *Reefer Madness* cult movie poster, Green Arrow's young ward Speedy was shown in the act of shooting up. DC had "bravely" decided to let Adams show Speedy's full kit of syringe, spoon, and wrap.

"MY WARD IS A **JUNKIE!**"

Perhaps Speedy's choice of a code name was an early warning sign of substance abuse, but now it was Green Arrow's turn to have his values challenged. Revealed as an absent father figure to his troubled ward, he was forced to confront his own narcissism, man up, and help his boy. The story began with this articulation of the "relevance" credo:

> SOME WILL SAY THE FOLLOWING STORY SHOULD NOT BE TOLD . . . THERE WILL BE THOSE WHO ARGUE THAT SUCH EVENTS HAVE NO PLACE IN AN ENTERTAINMENT MAGA-ZINE—PERHAPS THEY ARE RIGHT! BUT **WE** DON'T THINK SO—BECAUSE WE'VE SEEN THESE NOBLE CREATURES, HUMAN BEINGS, WRECKED . . . MADE LESS THAN ANI-MALS . . . PLUNGED INTO HELLS OF AGONIES! WE'VE **SEEN** IT—WE'RE **ANGRY**—AND **THIS** IS OUR **PROTEST!**

The ultimate villain of the piece turned out to be not the junkies and pushers but their supplier: a modish and witty multimillionaire named Solomon, who swanned around dropping bon mots in the company of willowy fashion models before being beaten senseless by an enraged Green Lantern. Like detective Popeye Doyle in *The French Connection 2,* our heroes were even pumped full of heroin (the unnamed drug in the story appears to be heroin but is often referred to as "snow," suggesting cocaine) and forced to fight crime on the nod for one or two pages.

"BROTHER—WHY DO PEOPLE USE THAT STUFF?!" moaned Green Lantern with his head in his hands.

After scrolling through its menu of hot-button issues, *Green Lantern/Green Arrow* eventually ran out of social problems to confront. It ended with its protagonists changing places and showed the damage an anarchist with a power ring might be capable of, when a Christlike environmental protester named Isaac ("YOU'RE AS BAD AS THE **REST** . . . RELEASING

FOULNESS INTO OUR PRECIOUS ATMOSPHERE!") expired after cru-
cifying himself (!) on the tail of a jet aircraft and Green Lantern's patience
with the Man finally snapped. With a shattering SSCHHAAAAKKKKKKK,
he raked his green energy beam along the full length of the plane, reducing
it to shrapnel.

"WHAT'S THE IDEA?" sputtered an outraged official. "THAT WAS A
NINE MILLION DOLLAR AIRCRAFT!"

To which a sickened, disillusioned Green Lantern, raising antiauthoritarian cheers across the Free World, replied: "SEND ME A **BILL!**"

One of the biggest and most significant achievements of the Green
Lantern/Green Arrow series was its introduction of race issues into the
comics in an unprecedented way. A heavily praised scene from 1970's *Green
Lantern/Green Arrow* no. 76, the provocative opening chapter of the O'Neil
and Adams run, drew the blood of the times with razor precision and was
often cited as an example of a fresh willingness to engage with real-world
issues in serial superhero fiction. After rescuing the tenants of a tenement
block from a fire orchestrated by the unscrupulous landlord, Green Lantern, and by extension the whole Silver Age of superheroes, was called to
account in no uncertain terms by an elderly black man who turned out to
be less than impressed with our hero's showy antics and had this to say:

"I BEEN READIN' ABOUT YOU . . . HOW YOU WORK FOR THE
BLUE SKINS . . . AND HOW ON A PLANET SOMEPLACE YOU
HELPED OUT THE ORANGE SKINS . . . AND YOU DONE CONSID-
ERABLE FOR THE PURPLE SKINS! ONLY THERE'S SKINS YOU
NEVER BOTHERED WITH . . . THE **BLACK** SKINS! I WANT TO
KNOW . . . **HOW COME?!** ANSWER ME **THAT,** GREEN LANTERN!"

(For the first time in DC superhero comics, black people actually
looked black and not like the traditional white men colored brown or
loose-lipped caricatures that were more common. Adams's photographic
accuracy left no doubt as to the ethnicity of his characters. Italians, Ori-
entals, Native Americans—all were given respect, dignity, and convincing bone structures by Adams's talent and sense of inclusion.)

In any real world where the laws of physics and some interstellar immortal judiciary permitted his existence, Green Lantern's response would
be all our responses to the same accusation: "I'VE BEEN SAVING THE
ENTIRE PLANET EARTH AND **EVERY LIVING THING** ON IT, RE-

GARDLESS OF RACE, COLOR, POLITICAL AFFILIATION OR SPE-
CIES, SINCE **GREEN LANTERN** ISSUE NUMBER 1!" Instead he hung
his head in shame as O'Neil subverted believability to hammer home his
powerful indictment of the superhero's role as weapon of the status quo
and the ruling elite. Green Lantern's sudden awareness of people suffering below the poverty line may seem almost farcical, but we can also
choose to view the Lantern as a representation of the typical white-
middle-class young reader and to see in the politically engaged Green
Arrow a "fiction suit" or mouthpiece for O'Neil, using his art to open a
few young eyes to some important facts of life.

Changing values have lent a hollow ring to O'Neil's sermonizing, but
in May 1970, when the only nonwhite face in a DC comic belonged to the
"glowing silhouette" character Negative Man, this felt like a challenging
and provocative call to arms—a timely demand for the paper universes of
DC and Marvel to acknowledge the human diversity of the real world in
which they continued to grow and develop.

The following issue was no less controversial, as O'Neal-Adams introduced a new substitute Green Lantern in the form of "Square" John Stewart,
a black, inner-city architect with a chip on his shoulder, whose first mission
was to protect a racist presidential candidate. This led to some slightly predictable but always amusing fun at the expense of "whitey."

The potential for tokenism was there, but Stewart was a strong character and has survived to the present day as a popular Green Lantern Corps
member. As the acting Green Lantern in the turn-of-the-century *Justice
League* animated shows, he reached a wider audience, on television, than
any of his predecessors.

Stewart was DC's first out-and-proud African American superhero.
Marvel, ahead of the curve on most things, had already introduced its
Black Panther character in 1966, and by 1973 he was starring in his own
title. *Jungle Action*, written by the radical Don McGregor (more about him
later), and drawn by Billy Graham, a talented young black artist, became
infamous for a controversial 1976–79 extended story line, "The Panther
vs. the Clan," which landed McGregor in hot water with the right wing.

The undeniable dignity and majesty of the Panther (T'Challa, the proud
king of Wakanda, a wealthy, culturally rich, and technologically advanced
Marvel universe African nation that was as far from the stereotypical

image of mud huts and scrawny goatherds as could be imagined in the sixties), was only marginally compromised by his failure to represent; T'Challa wore a full black body suit with a hood that covered his entire face. The completely masked black-hero trick was copied and improved upon to gruesome effect and great success decades later in Todd McFarlane's *Spawn* comic and its associated transmedia spin-offs, but without the taboo-smashing impact of the Black Panther and John Stewart.

Aiming a wink in the direction of the Black Panther's modesty, John Stewart made a show of ditching his Green Lantern Corps domino mask in the panel after he received it:

"I WON'T WEAR ANY *MASK!* THIS BLACK MAN LETS IT **ALL** HANG OUT! I GOT **NOTHING** TO HIDE!"

After architect Stewart tore down the barriers, Marvel revved up the relevance bandwagon with its own next-level take on the *Green Lantern/ Green Arrow* formula, teaming Captain America with a flying Harlem social worker who fought injustice as the Falcon. June 1972's *Hero for Hire* introduced blaxploitation hero Luke Cage, aka Power Man, whose dialogue bowdlerized urban argot into Marvel universe–friendly oaths like "SWEET CHRISTMAS!" "MOTHER!" and "JIVE TURKEY!" Cage was a rough-and-tumble enforcer with steel-hard skin and the semipermanent grimace of the framed and wrongly accused. He wore a length of chain around his waist to remind us of history's cruelties but soon outgrew his origins to develop as a rich and enduring character, still central to the ongoing Marvel story decades past *Shaft* and Jim Kelly.

DC earned progress points for John Stewart, but elsewhere in the line, the response to social upheaval was uncomfortable and tasteless. Leave it to Lois Lane to resonate most perfectly with the high-pitched confusion of the times in *Superman's Girl Friend, Lois Lane* no. 106. The cover illustration was a striking triptych with three vertical panels framed against a dramatic jet-black background. In the first, Superman was shown sealing Lois Lane inside some kind of sarcophagus perfectly molded to her size and shape. Both Lois and the Man of Steel appeared perfectly calm. Her face, in fact, was doll-like, expressionless. She'd dressed for 1970 in an orange minidress, orange Alice band, medallion, fishnets, and ballet pumps. Superman was talking:

"ARE YOU **SURE** YOU WANT TO GO THROUGH WITH THIS, LOIS?"

"YES, **SUPERMAN!**" replied the blank-faced Lois emphatically. "CLOSE THE **BODY MOLD** AND SWITCH ON THE POWER!"

The central wordless panel showed Superman operating the lever on what had to be the Body Mold's control box, while turning to look back over his shoulder at the closed door of the sarcophagus, through which we could now see the X-ray outline of Lois Lane, radiant and ghostly inside.

The third panel reversed the composition of the first, with Lois stepping from the sarcophagus while Superman fiddled with his controls and tried not to think about how he'd ended up here, endorsing *this* declaration of intent:

"IT'S **IMPORTANT** THAT I LIVE THE NEXT **24 HOURS** AS A **BLACK WOMAN!**"

And, indeed, Lois Lane, emerging from her techno-cocoon, was now a *black woman*. Her Alice band now contained a neat, clipped Afro, and her skin was a rich coffee-and-cream color. To emphasize the point, the eye-catching title banner in big letters below the triptych composition read:

"I AM CURIOUS (BLACK)!"

The title, of course, referred to the art house sensation of the permissive age, *I Am Curious (Yellow)*, a Swedish film made in 1967 and infamous for its extended graphic sex scenes. Using the name of what was considered by many at the time to be a notorious work of pornography disguised as left politics was confrontational enough in the context of a *Superman* comic book, but the paraphrase added a new touch of perversity.

Perhaps now we're grown-up enough to see Lois's attempts to be Everywoman and to bear every burden for at least eight pages as poignant, but I suspect in this case that relevance is a mask for a lack of originality and the kind of shock tactics editors hoped might draw attention to a book, like *Lois Lane*, with falling sales. Liberated Lois had turned her back on an obsession with supermatrimony that was now considered sexist and moved on to sci-fi-lite international adventures as a hard-nosed investigative superjournalist in a style that almost came close to justifying the premise of "I Am Curious (Black)." Unsurprisingly, the new, edgier stories were too adult for Lois Lane's traditional Silver Age audience of tomboys and kid sisters, and without the teen readership that kept "boy books" afloat, the book drifted wildly off course toward cancellation.

The relevance movement was short-lived, but stories like these, which legitimized superhero comics for older readers who'd begun to see not less but more depth and meaning in the pleasures of childhood, inspired a generation of teenage readers-cum–comics creators to restore and refine the methods of the realist school into purer and more potent forms in the eighties. The realist approach to superheroes appealed to teenaged male fans, but the general audience tended to look to comic books as a way of escaping from the mundane into worlds of the imagination possible only on paper. Pandering to the specialized tastes of older fans in lieu of the children, who began slowly but surely to drift away from these often stark and hectoring stories, was ultimately counterproductive for DC sales. Poor response to the award-winning experimental titles registered a general discontent that would soon be felt across the line, but the fan audience, small, articulate, vocal, prevailed for the moment, and comics began to be tailored to their requirements.

Marvel Comics led the way with its intensified development of an out-and-out virtual-reality fantasy world that came complete with maps, concordances, and charts of respective heights, weights, and power levels. It sold itself to collectors, geeks, and boy savants who prided themselves in knowing the secret identities of every single hero and villain, along with hair color, religious affiliation, and social security number. For all its free-form atmosphere of chaotic creativity, the Marvel universe could be trusted upon to make sense, and it even had a participatory dimension in the form of the letters pages, where mistakes could be pointed out and corrected, with praise or blame apportioned and appropriate steps taken. With its limited interactivity (fan opinion could guide story direction), the Marvel universe—and to its own lesser extent, DC's—prefigured the immersive worlds of computer gaming, such as Second Life and World of Warcraft.

Britain, meanwhile, was in a spiraling social free fall that would bottom out in three-day workweeks, with uncollected refuse piling in bin bag mountains and a nationwide electricity shutdown starting at six in the evening every day.

My own life, which had seemed generally golden, carefree, and ignorant, developed an acrid verdigris of cruelty and confusion. Dad's marital betrayals were more than Mum could handle. Like the cracked vases that she chucked in the bin for any sign of imperfection, Dad was irreparably fractured. He'd always dug the broken pieces out of the trash and painstakingly Scotch-taped them back together, but in his case the damage was irreversible.

In the winter months before the family tore apart, an injury I suffered in a sledding accident drew my doctor's attention to what turned out to be a seriously infected appendix. If not for the fall, the pain of the swollen abscess would have gone unnoticed until it burst. Within moments of diagnosis, I was in the back of an ambulance on the way to Southern General Hospital. Two hours later, I was shuddering out on cold lungfuls of sickly anesthetic oblivion. While I slept, they edited my appendix and preserved it in a jar, on account of the organ's misshapen, monstrous abnormality. I came to in a recovery ward in the threadbare hours of Monday morning, with raging thirst, a flat, green nightlight brooding over me like an alien eye, and a savage four-inch scar. Next day, Aunt Ina brought a stack of DC comics to my bedside, and I clung to them like a lifeline during the monotony of recovery and its endless bowls of hospital cornflakes. As if in solidarity, the cover of *Action Comics* no. 403 showed a single file of men, women, and children of all races wending all the way to the horizon as the inhabitants of planet Earth lined up to gratefully offer their blood to a dying Superman, who lay awaiting supertransfusion on a hospital gurney.

There followed weird, decelerated days of recuperation at home as spring broke through in that last, strange year at Mosspark Primary School, where the girls I'd known all my life became somehow hauntingly, achingly beautiful. There was still a big stigma around divorce, so I had to keep my parents' breakup secret from all but my closest friend. I don't even remember what our excuse was for Dad no longer living with us after we moved to a little flat above the Finefare supermarket on Glasgow's busy Great Western Road, but my sister and I kept it up for years.

The Dark Age outspread its shadowy wings. In my formative years, I'd bought wide-eyed into *Star Trek* and the promise of an Aquarian revolution of space travel, head trips, free love, and superscience. These visions had been sanctioned by the media, with color supplement pictures of London in 2001 as a city of jet-packed men in bowler hats, and artists' impressions of domed colonies flying the flags of the United Nations on Mars in 1985. I'd watched men leave footprints on the moon and saw no reason why humankind couldn't proceed to the immediate construction of time-traveling hyper-arks, but now everything was running in reverse. With no excuse or apology, I was being offered in place of Starfleet a bleak tomorrow of fuel shortages, urban decay, and economic and social unrest. If anything drove the anger of young punks like me with our disaffected "no future" rhetoric, it was partly this sense of absolute betrayal.

The superheroes were feeling it too. The antidrugs issues of *Green Lantern/Green Arrow* and *Spider-Man* had brought about the first relaxation of the Comics Code since its inception in 1954. Code-approved stories could now depict drug use, as long as it was shown in a negative light. Those perennial rascals the undead were also back in favor, and presumably a general permissiveness was responsible for their rehabilitation too.

Just as it had with EC after the first hero boom, the early Dark Age zeitgeist was for nonsuperhero fare that tended toward the shadowy, violent, and sexual. Horror comics became popular again, with Warren Publishing's successful *Creepy, Eerie*, and *Vampirella* titles leading a boom in black-and-white non-Code magazine publishing. The trend was for "weird" heroes, and characters such as Swamp Thing and his Marvel rival Man-Thing soared in popularity. *Morbius the Living Vampire, Werewolf by Night, Phantom Stranger, Tomb of Dracula, Ghost Rider, Weird Adventure Comics*—these were only some of the DC and Marvel universe titles as vampiric gloom descended.

The new superheroines clumsily explored the seismic shifts of women's liberation. The Black Orchid had no secret identity, no core personality, but assumed a series of masks and wigs, trying on and rejecting a parade of possibilities, role models, identities. Who was this new woman? Was she the glamorous enlightened Buddhist Moondragon, whose shaved head looked to the fetish catwalks and rave chanteuses of the nineties? Was she green-haired Polaris of the X-Men, ferocious Tigra, or rabid feminist Valkyrie in her tin bra?

Rose and the Thorn, was the perfect embodiment of the shape-shifting heroine. She was a schizophrenic vigilante heroine who snapped from timid blond Rose to feral sex goddess Thorn whenever the shadowy criminal organization called the 100 flexed its menacing tendrils. As drawn by Dick Giordano, she had a pouting, curvy sensuality that saw her slipping effortlessly into languid cheesecake poses every time she shrugged into her brief green hot pants, bra, and spike-heeled thigh boots—an outfit that turned out to be so remarkably effective in the crime-fighting arena, it's a surprise that policewomen didn't pick up on it. She seemed unable to prevent her naked back from arching provocatively whenever she had a shoe or a glove to put on, turning the hoary old comic-book cliché of the changing-to-costume scene from a private moment to a raunchy peep show, a slo-mo striptease of the Self. Peeling off her identity as shy, gentle Rose Forrest and replacing it with the flame-colored wig of the Thorn, her deadly and ruthless alter ego, she brought soft-core superheroics into the Vaseline-lensed age of *Emmanuelle* and Bob Guccione. Meanwhile, the modest Girl Scouts of the Legion of Super-Heroes were being made over by the artwork and costume design skills of artist Dave Cockrum into Studio 54 disco bunnies with bell-bottoms and bunches, belly cutaways, plunging necklines, and high-heeled, thigh-high Paco Rabanne space platforms. It was an equal-opportunity era and the Legion's substantial gay following was catered to with new costumes for characters like Element Lad, Cosmic Boy, and Colossal Boy that emphasized lurid cutaway panels and acres of rock-hard exposed muscle.

At school I vented my own teenaged libido in ferociously inarticulate rebellion. Every day was a tight-lipped war with authority, a crusade against learning that left furniture in splinters and resulted in the savagely orchestrated nervous breakdown of one gentle old physics master. I'd won a scholarship at one of Scotland's most prestigious boys' schools, but as the hormones began to kick in, a dawning horror confirmed that I'd exiled myself from sexual normality.

I didn't know any girls my own age. I lived a life far from the friends I'd grown up with at primary school, and my new friends at Allan Glen's School for Boys were in the same boat as I. We all converged on the school each day from the four corners of the city, so the chances of meeting up in the evening anywhere locally were few and far between, involving epic bus trips. As if to rub it all in, my mum broke off her affair with a glamorous Swiss airline pilot and I lost my opportunity to move to Zurich as the son of a millionaire. Had I become this alternative-life "ski-boy," surrounded by girls in bobble-hats and goggles, I'd probably never have written comics, or this book. But no dice—with dreams of escape on the wane, learning to make a friend of isolation and introspection was the only answer, and a rich and vivid inner life my only salvation.

With nothing normal to do in the evenings after school, I cooled my fevered imagination in the pages of fantasy novels and superhero comics, and compulsively created my own stories—my own evolving inner worlds—on pieces of folded cardboard and paper my dad supplied. Identifying more and more with the odd, the deviant, the different, I felt like a supervillain but tried to forge a moral code and some sense of an adult male self—with only comic-book heroes, barbarian warriors, and my dad's offscreen brand of committed proactive socialism to guide me.

My first serious attempt at creating an original superhero who could encapsulate this miasma of teenage angst was Monad, created when I was fourteen. He was a UK hero, who derived his powers from his "emotions." In his secret identity, he was a marine biologist who lived a lonely life in a cottage on a beach in the west of Scotland until a gorgeous hippie girl turned up on his doorstep, pursued there by a demented supervillain rapist. Our hero Iain Kincaid (named for my two best friends at primary school), aka Monad, wasted no time in thrashing the priapic bastard and sending him on his way.

With the rape plot and the shameless knight in armor fantasies of a teenage boy done and dusted, the story shifted wildly in tone and location to Northern Ireland, before swelling with my own brand of strained, uninformed "relevance"—in what I imagined was the O'Neil style. Northern Ireland was in the headlines every day, and my message was as heartfelt as it was ignorant: Not even a superhero could make sense of those awful Troubles. It was the first comic I almost completed after drawing twenty-five minutely detailed pages, some of which had up to twenty-six panels. (Most comics, you'll recall, have somewhere between five to nine panels per page.)

On weekends, I visited my dad, who, left to his own devices, had a habit of boiling all food; he preferred to boil whole chickens rather than roast them in the oven or fry them in a pan. He would boil steaks and lamb chops and liver, reducing even the most succulent cuts of meat to gray, zombie flesh. Hermetically sealed into my own little world for protection, I had no way of understanding how badly he was taking his divorce from my mum. He was drinking more, but I don't think I even connected any of his behavior to what we'd all just gone through.

I'd rejected the music of my peers—Tangerine Dream and Gong on one hand; REO Speedwagon, KISS, and Meat Loaf on the other—and found my own cockeyed route to authenticity via Tony Capstick's *Folkweave* radio program on a Wednesday night. Deep into the solitary hours, I built my own world to the skirl of the bagpipes and the crystalline cascades of Alan Stivell's Celtic harp. I encouraged my friends to draw their own comics and create their own characters and stories. On Saturdays we'd sit together in silence in Dad's bedroom, each painstakingly sketching out a new adventure for the others to read.

I had given up on *Monad* after coming up with a barrel scraper in which a sexy alien warlord disguised herself as Hitler and attacked the world with space Nazis. I knew I'd hit a wall with this half-formed brain splatter of a story, and it never made it as far as the paper. Russ Meyer would have been all over it, though. I was more interested in barbarian heroes now, like Conan, King Kull, and Bran Mak Morn, and barbarian stories gave me an excuse to draw near-naked dancing girls on every other page. Superhero comics couldn't compete.

By the midseventies, Marvel's writers had the monopoly on the kind of sophisticated superheroes I liked best. Marvel creators never talked down to me, and they helped me navigate and map my troubled inner landscape.

Best of all, Marvel had Donald McGregor:

"**BUTTERFLIES** TAKING WING, **OBLITERATING** THE NIGHT SKY. AN **AVALANCHE** OF COLOR, BLURRED, AS MEMBRANED APPENDAGES SLICE THE AIR, LIVING, **PULSING** STAINED GLASS ART EFFECTS. HE FEELS THE FIRST FAINT TRACES OF **FEAR**."

The narration here is characteristically McGregor: overwrought, stretched to the limits of conventional grammar, with a pained, self-analytical edge. This was comics' version of that progressive rock music my school friends liked and I despised—King Crimson, Greenslade, Yes—and yet I loved Don McGregor's writing.

McGregor's work burned with the holy fire of a just and loving wrath. His fan base was as passionate as its poet-shirted idol, and vocal too, but even it failed to save his arty books from cancellation when the ax came down at Marvel. The auteurs were replaced by businessmen establishing a house style where the rough experimental edges would be planed to a plastic finish. That made him even cooler, a martyr to his art, slaughtered on the altar of his stark refusal to compromise one drop of blood, sweat, ink, and tears. In interviews he was intense and clever, a hero to anti-establishment schoolboys everywhere.

THIS THEN IS THE FINAL WOMB. **DEATH! LOOK!** LOOK INTO THE **PIERCING** BLADES WITH A **VULNERABLE** EYE. M'SHULLA STANDS MIRED IN **MARTIAN GORE**...A **WAGNERIAN MUSIC DRAMA** COMPRISED OF VIOLENT LIBRETTOS THAT FLOW WITH **WHIRLPOOLS** OF MARTIAN DECAY. GO AHEAD, MINSTREL, EMBELLISH YOUR SONGS OF **BARBARIC GLORY** WHILE WE SIP THE **SOUR GROG** AND PRETEND OUR SLEEP WON'T HOLD **NIGHTMARES!**

Teetering off the razor edge of absurdity, lines like these (intended to evoke, in McGregor's defense, the delirium of characters in an abandoned virtual reality machine) thrilled me with their lyrical allusiveness and the images they conjured of a visionary writer throwing words at paper the way Pollock threw paint. Though his name has been all but omitted from the consensus history of the development of superhero comics, McGregor's influence on the next generation was immense. I grew up wanting to be the kind of writer who could let it all hang out like Don.

His *Jungle Action* no. 19 featured a brutal fight sequence—as T'Challa faced off against not the Klan but a Klan-like organization—set in a supermarket, during which the Black Panther's skull was split by a spiteful old white woman wielding a tin of cat food. It was an astonishing sequence; after years of seeing planets smashed together, the horribly believable two-inch gash on the Panther's head had a real visceral impact that Kirby's thunderous but all-too-familiar masonry-shattering punches could no longer match.

McGregor had another labor of love, entitled "Killraven: Warrior of the Worlds," the main feature in *Amazing Adventures*. He'd inherited the title from Roy Thomas and Neal Adams, who'd originated this sequel to H. G. Wells's *War of the Worlds*, in which the Martian invaders returned to Earth one hundred years later, applying the lessons they'd learned in Edwardian England to a successful planetary takeover bid that reduced mankind to a cringing, demoralized race of slaves. In Killraven's world, human beings were bred as gladiators for the entertainment of the Martian overlords or as food for their hellish dinner tables. Opposing the Red Menace was a band of ragged freedom fighters led by the red-haired messianic Jonathan Raven, aka Killraven—greatest of the gladiators—now doing the postapocalyptic Spartacus dance to great effect in a pre–*The Road Warrior*, prepunk leather-and-chains style that suggested a swiftly organized glam-rock response to the fall of civilization.

Swiftly, McGregor went to work adapting the series' promising but barely developed premise to suit his own wider concerns. Out went the by-the-numbers alien invasion plotlines; in came shocking violence, ethical ambiguity, intensely drawn characters, narrative formalism, and extended poetic digressions on love, morality, and suffering. McGregor had the perfect collaborator in P. Craig Russell, whose design-conscious and delicate psychedelic nouveau had developed from the Barry Smith school of Romanticism, with flourishes in the direction of Beardsley and Mucha that suited the series' lofty tone and aspirations.

Typical McGregor titles "Only the Computer Shows Me Any Respect!," "The Rebels of January and Beyond!," "The Morning After Mourning Prey," and "And All of Our Generations Have Seen Revolutions" were bold hand-wringing declarations that seemed to clang with conviction and portent. He was prescient too: A story published in 1975 detailed the breakdown of a Native American family whose social bonds were implacably severed by their immersion in personal virtual-reality synthetic worlds. Like the cold bad-dream clinics and dissecting rooms of the Martians, these human-built worlds of disconnected code and artifice were contrasted against the elemental heat, sweat, and fellowship best exemplified by Killraven and his crew. He ran with a surprisingly diverse gang of protopunks—Old Skull, M'Shulla Scott, Hawk, Mint Julep, Volcana Ash, and Carmilla Frost—who were a demographer's dream, including in their number a tough older man, a black gladiator, a Native American, three women, and ginger-haired Killraven. A tribe of like-minded freaks united in their outsider oddity and defiance. Pierced, shaved, tattooed, and idealistic, Killraven's gang were rebel heroes and role models for an embryonic alternative culture.

American Dark Age comics were deadly serious, with little room for the absurd. But there was one particular US writer who was more caustic, less tortured, and less solemn—though no less sincere and far more down-to-earth than any of his contemporaries. His work captured a strain of dark and skeptical Jewish surrealism that appealed especially to his young British fans, many of whom would bring our own strain of this sensibility back to Marvel and DC.

Steve Gerber was most famously the creator of *Howard the Duck*, which brought the influence of the underground comics and head culture directly into the Marvel universe. This tale of an anthropomorphic, highly intelligent cigar-smoking duck trapped in the world of "hairless apes" satirized hero comics, politics, culture, and human relationships from the ultimate-outsider point of view of its caustic mallard star. Howard, a combination of Donald Duck and stand-up comedian Bill Hicks, was drawn by artist Frank Brunner with a noncartoony photo-naturalism, which only served to heighten his poignant freakishness.

Howard the Duck was a big hit with college kids in particular. He even ran for president in 1976, only to be beaten out by Jimmy Carter, himself a living political cartoon. If Howard had set a precedent as America's first entirely fictional president, we would now undoubtedly be living in a world where the White House was occupied by the Simpsons; perhaps it was that looming threat that made the duck too dangerous to live. It's easy to shoot a president or smear a civil rights campaigner, but how do you go about killing a comic-book character? How do you destroy the credibility of a decent, honest, hardworking duck? A bad movie, it turned out, did the trick.

Gerber brought the same unique sensibility to the comic *The Defenders*, which teamed a group of Marvel's loner heroes—including the

Incredible Hulk, Doctor Strange, and Silver Surfer—and shared something of its deadpan surrealism with the humor of comedian Andy Kaufman. Plots included a self-improvement cult in clown masks called the Bozos; a bizarre game of musical minds that wound up transplanting the brain of an evil supervillain into an adorable baby deer; and a non sequitur recurring plotline about a murderous elf who was crushed underneath the wheels of a passing truck before he could make any significant impression on the story.

By that time the United States snapped out of its post-Watergate funk, celebrating the 1976 bicentennial and its aftermath with a determined confidence that was given its proper mythic expression in George Lucas's *Star Wars*. With its unabashed reliance on powerful archetypes, thrilling physical action, and simple high-contrast values and conflicts, *Star Wars* brought comics and the movies closer together. In a fearful world, the spacemen, cartoons, and superheroes of childhood began to seem comforting. *Star Wars* turned the material of the pulp stories and matinee serials into mass-market entertainment. Director George Lucas obliterated the ambiguities of seventies self-interrogating, auteur-driven Hollywood cinema culture with the pitiless efficiency of a Death Star razing worlds, when he turned his cameras outward to the infinite. Escapist epic fantasies populated with relatable archetypes were here to stay, and the comic-book auteurs found their absurdist existential fables losing favor with audiences who preferred robots to philosophy and space dogfights to politics.

As American superhero comics settled into another unchallenging rut, it was as if all those clever and literate stories had never happened. The heyday of grown-up mainstream comics appeared to be over but the lessons of the auteur era were not lost. Four thousand miles away in grimy Great Britain, the unforgiving sod was incubating the next phase in the progress of superhumankind toward the real world.

It was 1978 and I was determined to succeed in the comics business somehow, particularly after humiliation at the hands of my accursed careers guidance counselor, Mr. Shields. Seated in his claustrophobic office to discuss my future plans in that last year at Allan Glen's, I proudly produced my artwork and announced my intention to make a living as a comic-book-artist-slash-writer. The work showed some promise and skill for my age, so I expected him to be impressed and full of praise for my industriousness. Instead, and without the slightest flicker of curiosity, he handed back my lurid *Hellhunter* pages and told me to stop wasting my time. There were talented professional people in America who did this work, and I, a foolish boy from Scotland, could never hope to join their ranks, he assured me. I would, Shields continued evenly, be much better off considering a job in a bank.

Grimly repeating the "Fuck you" mantra in my head didn't seem to help; I was gutted like a cod. What if he was right, and I was deluding myself? My premature attempts to get work at Marvel and DC had resulted in polite "Thank you, but . . ." letters.

After the three-day weeks, the power cuts, the shit music, and the morbidly accumulating years without sex, Shields's dismissal was the last straw. Hate, that great motivator, kicked in. Nihilistic defiance became the order of the day, and my personal contributions to the ongoing psychological war of attrition between pupils and teachers developed a new guillotine edge of cruelty.

I'd applied to the Glasgow School of Art, convinced that my portfolio, based around comic-style illustrations and black-and-white graphics, would easily see me through. I couldn't wait to get among girls and start living to draw and drawing to live. Naturally, painting and figurative work were in that year, and graphics were out.

My art school rejection letter arrived as a cold manila fist that closed around my fragile hopes. When I closed my eyes, I saw the title animation for my TV favorite *The Prisoner*: Patrick McGoohan's scowling Buddha face inflating to fill the screen before two iron gates closed across it, eternally barring his escape. I imagined the walls of my room extending to the infinite horizon. I'd left a good school only to find myself washed up on the shingles of the dole queue. I was sure to die penniless, ugly, and a virgin. The Fear was practically edible. Nothing would happen unless I got out and made it happen.

Then, as if handing me the keys to the jet pack, my dad bought me a typewriter and taped a message to the inside of its case: "Son—the world is waiting to hear from you." Whatever had gone wrong in their lives, however oddly I'd been raised in accordance with their pacifist principles, my mum and dad had always given me the praise, the opportunities, and the tools to express myself, and I didn't want to let them down. And let's not forget the most basic drive of all: I would die or go mad if I didn't get laid. Reasoning that rich and famous writers were surely having sex all the time, I resolved to become one as quickly as I could.

The stars were right: Something was happening all around me as the grim decade accelerated to its conclusion with a scratchy burst of sunspot activity and a reversal of polarity in the solar magnetic field. Where dying hippie embers were, the incendiaries and flares of punk began to sputter into life. As if in a magical pass, everything cool was made uncool, and vice versa. I seized my chance as the door cracked ajar and stayed open just long enough for a "wierdo" (spelling courtesy of Scottish tabloid newspaper the *Sun*, describing me in 1988) like myself to sneak into the party. With one magic word, the angry outsider kids had merged to become the spearhead of a generational shift.

There were still interesting sci-fi and fantasy comics that were "adult" enough to appeal to my teenage sensibilities, but superheroes were in the doldrums. Many of the mavericks had moved on, and an air of listless nostalgia was all that remained. Journeymen turned out competent work to a safe house standard that rarely broke new ground. The superhero concept was running in place, like the Flash on a cosmic treadmill that took him nowhere but back to where he was, as a trail of afterimages, fossilized empty gestures now drained of relevance to anything but their own arcane, synthetic continuities.

The real action was in other fantasy genres: barbarians, horror, science fiction. Those stories could accommodate more grown-up content and showcase time-consuming, elaborate artwork in black-and-white magazines where the new cynicism seemed more at home. The flight of the superhero was stalled in a holding pattern. My homemade hero books and those of my friends seemed more contemporary and more relevant than any American comic.

My interest in comics was scribbled over with a revived, energized passion for clothes, records, and music. I'd wandered in late to the punk party—in 1978, when it was already over and the Sex Pistols were history. I'd kept my distance during the first flush of the new paradigm, when the walls of the sixth-form common room shed their suburban-surreal Roger Dean Yes album covers and grew a fresh new skin of Sex Pistols pictures, Blondie pinups, Buzzcocks collages, Clash radical chic. As a committed outsider, I refused to jump on the bandwagon of this new musical fad, which I'd written off as some kind of Nazi thing after seeing a photograph of Sid Vicious sporting a swastika armband. I hated the boys who'd cut their long hair and binned their crappy prog albums in an attempt to join in. I hated pretty much everybody without discrimination, in one way or another, and punk rockers were just something else to add to the shit list.

But as we all know, it's zealots who make the best converts. One Thursday night, I was sprawled on the settee with *Top of the Pops* on the telly when Poly Styrene and her band X-Ray Spex turned up to play their latest single: an exhilarating sherbet storm of raw punk psychedelia entitled "The Day the World Turned Day-Glo." By the time the last incandescent chorus played out, I was a punk. I had always been a punk. I would always be a punk. Punk brought it all together in one place for me: Michael Moorcock's Jerry Cornelius novels were punk. Peter Barnes's *The Ruling Class*, Dennis Potter, and *The Prisoner* were punk too. *A Clockwork Orange* was punk. Lindsay Anderson's *If . . .* was punk. *Monty Python* was punk. Photographer Bob Carlos Clarke's fetish girls were punk. Comics were punk. Even Richmal Crompton's *William* books were punk. In fact, as it turned out, pretty much everything I liked was punk.

The world started to make sense for the first time since Mosspark Primary. New and glorious constellations aligned in my inner firmament. I felt born again. The do-your-own-thing ethos had returned with a spit and a sneer in all those amateurish records I bought and treasured—even though I had no record player. Singles by bands who could often barely play or sing but still wrote beautiful, furious songs and poured all their young hearts, experiences, and inspirations onto records they paid for with their dole money. If these glorious fuckups could do it, so could a fuckup like me. When Jilted John, the alter ego of actor and comedian Graham Fellows, made an appearance on *Top of the Pops* singing about bus stops, failed romance, and sexual identity crisis, I was enthralled by his shameless amateurism, his reduction of pop music's great themes to playground name calling, his deconstruction of the macho rock voice into the effeminate whimper of a softie from Sheffield.

This music reflected my experience of teenage life as a series of brutal setbacks and disappointments that could in the end be redeemed into art and music with humor, intelligence, and a modicum of talent. This, for me, was the real punk, the genuine anticool, and I felt empowered. The losers, the rejected, and the formerly voiceless were being offered an opportunity to show what they could do to enliven a stagnant culture. History was on our side, and I had nothing to lose. I was eighteen and still hadn't kissed a girl, but perhaps I had potential. I knew I had a lot to say, and punk threw me the lifeline of a creed and a vocabulary—a soundtrack to my mission as a comic artist, a rough validation. Ugly kids, shy kids, weird kids: It was okay to be different. In fact, it was mandatory.

Almost at once, and with no previous or discernible talent for playing any musical instrument, I formed a band. My pals from the DIY comics weekends at Dad's were roped in and assigned temporary "punk" names like Awesome Toys and Simply Dimbleby. We recorded our first compositions using Dad's old acoustic guitar, with brown paper bags and cardboard boxes for percussion. Every time I painfully mastered a new chord, I'd write a new song to go with it. The others were doing the same, and our oeuvre became gradually more complex and ambitious. I never progressed beyond strumming but discovering a facility for making up original songs in any style was more rewarding to me than proficiency on the fretboard. Punk gave the pop cultural seal of approval to my efforts at self-expression. We were being told we could do anything, so we did. I still had no girlfriend, but I was learning how to make my fantasies into reality, and that was a start.

For all the lack of self-esteem that curdled in every other area of my miserable existence, I felt absolutely secure in my talent as a creator of comic books and fantastic stories. I had no doubt that I was good. Now that I had the whole stinking educational establishment telling me I had no chance, I really had a point to make.

I was given an opportunity to start making it at the first Glasgow Comic Convention. It was there, in the shabby modernist Albion Hotel, between the rail tracks and the River Clyde, that my life changed forever, and the road to this book began. I prepared my best *Gideon Stargrave* strips as samples and brought them with me in a fake leather zip folder I liked to carry based on a delusion that it made me look somehow "professional."

Rob King was part owner of the Science Fiction Bookshop in Edinburgh. Run by studenty young science fiction fans—a little too old for punk; a little too young to be sixties hippies—the Science Fiction Bookshop seemed an echo or by-blow of the underground scene. In fact, the opposite was true: The Science Fiction Bookshop was a piece of the future of comics retail. The new hippies were learning from their old enemy: the ever-reliable Man. Rob's decision to venture into publishing by assembling a new science fiction comic magazine was inspired by the sales success of France's *Metal Hurlant* and its American counterpart, *Heavy Metal*, as well as by former *Justice League* writer Mike Friedrich's anthology, *Star Reach*, which offered its own West Coast vision of censorship-free adult science fiction comics. This was the seventies formula in action again, with a particle-smashing collision of underground and mainstream effecting a transfer of novelty from the edges into the wilting center.

Rob King quite simply liked my pages and immediately offered me ten pounds for each one he printed in *Near Myths*. For the first time in my life, I was being taken seriously by a human being who wasn't my mum or dad, or five years younger than I.

I was eighteen, I was to be published, and they were offering me real money to write and draw my oddball, elliptical science fiction stories. If only Mr. Shields hadn't succumbed to cancer, I could have rubbed it in. It seemed too easy. Just like that, the door to the future unlocked and swung open, inviting me in.

The story of *Near Myths* doesn't belong in this book about superheroes, but it propelled me into the world of professional comics, which has sustained me ever since. In addition, it introduced me to Bryan Talbot, the creator of *The Adventures of Luther Arkwright*. I aspired to Bryan's professionalism, his command of his material, and his meticulous drawing style, which combined the etched line of Albrecht Dürer with the underground cartoon hatching of Robert Crumb. His figure drawing could be off sometimes, but his incredible eye for detail and obsessively researched costumes and backgrounds elevated his work far above its faults. He was a gifted writer, too—a better writer than he was an artist, perhaps. But I was a punk, and I didn't need things to be slick as long as they had conviction and personality.

Nearest to my age was Tony O'Donnell, who drew lush fantasy stories with dragons and warriors. As I saw it, Tony wasn't an out-and-out hippie like the others, so he became my anchor to the scene. Straight, uptight, and dressed in my Jerry Cornelius velvet jacket, with my No. 6 penny farthing *Prisoner* badge, I sat disapprovingly through dope-smoky editorial meetings that ran on and on until my head was swimming.

I'd left superheroes behind in favor of offbeat fables inspired by Moorcock, J. C. Ballard, and the New Worlds school of "speculative fiction." These were dreamlike improvised stories, free-associating and building to their crescendos through flash cuts and symbols. I was reading Jung, too, and finding in my own dreams and fantasies new ways to tell stories about things that mattered to me, favoring tales of sexy, brooding outsiders—with guns, unsurprisingly. No story was allowed to end without at least one gorgeous fetish girl wandering through the ruins of London or New York in search of some haunted hero with high cheekbones and a burden of enigmatic guilt.

Having defined the image of my hero, I attempted to become him by rewriting and editing my own life as if it were one of my stories. I began by combing my seventies side-parted mental-patient fringe across my forehead to make a sleek Beatles mop. One velvet jacket, some very tight trousers taken in by my sister, and a pair of Chelsea boots later, I looked like Jerry Cornelius, my nihilistic hero from Moorcock's stories and Robert Fuest's 1974 film of *The Final Programme*, starring Jon Finch as the main character.

Soon I was no longer a fan, queuing for tickets and autographs, but a guest at the big comic conventions. I was able to meet my heroes over dinner, on terms that put us on an equal footing. Somewhere in the tin-plated predawn hours of a Birmingham morning, I found myself stumbling from an all-night film show, in a construction site, waiting for the sun to come, wondering how it had come to this so quickly.

Superman vs. Muhammad Ali was released by *DC,* and turned out to be disappointing, marking the end of my teenage affair with superhero comics for a while. In hindsight, *Superman vs. Muhammad Ali* is a perfectly acceptable piece of daft science fiction well drawn by Neal Adams and his studio. But the shine was off. Comics and superheroes were boring. I was a sci-fi punk. Fuck you.

Ali won, by the way, but they shook hands at the end.

CHAPTER 12

FEARED AND MISUNDERSTOOD

AS THE DARK AGE progressed, the old superheroes coasted, reliving Silver Age glories in ever-diminishing circles. A set of gestures had hardened to become rules of the game, and the best hope seemed to gesture in the direction of operatic science fiction.

Star Wars borrowed from the comics as well as from a hundred other tried-and-tested sources, and expanded the appetite for fantastic and mythic storytelling.

Chris Claremont's *X-Men* was an early beneficiary of the sanction that *Star Wars* gave to science fiction stories. Bolting this aesthetic to Marvel's successful superhero soap formula yielded another winner. The world of *X-Men* was far from plausible, but Claremont cannily grounded his wide-open imagination in the engrossing and convincing emotional lives of his cast.

The mutant X-Men could be adolescents, or gay or black or Irish. They could stand for any minority, represent the feelings of every outsider, and Claremont knew it. He knew that there was a tidal wave of disgruntled teenagers out there ready to embrace antiestablishment victimhood and feelings of persecution and disillusionment.

The ever-inventive Len Wein started the ball rolling when he revamped the ailing *X-Men* title with the introduction of a new group of international heroes. Foreigners as well as mutants, they would be true outsiders in America. The twist revived interest in the book, but the concept really caught fire when it became a showcase for the talents of the flamboyant and theatrical Claremont, a young Marvel up-and-comer who had mastered the sleek and contemporary sci-fi pacing that was in vogue after *Star Wars.* Claremont took advantage of the possibilities that comics offered by embracing the widest possible canvas, sending his heroes across space and time and into the center of the earth. He created a new and even more compelling take on Roy Thomas's endlessly unwinding, self-revealing model of narrative inflation, enlarging the Marvel universe with a wealth of new concepts and characters. And when artist John Byrne replaced the departing Dave Cockrum, the writer was gifted with a partner whose clean, attractive lines and spacious layouts were state of the art in 1979 and made *X-Men* the best-looking superhero comic in the world—and the first in a long time that could also appeal to young women.

Claremont adored his female characters with a love that burned like that of Dante for his Beatrice. Women of all kinds—from idealistic teen Kitty Pryde; to the haughty, glorious Storm; to the witty, wicked psychic dominatrix Emma Frost—were richly drawn and allowed to drive the emotional twists and turns of stories that portrayed them not as background figures like the jealous girlfriends or calm, reserved Silver Age professionals of the past but as friends, warriors, mothers, goddesses, geniuses, and role models.

The same delicate touch transformed the Wolverine character from a one-note "feisty scrapper" to a layered portrayal of a man torn between nobility and savagery. Claremont gave a soul to his modern samurai, and Wolverine became a breakout hit character: Young men wanted to be him, while women wanted to tame him and cure his loneliness.

The Claremont-Byrne *X-Men* effect was of a seething virtual reality built up using accurate photo references and up-to-date travelogue descriptions of the exotic locales that the X-Men would visit in the course of each new headlong adventure. Claremont would often establish a foreign scene with the worldly, sophisticated air of a bore at an airport bar: giving his readers population data, climate statistics, and rundowns of main exports and imports. This kind of detailed scene setting, combined with an ever-open window into the ongoing thoughts of every single character, gave the comic a texture that was sticky like flypaper. It was impossible not to get caught up in the perfectly crafted, maddeningly compelling soap opera twists, turns, and shocking cliff-hangers. No story came without a shock revelation to rival Darth Vader's "No, *I* am your father." In *X-Men*, everyone was someone's father, long-lost brother, evil twin, estranged lover, mother, wife, or descendant from the future. Soon there was nothing random in the lives of these international mutant outcasts, which made the introduction of any new character a source of fretful speculation. Could this mystery masked man be Nightcrawler's missing sister or uncle? Or was it Colossus's evil counterpart from a parallel world? Or perhaps the long-lost son of Professor X?

If O'Neil, McGregor, and Gerber had been Scorsese, Robert Altman, and Francis Ford Coppola, Claremont was Steven Spielberg: the bridge between the fan-favorite auteur and the high-earning superstars of the eighties and nineties. His dedication to his characters was legendary and allowed him to weave a nightmarishly convoluted but internally consistent tapestry, or "canon," as he referred to it, that kept X-Men books at the top of the sales charts for more than twenty years. (Much to my distress, my teenage hero was unhappy when a new editorial regime at Marvel hired me to "reimagine" the X-Men franchise in 2001, and I became personally responsible for inadvertent irreparable damage to the canon. Ah, punk!)

When the time came to create Britain's very own Marvel superhero, Captain Britain, the avowed Anglophile Claremont was first in line for the job. Claremont, the pioneer, had intuited perhaps where the lightning would strike next. Something that felt like a movement was stirring in the fields of Albion and Caledon. Soon we wouldn't need Chris Claremont.

As film producer David Puttnam had proudly announced after the Oscar success of *Chariots of Fire* at the 1981 Academy Awards, the British were coming.

My beloved uncle Billy added another significant piece to my personal jigsaw puzzle with his gift for my nineteenth birthday ("Soon I'll be twenty! Thirty! Dead dead dead!" my diary entry wailed) of Aleister Crowley and Frieda Harris's beautiful tarot deck and its accompanying

The Book of Thoth. I decided that I would become a magician and sent away for *The Lamp of Thoth* magazine, my gateway into the postmodern "chaos magic" scene that was reinvigorating the occult underground. I liked the sound of the chaos method, which dispensed with traditional gods and rituals and encouraged practitioners to create their own personal systems of magic. Skeptical but willing to try anything that might improve my luck, I performed a traditional ritual and on cue witnessed the appearance of a blazing, angelic lion head, which gave me quite a jolt when it started growling out the words "I am neither North nor South." However, it confirmed my suspicions: There were states of mind that my education had scarcely prepared me for—and easily available printed instructions for how to trigger them using "ritual" behavior.

Alongside the free-form stories for *Near Myths*, which I considered my "personal" work, and the commercial jobs writing *Starblazer* science fiction adventures for the demanding ex-army editors of the august Scottish publishing giant D. C. Thomson, a third strand of paying work brought me back to superheroes when my dad scored me a gig with the local newspaper, the *Govan Press*, a paper that often provided him with another outlet for his incendiary social commentary. I was hired to provide the newspaper with its first ever homegrown comic strip, Glasgow's very own superhero.

"Captain Clyde" was a name suggested by the paper's editor, Colin Tough. If we'd lived in Newcastle, he'd have been Captain Tyne, of course. If this had been a New York local newspaper, perhaps he'd be Captain Hudson or Captain East River. The word *Captain* followed by any other word was an easy way to generate a new superhero: Captain Discount, Captain Clean, Cap'n Crunch. My friends and I thought the name was only slightly less pathetic than the kind of music our dads liked, but I'd already decided to redeem it by taking a new and more believable approach to the material, giving the stereotypical title an ironic kick. My editors imagined a "camp" superhero, with a secret headquarters under Glasgow's George Square and a spunky kid sidekick, but I was on a mission to show them how much superhero books had changed since they'd last looked, while testing some of my own ideas about how they might be developed into the future. I was determined to bring the self-important adolescent heat of my favorite comics into the traditional newspaper format.

When I presented the first completed episode in November 1979, my Captain Clyde was created to be a superhero I could relate to. Chris Melville was a twenty-three-year-old unemployed man living in the west end of Glasgow. A hiking holiday in the Peak District, tracing my own lonely steps earlier in the same year, brought him into direct contact with the ancient magic of Britain's pagan countryside. The "Goddess of the Earth Energy" endowed our hill-walking hero with the power to fly, superstrength, damage resistance, and speed, giving birth to a Glasgow Superman—a sensitive, witty young man on the dole who thought small and fought small.

As for me, I took the job and my six-pound-a-week salary dreadfully seriously. *Captain Clyde* began with a sci-fi-flavored, research-heavy story about mysterious monsters tearing up the newly renovated and reopened subway station in Govan. I jumped from there to the introduction of a tweed-jacketed headmasterly villain called Quasar, thence to the secret origin story of Captain Clyde. In time-honored fashion, I had my hero killed and restored to life with a new and better uniform and much-improved artwork.

As the strip progressed and my own fashion sense and social life began to improve, Chris got a sleek haircut and started to wear cooler clothes. He even went to nightclubs. His girlfriend Alison mirrored his transformation and blossomed from mousy student to styled sex kitten in high heels and tight jeans.

In one early episode, Captain Clyde made a visit to the dentist, who couldn't understand why his patient's teeth had become so tough and resistant to the drill. To keep it real, I referenced photographs of my own dentist, Mr. Paul, at work in surgery. The drawings stand as a record of a not-too-distant era of dental torture implements that appear to have been designed by experts for the exclusive use of psychopaths in haunted lunatic asylums or snuff porn films.

Chris liked to talk to himself about current TV shows and records as he flew around real-life city landmarks on his crime-fighting patrol. He shopped at local stores in Glasgow and tossed cars around the familiar streets of Renfrew, Clydebank, and Govan before widening his scope to the city center of Glasgow itself and finally to the surrounding countryside—including an adventure on a North Sea oil rig held hostage by superpowered terrorists. Fortunately for Captain Clyde, his enemies, no matter how powerful, tended to instigate their insane bids for planetary domination in the immediate environs of Chris Melville's rented flat in Hillhead. The madman Quasar, our schoolteacher turned star-powered monster, even dared to declare, "TODAY GLASGOW! TOMORROW LONDON! THEN THE WORLD!" without a trace of irony.

The stories turned darker and quirkier as I burned through material on a strict weekly deadline. Baby-eating demons and murderous skull-faced horrors began to stalk the pages of newspapers aimed at the elderly, the chronically unemployed, and other vulnerable members of society.

In the end, in 1982 the captain himself succumbed to full-scale diabolic possession before assuming a new identity as the self-proclaimed "Black Messiah." Poised to destroy the world, until redeemed by Alison's unswerving devotion, he killed the Devil himself before tumbling from the sky to expire in the arms of his beloved, accompanied by portentous valedictory captions. My rain-soaked, lightning-wracked epic of Fall and Redemption was a far cry from the real-life-local-hero strip that had started in 1979, and it was time to hastily move on, to be replaced on the paper's funny page by a syndicated, bloodless *Tom and Jerry*—a relief, no doubt, to traumatized readers who could once more consult the TV listings without being assaulted by satanic imagery and blasted skeletons. By the time of the overwrought operatic finale, I had reached the limits of Captain Clyde as an idea and was eager to create new and more contemporary heroes.

For all that, *Captain Clyde* ran for three years. I'd written and drawn 150 weekly episodes, and the discipline had improved my artwork and storytelling to a much more professional standard.

Odd or not, I was being paid to do what I loved. I continued to write *Starblazer* stories for D. C. Thomson, earning enough money to visit London on regular clothes-buying expeditions, while stocking up on musical equipment, comics, and sweets. My typical breakfast during these years was an ice-cream Arctic Roll and a family-sized packet of pickled onion flavor crisps. I ate this every single day in my first freelance period—or "unemployment," as it was known back then—and remained as skinny as a pencil. I still wasn't making enough money per year to be officially self-employed and was therefore technically a dole casualty, another of Thatcher's victims, a statistic.

The lack of traction on *Near Myths* and similar ground-level titles like *Graphixus* and *PSSST!* seemed to support the discouraging view that the market for adult comics in the United Kingdom was best described as "nonexistent." I was playing in a band now anyway, and as the Mixers (the name borrowed from *A Clockwork Orange*), we started publishing our own fanzine, *Bombs Away Batman*, which featured my drawings and collages. This mixture of local band interviews, gig reviews, weird cartoons, PC-baiting surrealist humor, and angry rants was lovingly assembled, printed, and distributed by me and the boys in the band. In search of any outlet for our restless, creative urges, we became part of a loose network of musicians influenced by Television Personalities, the Byrds, the Times, Syd Barrett, Swell Maps, and the Modern Lovers.

Our nameless, nebulous micromovement championed the band as lifestyle, as brand, anticipating Facebook and the spread of this variety of self-mythologizing into every corner of the networked life. The music was just a part of the show, along with the clothes, the homemade zines, and the photo sessions: a cargo cult re-creation of an imagined life where we were headlining stadia, not local cafés, with ten million screaming fans instead of no girlfriends and no money. So we made our own magazines, clothes, records, clubs, and private worlds of meaning and magic, hoping that our oddness would at least attract others.

Maybe making music was a better option after all. I had to earn a living and find a place for myself somehow in this ungenerous world. Unsure where to turn, I gave up on comics and concentrated on building up the Mixers, but the failure of the adult boom of the seventies was only the darkness before the brightest creative dawn comic books had seen yet. Be careful how you name things: *Near Myths* turned out to be exactly what it said on the tin. A near miss. But there were other people just like me, all over the country, looking for an outlet for their anger and their creativity and finding comics.

While my back was turned, as so often happened in those miserable teenage years, something wonderful happened.

If Superman had a wet dream, would he flood the world with indestructible supersperm capable of tunneling through women's bellies to reach the eggs packed within?

The answer is "no," if you believe that the Man of Tomorrow's essentially alien sperm wouldn't bother to seek out human eggs; and "yes," if you think that Kryptonian supersperm would naturally be capable of fertilizing anything, including cats, dogs, cattle, horses, and winsome squid—in which case we'd have a lot more to worry about than just undying spermatozoa.

And another thing: Does Superman go to the bathroom? If so, what the hell does his shit look like?

The slightly disturbing answer to that one is that Superman gets all the energy and sustenance he needs from the sun. When he does eat, his body is so efficient, it processes the food completely, leaving no waste.

Does this mean that his arse could eventually seal up after centuries of misuse?

Only time will tell.

The first example of real-world logic applied to the ridiculous comes from a 1971 short story entitled "Man of Steel, Woman of Kleenex," in which science fiction writer Larry Niven applied ruthless common sense to these questions of Superman's sex life. Niven's story influenced the next transformation of the superhero, turning at last to face the mirror and maturity.

And here it was again. The word of power, the lightning flash, the zap of invigorating voltage that never failed to strike.

The magic word was uttered, this time with a distinctly British regional accent, and the latest surge of imaginative current arced through the typewriter keys of a young, working-class writer from Northampton, sixty-seven miles north on the M1 from London.

Alan Moore was self-taught, ambitious, and fiercely, flamboyantly clever, and his greatest trick in an arsenal of great tricks was to appear utterly new, as if there had been no history of comics prior to his emergence. His witty, articulate, self-deprecating public voice—"I'm not saying I'm the Messiah . . ."—skipped hand in hand with a radiant self-assurance that renewed the comics scene. And his startling visual impact—six-foot-four, bright eyed, with a prophet beard that exploded in every direction, and cascading masses of abundant hair—gave fans a potent and charismatic figurehead. Moore became, in his own words, "Fandom's first girlfriend," and the love affair was intense and all-consuming. Not since the days of McGregor and Englehart had any writer been the center of so much attention and anticipation, but the adoration was so fervently uncritical that those antecedents and all others were forgotten in the flashbulb blast. Fans swooned, as if honored that someone so confident and funny had come along to prove they'd been right about the potential of comics all along.

Moore's work brought the superhero closer than ever before to reality with *Marvelman*, serialized in the United Kingdom's *Warrior* magazine starting in 1982. The strip that had ended in 1963 as a picaresque replacement for Captain Marvel's adventures on the British newsstands had been reborn into Thatcher's Britain, shivering under the cold arc lights. Carefree young Mickey Moran was now Mike Moran, a middle-aged, married reporter burdened by the nagging suspicion that once upon a time he'd been something more. Haunted by a mystery word he could no longer recall, Moran found himself covering an antinuclear demonstration that recalled the black-and-white grubbiness of Steel Claw, but updated for the eighties of Greenham Common, Trident, and Windscale.

Kidnapped by terrorists and manhandled through a glass door, Moran caught sight of the word *Atomic* written there in reverse. Mumbling the oddly familiar incantation "Kimota!" (the "keyword of the universe," once shouted out proudly by Mickey Moran), the shabby hack was transformed, in a blast of atom light and thunder, into the glorious superbeing Marvelman. The art of Gary Leach, combining the painstaking photorealist detail and precision ink lines of the British school with images of flying, battling superhumans in the tradition of the US comics, defined a look for "serious" superhero stories that would endure into the twenty-first century. Leach suddenly made American comics artists look as dated as Moore did their writers.

Moore neatly reversed the dynamic of Captain Marvel and his derivative, the original Marvelman. Moore's Mickey Moran had aged in real time so that Mike Moran was now an older man whose long-forgotten word of power made him young and perfect. As Marvelman, he was more graceful, more intelligent, leaner, and more muscular than his alter ego, the pudgy Everyman Mike Moran. Mike couldn't give his wife Liz a child, but after one magical night in the clouds with Marvelman, she was pregnant with a superbaby that regarded her with the disdain of an angel born from the steaming loins of a gorilla. (In *Miracleman* no. 13—the strip and character were both renamed for US publication at the request of Marvel Comics lawyers—readers found themselves with ringside seats as the simple miracle of birth was depicted in slow-mo, close-up, anatomical vérité style by artist Rick Veitch, with life-affirming poetic captions courtesy of Moore.)

Unlike the hero fantasy of the orphaned Bill Batson, Mike Moran longed with wistful, bittersweet nostalgia for the surging vitality and confidence of his youth. Captain Marvel and Marvelman were wish-fulfillment figures for children, but Moore transformed Marvelman into the dream of flying that haunted their older, more responsible selves.

Moran stood for the comics' aging demographic, its shrinking fan market composed of people in their late teens, twenties, and even thirties who'd grown up with these heroes and still found it hard or unreasonable to let go. Marvelman became the wish-fulfillment figure for a midlife crisis; a dream of the perfected self that eventually destroyed Moran the man, leaving in place of that frail, relatable character a supergod named Marvelman and a world that was barely recognizable.

Alienated and undermined by his own higher self, Moran eventually committed a kind of suicide by saying "Kimota!" for the last time and changing places with his magnificent alter ego forever. Marvelman's world of tomorrow would have no room for Everyman.

Marvelman's former junior partner Kid Marvelman, aka Johnny Bates, was depicted as a satanic corporate success story, a predatory superpowered yuppie in a tailored suit and tie who ultimately wiped out London in a savage onslaught that depicted the horrific consequences in the real world of a Marvel Comics–style all-out battle between superhuman beings as something akin to Pieter Brueghel's gruesome sixteenth-century painting *The Triumph of Death*. In a two-page aftermath-of-the-battle tableau, an eyeless woman stumbled through the ruins with her children clinging to her shredded dress, while thousands of Londoners were shown dead or dying, impaled, burned, or crushed in their cars. The villain even took the time to individually strip a family of their skins before pinning each of them like sheets to the washing line outside their terraced home. Moore wanted to show that cruelty too could have a superhuman dimension and to demonstrate the abject horror of what a psychopath with Superman's powers might do to ordinary people given a few hours to indulge his vast perverse imagination. It would be hard to look at a Marvel Comics superhero slugfest again after this. (The elemental climactic battle in a thunderstorm between Marvelman and his evil protégé was homaged extensively in the screen duel between hero Neo and the sinister Agent Smith in *The Matrix Revolutions*, but the filmmakers left out the severed heads and sodomy.)

The villainous corporate CEO with his smart black suit and tie was to become the default big, bad wolf of eighties comics. (Even mad scientist Lex Luthor was reinvented as a ravenous mega-tycoon.) The annihilated wasteland left in the wake of Bates's rampage showed us a world raped and violated by big business, greed, and self-interest. Following the epochal, culture-changing conclusion of the battle against the former Kid Marvelman, Moore's band of superhumans went on to establish a liberal-utopian new order on Earth, allowing the writer to indulge in the wish-fulfilling power fantasies of disenfranchised working-class intellectuals everywhere. Readers in Britain cheered when Marvelman and Marvel-woman gently removed a sobbing, disoriented Margaret Thatcher from office before rehabilitating Charles Manson to work with children. *Marvelman* closed with its beautiful, ageless hero gazing wistfully from his stainless-steel Olympus across a world redeemed into wonder, where the fantasies of the comic books had become the stuff of everyday life in a permanent, orgasmic Silver Age. Moore left his sexualized but still spandex-clad superhero stranded in a never-ending teenage dream world of flight, immortality, and supersex, mourning the ordinary and the everyday in a utopia too perfect to ever want to grow up.

The antics of the Marvel and DC superheroes who mindlessly and repetitively preserved the status quo were exposed as clichéd and dated by this masterly social sci-fi reevaluation of the basic assumptions of the comics. *Marvelman* can be seen to derive from the American superhero concept in much the same way that electronic dance music in the eighties evolved from rock 'n' roll, as unearthly, futuristic, and radical a departure from the template as Visage's "Fade to Grey" from Elvis's "Return to Sender." Moore argued that the arrival of a genuine superhuman being in our midst would quickly and radically alter society forever. The Justice League or Avengers could not be assimilated into any recognizable world as they appeared to be in the Marvel and DC universes. Superhumans would signal the end of the human and deform history itself with the gravity of their presence.

Moore's command of his material brought the disciplines and structures of drama, literature, and music to superhero comics in a way that made the familiar suddenly fresh. His was a challenging and articulate voice in a complacent field. Mike Moran's story began in a world that was recognizably Thatcher's Britain of nuclear power stations, strikes, terrorists, and moral ambiguity. Its hero was a shuffling, scruffy Everyman with bills, headaches, and dreams of flying.

I was drawn back to comics. For me, *Marvelman* was the next stage beyond the kitchen sink naturalism of *Captain Clyde*, and I couldn't wait to explore the new frontiers that were opening ahead. With my dream of adult pop comics becoming a reality, it looked like a good time to get back into the scrum. Perhaps at last, this could be a way of making enough money to quit the dole and get noticed doing something I loved. And I wasn't alone.

And so we arrived in our teens and twenties, in our leather jackets and Chelsea boots, with our crepe-soled brothel creepers and skinhead Ben Shermans, metal tattoos, and infected piercings. We brought to bear on the ongoing American superhero discourse the invigorating influence of alternative lifestyles, punk rock, fringe theater, and tight black jeans. We rolled up in anarchist hordes, in rowdy busloads, drinking the bars dry, munching our hosts' buttocks (artist Glenn Fabry drunkenly assaulted editor Karen Berger's glutes with his molars), and swearing in a dozen or more baffling regional accents. The Americans expected us to be brilliant punks and, eager to please our masters, we sensitive, artistic boys did our best to live up to our hype. Like the Sex Pistols sneering and burning their way through "Johnny B. Goode," we took their favorite songs, rewrote all the lyrics, and played them on buzz saws through squalling distortion pedals.

We arrived under the patronage of radical progressives on the publishing and editorial side at DC, like Jenette Kahn, Dick Giordano, and Karen Berger. We flourished in a culture where risk-taking women with taste were in charge—including Marvel editors such as Bernie Jaye, who worked with Alan Moore on the *Captain Britain* strip, and Sheila Cranna, who edited some of my own early work for hire on *Doctor Who* monthly. Most important for me, we were encouraged to be shocking and different.

Our arrival came at a time when the business practices of the comics industry were changing for the better, and in favor of the creative people for the first time since it all began with *Superman*. We were the first generation who could expect regular, lucrative royalties for our work and to see what had been ephemera validated in enduring hardcover bookstore collections. Karen Berger's Vertigo imprint was introduced and developed as a "mature readers" niche outside the "all-ages" DC universe. The Vertigo deal allowed creators to own a percentage of their own new creations and to profit from their exploitation in ways that Siegel and Shuster or Jack Kirby could never have dreamed of.

We arrived, most of us from the British Isles, from Ireland, Scotland, England, and Wales, dreaming of an escape from the dour drizzle of seventies Britain, the paranoid, war-haunted epic of the Thatcher years. America was jet cars and spacemen and film stars, and America wanted us. America's superheroes welcomed us and lay back while we took our scalpels to their sagging, exhausted bodies. We provided a lifesaving transfusion of nihilistic humor and wild invention, and restored a deadly serious, poetic narrative style that could veer effortlessly between the nightmare excesses of the grammar school prodigy and the genuine brevity and insight of those pop lyricists and Beat poets beloved by so many of the British New Wave. We dragged superhero comics out of the hands of archivists and sweaty fan boys and into the salons of hipsters. In our hands, the arrogant scientific champions of the Silver Age would be brought to account in a world of shifting realpolitik and imperial expansionist aggression.

The relationship of Britons to the figure of the US superhero came with a great deal of antagonism. Many of us were out for revenge and powered by the insurrectionist energy of the seventeen-year-old, sneering and demanding. The critique was often barbed, and, in some cases, clearly intended to be fatal. We had US missiles on our soil, at Greenham Common and Faslane and the Holy Loch, and that made us a red-pin target flashing out the seconds of an unending Cold War cold-sweat stalemate. We had good reason to be suspicious of America's power and influence, but there was the "special relationship" to consider and the fact that we'd grown up with best friends like Superman, Spider-Man, and Wonder Woman guiding our youthful senses of justice and equality. Now here were the proud Americans handing us their dream children, like Romans in Britain delivering their gods into the hands of the Celts for a revamp. The gray skies over Britain split. The superheroes arrived to save the day, and when the cape was dangled, we grabbed hold and were lifted into the golden clouds above the lengthening dole queues. We became known as the British Invasion.

It wasn't just Brits who were testing their wings on the winds of progress: One of the first of the predatory fledglings was a young writer-artist from New Hampshire. Skinny, hunched, and furtive, angular as a jangle of coat hangers in a trench coat, he plunged on past territory cleared by McGregor and Doug Moench (another thoughtful, well-read, and assured writer whose collaboration with artist Paul Gulacy on a title created to cash in on the Bruce Lee craze, *The Hands of Shang-Chi, Master of Kung Fu*, evolved into a delicate, literate, and perfectly composed fusion of cinematic techniques, zooms, interweaving inner monologues, and in-your-face symbolic content that only the comics page could safely contain) to uncover previously unsuspected vistas for exploration. His new adult superhero narrative drew as much from Jim Thompson, Sam Fuller, and Peckinpah as it did from O'Neil or Lee.

His name was Frank Miller.

CHAPTER 13

FEARFUL SYMMETRY

READERS MAY BE familiar with Frank Miller as the man behind *Sin City* and *300*, both of which began as acclaimed graphic novels before making the transition to the cinema screen. By 1985, he had established himself as the Boy Most Likely To in his field with a gripping, hard-boiled crime fiction take on Marvel's *Daredevil*, which he followed with experimental work like the science fiction epic *Ronin* at DC—an attempt to fuse Japanese *manga*, the influence of the French comics artist Jean "Moebius" Giraud, and Jack Kirby. When the wunderkind announced that his next project would be a radical reinterpretation of Batman, fans held their breath and feared for their bladder control, such was the anticipation.

Miller's first marketing masterstroke was to completely undermine the popular image of Batman as a camp pantomime. Much of the initial power of *The Dark Knight Returns* was derived from its bold dance with expectations. With their poker-faced insistence that the ludicrous Batman was worthy of this expensive, lavish, and tastefully packaged artistic accomplishment, Miller and DC intended to provoke a spectacular collision of opposites. This was how comics for grown-ups might look, using the cherished characters of childhood as a hook to draw in readers. Here was genuine American Pop

Art. It was a masterpiece capable of reaching back into the mainstream, past the newsstands and onto the shelves of legitimate bookstores.

The Dark Knight Returns so confidently and aggressively rebranded the Batman story as a violent operatic myth of eighties America—as much a definitive product of its times as *Wall Street* or *American Psycho*—that its influence became all-pervasive for decades, even bleeding into the style and tone of animated cartoons for children. *The Dark Knight Returns* portrayed the rise and fall and rise of a titan with a towering, nuanced portrayal of Bruce Wayne/Batman that was closer in spirit to Charles Foster Kane or Don Corleone than Bob Kane's wooden original. Miller's Wayne embodied the self-made American: ascendant, free, and accountable to no authority, yet haunted by guilt. In Miller's assured hands, the superrich capitalist Übermensch Batman turned his wrath against the corrupt and ossified power structures of a near-future America still run by an ancient Ronald Reagan, still under the protection of a true-blue Republican Superman. From the gutters of savage street crime to the fetid corridors of power, Miller's vengeful juggernaut Batman came complete with a Clint Eastwood sneer as he threatened pimps, kidnappers, neo-Nazis, and policemen alike with various kinds of beatings and/or permanent physical injury. He battled against steroid-enhanced monsters, muggers, armed soldiers, the Joker, and Superman with the same bloody-minded determination. In the fifty years since his creation, Batman had become a friend of law and order, but Miller restored his outlaw status to thrilling effect. A Batman wanted by crooks and cops alike made for a much more interesting protagonist, as director Christopher Nolan understood when he ended his 2008 film *The Dark Knight* with the same tension-fraught scenario.

Miller cut his narrative lean to the bone. Going beyond cinema technique to appropriate the rapid percussive editing of music videos, he crushed the ponderous narrative captions of the seventies down into hard-boiled nuggets:

"SOMETHING **EXPLODES** IN MY MIDSECTION—SUNLIGHT BEHIND MY EYES AS THE PAIN **RISES**—RIBS **INTACT**—NO INTERNAL **BLEEDING**—"

Frank Miller brought the Dark Age style into line with a newly confident right-leaning America. His monumental Batman was no bleeding-heart liberal but a rugged libertarian. Miller's captions were staccato bullet bursts

of hard-boiled grit. Compared to the florid poesy and hand-to-brow torment of McGregor, Miller's writing was direct and unpretentious.

The first issue of *The Dark Knight Returns* was released in the new "prestige" format, with card covers and spine. Even the jacket illustration looked as if it belonged on a paperback novel, owing nothing to the frantic, brightly colored, and trashy graphic overload of a typical super-hero comic in the 1980s.

The cover showed a small Batman silhouette leaping down from the top-left corner across a blue background split by a single lightning bolt (of course). No flashy carnival logo, just a simple modern Deco sans-serif font with the title and the DC bullet in almost transparent white against the central elemental flare. Batman himself was reduced to a hieroglyph, a blank sign, with no detail of his costume visible. The ears and scalloped cape were enough. What was important was the megawattage, the light-ning crack, with its promise of explosive energy and rejuvenation.

To ensure that the story inside was as radically different and as sophis-ticated as the jacket, writer-artist Miller had developed a whole battery of new tricks with layout, pacing, and narration that seemed to utterly dismantle and rebuild the form. Although written and penciled by Miller alone, the series was inked by Klaus Janson and colored by Miller's then wife, Lynn Varley, who replaced the traditional rainbow palette with somber blues, naturalistic grays, washed-out yellows, and shades of brown that perfectly evoked a dirty, crime-ridden city in high summer and inspired the look of every "dark" superhero and fantasy film of the early twenty-first century, from *The Lord of the Rings* to *Harry Potter and the Order of the Phoenix* and *Twilight.*

Each page was built around a repeating sixteen-panel grid structure that allowed Miller to slice and dice time and motion in a way that hadn't been seen since *Master of Kung Fu* or Walt Simonson's *Manhunter* strip. The closest cinematic equivalent was the split-screen technique, but there were only so many simultaneously moving images an audience could handle. A Frank Miller action sequence, on the other hand, could be comprehended not only as an analog full-page design but as a digital sequence—an animated mosaic of sequential tiles.

Tightly paced and timed cuts brought static images closer to animation than ever before. Miller might linger with a head shot of a single character over a dozen or more measured panels, focusing down on the maddeningly subtle gestures and changes of expression that helped build a tension so intolerable it could only be released like pressurized steam into an iconic full-page or double-page poster spread showing Batman and Robin in eye-popping visceral action. Miller paced the close editing of text and image to provide a galloping rhythmic beat, timing panels like the breaths and pauses of a heavy-metal symphony. Ever the innovator, he had developed another new art style for this project, and the line was blocky and aggressive, thrusting forward relentlessly through scene after scene of heart-stopping narrative choreography. From beginning to end, it was a tour de force that was not only conceptually bold but also tough and unpretentious enough to attract attention beyond its first enthusiastic audience of delirious geeks, who felt that Batman had finally received the truly serious treatment he'd always deserved. The book revived DC's fortunes and put the company at the forefront of an astonishing new wave of masterpiece-level material.

After decades of hallucinogenic sci-fi, anodyne detective stories, mocking irony, and formula, the Batman had returned to doing what he did best in a bleak world that was easily recognizable from any nightly news broadcast as our own, on steroids and PCP.

The Dark Knight Returns opened with the sixty-year-old Bruce Wayne's grudging survival following a race car crash, and it was clear from page 1 that here was a hero without a mission, and a hollow sham existence lacking in meaning. Without his Batman identity, which he'd retired after the death of Robin years previously, Wayne had become an aimless drinker, flirting with death while exchanging acidic repartee with his elderly butler. Outside, Gotham City boiled in a rising fever heat. The Joker had been reformed by a trendy psychiatrist who spouted pop-psych jargon and flaunted his successes on TV. The first image was of a burning, still speeding race car, and Miller took that elemental velocity as his gauge and standard.

The book was haunted by an all-pervasive media presence that marked its eighties origins. On dozens of pages, the sixteen-grid became rows of TV screens, each with a different media pundit spouting a different interpretation of the book's unfolding events, from the self-styled Dr. Ruth–like "sex expert" (who was first to die when the return of Batman triggered the murderous comeback of his archenemy, the Joker), to the right-wing and left-wing commentators, pop-psych, weather, and cultural analysts, and vox pops that peppered the action. The device of the multiple screens provided a recurring ironic Greek chorus in *The Dark Knight Returns*, satirizing the attempts of jabbering "experts" to explain or package the archetypal epic forces erupting all around them, which escalated from the first book's urban crime wave to all-out nuclear Götterdämmerung in *The Dark Knight Falls*. That fourth and final volume brought Batman's struggle into the realm of myth and symbol as he faced down Superman for an apocalyptic battle royal on Crime Alley, where Bruce Wayne's parents had been gunned down at the beginning of the Batman story.

The mercury rose as Miller gathered speed: Regular weather reports and carefully repeated establishing shots of the city's gargoyle-haunted rooftops and water towers blurring under a white-hot sky kept up the pressure until the storm broke halfway through, heralding Bruce Wayne's return to action as Batman, wearing the light blue and gray of the New Look and the Adam West years, even down to the yellow chest oval. Miller rationalized this as a target designed to draw fire to the hero's chest, which was revealed to be heavily reinforced under the familiar winged symbol. For many readers, this was Adam West, grown older in a more oppressive and violent contemporary world. By issue 2, the yellow oval had disappeared, Robin had arrived, and the bat uniform got progressively darker and more somber before its final incarnation as a chunky suit of armor. Batman's equipment was put through the same steroid filter, with the Batmobile emerging as a massive steel-plated tank with iron treads in place of wheels.

Miller's Batman was a monumental physical presence who seemed hewn and hacked from granite and India ink. His Robin was new; a fifteen-year-old girl named Carrie Kelly who deftly subverted the Wertham dynamic into a quirky, funny, and warm father-daughter configuration. He added a camp and decadent Weimar-era menace to the Joker, bringing a twisted hypersexuality and feral horror to the crime clown's arsenal of personality defects.

The thoroughly modern Batman of *The Dark Knight Returns* was an antiestablishment rebel and ruthless pragmatist, but Miller's Superman was an idealistic government stooge in the pay of an all but mummified Ronald Reagan, president forever and ever, amen. A memorable sequence of panels introducing Superman to the story depicted a visual dissolve of the flag on the White House roof, where the rippling stripes of Old Glory morphed into an abstract close-up detail of the famous *S* shield. Miller's Superman seemed a wry comment on the yuppie makeover of Superman. It was easy to imagine the clean-lined, hunky Clark Kent of John Byrne's *Man of Steel* revamp growing into this compromised champion of the powers that be, serving the letter of the law, no matter how corrupt its administration became.

Most important, *The Dark Knight Returns* was good. This two-hundred-page slab of grown-up, layered, and ambitious grand statement was no easily dismissed throwaway story for children. It was as formally ambitious as any novel, as well constructed and exciting as the best Hollywood blockbuster; as personal as a poem, yet populist. It was hundreds of hand-drawn pages from a uniquely gifted young artist who was both determined to realize the full potential of his beloved art form and blessed with the talent, discipline, and vision to make that possible. Miller blended his influences from *manga* and *bandes dessinées* into a voice that was so definitively American, so flinty and self-assured, it became the sound of an era. Here was the new way to do superheroes. The deadlock was broken.

With a taste of *Dirty Harry*, *Death Wish*, and *Taxi Driver*, inspired allegedly in part by Miller's own experiences as a young artist in the crime-ridden New York of the early eighties (including a mugging that some say provided the rage-fuel for this intense and driven piece of work), the artist single-handedly rebuilt the Batmobile, transforming High Camp Crusader to Dark Knight and paving the way for a grown-up acceptance of superheroes and the movies that were to follow.

As remarkable as *The Dark Knight Returns* was, the show had barely begun. The Dark Age was approaching the blue-sky peak of its trajectory and the purest expression of its spirit.

With revolution in the air, Alan Moore announced a new series that would change the way readers looked at superheroes forever.

The book was to be called *Watchmen*.

The "Watchman on the walls of Western civilization" was how the late novelist Kathy Acker generously and somewhat hyperbolically described Alan Moore. *Watchmen* had some of its roots in Moore's love of the elaborate self-reflecting fictions of Thomas Pynchon and the intricately structured films of Nicolas Roeg, like *Don't Look Now*. It had a lot in common with the work of Peter Greenaway too, recalling the British director's coded, perfectionist universes of puzzles, tricks, architecture, and symmetrical doubling. With *Watchmen*, Moore delivered a devastating "follow *this*" to American comic-book superheroes. In its clinical artistry and its cold dissection of self-serving US foreign policy decisions in the guise of an alternate history of superhumans and masked crime fighters, it was delivered directly to the heart of DC Comics itself and allowed to detonate there in the heart of the Man. *Watchmen* was a Pop Art extinction-level event, a dinosaur killer and wrecker of worlds. By the time it was over—and its reverberations still resound—the equation was stark for superhero stories: Evolve or die.

Watchmen began its stately, assured march toward the *Time* magazine Best 100 Novels list when Moore and British artist Dave Gibbons pitched DC a radical new take on a stable of characters that the publisher had acquired when Charlton Comics went bust in 1985. They included Steve Ditko's faceless Question, one of his early stabs at developing a ruthlessly objectivist crime fighter; Captain Atom; the Buddhist-influenced Thunderbolt; the gadget hero Blue Beetle; and Nightshade, who'd been cofeatured in the captain's book. Three of these were Ditko creations, and *Watchmen* would honor its debt to the artist with a reappropriation and intelligent deployment of Ditko's metronomic nine-panel-page grids.

When Moore's synopsis arrived, it outlined a twelve-issue murder mystery set against a familiar backdrop of Cold War nuclear paranoia, but located in an alternate history where the appearance of one single American superhuman in 1959 had deformed and destabilized global politics, economies, and culture itself. Constructed to be a complete novel, the original idea left DC's Charlton acquisitions in a position where their stories had been brought to logical conclusions, rendering them more or less unusable, and so Moore and Gibbons were asked to rethink their pitch, using new analogues of the original Charlton cast. In the process of reinvention and reexamination, both men created a masterpiece: a complete and coherent work of fiction that would have been impossible with the limitations of the originals.

In Moore's hands, the atomic-powered Captain Atom was rebuilt as Doctor Manhattan, a godlike blue naturist who wandered around naked for most of *Watchmen*'s three hundred pages, in another first for superheroes. Superman had worn his underpants on the outside; Manhattan dispensed with pants altogether. Moore rationalized the superman's decision to let his balls hang low with the argument that a being of limitless power and intellect would have neither the desire to wear clothes nor any requirement for warmth. Tell that to the magistrate.

Manhattan was the only superpowered being in *Watchmen*'s world. The book's other principals were all nonpowered crime fighters in the "mystery man" mold, with each character representing a bitter twist on a different superhero archetype, from Manhattan's dehumanized cosmic god to Rorschach's disturbed masked vigilante. Nite Owl was sixties Batman gone to seed—impotent and overweight, with his Owlship gathering dust alongside the rest of the owl-themed weaponry and equipment in his disused secret basement HQ. The Silk Spectre stood for every second-generation "legacy" superhero, from Black Canary to Kid Flash. Rounding out the cast were the world's stupidest smartest man, Ozymandias, and the Comedian, an amoral mercenary representing the supersoldier type and the less salubrious elements of American foreign policy in general.

Watchmen would subvert all expectations, we were told, and beginning with the title, it did just that: There was no superteam called the Watchmen. The name came from the epigram quoted at the beginning of the book: "*Quis custodiet ipsos custodes,*" or "Who watches the watchmen?," written by the poet and satirist Juvenal of ancient Rome. This implied an understanding that "watchmen" equaled "superheroes" equaled "America."

The "watch" invoked the nuclear Doomsday Clock, the book's primary repeating motif, which lent its shape to the circular structure of the narrative. The so-called Doomsday Clock has been maintained since 1947 by the board of directors of the *Bulletin of the Atomic Scientists* at the University of Chicago as a symbolic warning, its minute hand set closer to or farther from the midnight position, depending on the current likelihood of global catastrophe. In 1985, when Moore was writing the book, the clock was set at 11:57, but that would have spoiled his and Gibbons's injury to the eye motif, so in *Watchmen*, the minute hand stood at a more positively secure 11:50. (Following the murder of the Comedian, which launched the plot, five central characters progressed toward the midnight of *Watchmen*'s conclusion.)

Continuing the innovations of *The Dark Knight Returns*, the cover designs for *Watchmen* broke new ground by depicting a close-up of a single significant object; this doubled as the opening image of the narrative, so that each chapter began immediately on the cover.

The title *Watchmen* was written in a vertical strip on the left-hand side, reminiscent of police tape sealing a crime scene, and the first cover showed a detail on a smiley face badge lying in a pool of blood in the gutter. There was a single oddly shaped splash of blood at a 330-degree angle—or five-minutes-to position—across Smiley's right eye.

The image of the circular "face" was repeated across a multitude of graphic representations throughout the story, as a pulsing countdown toward utopia or Armageddon. Here it was a close-up reflection in a round goggle, with a fingertip smear drawn through dust on the lens to make the "minute hand"; there it was the moon, with a rising drift of smoke across the "right eye" cockpit window of the hovering Owlship, or the smudge of disintegrating human bodies, scoured to black powder in the same terrible five-to-midnight configuration. The scarred smiley motif also appeared as the murder victim's own disfigured face. The Comedian's scar was revealed, in harrowing flashback, as a gruesome reminder of his final encounter with a young Vietnamese girl he'd made pregnant. Callously dismissing her—"THAT'S JUST WHAT I'M GONNA DO ... FORGET YOU. FORGET YOUR CRUDDY LITTLE COUNTRY, ALL OF IT."—on the way to the first chopper out of Saigon, the brutal "hero" provoked the anger of a violated nation.

"I THINK YOU REMEMBER ME AND MY COUNTRY, I THINK YOU REMEMBER US AS LONG AS YOU LIVE."

Cracking a bottle against the table, Glasgow pub style, she slashed the Comedian's face, only to receive a hot bullet in the belly for her troubles. It was as if Captain America had gunned down a teenager carrying his child. The scar, the streak of blood, the minute hand, and the nuclear split in time were the cracks in the façade of the American Dream, and here were America's heroes, baring at last their unexamined hearts to the microscopic scrutiny of Moore and Gibbons.

The first page, like all the others, was laid out on Ditko-vintage nine-panel grids. This was especially appropriate to the introduction of lead character Rorschach, *Watchmen*'s Question–Mr. A analogue, who dragged the idea of the masked crime fighter into the dark alleyways of abnormal psychopathology, depicting the urban vigilante as a paranoid, antisocial loner. In spite of Moore's efforts to make Rorschach hard to like, the character's inflexible moral code and refusal to compromise his principles turned him into the book's star. In the gray-toned ambiguity of *Watchmen*'s bleak moral universe, Rorschach, with his dogged determination and clarity of purpose, was closest in spirit to the classic comic-book superhero—and, it must be observed, closest in temperament to his author, who opened the first historic issue of his masterpiece with a slow reverse zoom up from the smiley pin in the gutter to a broken penthouse apartment window overlooking a busy New York Avenue, accompanied by torn-edged caption extracts from "Rorschach's journal":

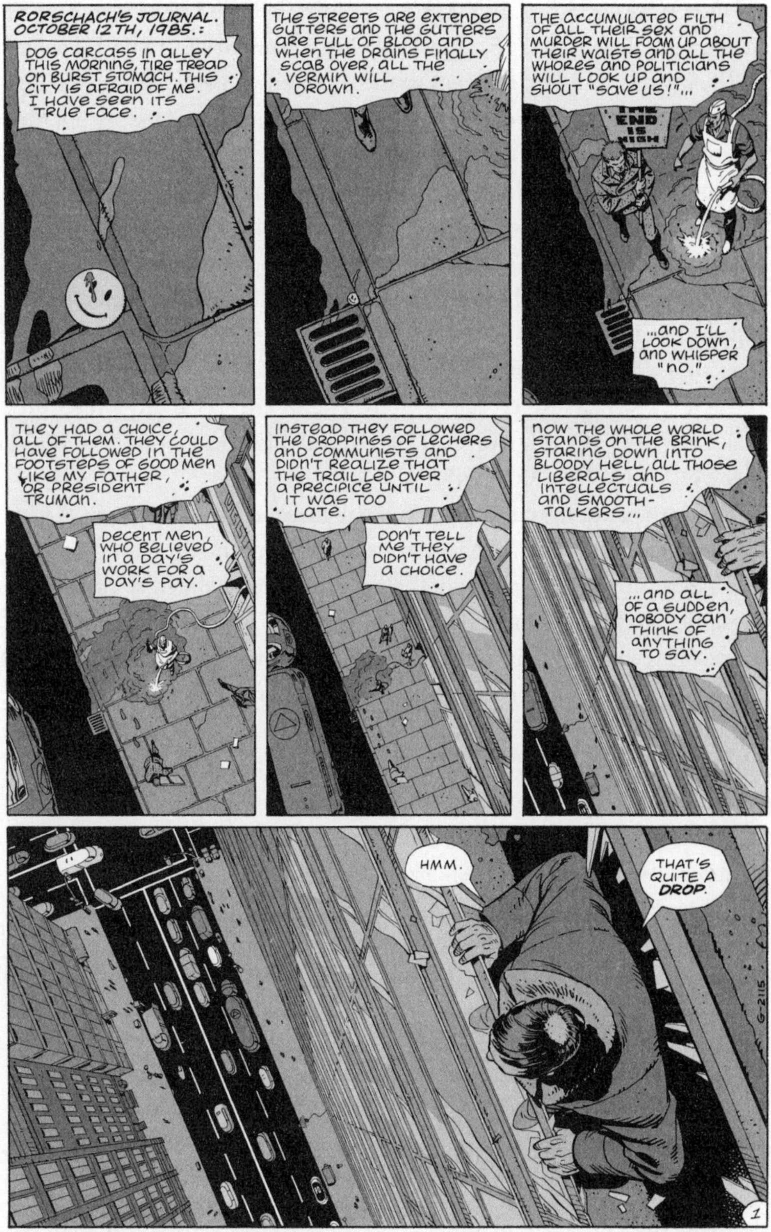
RORSCHACH'S JOURNAL. OCTOBER 12TH, 1985.:
DOG CARCASS IN ALLEY THIS MORNING, TIRE TREAD ON BURST STOMACH. THIS CITY IS AFRAID OF ME. I HAVE SEEN ITS TRUE FACE.
THE STREETS ARE EXTENDED GUTTERS AND THE GUTTERS ARE FULL OF BLOOD AND WHEN THE DRAINS FINALLY SCAB OVER, ALL THE VERMIN WILL DROWN.
THE ACCUMULATED FILTH OF ALL THEIR SEX AND MURDER WILL FOAM UP ABOUT THEIR WAISTS AND ALL THE WHORES AND POLITICIANS WILL LOOK UP AND SHOUT "SAVE US!"...
THE END IS NIGH
...AND I'LL LOOK DOWN, AND WHISPER "NO."
THEY HAD A CHOICE, ALL OF THEM. THEY COULD HAVE FOLLOWED IN THE FOOTSTEPS OF GOOD MEN LIKE MY FATHER, OR PRESIDENT TRUMAN.
DECENT MEN, WHO BELIEVED IN A DAY'S WORK FOR A DAY'S PAY.
INSTEAD THEY FOLLOWED THE DROPPINGS OF LECHERS AND COMMUNISTS AND DIDN'T REALIZE THAT THE TRAIL LED OVER A PRECIPICE UNTIL IT WAS TOO LATE.
DON'T TELL ME THEY DIDN'T HAVE A CHOICE.
NOW THE WHOLE WORLD STANDS ON THE BRINK, STARING DOWN INTO BLOODY HELL, ALL THOSE LIBERALS AND INTELLECTUALS AND SMOOTH-TALKERS...
...AND ALL OF A SUDDEN, NOBODY CAN THINK OF ANYTHING TO SAY.
HMM.
THAT'S QUITE A **DROP**.
G-2115
1

"DOG CaRCaSS In aLLeY THIS MORnING, TIRe TReAD On BURST STOMaCH. THIS CITY IS aFRaID OF Me. I HaVe SeeN ITS TRUe FaCe."

The most prominent element of the picture was the smiley face badge in its puddle of blood, poised on the edge of the drain's abyss, swept on a tide of gore, with its dumb, ignorant grin intact.

Panel 2 lifted us higher into the air above the drain so that now we could see the cracked flagstones of a city sidewalk. The badge was small but still clearly visible below; sunshine yellow contrasting against a sea of red. With ankles and shoes entering from the top of the panel, a man began to walk through the watery blood as it was sluiced off the curb by a jet from a hose. The journal entries continued:

"THe STReeTS aRe eXTenDeD GUTTeRS anD THe GUTTeRS aRE FULL OF BLOOD anD WHen THe DRaInS FINALLY SCaB OVeR aLL THe VeRMIn WILL DROWn."

The third panel, the last of the top tier of three, elevated our point of view to twenty feet above the sidewalk scene, with the drain, the gutter, the now tiny badge, the puddle of blood, the angry man with the hose rinsing the flagstones, and the second man, marching from top to bottom through the red puddle, with red hair and a homemade banner reading THE END IS NIGH—a detail with its own cascade of double and triple meanings.

"THe aCCUMULATeD FILTH OF aLL THeIR SeX aND MURDeR WILL FOaM UP aBOUT THeIR WaISTS aND aLL THe WHOReS anD POLITICIaNS WILL LOOK UP aND SHOUT 'SaVe US' . . . aND I'LL LOOK DOWn aND WHISPeR 'NO.' "

In panel 4, both men were small and far below. The red-haired man with the placard left bloody footprints as he marched across the swirling mix of blood and water. An oddly designed delivery truck with a pyramid logo could be seen on the road, sending the first subtle signal that this seemingly familiar world of smiley badges and religious nuts might not be what it seemed. The accompanying captions talked about following " . . . In THe FOOTSTePS OF GOOD MeN LIKE MY FATHER anD PRESIDeNT TRUMaN." (Rorschach never knew his violent, absent father, and President Harry S. Truman gave the order to drop the atomic bomb, the specter of which haunted the book.)

By the time we reached panel 5, the figures were antlike, although the blood and the placard man's trail of footprints were clearly visible as the caption rolled on with phrases such as "FoLLoWeD The DROP-PInGS . . . THe TRaIL LeD OVeR A PReCIPICe . . ."

Panel 6 brought us to several hundred feet above the tiny bloodstain, now smaller than a letter *o* in the accompanying journal entry:

"nOW THe WHOLe WORLD STanDS On THe BRInK STaRInG DOWn InTO BLOODY HeLL, aLL THOSe LIBeRaLS anD InTeLLeCTUaLS aND SMOOTH-TaLKeRS . . . aND aLL OF a SUDDeN nOBODY Can THInK OF anYThING TO SaY."

As the mad malarkey went on, a man's hand entered the scene from the top right-hand side. Far below there were more podlike "futuristic" cars. If you've been paying proper attention to Rorschach's rambles—and no one will condemn you if you haven't—you may have noticed how everything he says has some visual echo: the "TRUe FaCe" and the smiley pin, the gutters and drains, the looking down, footsteps, precipice, the brink of bloody hell.

The final panel occupied the entire lower tier to punch home its impact and pay off the series' first blank gag setup:

"Hmm, that's quite a drop," observed a balding man from the vantage point of a broken window high above the busy city street below. (The final page had another seven-panel reverse zoom from a smiley badge and ended the chapter with a joke about Rorschach dropping a criminal down an elevator shaft—another abyss, another fall, another mordant gag.)

The self-reflecting cross-referral of image and text reached fever pitch as *Watchmen* unfolded: A drawing of Doctor Manhattan telekinetically looping a tie around his neck for a rare clothed appearance in a TV interview had his estranged lover Laurie Jupiter, the former second-generation Silk Spectre, ask in voiceover, "How did everything get so *tangled up*?," while a scene in which she crushed a mugger's balls in her grip was cross-cut with another character's words to Doctor Manhattan: "Am I starting to make you feel uncomfortable." The parallel narrative threads of Manhattan and Laurie reflected and commented upon each other in a kind of remote quantum entangled conversation that perfectly suited Manhattan's nature and dramatized the breakdown of a relationship. This relentless self-awareness gave *Watchmen* a dense and tangible clarity. Everything connected in a dazzling, elaborate hall of narrative mirrors.

In 1985 the steady, constant-focus reverse zoom that opened *Watchmen* (a "camera" move that became possible on-screen only with the advent of computer-manipulated images)—from a microscopically detailed, thematically charged close-up on a single object to a scene-setting overview—was a technical effect that only comics could achieve. From the extreme close-up on the blood-streaked yellow idiot face on the cover to our balding Everyman joking at the splintering edge of the existential chasm, this deft sequence summed up the themes of the entire book and gave warning that its range would extend from the drains of death and disillusion to the holistic heights of cosmic overview awareness.

The opening daytime scene of slightly slapdash police work was followed by a neat four-page night sequence of vigilante professionalism and investigative efficiency as we met the feared Rorschach himself, scaling the sheer face of a skyscraper with his grappling gun line (in a nod to Adam West, who'd simulated his daring rope climbs by having the camera turned on its side while he inched along a taut rope on a horizontal stage set with windows in the floor). Rorschach wore a fedora and a tightly buttoned and belted trench coat that was stained, grubby, and torn, but he got things done. His trademark was a gimmick mask that covered his whole face like the Question's synthetic skin or Mr. A's blank mask. Unlike the featureless heads of Ditko's objectivist judges, Rorschach's mask had black liquid trapped between sheets of latex to make ever-changing symmetrical inkblot patterns that reflected the character's moods or dramatized story beats. The plot of *Watchmen* no. 1 followed Rorschach's dogged investigation into the death of the Comedian, which brought him into contact with the book's cast of retired crime fighters and set them on the road to uncovering a massive international conspiracy.

Moore became notorious for writing immense scripts filled with pages of detailed panel description in which every stray matchbook or record sleeve would be described, along with the precise angle of its placement in the picture as well as its color, shape, state of wear and tear, and symbolic meaning. In *Watchmen* there were no comic-book sound effects, no thought balloons or scene-setting captions, although Moore used interior monologues in later chapters. The pace was measured and hypnotic, incorporating flashback, flash-forward, and simultaneous narrative to disconnect time from the clock face and make it cyclical, endless, and all at once.

The themes of the entire work were contained in *Watchmen*'s iconic first cover: The childlike cartoon smile of innocence bloodied by real life and experience was a sour glyph that distilled Moore's whole approach to comic-book fantasy. He would compel the comic-book medium to grow up even if he had to elegantly violate its every precept in front of a cheering crowd of punks and perverts.

The book's final image—in the last panel of *Watchmen* no. 12—was of the same face, seen now on the T-shirt of a young man named Seymour, who stood poised to undo the book's entire plot. The story became a perfect circle, inviting us to complete its circuit by returning to the first page and "Rorschach's Journal," and suddenly we were reading the words again—"DOG CaRCaSS IN aLLeY . . ."—implicated in a new and terrible understanding: *We* were Seymour, reading the journal, joining the story right here where, as we'd been reminded the first time, "The end is nigh." And indeed, the end, which still lay three hundred pages away in the forward time axis of the story, was always a mere two panels "nigh" in the past-time direction of *Watchmen*! That glance back to page 1 made us all readers of Rorschach's journal, opening it for the first time. The end was nigh from the very beginning.

The book's last words are "I LEAVE IT ENTIRELY IN YOUR HANDS," and if the reader asks, "What?," the answer awaits on the first page of the journal. The responsibility for completing the story may seem to be our own, but we are guided to its inevitable end by the ever-present Watchmaker. Moore and Gibbons know that their complex masterpiece will be reread. They have set up their readers to pull the fatal switch, drafted them as executioners to undermine the world's greatest superhero's ultimate utopian triumph. We were made complicit in Moore's final mean joke, with a story that was completed beyond the page—in the reader's mind—and where the chance discovery of Rorschach's crazed journal undid the perfect plan of the perfect man.

I imagined that any story of real-life superheroes in the world where I lived would wind up in a welter of embarrassment and misunderstanding. I liked superhero comics because they weren't real. For all its pretensions to realism, *Watchmen* laid bare its own synthetic nature in every cunningly orchestrated line, lacking in any of the chaos, dirt, and non sequitur arbitrariness of real life. This overwhelmingly artificial quality of the narrative, which I found almost revolting at age twenty-five, is what fascinates me most about it now, oddly enough.

I preferred the sprawl and turbulence of *Marvelman*, which felt more like the real, messy world than the stifling, self-regarding, perfect yet mean-spirited microcosmos of *Watchmen*, but I was alone in my negative judgment.

Dazzled by its technical excellence, *Watchmen*'s readership was willing to overlook a cast of surprisingly conventional Hollywood stereotypes: the inhibited guy who had to get his mojo back; the boffin losing touch with his humanity; the overbearing showbiz mom who drove her daughter to excel while hiding from her the secret of her dubious parentage; the prison psychiatrist so drawn into the dark inner life of his patient that his own life cracked under the weight. The *Watchmen* characters were drawn from a repertoire of central casting ciphers to play out their preordained roles in the inside-out clockwork of its bollocks-naked machinery. Moore's self-awareness was all over every page like fingerprints.

The God of *Watchmen* was far from shy. He liked to muscle his way into every panel, every line. He strutted into view with his blue cock on proud display, and everywhere you looked, the Watchmaker was on hand to present his glittering structure for our approval and awe, just as Manhattan erected his own flawless crystal logic machine to lay out the law to a distraught Laurie in this maddeningly intricate engine of a story. The God of *Watchmen* could not hide and begged for our attention at every page turn. He was a jealous Maker who refused to allow any of his creations to be smarter than he was, so the pacifist genius became a genocidal idiot; the confident trained psychiatrist was reduced to a gibbering wreck by the darkness in the soul of his patient; the detectives stumbled through the plot to their doom; and even the more or less divine superhuman was shown to be emotionally retarded and ineffectual. It was as if God had little more than contempt for his creations and gave them no opportunity to transcend the limits he'd set for them.

Moore's love of obvious structure never left his work, although he tried in the nineties to approximate the looser, funkier style of the young pretenders to his throne. Later work like *Promethea* was built around the arrangement of the twelve *Sephiroth* of the Kabbalistic tree of life, but that was found structure. *Watchmen* built its own splendorous crystal labyrinth, conjuring from the red Martian sands of Moore's imagination an unending object of wonderful contemplation. (This is not to downplay Gibbons's hard work, but he was very faithful to Moore's immensely detailed scripts, and I presume from the depth and detail of Moore's typewritten art instructions that the writer saw most of *Watchmen* in his head.) Its bolt-from-the-blue impact meant that from that moment on and no matter what else he did, he would be Alan (*Watchmen*) Moore.

The film version of *Watchmen* as directed by Zack Snyder in 2009 (after several aborted attempts by directors like Terry Gilliam to bring the project to the screen) was a bizarrely accurate reconstruction of the comic's purely visual dimension, which added to the story flaws of the original some glaring errors of its own devising. Audiences unfamiliar with Roeg, Pynchon, Greenaway—any of the varied precursors to *Watchmen*'s naked structural and philosophical preoccupations—were confounded.

Moore had always claimed that it was essentially unfilmable. The film's very existence proved him wrong to some extent and was a respectful adaptation, but by the time of its release, an angry Moore could afford to sever all ties with Hollywood. He'd been burned by previous poor adaptations of his work and refused to endorse or even attach his name as original creator to the film of *Watchmen*, giving his share of the buy-out to his artist before returning to his underground roots in high dudgeon. While the filmmakers failed to capture the essence of Moore's writing, they duplicated Gibbons's artwork with an almost supernatural fidelity that was made possible by the development of computer-generated imagery (CGI) to a degree where it could render an infinite depth of field in which every tiny holographic shard of background detail was visible in crystal clarity in high definition.

Ultimately, in order for *Watchmen*'s plot to ring true, we were required to entertain the belief that the world's smartest man would do the world's stupidest thing after thinking about it all his life. It's there where *Watchmen*'s rigorous logic runs out, where its irony is drawn so tight that the bowstring gives. Its road ends. As the apotheosis of the relevant, realistic superhero stories, it had to come face-to-face with the bursting walls of its own fictional bubble, its fundamental lack of likelihood. No real world could be as beautifully designed and organized as *Watchmen*'s 4-D jigsaw puzzle.

With Moore as comics' fire-flecked prophet of apocalypse and Miller as its sensitive would-be tough-guy, the medium had made it all the way to college, where some unlikely characters were now rooming together. The audience was still aging along with the books: These were teenagers and twentysomethings who wanted superhero stories that spoke to them about their sense of alienation, their sexuality or anger. The New Wave was eager to oblige.

The superheroes fed on this new energy, and the strands—US underground and UK art house—diverged, each growing toward a decadent phase that would prove more successful for the American brand of alternative than the androgynous eyeliner Goth of the British Invasion.

And there was a new audience willing to buy comics in expensive hardback collected editions sold in bookstores. The term "graphic novel" became a buzzword overnight, heralding a new dawn for coffee table editions of *The Dark Knight Returns* and *Watchmen* made to adorn studio apartments as evidence of serious hipster credentials in the late eighties. In France, comics were accepted as the Ninth Art and sold to adults in expensive hardbound collectors' editions. In Japan, they were everywhere.

Perhaps it could happen here.

CHAPTER 14

ZENITH

THERE WAS NOTHING else for it: The shyness and diffidence that held me back were ruthlessly expunged in the service of earning a living, and I began to make regular trips to London in search of work in the comic-book business. I was a rock kid now, released like a rat from a trap from the cage of virginity, and beginning what became a nine-year relationship with a fashionable, funny, and attractive nurse. We soon found there was no money in looking gorgeous down at the pub so, skinny, spectral, I hung around the offices of Marvel and Fleetway, publishers of *2000 AD*, at that time the official stepping-stone to overseas recognition. I'd never been a *2000 AD* fan, but they were always on the lookout for new sci-fi comic writers, and I was happy to read through a few back issues and see if I could simulate the style. I wrote endless letters, including script ideas. I made a point of attending every monthly meeting of the Society of Script Illustrators. I traveled four hundred miles for interminable lunch hours in South Bank bars, watching the editorial staff play pool as I declined rounds and beers.

I scored some work with Marvel Comics' UK division, writing a toy tie-in serial entitled *Zoids*. I took the job seriously and set about transforming the undemanding source material—a group of astronauts stranded on a planet of warring alien robots—into a showcase for my peculiar talents in an action-and-angst-fueled take on East-West politics and how it felt to be part of a group of ordinary people trapped between the titanic struggles of very large opponents who couldn't care less about your hobbies or your favorite books.

At twenty-four, well beyond any awkward geek years, I was still convinced my life was ebbing away with nothing much to show for it. As far as I was concerned, heroes like Keats and Rimbaud had already done their best work and left inscriptions on headstones or given up by the time they got to my age. My own achievements seemed to count as nothing by comparison. The Mixers, meanwhile, were spinning in multicolored circles, devolving to nothing more than posters, threats, and endless vague rehearsals with a carousel of drummers who never stuck around, smelling our lack of commitment to actually playing live. I was still on the dole and living at home, a sitcom character disturbing the fragile peace between my mum and my increasingly depressed stepdad, a sea captain.

Eventually with a recommendation from *2000 AD* founder, fellow Scot, and future *Batman* writer Alan Grant, Fleetway hired me to write a trial *Future Shocks* twist-ending story with the promise of more. It meant that I could afford to be self-employed and say farewell to the Department of Social Services. My first *2000 AD* deadline, the next big step up toward the US superhero universes, coincided with the epochal eruption of the sea captain's by-now-volcanic inner demons. My stepfather needed a small, soft scapegoat and chose the innocent feral kittens I'd rescued from the garbage bins outside. He lost all patience when he realized that the tiny orphans were behind the infestation of ringworm that explained the stink of disinfectant and why Mum was wearing polo neck sweaters that hid her scabby neck in the hot middle of August. I was told to have those kittens "put down" several times, but I persevered with them, and they got over the ringworm and the diarrhea and vomiting, growing to fine cathood, even appearing on the cover and in the pages of DC Comics' *Animal Man* title, thereby securing themselves some little immortality.

In exile at my dad's place, I wrote the first of seventeen *Future Shocks* stories as my apprenticeship with *2000 AD*. These were short, done-in-one science fiction stories—anything from a single page to five pages long—

with O. Henry twists or shock endings. Like so many others, I honed my skills on these odd little haiku-like pieces, for which I'd developed a kind of English middle-class sci-fi twang based on the writing of Douglas Adams of *The Hitchhiker's Guide to the Galaxy* fame, which seemed to fit with *2000 AD*'s brand of playground rebellion. After working one's way through a few years of *Future Shocks*, it was customary to be offered a series to write, usually one devised by the editors. So I was lucky enough to be in the right place at the right time with the right subject when it was announced that *2000 AD* planned to take on the Americans at their own game with a big, revisionist superhero story set in Britain and featuring all new characters. All eyes were back on the superhero. What happened next? What came post-*Watchmen*?

I'd waited all my life for this moment, and my offering was *Zenith*, which used a few characters and concepts I'd created for an earlier and mercifully unpublished strip about glum British superheroes. I re-thought the entire concept to bring it into line with a sensibility I hoped could bridge the gap between *Watchmen*'s Saturnian heaviness and the breezy shallowness of eighties pop culture. I saw it not as art but as a freelance gig, a step up the ladder toward the American super-heroes I wanted to get my hands on, so I constructed *Zenith* quite care-fully. I was resolutely straight edge, no drink, no drugs, no caffeine. In the strictest sense of the coinage, my girlfriend Judy and I were Young Upwardly Mobile People, doing uncommonly well under a prime min-ister who fronted a political party I'd been raised to despise as my class duty, still identifying with roots I'd long ago outgrown. I needed my own new direction away from leaden politics and humorless social realism.

In 1986 I was invited to the Birmingham Comic Convention. There I met the one-of-a-kind artist Brendan McCarthy, who complimented me on my *Brideshead Revisited* fringe and floppy cuffs. McCarthy was a styled and prickly genius whose hand had and still has a direct line to his unconscious mind. Imagine that you could take photographs of your dreams, and you will have some idea what McCarthy is able to do with his art. I liked him immediately, recognizing a far-flung überspecimen of my own odd and difficult breed, immediately tracking down the three Day-Glo issues of McCarthy's *Strange Days* comic-book series from 1982. In it, he and two other early exports to the United States, Brett Ewins and writer Peter Milligan, had created something that now opened my eyes to the horrible bargain I'd made: I'd been chasing the dollar by aping the styles of popular writers, but *Strange Days* took me back to the *Near Myths* days and reminded me of the pride that I took in the madcap, personal comics I still wrote and drew in my free time.

Strange Days' superhero character Paradax was a pompadoured poser who could walk through walls as long as he was wearing a banana-yellow skintight one-piece that married the Kid Flash design to glam rock and Ziggy Stardust. Paradax was a slacker superhero, interested only in fame and sex, manipulated by his manager into aimless struggles with living abstractions like Jack Empty, the Hollow Man, or "*SHUDDER* . . . THE MADNESS OF A WARM TOILET SEAT . . . AND *TWITCH* . . . THE HEINOUS SCAB ON THE CROTCH OF YOUR DREAMS." This was a comic created by art students to be a sexy, funny, and clever deconstruction of superhero and adventure tropes. McCarthy's melting superpsychedelic visuals could sprawl across pages in a trancelike pageant of phosphorescent dream imagery, conjuring epic post-Kirby aboriginal visions of city-sized, floating, three-eyed Kennedy heads and a runway parade of fabulous, ludicrous supervillains as easily and lovingly as he captured the bustle and life of the East Village arts scene. Imagine *Yellow Submarine* grown up androgynous on mushrooms in the Dreamtime, and you may get some distant flavor of the flashing colors and textures of Brendan McCarthy's inner territory. Milligan's arch, knowing voice suggested an author at home on the chaise with a hookah in one hand and a hooker in the other, and together they made a formidable team—as well as making all the other adult superhero comics look decidedly adolescent.

Strange Days was a bracing dose of sunshine-yellow and petrol-blue exuberance in a landscape of postpunk industrial-gray tones. It had a relaxed and amused sexuality where *Watchmen* was stiff and uptight. McCarthy mined his living dreams, and I was reenergized by my encounter with his work, and rededicated to pursuing my own obsessions and consolidating my own style.

I'd already separated out the strands in my head: There were my own, unpublished drifting dream logic stories in the *Near Myths* style, and there were the commercial jobs for which I wrote about warring toys or absurd alien races in order to pay the bills, hone my commercial storytelling skills, and build a reputation as a freelance writer. There I tried to toe the line, follow trends, and do a passable copy of the latest fads and fashions with just enough of my own sauce to make it individual. But I always considered this work inferior to the expressive avant-garde material. *Strange Days* encouraged me to put more of myself into the commercial work and to enliven even those jobs with the things that really mattered to me.

Having seen what was possible, I decided to write about the kind of superhero that *I* would be and the kind of world it would take to have made me. *Zenith* consciously attempted to occupy my own imagined middle ground between the extremes of Gibbons and Moore's serious formality and Milligan-McCarthy's visionary remixes of modern culture high and low.

The superhumans of *Zenith* were designed by a mostly disinterested Brendan; the hero's lightning-bolt Z motif—I never forgot to honor my divine inspiration—was borrowed wholesale from the well-known TV company logo.

Zenith had no secret identity; he was too famous for that. Nineteen-year-old Robert McDowell was the world's first thoroughbred superhuman being, and only son of sixties iconoclasts White Light and Dr. Beat, the Julie Christie and Terence Stamp of Cloud 9, a psychedelic British superteam. The surviving members of Cloud 9 were Ruby Fox, the former Voltage, now a fashion magazine editor; and Peter St. John, a one-time hippie idealist with a new job as a Conservative MP in Margaret Thatcher's cabinet. (He turned out to be the strip's most popular character.)

Like Captain Clyde, Zenith lived in a recognizable fictional facsimile of late-eighties Britain, with familiar programs on TV, and well-known politicians and celebrities taking incidental roles, but *Zenith* took the world-building detail to new heights. I wanted to include all the tropes of Brit superheroes, too, so no costumes, and although Zenith's history clearly wasn't our own, everything else was interwoven with real current events as they happened. I composed pastiche George Formby Jr. songs about World War II superhumans, and the strip was peppered with British youth and pop culture references: Jonathan Ross. *Network 7*. Comic Relief. Bros and *Betty Blue*. Unlike Captain Clyde, Zenith was incredibly famous and used his special powers not to fight crime or injustice but to bolster his reputation as a shallow, party-loving pop star who could fly and bite off the tops of beer bottles without breaking his perfect teeth. Instead of costumes, the Goth, punk, skinhead, soul boy, and fetish supermen, superwomen, and supertrannies wore fashions influenced by designers Jean Paul Gaultier, Thierry Mugler, and Vivienne Westwood.

Another unique flavor of the Zenith strip was the lead's complete lack of interest in committing his inherited abilities to the endless fight against crime or evil. I wondered why we automatically assumed that having superpowers would encourage a person to fight (or commit) crime. Zenith was a talent-free chart singer with a callous wit who hid his superhuman intelligence and perception under the sneering veneer he figured would get him by in a superficial world. He acted like a brainless oaf in order to get through life without the persecution that had led to the deaths of his gifted parents. He shagged Page 3 Girls and pursued a vapid, style-conscious, utterly vacuous existence of the kind that I was still convinced I coveted, all under the watchful gaze of his manager, Eddie McPhail. Artist Steve Yeowell and I based the gay Scot on Richard Wilson's portrayal of Eddie Clockerty in the 1987 TV series *Tutti Frutti* by John Byrne—not the superhero comics artist, but the playwright, artist, and husband of actress Tilda Swinton.

The elaborate alternate history of *Zenith* was constructed around the idea that the Americans had dropped the first atom bomb on Berlin, not Hiroshima, in order to kill a fascist superhuman engineered and empowered by the Nazis as a living weapon to win the war against the Allies. This backstory, with its grubby roots in popular Nazi occult lore, eugenics, and the CIA's clandestine LSD research program, had Lovecraftian monsters teaching the Nazis how to turn humans into superhuman vessels—ostensibly supersoldiers but in reality to be used as bodies for higher-dimensional entities whose mere presence caused fatal hypertension and hemorrhaging in ordinary flesh-and-blood men and women. It had the flavor of Robert Anton Wilson and Robert Shea's *The Illuminatus! Trilogy*, too—everything including the kitchen sink.

High-contrast Western *manga* art by my *Zoids* partner Steve Yeowell made *Zenith*'s world a frantic modernist blur of speed lines and contemporary fashions and haircuts. We announced to the world that *Zenith* was intended to be as dumb, sexy, and disposable as an eighties pop single: Alan Moore remixed by Stock Aitken Waterman. Keeping all the self-awareness outside the story, we used interviews and forewords to admit to our sources. In them we praised creative theft and plagiarism, quoted the French playwright Antonin Artaud and sneeringly suggested that the likes of *Watchmen* were pompous, stuffy, and buttock-clenchingly dour. The shock tactics I'd brought with me from the music world, delivered with the snotty whippet-thin snideness of the hipster, had helped me carve out a niche for myself as comics' enfant terrible, and Steve was happy to play along as the handsome nice one with nothing controversial to say.

My public persona was punk to the rotten core. Outspoken and mean spirited, I freely expressed contempt for the behind-the-scenes world of comics professionals, which seemed unglamorous and overwhelmingly masculine by comparison to the club and music scenes. My life was rich, and my circle of friends and family was secure enough that I could afford to play a demonic role at work. Reading interviews from the time makes my blood run cold these days, but the trash talk seemed to be working, and I was rapidly making a name for myself. Being young, good-looking, and cocky forgave many sins, a huge hit British superhero strip did the rest and proved I could back up the big talk.

Over four volumes, Steve and I chronicled our hero's reluctant entry into a massive parallel-worlds story that led inexorably to the origin of everything and one of those apocalyptic final battles so beloved of comic-book creators. In our version, instead of banding together to save the multiverse, the superheroes of the various parallel worlds spent twenty-six installments arguing and losing the plot. In one macabre twist, *Zenith* even predicted Labour Party leader John Smith's unexpected death of a heart attack. In *Zenith* the fatal coronary was brought about by the telekinetic meddling of Peter St. John, but it was no less terminal when the real-life leader was struck down by myocardial infarction on May 12, 1994, at age fifty-five.

DC's rising fortunes were due in great measure to a new publisher who had replaced Carmine Infantino in 1978. Jenette Kahn was a go-getting, well-connected socialite with a progressive editorial team that included the dapper, elegant, and erudite Dick Giordano, the artist on *Rose and the Thorn*. Giordano, a much-respected editor at Charlton in the sixties, had set up in business with Neal Adams as Continuity Associates. In addition, he'd made a name for himself as an inker and artist in his own right, and now here he was green-lighting DC groundbreaking projects one after another.

By the time I met both of them in the back of a London taxi in 1987, Giordano was deaf, and my Scottish accent, churned to the consistency of a guttural porridge by my years in the tenement glens, left him smiling but clearly none the wiser.

Under the strict guidance of Jim Shooter, former teen prodigy, Marvel Comics had shed its counterculture trappings to corner the mass market for well-produced but mostly formulaic superhero books. Although that war was over, DC could take advantage of the growing older audience— the Alan Moore and Frank Miller fans—the people who remembered the relevance and cosmic movements and wanted something a bit more underground and edgy.

While Marvel gathered the abundant dollars of the lowest common denominator geek market, DC occupied the high ground with a series of projects that would redefine what superhero comics could look like, be about, and command, price-wise. Jenette identified the bookstores as an emergent market for DC collected and original hardcover or paperback books.

In the stuffy, aging microuniverses, change was afoot. *Crisis on Infinite Earths* (1985) had begun in the DC universe as an elegiac continuity audit made to purge all story meat that was seen as too strong for the tender palates of an imagined new generation who would need believable and grounded hero books. There were complaints that the parallel-worlds system was too unwieldy and hard to understand, when in fact it was systematic, logical, and incredibly easy to navigate, particularly for young minds that were made for this kind of careful categorization of facts and figures. There was Earth-1, where the regular DC superheroes lived; Earth-2, where their revived Golden Age counterparts, now twenty years older, existed; Earth-3, where all the heroes had evil counterparts;

Earth-X, where the Nazis had won the war and where the characters that DC had acquired from Quality Comics—Uncle Sam, the Ray, Phantom Lady, Doll Man, and the Black Condor—were stationed in a never-ending battle against robot Hitler and his nightmare brand of techno–National Socialism. Is that really so hard to follow?

The new status quo mashed these infinite Earths of the Multiverse together in a yearlong maxiseries written by Marv Wolfman and drawn with meticulous perfectionism by George Perez, who managed to include every single DC Comics character ever created.

The Superman of the Silver Age had been given a teary farewell in a typically thorough, intelligent, and ruthlessly logical Alan Moore script entitled "Whatever Happened to the Man of Tomorrow?," which lost points for its weeping Superman, but otherwise it brought the necessary gravitas and a satisfying twist to the conclusion of an era.

The next month, Superman was reborn as a clean-limbed, square-jawed twentysomething quarterback. Even as Clark Kent, he stood tall, dressed well, and was, for all intents and purposes, a yuppie—all thanks to the notoriously cantankerous, restlessly reinventive Canadian superstar writer-artist John Byrne, collaborator on *X-Men* with Chris Claremont. Byrne's *The Man of Steel* binned the bottle cities and superdogs in the first serious housecleaning for almost fifty years. The entire *Superman* franchise was rebooted back to its roots; the story told as if new, erasing all prior continuity. Everything felt fresh, and the skies were wide again in Metropolis. Byrne's spacious layouts and horizontal compositions gave the hero space to breathe and rediscover his youthful sexuality. Freed of the baggage of the past, eighties Superman was no longer your dad but your big sister's horny beefcake boyfriend. He snarled and got torn up a little. He faced terrible moral dilemmas in a way that gave them a contemporary dimension—even going so far as to execute three deadly rogue Kryptonians whose homicidal rampage destroyed an alternate universe.

Backing Byrne was the accomplished Marv Wolfman, who brought a new evil-eighties-businessman incarnation of Lex Luthor. The Superman revamp had the whiff of prefab plastic smugness that characterized a hit primetime TV show in the eighties, but in its day it felt like another bold and fresh move away from the expectations of superhero fiction, and that was what mattered. Superman was no longer a forty-five-year-old alien or a troubled counterculture outsider seeking meaning in post-Watergate America; he was confident and assimilated, like Byrne himself. In the revolutionary eighties, it seemed as though everything DC touched turned to gold and glittery awards.

The Batman franchise, following Frank Miller's groundbreaking turn, was locked into increasingly bizarre, shrill, and distorted parodies of his voice, relieved only by a charming, nonconformist take from Alan Davis and Mike Barr that effortlessly updated the Adam West aesthetic to suit the new DC but which was counter to the prevailing trends and went largely unlauded. Batman was waiting for Hollywood to bring him back into the global mainstream, and he wouldn't have to wait for very much longer.

Far from delivering the rational death blow and beautiful eulogy that he and many others assumed he'd dealt, Moore had instead opened the door to a new kind of superhero. Take out Moore's passion, his excellence as a wordsmith, and his formal obsessions, and save only his cynicism, his gleeful descriptions of cruelty, and his need to expose the potentially wounded sexuality of cartoon characters, and you had the germ of a strain of superhero-porn comics. Unlike *Watchmen*, which was written for a wide mainstream audience, the new superhero comics were pitched at fans in the direct market, who were tired of all the old tricks and craved shock-therapy versions of all their old favorites. In this atmosphere of self-flagellating manly guilt and doubt, even Batman's inner monologues had come to read like the diary of the madman in the 1995 film *Se7en*.

Eliminate Miller's talent as a cartoonist and satirist, his skill as an action storyteller, and leave only his reactionary "bastard" heroes—all those psychologically damaged sociopaths in trench coats, jackboots, and stubble—and you had the new model superhero in the late-eighties American style. Humorless cyborg assassins, crazed death machines, amoral and carnage-loving sadists became the heroes of the Dark Age's decadent phase; for instance, the Punisher, a *Death Wish*–inspired Spider-Man antagonist who'd seen his wife and family gunned down by the Mob and responded by waging a one-man violent war against criminals. Created for Marvel in 1974 by Gerry Conway and John Romita, the right-wing antihero Frank Castle became the template for a new generation of cookie-cutter no-compromise superthugs. The superheroes were exposed as kin to the serial killer, deranged fascist loners, delusional narcissistic nut jobs who were barely above the level of the scum upon whom they preyed night and day. Was this what America's role models had become?

Oddly enough, Britain had outgrown all that. Its new comics seemed keener on old-school Lewis Carroll–John Lennon surrealism, Smiths-style kitchen-sink kitsch, and druggy absurdity. As the no-longer-excluded Brits partied and surveyed the flag-planted beachhead, Americans were in retreat as if through the flaming hooches of Southeast Asia.

When I got the call to join the DC orchestra, I was living with Judy and four cats in a rented flat near Observatory Lane, doing well on my *Zenith* paychecks and her nurse's wage but hungry for bigger opportunities and more creative control. Now at last the Americans were on the phone, and I'd never been more ready.

On the nail-biting train journey south to the London meeting, I worked up a four-issue miniseries pitch for Animal Man, an obscure superhero from the sixties. I'd seen him in reprint comics and I figured no one else would remember him. I even saw a way to give the character a fashionably Moore-esque spin that would hopefully make him appeal to DC editorial. I'd been horrified by harrowing scenes from the animal rights documentary *The Animals Film*, and a single viewing was enough to bring about my conversion to vegetarianism. And I saw how to use Animal Man as a mouthpiece against cruelty to animals and the general degradation of the environment as well as for deeper explorations of the superhero as an idea.

Alan Moore's magnificent costumed deities in *Marvelman* and *Watchmen* were flawed by the same familiar human doubts and failings we all shared. They were Olympians but not comic-book superheroes like Superman and Batman. So what were comic-book superheroes, really?

Even Moore's view of planet Krypton showed a world riven by racial tensions, religious fanaticism, and brutal street violence, but I could see all that on TV and longed for mind-expanding tales of a world so far beyond my own in development and learning that it would have no need for conflicts of this ordinary kind, except perhaps as games. Eighties leftist politics, with its regular recourse to incoherent angry victimhood, was no longer blowing my mind the way that situationism, the occult, travel, and hallucinogens had begun to. I was tired of grids and imposed structures.

For me, the answer lay in pushing "realism" to its next stage. What *was* the proven tangible reality of comic-book superheroes? What was a superhero, really? What was the exchange—the relationship—between our real world and their printed universes? What was going on when we hung out with superheroes in our hands and in our heads?

If they were *really* real, what would they look like?

The answer turned out to be as simple as it was obvious.

In the real world, superheroes looked like drawings or special effects. As artist David Mazzucchelli would one day state so succinctly: "Once a depiction veers toward realism, each new detail releases a torrent of questions that exposes the absurdity at the heart of the genre. The more 'realistic' superheroes become, the less believable they are. It's a delicate balance but this much I know: superheroes are real when they're drawn in ink."

My experiments on *Animal Man* were described by critics as "metafiction," or fiction about fiction, and perhaps that was an easy way in for some readers, but I felt that I was onto something more concrete and less rooted in abstraction or theory. The fictional universe I was interacting with was as "real" as our own, and as I began to think of the DC universe as a place, it occurred to me that there were two ways to approach it: as a missionary or as an anthropologist.

I chose to see some writers as missionaries who attempted to impose their own values and preconceptions on cultures they considered inferior—in this case, that of the superheroes. Missionaries liked to humiliate the natives by pointing out their gauche customs and colorfully frank traditional dress. They bullied defenseless fantasy characters into leather trench coats and nervous breakdowns and left formerly carefree fictional communities in a state of crushing self-doubt and dereliction.

Anthropologists, on the other hand, surrendered themselves to foreign cultures. They weren't afraid to go native or look foolish. They came and they departed with respect and in the interests of mutual understanding. Naturally, I wanted to be an anthropologist.

In *Animal Man* I created, with the help of my artistic collaborator, Chaz Truog, a paper version of myself that could be integrated with the 2-D DC universe. I sent my avatar onto the page surface to meet the Animal Man character and confirm suspicions he'd been having that his life story was being written by some demiurgic Gnostic overlord. I explained to my character how the people who wrote his life needed drama and shock and violence to make his story interesting. The implication was that our own lives might also be "written" to entertain or instruct an audience in a perpendicular direction we could never point to, interacting with us in ways we could scarcely understand but that could be divined in the relationship of the comic world to the world of the creator and audience.

I tried to condense the painful adolescent self-awareness that had come to superhero comics into a single image: as Animal Man's alter ego, Buddy Baker, turned to look back over his shoulder, sensing the uncanny presence of the reader, he yelled, **"I can see you!"** It was the violated superhero finally confronting the voyeuristic reader. I wanted the superhero to face up to us—to challenge the zealous missionary work that had inflicted real-world tortures and judgments upon the ethereal, paper-thin constructs of unfettered imagination.

Buddy's face, filling the whole page so as to seem almost life sized, was drawn in a simple cartoonish style that ultimately made him seem more human: unshaven and unprepared, perpetually startled by the old intruder at the door.

Animal Man was dedicated to my childhood imaginary friend Foxy, as I entered what I can describe only as the freewheeling "shamanic" phase of my career. I wanted nothing less than first contact with fictional reality, so I set about making it happen by truly immersing myself in my work. The results were literally life altering.

I chose to take comic-book characters at face value. There was no Batman in the real world and probably never would be. The chances of a humanoid infant alien growing to maturity with extraordinary superpowers in midwestern America were infinitesimal. These were fairy-tale creatures; they could never be flesh and blood, and the breakdown in plausibility required to make the machinery of *Watchmen* work suggested that any further attempts to pursue that line of thinking would be fruitless.

I agreed that superhero comics could always use a little more realism, but that didn't mean scenes of Batman on the toilet or the X-Men failing to feed the starving millions of Africa. It meant, instead, an acknowledgment that anything we could experience was by its nature real and a corresponding rejection of the idea that fiction had to behave like flesh. The presumption that superheroes could literally show us how to end hunger or poverty seemed as naïve as a belief in fairies.

There were real superheroes, of course. They did exist. They lived in paper universes, suspended in a pulp continuum where they never aged or died unless it was to be reborn, better than ever, with a new costume. Real superheroes lived on the surface of the second dimension. The real lives of real superheroes could be contained in two hands. They were so real they had lives that were longer than any human life. They were more real than I was. They say most human names and biographies are forgotten after four generations, but even the most obscure Golden Age superhero is likely to have a life and a renown that will last as long as trademarks are revived.

There was no physical Marvel universe New York. You couldn't buy a ticket and fly there, yet you could buy a comic that would instantly transport you to the only real Marvel universe New York there could ever be—a paper-and-ink virtual-reality simulation—on the pages of the comic books themselves. A wholly alternative, fully functioning duplicate of New York now existed on the paper skin of the next dimension down from our own: a city populated by drawn figures of Daredevil, Spider-Man, and the Fantastic Four. That New York had its own history of alien invasions and tsunamis from Atlantis, but it also kept pace with changing fashions in the "real" world, and it had the capacity to grow in complexity and depth over decades. It had a continuity that was separate from our own. Its characters outlived real people, including their creators. The Baxter Building could outlast real houses made of stone. In my attempts to see beyond preconceptions to the undeniable actuality of things in *Animal Man*, I was drifting closer to what could only be termed a kind of psychedelic hyperreality. I used my next assignment to go deeper into the rabbit hole in search of a little conceptual allotment to call my own and cultivate. When I was offered the ailing *Doom Patrol* title, it turned out to be the perfect venue for my new approach.

The *Doom Patrol* feature had been launched in 1963 in the pages of *My Greatest Adventure* as the brainchild of writer Arnold Drake and artist Bruno Premiani. A group of outcast, freakish superheroes, led by a genius in a wheelchair, they debuted almost exactly and quite coincidentally at the same time as the similar X-Men and had been revived in 1990 as a pallid imitation of the Claremont school. I went back to first principles in an attempt to define an alternative to the dominant *X-Men* superteam model.

Originally billed as "the World's Strangest Heroes," the Doom Patrol had always been played as misunderstood outsiders, so I gave them a new purpose as the only superheroes disturbed enough to deal with the kind of menaces to sanity and reality that not even Superman could hope to confront. With artist Richard Case and some design assistance from Brendan McCarthy, the spiritual father of my take on the book, *Doom Patrol* cornered the market in "strange" and picked up the baton Steve Gerber had passed in the form of *The Defenders*.

Carefully composed pastiches of Thomas De Quincey, Sylvia Plath, Italo Calvino, and F. T. Marinetti jostled for attention alongside fight scenes, wild action, and quotes from avant-garde art or the wilder frontiers of philosophy and the occult. *Doom Patrol* stories took childhood fairy tales (most of them from the gruesome school readers I'd had forced on me when I was six and too young to defend myself: monsters like the Scissor Man or the Hobyahs) and transformed them into grown-up nightmares for my disturbed heroes to fight.

I kept dream diaries, and made characters of the imaginary friends with whom my real friend Emma had shared her own childhood. Emma had imaginary friends called Darling-Come-Home and Damn-All, and when she got old enough to tire of them, she took them both outside and shot them. "What did you shoot your imaginary friends with?" I asked her. "An imaginary gun," said Emma, and it went straight into *Doom Patrol*.

I used material from fairy stories, and discovered the weird, paranoid fairy tales of Lucy Lane Clifford, whose cosmic horror tale "The New Mother" was written as a bedtime story for her children. After I brought the piece to Neil Gaiman's attention, it went on to influence his *Coraline* and the movie that was based on it. I was using surrealist methods: automatic writing, found ideas, and even my word processor's spell-check functions to create random word strings with syntax. I'd type in strings of nonsense words, which the computer would dutifully correct to the nearest equivalent, giving my dream horrors dialogue exchanges like this: "DEFEATING BREADFRUIT IN ADUMBRATE." "CRASHLAND FOR AWARD PRIMATE." "YUCCA OR PRIORITY?" "LEMUR NEVER HIBERNATE."

The Brotherhood of Evil from the sixties Doom Patrol stories were recreated as Mr. Nobody and the Brotherhood of Dada, a group of absurdist supervillains who began their war on reason with the following words:

> LOOK AT US! ARE WE NOT PROOF THAT THERE IS NO GOOD, NO EVIL, NO TRUTH, NO REASON? ARE WE NOT PROOF THAT THE UNIVERSE IS A DROOLING IDIOT WITH NO FASHION SENSE?
>
> FROM THIS DAY ON WE WILL CELEBRATE THE TOTAL ABSURDITY OF LIFE, THE GIGANTIC HOCUS-POCUS OF EXISTENCE. FROM THIS DAY ON, LET UNREASON REIGN!
>
> THE BROTHERHOOD OF EVIL IS DEAD! LONG LIVE THE BROTHERHOOD OF DADA!
>
> AND THE PANTS OF THE VICAR ARE CLOSING RATAPLAN RATAPLAN *RRRRRRR.*

Gaining possession of a mysterious painting, the Dadaists sucked Paris into its recursive structure. Each of the levels inside the Painting That Ate Paris was rendered in prose and illustrations evocative of different art movements, and even the storytelling structure was a recursive sequence of nested flashbacks. Encouraged by *Doom Patrol*'s cult following and a healthy readership, in 1990 we introduced Danny the Street: a sentient transvestite street, inspired by the popular British drag artiste Danny LaRue, that roamed around the world inserting itself quietly and unobtrusively into the street plans of different cities. This was the product of a conversation I'd had with Brendan McCarthy in Dublin.

I began to receive letters from MPD and abuse survivors or from gay kids thanking me for introducing them to the queer slang vocabulary of "palari," a hitherto unheralded aspect of their culture but familiar to any-one in Britain who'd grown up listening to the camp characters Julian and Sandy on the BBC radio comedy *Round the Horne*. I felt I was finally con-necting with my own people, an imagined secret constituency of glamor-ous oddballs, and I pressed on deeper into the bush.

As a fan of the Beatles, the Doors, Jim Starlin, and *Doctor Who*, I also loved sixties movies, trippy comics, and more or less anything that could loosely be described with the word *psychedelic*, and so in 1988, after a lifetime's puritanical denial in the face of this fascination, I took the plunge and sampled a fistful of psilocybin mushrooms. Listening to a preview tape of the Bachelor Pad's first album while reading *Doom Patrol* brought about an epiphany right on cue.

In the eerie lantern-lit mushroom high—where every object in view had the lambent, numinous singularity of the murder weapons on Cluedo cards—I became aware of something new and interesting about the comic in my hands, and it brought the breakthrough I'd been seeking. Somewhere around page 17 of a particularly engrossed reading of *Doom Patrol*, a reference to an earlier plot point made me turn back to page 8. The shock was profound: It was as if I had time traveled backward. The characters had no idea I was there, but I had come from their future to observe their past, which I had already experienced in my own past. I flipped forward again, jumping to page 17, where the timeline of the characters was stalled awaiting my return to the exact moment I'd left and where page 18 was still about to happen.

Although each isolated panel seemed posed and angular, the charac-ters were filled with life and charged with meaning. They interacted with us: made us laugh, cry, feel afraid, anxious, or excited. They were living characters, and their reality was pulp and ink. What real world was this paper slice of the living DC universe? A 2-D universe, hidden in plain sight, growing and breathing in a strange symbiotic relationship with its audience in the "nonfictional" world above it.

From what little reading I'd done, I concluded that I was possibly wit-nessing the activation of some kind of hologram. Inert materials primed by artists and activated by readers brought this universe to life and allowed it to move on another week, another month, another year. Every time you interacted with it, you were different, and it became different in response.

You saw new things, gained new insights. The best comic stories never stopped delivering surprises.

I held in my 3-D hand a 2-D replayable slice of the ongoing DC universe continuum in module form. It felt like there was a whole new cosmology waiting to be explored. My dedication to a new absolute realism was unconditional, and demanded that readers acknowledge the object in their hands and their participatory role in generating the meaning of the story.

Comics' fiery adolescence continued, and the turbulence subsided a little as the hunched defensive loner relaxed into his own skin, got laid, got a haircut, chilled out, and began to dance with cute girls. The brief era of art superheroes had arrived.

By the end of the decade, I was clambering out of my shell. I was earning a living as a comic-book writer, living in a flat in Glasgow's West End with my beautiful girlfriend and the four cats, playing in a band, and making art with my sister and our coterie of glamorous and creative friends. I was successful. We dined in London restaurants with beautiful transvestite waiters. The French culture minister invited me to a dinner in Angoulême. I was courted by filmmakers, producers, and their glamorous assistants. Comics and the arts. Bridges were being built. The Brits would try anything. They had friends in bands. When Pop Will Eat Itself sang "Alan Moore knows the score," it brought the full thrill of acceptance into the mainstream of the pop chart.

With *Doom Patrol* I was drawing on the art, culture, and hallucinogens I'd been exploring. With the fractured, angular art of Richard Case, *Doom Patrol* reconnected the World's Strangest Heroes with their roots and gave me the freedom to be myself at last. My efforts attracted the attention of postmodern analysts like Steven Shaviro, whose book *Doom Patrols* drew flattering connections between my work and some of the great currents of postmodernist thought. This was what I'd always wanted. I appreciated the high-level engagement with what to me were high-level attempts to communicate. The old art school dream was coming true at last. The success of the graphic novel had created a demand for new material worthy of the superior format, and I had a project I thought might be appropriate. *Watchmen*, like the structured, precious films of Peter Greenaway, no longer suited my tastes. My peers and I were upstarts with big ideas and unlikely ambitions. The grim 'n' gritty comics had nothing to say to me about my life anymore. I chose to turn away from the mean streets, the fire hydrants, and the steaming manhole covers of Miller, and I found what Mort Weisinger had found: gleaming gold in the underpants of the interior. While everyone else was struggling with the nuts and bolts of how superheroes might function in a strictly real-world setting, I decided I would plant my flag in the world of dreams, automatic writing, visions, and magic, where I felt suddenly more comfortable after the Puritan years. With its subtitle filleted from Philip Larkin's poem "Church Going," my dark Batman story *Arkham Asylum: A Serious House on Serious Earth* was deliberately elliptical, European, and provocative. It was produced especially for the era of the coffee table superhero graphic novel and it looked like nothing DC Comics had done before.

Arkham Asylum, created in collaboration with artist Dave McKean, was pitched as a sixty-four-page story in the "prestige" format, as it was known, and aimed at the new mainstream audience for art superheroes. This meant better paper, cardboard covers, and a spine like a real book. The prestige format project was one of the new signifiers of success, and I hoped it would get me noticed. In the end, we had a new format created especially for the project, which broke ground in areas of production design and lettering, but which boasted a binding that came apart in the reader's hands as soon as the shrink wrap was off one of these otherwise lavish $15 items, making it a cruel coincidence that the book's story is set on April Fools' Day.

I had a lot to prove, and I wanted to make my mark. *Arkham Asylum* would be dense, symbolic, interior—a deliberate response to the prevailing current of Hollywood realism. Instead of Orson Welles, Alfred Hitchcock, Scorsese, and Roeg, we'd be influenced by Crowley, Jung, Artaud and *Marat/Sade*, by the Czech surrealist filmmaker Jan Svankmajer, and by his disciples, the Brothers Quay. Our story would be heavy with tarot meanings, allowing a hieratic, allusive, and quite deliberately un-American exploration of an American icon. A story of the mad and excluded. A story not of the real world but the inside of a head—Batman's head, our collective head. *Arkham Asylum* somehow struck a chord.

It took a month to write, with very few distractions, in 1987. I stayed up late to induce delirium. Drug and alcohol free, I was forced to find derangement in all the old familiar places: At four thirty in the morning after fifty hours writing without sleep, I ransacked my dream diaries and my most frightening childhood memories for content. In the end, I delivered what felt like a coherent statement of intent. It felt like the kind of high-level comic book I knew was possible and showed that the serious superhero story didn't always have to be realistic.

The first shock came when I was told that the book had been canceled. Eager to embrace influences from *Cabaret* to the Theater of Cruelty, the Joker was to have been dressed in the conical bra worn by Madonna for her "Open Your Heart" video. Warner Bros. objected to my portrayal on the grounds that it would encourage the widespread belief that Jack Nicholson, the feted actor lined up to play the Joker in an upcoming $40 million Batman movie, was a transvestite.

I wrote a long, impassioned letter to Jenette Kahn, and after some tense negotiations, we managed to keep the Joker in high heels at least, and *Arkham Asylum* went back on the schedule. I was sure that Nicholson would have loved it even more if he could have played the Clown Prince of Crime in a dress, but in the end, it was Heath Ledger who immortalized the tranny Joker in 2008's *The Dark Knight*, vindicating my foresight.

Before the book went on sale Karen Berger called to tell me I was rich. Initial orders were for 120,000 copies, with Dave and me on a dollar royalty for each. To date, we've sold over a half million copies, making *Arkham Asylum: A Serious House on Serious Earth* the bestselling original graphic novel of all time.

The book reads up and down rather than left to right, McKean's tall, narrow panels evoke church windows, test tubes, the cracks between shutters, and the spines of books, and they create a bad fairy-tale sense of confinement and of toppling, falling dominoes set in motion a long time ago.

Dave McKean was bearded and intense. I was beardless and slow to make friends, but we bonded on the *Arkham Asylum* tour and found some common ground in our love of art, fringe theater, and Dennis Potter drama. DC had never organized a countrywide signing tour before, so Dave and I became helpless glazed guinea pigs in an experiment to see how far, how fast, and how many stores we could visit in a week. I recall a delirium of snow-struck plane flights, fitful microsleeps in cars that rolled through backgrounds of endless fields that never seemed to change until it was time to decant into another cheesy hotel, another comic store. I remember Minneapolis and the statue of Ho Tai, the so-called laughing Buddha, in the restaurant where we had our only decent meal in the midst of a nightmare of fast-food joints and gas station kiosks. I still dream of the rotten stink of syrup and electricity that was my first impression of the United States. And I gagged on the inedible chocolate bars, but America was another world, another open door through which I could see a new version of my life. America was promise and adventure. I felt revitalized, inspired, as I watched ice crystals form within seconds in Dave's beard while we scuttled across the frozen sidewalk between our cab and the front door of some Chicago hotel looming in a blizzard.

In winter 1989, with comics and their creators appearing in Britain's *The Face* magazine and on TV, we crossed the American continent and back in the time it takes to scrawl a page or two of hallucinatory recollections. A day in Los Angeles, signing in Golden Apple on the exotic sidewalks of Melrose Avenue, where we discovered that actor Anthony Perkins—Norman Bates himself, and one of my pantheon of neurotic boy outsider heroes—loved *Arkham Asylum*. Then San Francisco, days after the big quake, with the lights of the Bay Bridge slicing by as REM played on the car sound system scoring my semiconscious awareness. I loved to travel. Hailing taxis on Broadway, black coated, newly born as the star of my own biography at last, I wondered where I could go next, what I could be. Jimmy Olsen's "disguise kit" beckoned.

Arkham Asylum seems to have maintained its appeal over a generation, inspired the most successful superhero video game ever, and is number five on the *New York Times* graphic novel bestseller list as I write this, two decades after its first release. Dave McKean, who has gone on to produce innovative fine art comics, films, and music scores, remains slightly embarrassed by it, but I've always secretly loved its shrill, suicide eyeliner version of the Dark Knight.

Acclaimed by audiences outside the community, the book was often described as incomprehensible, meaningless, and pretentious by many of those within, who tended to get prickly when I insisted that there were no rules to making superhero comics. Alan Moore scored payback when he praised Dave McKean's efforts but described the result as "a gilded turd" nevertheless. This was, I must add, after I'd cruelly dismissed *Watchmen* as "the 300-page equivalent of a 6th form poem" in a semispoof interview with style magazine *i-D*, so I felt compelled to take my lumps with a grin.

Nevertheless, the accusations of pretension stung horribly. I was a working-class dropout pretending to be the art student he never was. I was full of big talk, but big talk was all I'd ever had. The moon mirror of *Arkham Asylum*, held up to me, revealed the grotesque mask of snide contempt I'd constructed to mask my uncertainty. The obsession with art and fashion, myths, and popular music with which I'd separated myself from my roots now seemed as false as Granny's teeth. No more "influences," I decided; no more plagiarism or quotes from the Romantics. I would shave my head before male pattern baldness could ruin my Beatles cut and be my own naked self.

CHAPTER 15

THE HATEFUL DEAD

IN HIS INTRODUCTION to the Graphitti Designs collected edition of *Watchmen*, Alan Moore had bid a typically thunderous farewell to superheroes, declaring *Watchmen* to be his last word on the subject: "I wish the superhero well in whatever capable hands guide his flight in the future, but for my part, I'm eager to get back to earth." It turned out to be only the first of a series of hyperbolic retirement announcements that would enliven Moore's career as a writer of superhero comics, but there was no doubting the intent; if Alan Moore was closing the book on a fifty-year story, there was nowhere left to go. After pushing his fastidiously logical approach to two very different conclusions in *Marvelman* and *Watchmen*, there was, Moore implied, simply nothing left worth saying. Both books were complete and definitive statements, both absolute in their finality. One took the realistic strand to its natural limit; the other took the poetic, utopian strand to its own logical conclusion.

Most professionals in the superhero comic-book industry gloomily agreed with Moore's sonorous valedictory address; the endgame had been played, conceptually, formally, thematically. After Moore, there was nowhere to go that didn't feel stupid and self-conscious. The big man had spoken. The superheroes had been cast from Eden by their bearded judge, made to confront their silly clothes and denounce their own outmoded values. Condemned from the pulpit, stripped of their protective, self-deceiving masks and hoods, they stood naked, ridiculous, and obsolete.

How would they get out of this one?

A kind of exhausted resignation soaked in as the comics industry tried to deal with *Watchmen* by stoically refusing to recognize what made it great, concentrating instead on the violence and sex and perceived realism. Themes of brutal urban vigilantism were playing out in an increasingly stylized set of post-Miller gestures. It was felt that no one could possibly follow these great milestones without asking why anyone should have to. The smart money had moved on to create graphic novel projects aimed at a fondly imagined emerging market of adults with no real interest in superhero stories. People were making comics inspired by literature, theater, and poetry, and I wanted to be part of that too. But I was also accepting well-paid superhero projects at DC and had no intention of approaching them as the last embers of a spent blaze, or the dying coals of the house that Moore Burned Down.

Some of the earliest notable responses to *Watchmen* offered very different attempts to frame the superhero concept in adult terms.

Pat Mills was one of the team of writers responsible for creating *2000 AD*. He had a Kirbyesque world-building talent and was capable of effortlessly generating massive, well-thought-out fictional realities with iconic, memorable central characters, unique story locations, and original plots. A vicious streak and a strange sense of humor completed the picture. It was Mills who turned the sixteenth-century painting *The Garden of Earthly Delights* by Hieronymus Bosch into a spooky and unnerving role-playing adventure for the comic *Dice Man*.

Where *Watchmen* was scholarly and elegiac, *Marshal Law* by Mills and his regular *2000 AD* collaborator, artist Kevin O'Neill (first published by Epic Comics), specialized in spite and savagery. The logo was contained in a US flag shaped like an automatic pistol. Mills and O'Neill's Superman stand-in, the Public Spirit, was shown injecting himself in the arm on a grubby toilet. The sole mordantly spare caption read, "I'M WORRIED ABOUT BUCK." Another opening page had a crucified Jesus painted on the underside of a US bomber as it rained napalm death on a South

American village. The saga was a tortured, frantic torrent of Mills and O'Neill's primal scream storytelling. Since the days of Weisinger, no superhero stories had come this close to bugging out on the analyst's couch. Mills seemed too intelligent to be serious, but there was something raw and real about the psychological insights of *Marshal Law* that gave its cynicism a genuine, edgy authority as Marshal Law worked through his hatred of women, his job, and, above all, superheroes.

Where Alan Moore had peered beneath the masks to find frightened, confused, hopeful people very much like the rest of us, Mills found only deviants, perverts, liars, and monsters. He saw superheroes as emblematic of regressive reactionary forces and disastrous foreign policy. They were America's self-delusion, a fantasy of US omnipotence that Mills despised and set about eviscerating with the glee of a revolutionary on a purge. If superheroes were the face of mythic America, Mills planned to rub their noses in the shit of real-life America—which he exposed with meticulously researched, coldly delivered info-dump captions detailing a world of CIA dirty tricks, torture camps, denial, vivisection, corrupt politics, and ruined lives. This was hard-core lefty comics, taking the superhero back to his socialist roots with a shot of sleazy antisocial satire.

Weisinger's were the fantasies of a buttoned-up postwar drive to act normal and get on with the future. Mills was bursting a boil. In Kevin O'Neill he had an artist who drew bursting boils like no artist before or since. Among his other accomplishments, O'Neill is the only artist whose style itself has been banned by the Comics Code Authority on the grounds that simply looking at his work is liable to disturb or offend! O'Neill follows in a tradition of the cartoon grotesque that goes back via Gerald Scarfe and Ralph Steadman to William Hogarth and James Gilray rather than Jack Kirby. O'Neill's scabrous imagination matched Mills's volcanic outpouring of venom and he designed hundreds of distinctive costumed characters only to humiliate, burn, torture, eviscerate, hang, crucify, or drown them all in scenes of visceral close-up violence descended directly from the excesses of EC. His malignantly ugly superheroes were covered with slogans, branded and colonized by semiotic debris in the form of boastful graffiti, reconstituted ad jingles, and filthy nursery rhymes. O'Neill's world, a riot of jagged stained glass, faces, and distorted stressed anatomy, mocked the athletic hero body with drawings of engorged steroidal deformities that mirrored the ruined personalities beneath. Heroes and villains alike could contort on a beat into Francis Bacon's screaming popes, all teeth and gums and pain, bulging, veiny muscles, and cracked bug eyes.

Mills plunged the ponderous, trendy self-analysis of superheroes past its ultraviolet limit and on into the crazy black beyond. He dragged the corpse of superhero comics into a dark alley and mutilated it with exquisite finesse.

Marshal Law's credo might have been Mills's own: "I HUNT HEROES. HAVEN'T FOUND ANY YET." And, like Mills, the hero was unable to deny his unhealthy entanglement with a world he despised.

In *Marshal Law Takes Manhattan,* Mills and O'Neill gave us barely obscured parodies of the Marvel heroes in therapy, deconstructed into a set of pop-psych complexes as a parody of *Arkham Asylum.* With customary relish, they dissected the Marvel stable, all of whom were conceived and sold as "heroes with problems." Mills and O'Neill set about making these problems explicit, forcing them into seedy, contemptuous close-up. Their "Spider-Man" became a compulsive masturbator; a shy science student who only came to life when he dressed in his bristling bug suit and sprayed spurts of sticky white webbing across the rooftops, ejaculating wildly as he somersaulted across the Manhattan skyline. The "Daredevil" character was ruthlessly mocked for his blindness and dressed in clashing colors. "Doctor Strange" spouted glossolalic gibberish while his hands jerked in cruel spastic parody of the original's magical passes and gestures.

Mills's attitude toward the US-inspired nostalgia market that was keeping outmoded, outdated characters alive was no more unambiguous than when Marshal Law went up against a plague of superzombies, all drawn to resemble Golden Age characters, and portrayed Zenith/me as a character called Everest, who was morbidly obsessed with cadaverous American heroes. This definitive story produced the single line that seemed to encapsulate the entire series when our hero split the skull of an undead hero with a cry of "*EAT SHIT AND LIVE, ASSHOLE!*"

With Mills unable to sustain his rage, *Marshal Law* sputtered off the boil in a series of unfinished stories. The pressurized avalanche of righteous pus had to drain eventually. A crossover with Clive Barker's *Hellraiser* characters delved into pleasure and pain like a letter to *Forum* magazine written by a middle-aged man experimenting with S/M for the first time.

It was said of *Marshal Law* that *Watchmen* killed the superhero but that *Marshal Law* danced on its corpse.

Yet try as they might, the superhero would simply return from the dead with new powers, as he always did, to wreak vengeance on his would-be destroyers. Far from killing the superhero, *Watchmen* had opened up the concept for examination and reinvigorated its potential. My friends and I were young enough to feel quite differently from the old pros. We didn't think the superheroes in their gaudy outfits looked stupid at all. We thought they looked cool, and, like Ken Kesey in the 1950s, we saw them as vehicles for the transcendent spiritual values that were coming back into vogue in a connected global-travel culture after the fall of the Berlin Wall at the dawn of nineties.

I wanted more from my fictions. Naturally contrary, I'd tired of hearing about what superheroes would be like if they were real, only for it to be exactly the same as us at our worst: venal, corrupt, bemused, and stupid.

Realism had become confused with a particularly adolescent kind of pessimism and angry sexuality that I was beginning to find confining.

What would happen if all those macho men superheroes came out of the goddamn closet?

Britain's comic-book writers were comfortable with ambiguous sexuality, and they saw in the notion of the costumed identity—so fundamental to the appeal of the superhero—a strain of narcissistic display not too far removed from the world of the fetishist or transvestite. The performer.

Our approach to gay superheroes was knowing and nonjudgmental. Alan Moore, after all, had slipped hints of an affair between Hooded Justice and Captain Metropolis, two of his first-generation *Watchmen* heroes. Most comic-book creators had a natural sympathy for outsiders and underdogs, and support for the gay community tended to be decisive but often unobtrusive in the more progressive titles. The eighties saw a number of well-meaning attempts to introduce gay superheroes such as the ludicrously over-the-top Extraño (a kind of Rio Carnival twist on Doctor Strange) and the militant Northstar, who announced his tastes to the world in the heat of battle with a clarion call that set the gay cause back by at least thirty years.—"*I AM GAY!*"

In Britain, Don Melia and Lionel Gracey-Whitman published *Matt Black,* the adventures of the UK's first "out" superhero written and drawn by gay men, before launching *Heartbreak Hotel*—another Brit Com anthology title with comic strips and articles based around musical themes. When Don died of AIDS in 1992, it felt like another nail in the coffin of an era of art and experimentation. The Americans were already wresting control of their beloved superheroes away from the cynical Brits and rebuilding them for a future based on Hollywood action movies, not literature and poofy Euro cinema.

Combining Detroit dance music with British psychedelia, offshoots of the acid-house music scene were infiltrating all areas of UK artistic culture. I'd always been too cool to dance, but this music had me on the floor, and I loved it.

The new superheroine of the age was Tank Girl, drawn by Jamie Hewlett and written by Alan Martin (and eventually published by Dark Horse Comics). Tank Girl had a shaved head, lived in a strange cartoon Australia, and fucked a talking kangaroo. With its spiky, exuberant line, its influences from Saturday morning cartoons and *manga,* Hewlett's work was fresh, sexy, and playful—miles away from the ponderous gloom and political pessimism of Moore and Miller, or the vicious cynicism of Mills. These were comics by bright and bushy-tailed young people designed to entertain others like themselves on sunny lysergic afternoons.

Jamie went on to find further fame as one-quarter of the band Gorillaz, providing the artwork and animation for its videos, shows, and CD packaging.

When Hewlett and Alan Martin ditched the Riot Grrrl elements and re-created *Tank Girl* with a dizzy, south coast Brighton beatnik style, out went the Doc Martens boots and in came minidresses, flowers, and Tree Top orange spiked with MDMA. The influence of ecstasy culture brought a fuzzed-out stream-of-consciousness raga-drone to the material that gave it a new direction, while alienating many of the tough girls and dykes who'd made Tank Girl an icon of their culture.

The United Kingdom Comic Art Conventions ("Yoo-kak" as it was known) became riots of alcohol, drug abuse, and suspect behavior. There were more girls now, attracted by the youth, the energy, and the style-mag write-ups. I even had my own gang of friends—Steve Yeowell, Mark Millar, John Smith, Chris Weston, Rian Hughes, Peter Milligan, Jamie Hewlett, Philip Bond, Simon Bisley—and didn't feel the need to hang about outside the hospitality suite anymore. We felt different, we felt like pioneers. We were making a wedge in the final years of the Thatcher Götterdämmerung, and we considered ourselves artists, free to express the new spirit of the age using the freshly sharpened tool of the comics. The now ponderous political seriousness of the eighties was about to be overturned by a new flippancy and a cartoon optimism that seems, in hindsight, poignant.

The Berlin Wall and everything it represented now crumbled with a surprising lack of resistance, like stale meringue. It was as if we'd woken up in the plot of a utopian sci-fi story. The future was back in vogue, and perhaps because the last time the future had really been popular was somewhere in the Silver Age sixties, there was a revival of styles and attitudes from that era.

The gender confusions and reorganizations of masculine-feminine boundaries that marked the eighties had outgrown their welcome, so men became lads and women were babes. There was a new infantilization of culture as the idea of what was "adult" gave in to the desire of baby boomers to never outgrow their childhood pleasures. Geek culture and collector culture began slowly to infiltrate the mainstream with videos and later DVDs. The popular recreational drug of the day gave rise to a sunlit, cheerful Zen togetherness that recalled hippie afternoons in a playful recapitulation of a generation's childhood. Even Margaret Thatcher was gone, betrayed by her party. Frail and shell shocked, the Iron Lady shuffled offstage as she had in *Miracleman* no. 18. In an age of glasnost and perestroika, the nuclear fears of *Watchmen* and *Marvelman* seemed quaint. It was time for superheroes to wipe the tears from their eyes and rediscover fun.

Endless vistas seemed to stretch into chromed and kinky-booted futurity: The world of the Legion of Super-Heroes was on its way, almost visible on the electric blue horizon. Girls who looked like the citizens of my daydreaming future meta-republics had arrived on the dance floors of the local nightclubs, as if from Time Bubbles launched in the thirty-first century—the hair bunches, bell bottoms, and crop tops, the fetish vinyl, high heels, Goth eyeliner, metallic wigs, and MDMA turned ordinary discos into meetings at the Legion Club House as tailored by Dave Cockrum.

The world of "Cyberia," as Douglas Rushkoff dubbed it in his book of the same name, had arrived.

The superheroes responded by mutating into more colorful and baroque forms than before. *Watchmen* wasn't a headstone after all, just the end of one particular line of inquiry.

Back in Britain, Milligan and McCarthy brought their collaboration to a pinnacle with the sensuous *Rogan Gosh*, a perfectly timed piece of multicultural psychedelic surrealism. Published in six parts in the anthology title *Revolver,* the dance-era successor to the punk *Crisis,* Rogan Gosh was a true supergod, a blue-skinned "karmanaut" enmeshed in the tacky snares of samsara in the company of a brutish South London boy named Dean.

Rogan Gosh addressed the nature of life, death, consciousness, and meaning with the characteristic wit of Milligan's voice at a fresh peak and the boundless supercompressed natural originality of McCarthy. It was of its time and ahead of its time and timeless. It flowed between several narrative voices, including Rudyard Kipling and an unnamed dying youth representing the voice of bleak rational existentialism in the face of the uninflected void. Blending their stories like spices, Milligan and McCarthy summoned all the flavors of human experience from the gutter to godhood in forty-eight dazzling pages.

McCarthy reprocessed the lush, painted look of the Amar Chitra Kathra comic books from India. Using then new color-distortion effects made possible by more sophisticated laser printers and scanners, the artwork exploded in a dozen directions, each carrying a strain of the fugue weaving it tighter to its conclusion.

Like the cosmic comics boom of the early seventies, this new psychedelic period came about as a direct response to a preceding period of realism. The focus turned again from outer concerns to inner ones, along with the presence in many of our lives of the new psychedelic drugs. There was John Broome on weed in the sixties, Starlin on acid in the seventies, Milligan and me on mushrooms, ecstasy, and champagne in the nineties.

Enigma told the remarkable story of boring Michael Smith and his life-changing encounter with the world's most powerful living being. This was Moore's Doctor Manhattan born as a hillbilly and thrown into darkness, dropped into a well at birth, where he created his own world based on nothing but the objects and animals in his immediate environment. It opened in typical Milligan fashion with a single image of a well and three captions.

"YOU COULD SAY IT ALL STARTED IN ARIZONA. TWENTY-FIVE YEARS AGO ON A FARM. IT WAS AN ORDINARY SORT OF FARM IN ARIZONA. THE KIND OF PLACE WHERE YOU'D HAVE SEXUAL RELATIONS WITH YOUR PARENTS AND END UP SHOOTING SOMEONE."

This autistic superman discovered his humanity when he fell in love with Everyman Michael Smith and transformed himself into an image of Michael's childhood comic-book hero the Enigma. The routines, deadlines, and expectations that had set limits on Michael's life disintegrated under the influence of the Enigma, until even his sexuality was reconstructed when he and the Enigma became lovers.

Enigma's narration was provided by a sardonic voice-over commentary:

"IT'S LIKE THE **BOOK OF REVELATIONS** BUT FUNNIER. IT'S LIKE THE **LAST TRUMPET** BUT HOPELESSLY OUT OF TUNE. IT'S LIKE THE PERENNIAL BATTLE BETWEEN **GOOD** AND **EVIL** BUT NO ONE CAN QUITE WORK OUT WHICH IS WHICH ANYMORE AND MOST PEOPLE DON'T EVEN KNOW WHAT PERENNIAL **MEANS**."

It was a voice that could never quite disentangle itself from the text or remain truly omniscient in spite of its mocking detachment. *Enigma* subverted genre by having its all-powerful central figure on a quest to find in himself the humanity and compassion that will allow him to confront the ultimate enemy in the form of his own deranged mother (building up to a climactic confrontation, a "fight scene" that occurs after the last page of the story). When Michael finally discovered that it was the power of the Enigma that made him gay and was given the opportunity to return to his previous life of routine straight sex and boredom, he elected to remain the person he'd become.

Duncan Fegredo's art had a fluid grace and delicacy that brought the world of Enigma to life across panels swirling with the serpentine spirals of the lizards and wells and searing suns of Arizona. Enigma was a godlike superbeing born from the lowest depths, culturally, socially, and physically. Autistic, omnipotent, bereft of role models, the character known as Enigma spoke of the strangeness and isolation of being special in a way that Doctor Manhattan could not match. And when the identity of the series' sardonic narrator was finally revealed on the second-to-last page of the story in a breathtaking masterstroke that changed everything, the effect was of a lightning strike of bright comprehension that compelled us to return to the beginning with a heartbreaking new knowledge that refreshed every line of the text.

I'd reached the point where I didn't feel I had to do any more superhero comics. I felt I could be myself and open up new territory to explore. I preferred a bit of absurdist humor with my superheroes, too. I saw life as essentially ridiculous and inexplicable and found it hard to get into the minds of truly evil characters. My villains were all delusional, ultimately preposterous, as I imagined myself to be.

Meanwhile, in Barcelona, I learned to drink screwdrivers and munch on hashish in the company of DC editor Art Young and Peter Milligan and found that intoxication agreed with me and cured what had seemed a natural state of mild anxiety and depression. Milligan and I traveled to a comics convention in the gorgeous walled town of Lucca in northern Italy near Pisa to perfect the art of spending all day in the bar, making ourselves unavailable to the press.

"I'm afraid Peter Milligan can't come to the phone right now. He's dizzy," I'd say gravely in response to every anxious inquiry from the media. "Very dizzy."

Across the room, Milligan ordered a fourth round of drinks—on the convention organizers' tab, of course.

"Tell the TV people perhaps tomorrow will be better. It's just with the travel. The dizziness is getting worse. Even I'm starting to feel it . . ."

Together we stood on the rocks at Lerici, not far from where our mutual hero the poet drowned in 1822, with Milligan drunk, yelling defiantly at the surf, "You've had Shelley but you won't have me!" as it broke over our feet, sending the two of us stumbling back to safety like a couple of big Romantic jessies.

Art Young replaced Tom Peyer as my editor on *Doom Patrol* before accepting an offer to move to London to head Vertigo's British office. Ensconced in a well-appointed Soho apartment, the tall, handsome twentysomething came out (as no surprise to any of us, it must be said) in the hedonistic fireworks party of MDMA and thumping trance. In its brief life, Vertigo London blossomed into a glittering mirror-ball where the future of comics was cooked and served by cackling pranksters on shiny chemicals.

The Sandman—Neil Gaiman's revisioning of the superhero team as contemporary mythology—was the last and biggest success of the Brit-lit comics wave. Sandman was a Gardner Fox concept from 1939, which had already passed through several iterations: originally clad in a suit, tie, cape, and gas mask, he slipped into gold-and-purple tights for a few adventures with kid partner Sandy the Golden Boy and the new creative team of Joe Simon and Jack Kirby. In 1974, Kirby retrieved the name and stuck it on a fresh creation. This cosmic Sandman was the protector of the Dream Dimension in stories that aimed at an audience of younger children and failed to attract the teens and college kids who were now buying comics.

Gaiman stayed with the dream theme for his own update, but everything else was fresh. His Sandman borrowed the traditional trappings of superhero comics: the skinny, pale hero had a cape and a helmet that he sometimes wore; he had a magical ruby of destiny; he had a castle in the Dreaming; and he even had a kind of team of his own in the form of the Endless, a group of anthropomorphized eternal principles with names all beginning in D—like Delirium, Destiny, Despair, Destruction, and the series breakout star, Death, re-created by Gaiman and his artists as a funny and wise teenage Goth girl with spiky hair, an ankh necklace, and spray-on black jeans. From familiar foundations he built something brand-new. *The Sandman* ran for seven years, during which the idea and Gaiman's ambition grew so far from their roots in superhero comics that the book basically invented a new genre at the intersection of fantasy fiction, horror, and literature.

The Len Wein–Don McGregor school of poetic narration rose to a new prominence in the hands of delicate stylists such as Moore and Gaiman, whose lapidary prose captions attracted a new, hip audience from outside the traditional comics fan base. Gaiman's friendship with singer/

songwriter Tori Amos inspired the lyric "Me and Neil'll be hanging out with the dream king" from the song "Tear in Your Heart" on her 1992 album *Little Earthquakes*, and soon the writer was to be found working and playing golf with Alice Cooper and Sammy Hagar. A confident and clever young man with a plan, Gaiman carefully polished and promoted his brand while so many of us were spending our money on drink and drugs and acting as if it would always be this way, always this easy.

But these live dissections, these autopsies of the American Dream conducted on the operating tables of chic Brits, would soon come to an end. Nobody wanted to read about miserable, wimpy emo superheroes anymore anyway.

The Americans had figured out how to fight back.

CHAPTER 16

IMAGE VERSUS SUBSTANCE

THE ART SCHOOL invasion defined one strand of superhero development, which mostly refined itself in the Vertigo imprint established at DC. Vertigo books were owned by their creators, and there was no bar on content. In celebration of the new latitude, my comic *The Invisibles* opened with a character screaming "*Fuuuuuck!*" Karen Berger had established herself as the go-to girl for securing British talent. She seemed to genuinely like us, and the respect was mutual. She'd been rewarded with her own imprint where new content and more contemporary ideas could be generated away from the DC universe, with its monolithic continuity and its caped characters dating back to times and attitudes that barely anyone left alive could recall or comprehend. Fantasy, sci-fi, Gothic, and political were in, superheroes were out—in a moment equivalent to the "weird" comics boom of the early seventies or the blossoming of EC in the fifties.

We Brits rode in on a wave of self-belief and arrogance and now we were off to do our own thing. We were quitting the superheroes, leaving them to the Americans, who would not suffer our changes for long or gladly. US comics' response was devastating when it came and effectively ended the art school phase of mainstream superhero comics.

Rob Liefeld and Todd McFarlane had both apprenticed to little fanfare at DC. There they perfected their styles before being snapped up by Marvel, which could always offer more lucrative deals and was always happy to watch DC do the work of developing talent.

McFarlane's *Spider-Man* run sold nine million copies. Not since the heyday of comics in the sixties had sales peaked like this, bumped up by the multiple variant covers, the collector's item limited-edition foil, or holographic enhancements. The decision to target the collectors' market seemed to have paid off handsomely.

By anyone's reckoning, this was crazy money.

Chris Claremont had shown the way. He'd stuck with *X-Men* to deliver a steady, ongoing, bizarre soap opera in which the characters could become children or animals or travel across time, space, and alternate dimensions with ease. His stories had taken on the anything-goes quality of Weisinger-era Supermen but with an added twist of S/M role play that gave it a gloss of adult wickedness.

The sales were consistently high, and Claremont's royalties were piling up. Soon he was able to buy his mother a Learjet, or so the story went. This was no longer a business for out-of-work pulp writers or I'd-do-it-free fans turned pro; this was a medium where outsider artists could work out their kinks on a regular basis, in public, and make big money in the process.

So the star system developed. Once it had been Batman who mattered; henceforth it would be the combination of character and creator that really made the difference. It would be Frank Miller's Batman or Brian Bolland's Batman that brought in the audience dollars. And after a decade in the hands of the writers, it was time for comic-book artists to remind the world who really made the rules in this "visual medium," as it was so often described whenever we writers got too big for our brogues. The backlash, when it came, took the form of severing of the cord linking American superheroes and the UK alternative arts scene. The previous few years had been dominated by superstar writers, and mainstream press attention had tended to focus on the improvement of story content and narrative technique—at the expense of the drawing. Now the visual constituent was wrenching its domination back with an

unabashed return to old-school punching, kicking, and exploding superhero comics.

While the Brits remained foolishly intent on creating comic stories
worthy of review alongside the latest novels in the *Guardian* literary
section, a group of young American artists were preparing undeniable
proof that comics would do much better business if they just looked cool
and stopped trying to be so goddamned clever. At the time, it was a
dreadful setback for the idea of "grown-up" superhero comics. In hindsight, it was America's inevitable reaction to *Watchmen*, and the only response that could possibly be effective: Fuck realism, we just want our
superheroes to look cool and kick ten thousand kinds of ass.

Image Comics was a different kind of punk. Founded in 1991 by a group
of successful and popular artists—including Todd McFarlane, Jim Lee,
and Rob Liefeld—who'd made their names on Marvel properties before
tiring of their treatment at the hands of the company's accountants, this
was no po-mo ironic art school sneer. The Image gang were the Ramones,
all gabba-gabba glorious incoherence. Image comics seemed tailored toward bored, cynical kids in the Valley or heartland suburbia, post-ironic
Bill and Ted Gen X airheads who'd grown up privileged on a diet of *Star
Wars*, MTV, McDs, mosh pits, and metal. Image had a lot in common
with European house music, too. Like hard-core dance, Image stripped
away all the frills—all the boring bits—and left only a straight-ahead,
hard-punching beat.

Artists had learned that they could make ten times their page rate by
selling the original pages to collectors, and the more iconic the page, the
more money it would fetch. A full-page or double-page shot of the title
character or team was best. A similar shot of a new character or team
was almost as good—better if the new team graduated to its own spin-
off book. Soon Image comics came to resemble pinup catalogues. Rob
Liefeld in particular developed a hyperkinetic narrative style where a
new superteam would be introduced on almost every other double-
page spread. Creating characters was easy for Liefeld and the Image
boys. The fragrantly poetic hero and villain names of the past—the
Doctors and Professors, Lads and Lasses—were replaced by punchier

names ripped raw and unprocessed from the pages of nearby dictionaries; there were "tough" names like Barricade, Brigade, Thrust, Magnum, Grifter, and Pulse for the men, while the women were called things like Vogue, Zealot, and Catwalk.

Villains now had to compete with the heroes for tags like Deathshead or Blood Pack. Image superheroes led the howling horde with permanent enameled snarls and pinpoint eyes. Consumed by rage or grief or rage or sometimes grief, they romped across outlandishly nonnaturalistic artistic landscapes, rippling with muscle meat and steroidal attitude. The kind of direct copying that would have been impossible in 1945 was now a profitable business model. Anyone could, and many did, create "analogues" of DC and Marvel superheroes in ersatz "universes" photocopied from the structural gestures of the old originals. Superman could become Supreme in Liefeld's hands, or Mr. Majestic in Jim Lee's. Lee's Wonder Woman was a warrior nun named Zealot; Liefeld's was a princess named Glory. Mc-Farlane, to his credit, forged a style of his own by uniting horror and superhero comics in a way that was designed for transmedia exploitation, but many of the others were happy to use tried-and-tested concepts with new names and costumes that were crisscrossed with a bewildering, nonfunctional tangle of straps, pouches, buckles, harnesses, and leather garter belts (on men). It was how Batman's utility belt might look if it was left to grow wild and free in every direction.

There was a science to some of this: The Image artists had made their names on high-profile Marvel comics, and readers expected to find those comics at certain predictable places on the shelves of specialist stores, so it's no coincidence that Todd McFarlane chose the name *Spawn* for his first venture after *Spider-Man*. He knew where in the alphabet readers looked for his book's name. Unable to infringe on the X trademark, Jim Lee was still able to occupy a nearby space on the shelves with his new *WildC.A.T.S* title. Rob Liefeld went from *X-Force* to *Youngblood*. The art school crew had sought validation in the literary columns, only to be dismissed by media tastemakers as a lurid, passing fad. Image couldn't care less what authors Iris Murdoch and Martin Amis, or the readers of the Sunday newspaper supplements, thought about them. They were here to have fun and make money—enough money to play endless Mega Drive, hang out at the beach, buy a car, fuck cuties, whatever. Then retire.

If the whole process could be accomplished within a span of months, so much the better.

Variant covers appealed to the speculator market. Driven by collectors convinced that these trashy foil alternatives, printed in their thousands, were in some way going to be scarce or valuable in the future, prices were briefly inflated, and comics stores enjoyed a boom time that left the Image crew very wealthy indeed. By appealing to the lowest common denominator, they had identified and then supplied a huge, new market: bored teenage boys growing up with *The Terminator*, PlayStation, and Mega Drive who wanted no-nonsense action heroes in the Arnold Schwarzenegger–Bruce Willis style.

Jim Lee had absorbed Adams and Byrne, then added his own steely refinements to the Romantic style. His men were impossibly handsome, with high angular cheekbones, piercing eyes, and permanent Clint Eastwood stubble. His women were all outlandishly long-legged supermodels, untouchably perfect in their glossy makeup and barely there costumes. Lee was a Princeton University physics graduate, and his *WildC.A.T.S* can be seen as an equation: Conflicted leader plus big guy plus man with claws plus ice maiden plus fiery sex kitten plus physically challenged mentor equals megasuccess. It was as if someone somewhere had handed out a superhero team assembly kit to several different men and asked them to create their own Frankenstein. Lee cleaned up. They all cleaned up, of course, but of all the Image artists, his drawing skills improved the most dramatically from an already strong base. And he was a natural businessman. In 1998 he sold his Image offshoot, WildStorm Productions, to DC before being promoted to copublisher in 2010 alongside Dan DiDio. He got back to work developing the next-generation version of the DC universe online and drawing Frank Miller's flip and divisive *All Star Batman and Robin the Boy Wonder* comic, which brought back a bracing dose of farce to the strip and drove the purists wild with its depiction of a cackling Batman yelling lines like "WHAT, ARE YOU **DENSE**? ARE YOU **RETARDED** OR SOMETHING? WHO THE HELL DO YOU **THINK** I AM? I'M THE GODDAMN **BATMAN!**"

Rob Liefeld was the poster boy for Image. Certainly no physics magna cum laude but as shrewd an operator in his own way as Lee, he had the cornflakes-fed grin of a twelve-year-old California surfer. He looked like his name should be Skip or Spanky, but it was Rob, which was good enough. With his baseball cap and his wide-eyed love of trash culture, Liefeld spoke for a new generation of American kids. Not outsiders, not punks, not hippies or geeks; they were the Gen X-ers, the forgotten demographic, the kids too ordinary to merit their own movement, too depoliticized for manifestos. Their power fantasies were not of social justice or utopian reform but of nihilistic, aimless hedonism or revenge. Like so many of my favorite punk bands, however, Liefeld's enthusiastic, arrogant amateurism enflamed a generation of young artists. If Rob could get away with his barely original characters, his blizzard of crosshatched lines, the heroic legs that tapered to tiny screwdriver feet, and the multitudinous array of new muscles he'd invented for the human forearm alone, anyone could do it. He was mocked, but his style was his own.

Image made Liefeld rich, and an appearance in a Spike Lee–directed Levi's jeans commercial even made him briefly famous. His drawings never missed any opportunity to inflict some elaborate new deformity upon the human physique. His ideas were secondhand, his research nonexistent, his vision eccentric and quite unique in every detail. He was a superstar. When the script called for the appearance of a group of Nazi scientists, he drew them as modern men in modern clothes with background detail only where he could be bothered to sketch in a vague wall, screen, or rock. Period detail would only get in the way of another shot of a clenched-teeth hero crashing through a window in a shower of unconvincing glass shards, to disembowel foes with names like Stryfe, Carnyge, and Murdy'r.

The Image heroes *killed*: readily and without mercy. They understood that Gen X didn't want super Boy Scouts. They were post-Miller superheroes, off the leash, finally able to hit the bad guys where it hurt. When the talented Jim Valentino unveiled the pallid, Batman-inspired *Shadowhawk* title, it was distinguished only by its hero's rampaging AIDS infection and a crime-fighting specialty that amounted to snapping the spines of any thuggish ne'er-do-wells who made the mistake of crossing his path. While UK youth celebrated the fall of the Berlin Wall by dancing to anything that ticked or pulsed, American indie kids were snotty and uncomfortable in the midst of plenty, willing the whole world toward some kind of vague suicide pact, some love affair with a shotgun. Young middle-class Americans became ever more captivated

by the violent lives of lower-income gangsters or contract killers, policemen, and soldiers.

Like those young readers, Image heroes suffered like no others had ever
suffered, and none more so than Spawn. Disfigured, diseased, outcast, he
personified the scarred America of *River's Edge*, Marilyn Manson, and *The
Crow*. Grunge music emerged as a prowling, whining, snarling soundtrack
to the lives of kids who had to pretend really hard to be scared anymore.

Every band has its own defining couple of notes: The Beatles' orgasmic
"Whoooh!" said everything you need to know about their androgynous
upbeat appeal. Johnny Rotten's "Nyaaaa" was a sneer of disgust and disillusion. The defining sound of grunge came as a nasal whine of pain, a
suicide psychedelia. The Crying Boy was back in a new guise, hiding his
fear behind a moist and inwardly directed rage. Skinny boys with cigarette
voices and mournful beauty called us to witness their immaculately
scored dramas of self-extinction. With no more Red Menace, the American
psyche seemed to turn on itself again with a renewed determination and
fury, as if it had been gnawing on its own foot for so long that it couldn't
deal with the disappearance of the trap and just kept on going all the way
down to the marrow.

Todd McFarlane's art was the sound of death metal rendered into jagged lines and claustrophobic verticals. Spawn's immense crackling cape
echoed the crazed storm of webs surrounding McFarlane's stylized depiction of Spider-Man for Marvel. McFarlane pages offered full-size images,
two-panel spreads. His writing strained like a team of rabid huskies
against the leash of the English language.

McFarlane drenched his superhero stories in a suffocating miasma of
violence and bad religion, where cold-eyed angels and demons played
out their amoral struggles with doomed human beings trapped in the
middle. Unlike the gods and demigods of Kirby and Starlin's stories,
these sci-fi angels and demons had no interest in people as anything
other than cannon fodder in their vicious struggles. The angels were
every bit as devious, violent, and murderous as their infernal counterparts. The dial was never tuned to anything less than "total bugfuck
hysteria" in a given Spawn story, and the agony was palpable in the
slashing lines and black ink shadows. Spawn's was a world of gaping
graves, steeples backlit against flaring lightning, leering obese demons,

trash cans, and overflowing gutters. It was the world behind the strip mall, the world of the homeless, where Spawn lived as king of his own garbage heap: a mountainous, fuming haunt of child molesters, rats, and emissaries from hell.

I managed to write three issues of *Spawn* in 1993, as a result of a misunderstanding. It happened after the trade magazine *Comics International* ran a cover story claiming that I was one of several names asked to contribute the first non-McFarlane-penned stories to *Spawn*—the others being Alan Moore, Neil Gaiman, Dave Sim, and Frank Miller. It was true for the others, but not for me. When I called McFarlane to check on the rumor, he asked me to write *Spawn* anyway. It was some of the easiest work I've ever done and the most lucrative. I found a tone that seemed faithful to McFarlane's voice and followed it through to the end. McFarlane paid ten times more than anyone else at the time and reinflated a bank account that was beginning to diminish, as I blew the *Arkham Asylum* royalties on champagne, drugs, and spur-of-the-moment expeditions around the world.

Spawn appealed to kids who were desensitized to horror and violence but couldn't get enough of it. Spawn was a black hero, but his face was completely covered by his mask to ensure that his ethnicity would never become an issue. When we did see him unmasked, he was so badly burned as to be unrecognizable as anything but a noble monster, allowing McFarlane to make his point and obscure it at the same time.

Alan Moore returned to the mainstream of superheroes with a curious and telling piece entitled "In Heaven" from *Spawn* no. 8. After the collapse of his own Mad Love self-publishing venture and the abandonment of the ambitious, nonsuperhero series *Big Numbers*, there was nothing left for Moore, then in his early forties, but to go back to the place where everybody knew his name. He had branched out into performance and declared himself a magician—describing it as an alternative to going mad at forty—but when he returned to the superheroes he'd made such a show of leaving behind it was clear that he needed money to back up his small press experiments. "In Heaven," written by Moore and drawn by McFarlane, told the heartwarming story of Billy Kincaid, a sweating, unshaven child molester who'd made his first appearance in *Spawn* no. 5, as the lead in "Justice," a typically shrill and insensitive story of child murder. Billy had indulged himself with a series of brutal kiddie killings before Spawn arrived to exact unholy vengeance and send the unrepentant bastard on his way to a well-deserved eternity in hell.

Alan Moore picked up the story where McFarlane left off with Billy waking up in hell to begin a Dante-inspired journey down through the trenches and rings of the inferno toward the domain of the grand devil, the *Malebolge*, here called Malebolgia. Moore posited other hells, other devils—enough for everyone to have a special customized one of his own, with a personal Satan.

In the end, the murderer's soul was consumed by a sentient, demonic Spawn costume. The cape wrapped around him, while the mask sealed over his head and mouth to finish the job. Together with a horde of other damned souls, all swaddled head to toe in their own versions of the parasitic outfit, Billy trudged hopelessly toward his towering, chuckling satanic master in a chilling full-page image of final damnation. The end.

It was hard to read this and not imagine Alan Moore in that throng, sealed inside a superhero suit he couldn't seem to peel off, manacled and bound as he was frog-marched back into the tenth circle of the abyss, the factory, the cold engines of the Industry. In the end, superheroes were bigger than he was. Bigger than all of us. What had seemed a gravy train was now pulling into a dreary Eastern European station with conformity cops waiting on the platform. For a freelance writer, the only money left in comics was in superhero stories.

Some factions credit Moore for signaling the beginning of the end of Image with his follow-up *1963* project. In a mildly satirical sequence of pitch-perfect pastiches of the early Marvel style, Moore reinvented the Fantastic Four as Tomorrow Syndicate, while Spider-Man became the Fury. With the help of the chameleonic artist Rick Veitch, he devised meticulous reconstructions of the early Lee-Ditko-Kirby Marvel comics that went so far as to reproduce the acidic yellowing of the pages on old comics, so that each *1963* issue came pre-aged, precollected, nostalgic on the day of release.

These imitations were intended to contrast the fallen superhero comics of the Image era with their allegedly more inventive forebears, but the curmudgeonly attack on changing tastes backfired to make Image look old-fashioned—no longer young, dumb, and full of cum, but backward-looking, bitter, and, worst of all, *arty*. The comic *1963* was a water-treading joke aimed squarely at jaded adult comics readers. It was easy to tell that he'd rather be somewhere else, stretching his wings, but even the stentorian Moore had capitulated to the Image juggernaut.

All in all, Image was comics' greatest success story since Stan Lee stuck the Marvel logo on Fantastic Four. What Image Comics lacked was stories, relatable characters, and any real sense of emotional involvement with the events being depicted on the pages. It was cocaine comics, emotionally dead, creatively limited, and perfectly timely—but only for a short time. In the first rush of energy, glossy paper, and glowing color, the deficiencies barely showed, but they soon became apparent as the wait between issues that could barely be recognized apart from one another grew longer. Super Mario and Sonic the Hedgehog video games consumed the artists' time, and they were all rich enough to step back from the wage-slave production line ethic, paving the way for new talent and clearing the field for yet another new take on superheroes in this turbulent time of restless change.

Back in the Marvel and DC universes, the Dark Age heroes got darker and more unhinged, and the villains became increasingly and laughably more grotesque to keep pace. Villains became serial killers with bizarre MOs: One mummy's boy murderer might employ china dolls in his crimes, another could be equally obsessed with martyred saints or letters of the Greek alphabet—and they all had troubled childhoods. The tittering prankster of the TV series had become the eighties Joker, a psychopath who'd already demonstrated his commitment to the new sadism by using a crowbar to comically smash out the brains of Jason Todd, the second Robin, before shooting Batgirl in the spine (she's still paralyzed in a wheelchair) and taking naked pictures of her agony—which he then showed to her father, Commissioner Gordon (courtesy of Alan Moore and Brian Bolland in *The Killing Joke*).

Kyle Rayner, the new, young Green Lantern of 1994, came home one day to find his girlfriend chopped into pieces and neatly stacked on the shelves of his refrigerator by an atom-powered supervillain named Major Force. Green Lantern was angry for as long as it took to defeat the villain and somehow managed to avoid being scarred for life. He took the gorgeous Alex's gruesome death in his stride before proceeding without guilt or too many backward glances into a series of relationships with hot alien babes. The subtle psychological insights of the Moore advance were replaced with feverish inner monologues detailing the inner agony of being a superhero crime fighter in one more crumbling sewer of a city. Or worse, the hero's psychotic opponent, who more often than not thought in scratchy, oddly angled, misspelled letters. No story could pass without at least one sequence during which an unlikely innocent would find herself alone and vulnerable in some completely inappropriate inner-city back alley setting. If the victim could be a scantily dressed prostitute, the jackpot was in sight, with bonus points for a transvestite hooker. Within a few panels of any such skimpily attired naïf penetrating the seedy underbelly of the urban nightmare, a pack of human wolves would slink inevitably from the shadows with grins and glinting knives. Part *A Clockwork Orange*, part Kings Road punk, the leering thugs would encircle their busty prey, and gibber in some private rapists' pidgin. Only at the very last moment would Batman/Wolverine/Daredevil swoop down from the shadows to deliver a righteous display of satisfyingly brutal bone-breaking vengeance. The modern vigilante liked to leave his criminal enemies hospitalized or even permanently disabled.

"YOU DON'T **GET** IT, BOY . . . THIS ISN'T A **MUDHOLE** . . . IT'S AN **OPERATING TABLE.** AND I'M THE **SURGEON**," Batman had boasted in *The Dark Knight Returns*, clearly superior to his opponents in every department, from class, privilege, and style to athletic ability, even as he menaced them with paraplegia. The idea of a terrorist threat to America was ludicrous in those halcyon days, so superheroes tended not to stretch themselves too far, content with beating up more than their fair share of unfit, unhealthy junkies and muggers.

This was noir condensed to a jet-black absurdity. Alone in its bedroom with overblown fantasies of grand agency, the adolescent comic book, the result of cloistering in direct-market retail outlets, had attenuated into a refined and specialized product, but the geek superhero was about to glimpse itself in the mirror, standing there in stained underpants and playing air guitar. The deep earnestness, the crass sensationalism, the aching desire to be taken seriously had become a ridiculous posture, and things would have to change. Hormones were beginning to subside. Calmer voices were breaking through.

The Dark Age period of adolescent introversion had yielded spectacular transfigurative insights that could now be put to more positive use. After facing his darkest dark night of the soul, the superhero was back, stronger than ever. Now it was time to get out there and meet some girls. In their coming Renaissance period, the superheroes would not only recover their dignity but also begin the journey off the page and into our lives.

CHAPTER 17

KING MOB—MY LIFE AS A SUPERHERO

IN THE YEARS after 1996, the impatient energies of transformation that had dismantled the Berlin Wall, brick by painted brick, and dethroned eternal Thatcher, began to pry apart my own personal status quo with the same restless diligence and attention to detail.

Having missed out on the imagined tilt-a-whirl of teen life, I was tormented by regrets. I felt my own existence had grown stale and repetitive. My own personality seemed crudely fashioned, and often ill-fitting. I was sick of chronic vague depression, and chose to treat myself as another poorly conceived and barely developed character in need of a revamp. After much agonizing, I split from Judy after nine years together.

I'd already made my mind up to accept complete surrender to a process of transformation, an ego-dissolving ordeal that I felt sure would give me new things to write about, new things to say, and a new way to see the world.

Growing up, I'd immersed myself in the life stories of Byron and Shelley, Rimbaud and Verlaine, and the Beats, and knew by heart the biographies of the sixties psychonauts like Kesey, Timothy Leary, and John Lilly. They were my perhaps dubious role models in my project of reinvention. I set about debugging my glitchy personality with Robert Anton Wilson's *Quantum Psychology*, NLP, acting classes, tae kwon do lessons, and yoga sessions. The *Arkham Asylum* royalties gave me an opportunity to play the part of "writer" to the hilt. I pictured myself lolling with floppy, frilled cuffs like Thomas Chatterton, suicidal and glamorous on a chaise, quaffing absinthe and laudanum as I dipped a peacock quill into luminous green ink and scrawled feverish fantasies by black candlelight. Insensate on the South Seas, scandalous in the Forum. I longed to experience the full freedom and scale of the archetypal writer's world and made up my mind to leave a biography as good as the ones I was consuming so avidly.

I'd already contrived to meet Animal Man in his own environment, creating with the help of artist Chaz Truog what I came to call a "fiction suit." This was a way of "descending," as I saw it, into the 2-D world, where I could interact directly with the inhabitants of the DC universe on their own terms, in the form of a drawing.

I wanted to take that direct contact idea further, to explore the interface between fact and fiction in a more personally involving way. I wondered if I could arrange an exchange that would affect my life and real world as profoundly as it would the paper world.

As I brought *Doom Patrol* to a close after four years of monthly surrealist folderol, *Lonely Planet* guides were being spread on the carpet to help map out a year away from comics and routine.

I plotted an immense path around the world via India, Thailand, Indonesia, Singapore, Java, Bali, Australia, Fiji, Los Angeles, and New Mexico before coming home, I hoped, transformed.

On my first night in the dull hotel near the airport, I celebrated this personal rebirth by taking an electric razor to hair that was undeniably thinning. It felt ritualistic; my fear of going bald and becoming immediately unattractive was faced with a drift of brown shavings on the floor. In the mirror was a blank character design, a smiley face. I could now revamp myself as I had Animal Man, the Doom Patrol, and Batman. I was becoming a superhero.

It didn't begin as well as I'd hoped. Culture shocked, dripping in the heat, and unable to move in the ramshackle dream city streets of New Delhi without attracting a thousand touts offering water, shoe shines, or ear cleaning services, I'd never seen beggars with noses munched down to knotholes by leprosy. The days were spent staggering through the over-load, the nights were homesick and lonely in a windowless room, at the soul's lowest sump, and far from home, bald, thirty-two, out of my depth.

It all started to get better on a taxi ride to Agra. I'll never forget the turtle crawling laboriously across a road between thundering eighteen-wheel juggernauts. I began to enjoy myself. Nobody knew me, nobody expected anything from me, and I was forced to rely on resources I never knew I had.

Three days on the state bus from Leh to Manali down through vertigi-nous Himalayan passes with no guardrails and the burned-out shells of state buses evenly spaced, far, far below.

A train ride from Bangkok, through the mountains of Malaysia. The Snake Temples on Penang. On a bus ride to Singapore via Kuala Lumpur, its multicolored Futurist pinnacles as fabulous as Oz in the nighttime half-awake.

There were magic mushroom omelets in Jogjakarta, motorbike rides to the scrolling, humid ruins of Prambanan and Borobodur, that colos-sal grounded flying saucer mandala where the story of life is cast in terraced stone.

In a tropical garden in Bali, glad to be alive, drunk on oxygen and the explosive fragrance of tropical flowers, I imagined myself going around and around the world like a satellite, resting up in hotel gardens between fleapits, sending scripts from Pacific atolls and rain forest villages. My friend Emilio, from the homemade-comics afternoons in the seventies, had relocated to the USA to meet his estranged father before winding up just outside Santa Fe, where he found work and accommodation with a young and prominent Zuni ceramic artist. I spent a life-changing few days on the Pueblo, ending with an acid trip on the sacred mesa overlooking the Rio Grande, as it flowed like a river of chocolate through a dawn Eden. My mind felt ten thousand times bigger. I'd found my SHAZAM!

Back home, I felt reborn, more confident, creative, and alive than ever before. To my surprise and delight, the girls loved my bald head and constantly wanted to touch it. So much for all those years worrying about hair loss.

I had to get deeper into the magical experiments, too. I'd read about the cross-dressing berdache tradition of shamanism, and decided I could do a glossy, chaos magic, nineties version of that as a way of shaking out my identity and becoming my own complete opposite. A few fetish-wear catalogues later, and I'd assembled a shiny disguise kit that put Jimmy Olsen's to shame. The clothes and makeup allowed me to transform into a female alter ego I now created to stand in for me during the darker magical operations I was undertaking. I was entering some very bizarre areas of consciousness and found that the "girl" was smarter and more courageous and could more easily negotiate with and fend off predatory "demonic" entities. At least that was my personal justification for some epically odd behavior. If it helps, consider demons to be "bad" states of mind, crippling neuroses or fears. Dressed in black vinyl with six-inch heels, showgirl makeup, and a blond wig, I began to traffic freely with angelic forces, Voudon *loa*, Enochian Kings and Seniors, the scum of the Goetia and the Tunnels of Set, Lovecraftian entities, and other fictional characters and aliens. I performed rituals of all kinds to see if they worked, and they delivered every time. As mad as it sounds, and it sounds a bit mental even to me these days, all of this was done with the rigor and precision of scientific experiment.

If I found some dangerous or interesting ritual in a book, I'd give it a go to see what effect it would have on my consciousness. The results were never less than revelatory. Psychedelics gave these experiences the fidelity of a *Star Trek* 3-D holodeck experience. Demons and angels had faces now of white-hot, razor-edged purity or grotesque puzzle box monstrosity. Gods and fictional creatures had forms that seemed tangible. These beings could be painted and rendered from memory, and they fit the descriptions left by intrepid psychonauts who'd been this way before me.

I have no real explanations for a lot of this but numerous speculations that may find their way into another book one day. I simply allowed all this to happen under some vague direction from a diamond-interior Protestant straight-edge self that seemed to never lose control. I carefully filmed and recorded these rituals, during which I could be heard to speak in tongues, and with multiple voices—some male, some female, some utterly inhuman. Every day was a party. I would drink champagne or take mushrooms and write comics. My friends came around to drink, take mushrooms, and make music. Every fortnight my teenage girlfriend would visit from London to join in the fun or otherwise. When I got bored, I'd buy a plane ticket and fly somewhere I'd never been before. The world felt intensely awake and alive, as if I'd somehow learned to dance with it a little. My comics began to reflect this new freedom, becoming looser, more personal, and more psychedelic in that word's literal sense of "mind manifesting." It was hard to believe that people were paying me for what I soon came to realize was something close to self-therapy. I could assume only that my problems and doubts, my hopes and dreams, were shared by many others who could relate to the way I was framing them as fiction.

In 1993 I toured America in the company of my *Zenith* collaborator Steve Yeowell and artist Jill Thompson. Jill was a striking alternative girl in her early twenties who drew herself into everything she did. Her work had a quirky cobwebby line with an instinctive grasp of composition and character acting. Together the three of us lurched across the States, winding up in San Francisco to live out my undemanding dreams of visiting the famed independent City Lights bookshop dressed in a hooped black-and-white T-shirt, leather jacket, peaked cap, and Beatle boots. I'd decided to let my hair grow back, and it had reached a particularly wispy stage of its return, like cat grass sprouting from a window box, hence the leather hat, which I'd convinced myself made me look like a Beat writer. Drunk in the Vesuvio Café, where heroes like Ginsberg, Kerouac, and Burroughs had gathered before I was born, I felt I'd finally become who I was meant to be and I no longer cared what anyone thought.

"You should be in a cage," the writer Tom Peyer observed as we all danced like strippers on MDMA during the "50 Years of LSD" celebration commemorating Albert Hofmann's synthesis of the wonder chemical.

Next day, still sparkling merrily and wafting through Golden Gate Park, pinning flowers to Peyer's curly locks, we all vowed to work on something new and amazing together, something that could change the world. Reading Terence McKenna's *True Hallucinations* in Chicago's O'Hare International Airport, tripping at thirty-three thousand feet, aged thirty-three, like Jesus in a post–Cold War international thaw, at large in a charmed era of dancing and hugging and doing what thou wilt in exotic latitudes, I was happy, I was cured all right, and my straight-edge years had left me looking ten years fresher than I actually was.

Another minifortune arrived in the mail courtesy of those three issues of *Spawn* for Todd McFarlane, and it looked as though I could fund this boho lifestyle indefinitely. I imagined writing one hundred pages of comics a year and making enough wedge to live large for another five, but the bubble was already popping, and I had to admit that this period of grace was unlikely to last for much longer.

The media interest in comics had subsided. The speculators who had entered the comics market now began to leave, pulling the business down around them as they beat a hasty retreat. The boom, like the Dutch "tulip mania" economic bubble of 1636–37, had been artificially generated. There was big money, it was true, in collectibles, number one issues, and special printings, but the inflated prices relied on scarcity and the endless multiple-foil-enhanced, 3-D holographic variants put out by Image and Marvel in particular were in anything but short supply.

The good times were coming to an end, but more important for me, I missed the discipline of regular writing and needed a forum to express my newly forming worldview. I was happy to get back to work on a new kind of comic book.

I decided to do a book where I could contain and address all my interests. I already had the vague concept of a vast occult conspiracy thriller set in the real world, in the present day. I flipped through the ever-reliable *Brewer's Dictionary of Phrase and Fable* in search of odd character names and interesting ideas, and that's where I found the title *The Invisibles* and the names of several of the lead characters, like Ragged Robin—who Jill drew to resemble herself—King Mob, and the transvestite witch Lord Fanny.

The characters were all parts of me mixed with people I knew: Dane McGowan, the Liverpool street punk destined to be a bodhisattva, was the working-class cynic who still kept me in check. King Mob was the art school fashion-conscious chaos magician. Ragged Robin was my sensible anima; Lord Fanny, my indomitable tranny witch disguise; and Boy, the practical, pragmatic voice of reason that made sure I always paid my bills and taxes and fed the cats. Even the villains, blind Gnostic forces of repression, tyranny, and cruelty, were my own self-hate and fear given form, named and tamed like demons.

King Mob was the action lead. He was shaven headed, my age, and he'd made his money as a writer. As an anarchist activist, he borrowed some of his praxis from my dad. He was a Tantric sex adept, a kung fu master, and wore slick leather coats, PVC pants, and mirror shades. King Mob was the punk James Bond, the archetypal *Matrix* dude five years before the release of that movie, and like Neo, like Morpheus, he had come to understand that his entire universe was embedded in something bigger and stranger. I intended to blend my life, my appearance, my world with his until I could no longer tell us apart. I had no idea what I was letting myself in for.

The world of *The Invisibles* was our own. I took care to keep it current, with the names of bands and movies and references to events of the day. It was a world so close to our own, it even had the comic *The Invisibles* in it, in a scene where King Mob reads and comments on the comic as a glamorization of his own real life. The model had to be perfect. The voodoo doll universe I was making needed to map our own closely to allow me to slip between them across the permeable page surface.

Having set this up, I wanted people to keep reading. I had to promise revelations, and so I promised the Secret of the Universe—not quite sure what I was going to deliver but certain I'd figure it out.

In February 1994, depressed and becalmed in Scotland's winter monochrome, I bought a plane ticket to New Zealand with the intention of bungee jumping my way back to happiness.

As I stood, questioning my impulsiveness, on the edge of a short plank of wood extending from the Kawarau River Bridge, heavy elastic rope tied around my ankles, I held in my tightly clenched fist a magical sigil drawn on paper. The idea was to launch the *Invisibles* project with a bang, "lighting the blue touch paper," as it were, of a dynamic "hypersigil"—a magical spell in comic-book form that would have the power to change lives, and maybe the world.

"What do you do for a living?" the operator asked, in an effort to distract me from the single shrieking note of fear in my head.

I had to think about it.

"I'm a writer," I remembered through the squall of neuronal white noise. "I write *Batman* comics."

"Well, this'll give you something to write about, mate." He grinned, counting down from five.

By the time he reached "three," I could feel the last scrappy "Don't do it!" thoughts raining like numbers off a screen. Then there was nothing going on in there at all.

"One!" he said. The whole horizon took on the static, eternal quality of a print on a hotel bedroom wall.

And off I went.

I hurled the sigil down into that moment of whipping chaos, before being bounced to a stop like a yo-yo under the arched eyebrow structures of the bridge above me. The surge of endorphins afterward brought an ecstatic rush that powered me all the way to Auckland, where I stumbled across a rare copy of Michael Bertiaux's fabled grimoire *The Voudon Gnostic Workbook,* containing descriptions and names for the scorpion gods I'd encountered the year previously. The spell was off to a good start, I reckoned.

Then, in spring that year, came Kathmandu. The idea for this expedition had been triggered by a Dan Cruickshank documentary that my friend and Mixers bandmate Ulric and I caught on TV one night, in which the veteran TV host tramped his way through India, Nepal, and Tibet in the footsteps of the Buddha. We were particularly intrigued by Cruickshank's description of the Shwayambunath temple in Kathmandu valley. There are 365 steps leading up the hill to the temple on top, and it's said that any pilgrim who is able to ascend the steps on one lungful of air will attain enlightenment in this life.

The climb was so easy as to be barely remarkable for two fit young men. Beyond a beaming smile from a wizened Buddhist monk that felt like a brief audience with Yoda, nothing much happened that day. We sat drinking lemon soda, or wandered the refuse-mountain embankments of the Bagmati River, where huge black boars immersed their bodies in the sour fumes, cooling off in the yellow fever heat of another yelping, clattering, reeking day.

After a few drunken days in Thamel, the town's tourist sink, we crawled back to our room at the Vajra Hotel, the House of the Lightning Bolt, where on our last day before leaving, Ulric felt ill and retired to bed. The bell-ringing, dog-barking cacophony of Kathmandu life went on, as it did all day and all night. I went up to the roof garden with my notebook. The Kathmandu football team was playing Bhaktapur in a nearby field, like a cargo cult version of the World Cup—the impromptu pitch marked out by the spectators, the teams in T-shirts and shorts.

I watched for a while, then retired to my deckchair, where I started writing an introductory text piece for the second issue of *The Invisibles* at the same time as composing an essay I'd been commissioned to write for the late Simon Dwyer's much-missed alternative culture journal *Rapid Eye*.

And then it all kicked off as the cheers from the crowd warped into a high-powered whine that might have been starship engine turbines. I looked up from my notebook to see the Shwayambunath temple rearrange itself like a Transformer into some kind of chrome lionlike configuration with exhaust pipes and tubular spirit conduits, seeming to blast its raw holiness into the sky as raging searchlight storms. Overwhelmed, I stumbled back downstairs in the grip of an immense seismic shift in awareness that I could not, hand on heart, attribute to the sole action of the tiny piece of hashish I'd ingested. I negotiated wildly distorting spiral stone steps and candles on the way down from the roof, to flop on my bunk and hang on tight. Ulric was asleep on the other side of the room. I could feel something enormous, unseen, squeezing down the narrow corridor of oncoming moments, looking for me.

I began to lose contact with the physical reality of the room, seeing in its place cranky ancient streets, and leaning ceramic houses haunted by gnomish presences, the current dragging me deeper through hallucinatory ancestral wynds and crabby cobbled alleyways that felt like the archaic half-remembered dreams of childhood.

The effect intensified.

Now there were what I can describe only as "presences" emerging from the walls and furniture. Perhaps someone else would call these rippling, dribbling blobs of pure holographic meta-material angels or extraterrestrials. They were made of what might have been mercury or flowing liquid chrome and informed me that I had caused this to happen and now had to deal with the consequences of my actions. Where did I want to go?

I had no idea. Alpha Centauri was the first thing that came to mind, and the thought was followed by a toppling, spiraling "stargate" effect that completely erased the room from my consciousness and replaced it with another reality.

© DC COMICS

I saw in front of me a perfect astronomical vista with three nearby suns of different sizes. I became aware of a huge pond-water-green planetary horizon, which I plunged toward. There I met intelligent sculptures made of what appeared to be ultraviolet neon tubes, which fanned and changed configuration as they attempted to communicate with me. My "angels" dragged me out of there, admonishing me for offending the cultural sensibilities of the Alpha Centauri. (I included a version of them as the Electrokind in All-Star *Superman*—tungsten-gas aliens with brittle glass exoskeletons.)

"Okay," they said. "This is what you wanted. The secret of the universe."

I was *turned around*, is the simplest way of thinking about it. My sense of being was rotated through a plane I could not now point to, turning my attention to an environment that was not entirely incompatible with theoretical physics' descriptions of hyperspace, or the bulk, a hypothesized mega-medium in which entire universes are suspended. This was like that, but real—more real than anything I had ever experienced.

Whatever it was, I had fully entered a space that felt both vaulted and enclosed, like an immense cathedral but also infinite in horizon. It was as if infinity and eternity could be contained and bottled inside something much bigger than both. The space was profound azure blue in all directions, laced with bright silver lines and grid traceries that came and went, ghost blueprints zipping up and down an invisible monofilament scaffolding all around me. I could not feel my body or open my eyes in the physical world. I wouldn't have wanted to. My real eyes were wide open here. Stranger yet, my arrival in this place felt like a homecoming. All the cares and fears of the mortal world were gone, replaced by the hum of immaculate industry, divine creativity, and, through it all, that unmistakable always-known sense of deep familiarity, of belonging and completion.

This was as weird as anything that Batman or Superman had faced in the pages of *World's Finest*.

Continued same time, same channel, next chapter, new age!

PART 4

THE RENAISSANCE

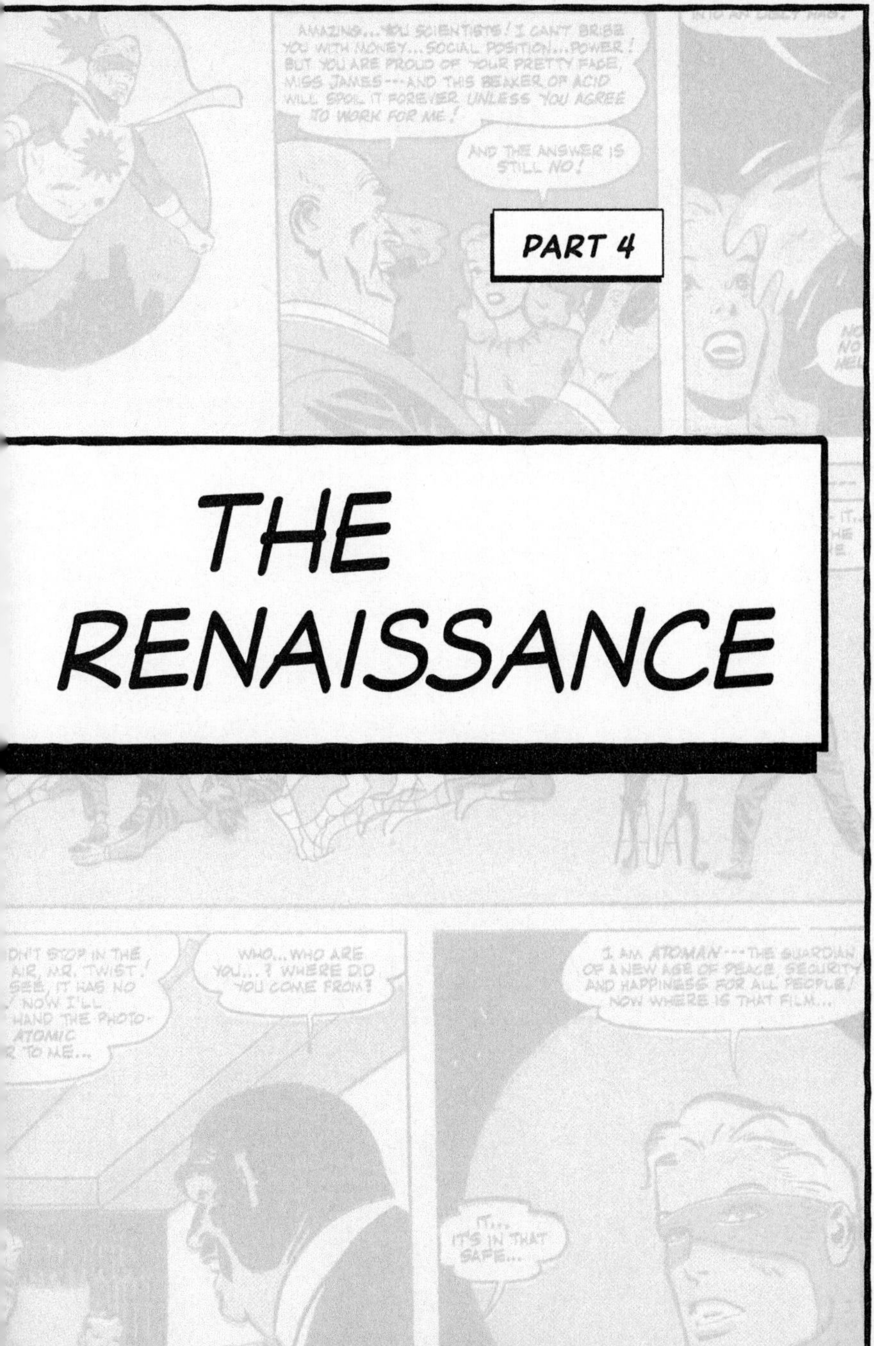

AMAZING... YOU SCIENTISTS! I CAN'T BRIBE YOU WITH MONEY... SOCIAL POSITION... POWER! BUT YOU ARE PROUD OF YOUR PRETTY FACE, MISS JAMES---AND THIS BEAKER OF ACID WILL SPOIL IT FOREVER UNLESS YOU AGREE TO WORK FOR ME!
AND THE ANSWER IS STILL NO!
WHO... WHO ARE YOU...? WHERE DID YOU COME FROM?
I AM ATOMAN---THE GUARDIAN OF A NEW AGE OF PEACE, SECURITY AND HAPPINESS FOR ALL PEOPLE! NOW WHERE IS THAT FILM...
IT... IT'S IN THAT SAFE...

CHAPTER 18

MAN OF
MUSCLE MYSTERY

AFTER *DOOM PATROL* and *Arkham*, I felt I was all but done with traditional costumed superheroes. New forms could be created, new kinds of heroes and more experimental work like *The Invisibles* was possible. However, I found myself drawn back to superheroes.

Flex Mentallo, Man of Muscle Mystery, published in 1996, was the result. It was the story of the finest, noblest, most selfless hero of all; an exemplar of a type of hero who had all but disappeared. With one tremendous curl of his bicep, he had transformed the Pentagon into a circle, in the pages of *Doom Patrol* no. 44, thereby negating its occult energies.

In *Flex Mentallo* I wanted to answer the question that writers are always asked: "Where do you get your ideas?" It's always seemed quite obvious to me: I look inside my head and there they are. Flex was an attempt to lay out that process on the page. This was my chance to show what I meant when I talked about realistic superheroes.

Flex Mentallo, Man of Muscle Mystery also turned out to be the first of many successful collaborations with my long-term friend and partner, Frank Quitely. I'd seen the artwork of the pseudonymous Quitely ("Quite frankly") in the Scottish underground dope humor magazine *Electric*

Soup, where his clean-lined, detailed, and expert draftsmanship stood head and shoulders above the gifted R. Crumb and Gilbert Shelton wannabes with whom he shared page space. Quitely's drawing style reminded me of Winsor McCay, Arthur Rackham, Harry Clarke, and other great illustrators of the early twentieth century, with touches of Norman Rockwell, early Disney, and the Max Fleischer Studios animators. Best of all, he seemed to have taken the majority of his inspiration from Dudley D. Watkins, the genius behind D. C. Thomson's *The Broons* (*The Browns*) and *Oor Wullie* (*Our William*) newspaper strips that were such an indispensable part of a Scottish childhood. The idea of Watkins-style American superheroes appealed to me greatly.

Frank Quitely was the artist I wished I could be. He had a command of anatomy, movement, and expression that gave every character a nuanced life and personality that leapt off the page, and unlike many of his peers who used extensive photo reference, Quitely's world was generated inside his head; he was able to draw anything from memory and imagination. Even better, Quitely had no particular interest in or love for superhero comics and their conventions, which meant that he could approach them with a fresh eye and few assumptions.

Flex Mentallo made his debut in the pages of *Doom Patrol* with an origin story that was a surreal take on "THE INSULT THAT MADE A MAN OUT OF MAC," a famous single-page comic strip advertisement for the Charles Atlas bodybuilding course. Aimed at the skinny and obese, this ad was a perennial in the back pages of Silver Age superhero comics. Atlas promised that he could "make a man out of you" if you only had the guts to "gamble a stamp."

"DARN IT! I'M SICK AND TIRED OF BEING A SCARECROW! [THINKS] WHY CAN'T I BE A REAL HE-MAN LIKE THOSE OTHER FELLOWS ON THE BEACH?"

I sampled the beautiful, muscular prose of the Atlas pitch and put it in the mouth of a Captain Marvelesque "mysterious stranger" outside a gents' public toilet, to continue and elaborate upon the story of young Mac's determination to "get even."

LET ME PROVE I CAN MAKE YOU A NEW MAN! ARE YOU "FED-UP" OF SEEING THE HUSKIES WALK AWAY WITH

THE BEST OF EVERYTHING? SICK AND TIRED OF BEING
SOFT, FRAIL, SKINNY OR FLABBY—ONLY HALF-ALIVE?
YOU WANT THE "GREEK-GOD" TYPE OF PHYSIQUE THAT
WOMEN RAVE ABOUT AT THE BEACH—THE KIND THAT
MAKES OTHER FELLOWS GREEN WITH ENVY. THEN FILL
IN THIS COUPON NOW.

With these words, the mysterious stranger handed young "Mac" a coupon entitling him to a free book, *Muscle Mystery for You!*

I DON'T SUPPOSE I'LL EVER KNOW WHERE THAT BOOK
CAME FROM. IT CONTAINED **TECHNIQUES** THAT I CAN'T
EVEN BEGIN TO HINT AT. MUSCLE POWER DEVELOPED TO
SUCH A DEGREE THAT IT COULD BE USED TO **READ
MINDS,** SEE INTO THE FUTURE, INTO **OTHER DIMEN-
SIONS**, EVEN.

Flex was the pre–Dark Age superhero delivered—with his simple morality, his kind and friendly nature, and his hatred of bullies—into a more
sinister world. Rather than succumb, as the *Watchmen* characters did, to
real-world pressures, he would overcome them with the sheer power of
muscle mystery.

Each of the four issues took its thematic cue from a different age of
comics, so the first, entitled *Flowery Atomic Heart,* dealt with the golden
age of childhood memories and lost Edens. The second was the silver age
of transformation and young adulthood, *My Beautiful Head.* The dark
age and late adolescence were represented by issue no. 3's bleak *Dig the
Vacuum*, while *We Are All UFOs*, the final installment, anticipated that
coming, as yet unnamed, age, which almost twenty years later we're calling the Renaissance. In that respect, *Flex Mentallo, Man of Muscle Mystery* can be seen as a template for *Supergods.* Together, the four issues told
the story of the titular superhero's quest through a night city built from
what appeared to be the debris of half-forgotten comic-book memories,
in search of his lost teammate, the Fact.

But these might also have been the dying hallucinations of a suicidal
rock star tripping in a grimy back alley in the rain, while rambling over
the phone to what he thinks is a Samaritans help line.

The book was part biography, real and imagined—the story of a life I might have led if the Mixers had been successful. I saw it as the memoir of an "Earth-2 Grant Morrison," so I gave him my own childhood, and he inhabited a rough facsimile of my West End terraced town house. He was me with my cat and visiting girlfriend, my comic books, aliens, and white-hot blitzkrieg visionary nights. An odd, liminal alleyway near Charing Cross in Glasgow had often caught my eye on buzzed-up walks at three in the morning and became the setting for the main character's life-saving hallucinations—or perhaps they were his genuine contact with a departed superworld that had always existed all around us, surfacing only in our fantasies. The book showed the influence of my occult experiences too, and tried to resolve them in the context of superhero fiction, using the symbols, archetypes, and characters that had formed in my imagination to construct a kind of superhero alternative to religion.

The first cover was plastered with graphic bursts and exclamations in a frantic Pop Art saturation that quoted Infantino's great *Flash* no. 163 cover illustration: the hero's hand outstretched to make direct contact with the reader.

"STOP! YOU MUST BUY THIS COMIC OR THE EARTH IS DOOMED!"

It opened with a nine-panel grid showing a Ditkoesque "hat and trench coat" character with a fizzing cartoon bomb in his hand. The thrown bomb arced into 3-D foreground in the second panel, to explode in the third.

This explosion was the big bang itself, as we understood when cosmic expansion slowed in panel 5 to show the familiar configuration of the constellation Orion and its brightest star, Sirius.

"FLIGHT 23 IS NOW DEPARTING THROUGH THE K-9 DOORWAY."

Panels 6 and 7 began an immense reverse zoom from Orion out to the galactic spiral, seen from a distance of one hundred thousand light-years.

Panel 8 was blackness, with a single tiny white dot containing the whole universe, and in panel 9, the light of the universe itself vanished into what seemed eternal darkness.

But page 2's continuation of the disorienting reverse showed that not even the darkness can claim absolute sovereignty, when the first three panels slowly revealed it to be nothing more than the shadow in the dimple of a felt hat. The same hat, in fact, worn by the bomb-wielding mystery man we met on the first page.

Now he was a drawing of a different kind on a different scale: a spindly pen sketch on the shell of an egg, which, in panel 6, was cracked against a pan's iron rim.

"THIS IS YOUR BRAIN ON DRUGS."

Panel 7 showed a hand emptying the egg into a frying pan.

"HAVE YOU SEEN THAT ADVERT?"

Panel 8 revealed a smiling chef who turned to look directly at the reader just as Animal Man had done but without the same alarm or existential confusion.

"EGGS, EGGS, EGGS." He grinned. "WHO WANTS EGGS?"

The title page 3 was a full-page picture of our hero, smiling and winking. Flex was the superhero stripped back to his core appeal as an all but naked muscleman in leopard-print trunks and lace-up wrestling boots. He was as ludicrous, camp, serious, and completely dependable as we could possibly make him.

"EGGS? THAT'LL BE ME!"

Every single character was given his or her own distinct body language, and Quitely included twenty-three separate and distinct airport diners in the background of his splash, each reacting to the presence of this outlandish, grinning, egg-ordering muscleman with the notebook for recording his impressions. As the unreconstructed, good-hearted, unself-aware superman stood among them, some were disgusted, some were mocking, some were impressed, and some were frightened or surprised.

When a terror cell known only as Faculty X (British author Colin Wilson's term for the hidden potential of the human mind) left a fizzing cartoon anarchist bomb—like the one from pages 1 and 2—in the airport concourse, Flex leapt in to save the day, only to discover the bomb was designed not to explode but to frighten and confuse. Faculty X used bombs to "destroy not objects but certainties."

As we looked down on Flex pondering the airport bomb in a majestically composed overhead wide-angle view, the story switched on a page turn to a detailed close-up re-creation of a tabletop in a well-heeled stoner's apartment: bong, hash block, rolling papers, and a scatter of superhero comic books with titles like *Outerboy* and *Lord Limbo*, published by the fictional Stellar Comics line (named for my own DIY boyhood comics imprint). Here we were introduced to the real hero: the nameless, aimless unshaven rock star, drunk and on drugs, manically clearing out cupboards containing boxes of old comic books and his own youthful drawings of what turned out to be the adventures of Flex Mentallo. A realistically rendered scene of Mentallo in police headquarters blended into the same scene drawn by a talented ten-year-old as the story's levels of fantasy and fiction began to interact.

Flex set out through a seedy, fallen Limbo that stood for the devastated postdeconstruction landscape of superhero fiction, where kid sidekicks bereft of adult hero supervision haunted the backstreets as brutal costumed gangs, part–Burroughs Wild Boys, part–Burgess droogs, or where junkies searched for an elusive kryptonite high that would confer upon them Captain Marvel–style cosmic consciousness and apocalyptic revelatory visions of superheroes swooping in their thousands from a hole in the clouds on the Day of Judgment. I imagined superheroes had become hearsay, glimpsed in blurred photographs like Bigfoot or the Loch Ness Monster.

A third tier of the story was set in a Platonic superhero universe that was being eaten out of existence by a godlike entity known as the Absolute. The surviving superheroes, known as the Legion of Legions, had devised a desperate plan that required the creation of a whole new universe into which they could escape. The only catch: The superheroes would have to become fictional in order to survive in this new universe with its less forgiving physics. The new universe they created was, as you may have guessed, our own. Our superhero stories were race memories of our own origins in this lost world.

Like *The Invisibles*, *Flex* was a direct product of that Kathmandu experience, to which we can now return and where, if you remember, I'd just been twisted off the surface of the universe into the fifth dimension.

Moving through the rich blue space of the beyond were more creatures like the silver blobs who'd brought me there. When one of them passed right through my substance, trailing a tidal wash of emotions, I heard my mother's voice saying, "Next time I'll be you and you can be me." I saw from my own reflection that I was a mercurial hypersprite too and remembered that I always had been. I was fine with that. I understood that we were all holographic sections of something invisible to me in its entirety; I was reminded how to "plug into" the silver grid lines that zipped and glistened in and out of being all around me. These lattices, I knew, were for the input and output of pure information. There was time and space, but those were lower dimensions, useful for creating worlds in the same way that comic artists drew living worlds on paper. Here was an unending perfect day of absorbing eternal creation.

To help explain to my blown senses what was happening and why I was here, the beings were keen to show me the universe I'd just come from and how it looked. When they did, it was one of several, inside something I recall as a kind of stall of incubators.

The universe—the entire space-time continuum, from big bang to heat death, no less—was not a linear stream of events with beginning, middle, and end. That was only how it felt from the inside. In fact, the totality of existence looked more like a ball of sphincters, constantly moving through itself in a way that was hypnotic and awe inspiring to observe. There was Shakespeare scribbling *King Lear* on one wrinkled fold, and just around the corner from him, forever out of his line of sight, was the Cretaceous period and tyrannosaurs padding past his wife Anne Hathaway's cottage.

And, as if to confirm that ours was not the only universe, it was explained to me that what I was seeing was a nursery of some kind. In order to grow their "offspring," the chrome angels had to "make" time, because, as they pointed out reasonably, only in time were things able to grow as I understood it. Time was a kind of incubator, and all life on Earth was one thing, a single weird anemone-like mega-Hydra with its single-celled immortal root in the Precambrian tides and its billions of sensory branches, from ferns to people, with every single detail having its own part to play in the life cycle of a slowly complexifying, increasingly self-aware superorganism. It was as if I had been shown an infant god, attached to a placental support system called Earth, where it could grow bigger, more elaborate, more connected, and more intelligent. Growing at its tips were machine parts; cyborg tools made from the planet's mineral resources. It seemed to be constructing around itself a part-mechanical shell, like armor or a spacesuit. "It" was us, all life seen as one from the perspective of a higher dimension.

I was told to return and take up my duties as a "midwife" to this gargantuan raw nervous system. It was important to ensure the proper growth and development of the larva and to make certain it didn't panic or struggle too much when it woke up to its true nature as a singular life form. Incidentally, what we experienced as "evil" was simply the effects of inoculation against some cosmic disease, so I wasn't to worry much.

I felt slammed into the sudden weight of my meat on the bed, the rasp of breathing, reeling as sounds returned and the room jigsawed itself backward out of the void, like a kit assembled by my opening eyes. The sense of loss, the fall from heaven, was heartbreaking, but it was my origin story too—my personal induction into the cosmic corps, the army of light.

My experiment was going very nicely indeed.

The next day, Ulric and I flew home via Frankfurt, where I locked myself in an airport hotel room to fill dozens of journal pages with my attempts to describe what had just happened to me in Nepal. If nothing else, I was left with enough ideas for comic books to keep me working for another fifty years.

But there was much more: I soon discovered that I'd been sent back to Earth with my very own superpower. I was now able to "see" 5-D perspective. It became impossible to look at a cup, for instance, without seeing it as the surface of something much bigger and even more astounding; an elongated physical object that was winding back through its progress toward my table and beyond, back through its manufacture. The cup was the tip of a string that, if it could be followed back through time, had an immediate physical connection to origins in prehistoric clay beds created by the weathering of primordial rocks, composed of elements spun from a cooling star that was itself one blazing spark of an unimaginable, still-occurring explosion at the dawn of time. This one cup was all of those things in time. One day it would break, but the fragments would continue forever. And if a cup was a spectacular, constantly shape-changing, disassembling, re-forming, never-ceasing process, what about the human body itself, morphing extravagantly and more totally than any special-effects werewolf, from small, soft infancy, to hard-bodied teenage self-replicating self-aware maturity, to sagging middle age, and decomposing dry-leaf seniority? How completely has your own body changed since you were five years old? Even when we die, our physical process continues; centuries reduce our bodies to dust, recycling every atom so that the air you breathe today might contain a particle that was once Napoléon. An atom of iron in your body might once have spilled from the brow of Jesus Christ.

I could see the shapes of things and of people as the flat plane surfaces of far more complex and elaborate processes occurring in a higher dimensional location. Every human life became a trailing extension through time, not just four-limbed and two-eyed but multilimbed and billion-eyed as it wormed back from the present moment and forward into the future: a tendril, a branch on this immense, intricately writhing life tree. This biota, as science calls the totality of life on Earth.

Adding time to the world picture was like adding perspective to Renaissance paintings or finding space in the spectrum for a billion new colors, or room on the airwaves for a trillion new TV stations. There didn't need to be spirits or aliens. Everything was immortal and holy not as a result of some hidden supernatural essence but as a consequence of its material nature in time. We ourselves were miraculous, already divine in our glorious, ordinary impossibility. And it was consciousness that brought the whole thing to life, finding structure and symmetry in it, making it sing and weep and dance. I felt sure that in some way what we call consciousness would turn out to be the long-sought unified field.

I could see that the past had to exist somewhere in order for us all to be here today, but no one could take us there or even point to it. I was now very aware of myself as the front end or leading edge of something that was pushing forward into time. But more important, it stretched *behind* me, thirty-four years long, diminishing at the baby tail where it twisted up into my mother's belly and curled inward to a seed, a bud, grown from my mum's own thirty-year-long, multilimbed total physical existence from her birth to mine. She branched back into her own mother; and so it went all the way down to the dawn of life on Earth in a single unbroken line.

And the same was true for all of us. Everything that had ever lived was a twig off the same tree, a finger on the same hand. Add time, and it became blindingly obvious that the entire tree of life on Earth was alive and physically connected, across three and a half billion years. Not in any metaphysical way but literally, materially, back through all time toward the root. The same primordial mitochondrial cell that began its eternal self-cloning process in the primordial ocean was and is still dividing inside each and every one of us.

Could *mitochondria* be science's secret word for "soul"? Could the presence of an asexual immortal organism in the depths of our physical being be responsible in any way for the sensation we have of some indwelling, undying, and infinitely wise and fulfilled essence? Had my entire experience been some kind of dialogue with my own cellular structure? Was it some literal understanding of the Hermetic axiom "As above, so below"? Was I really just a cell, in the body of the earth's sole life-form? Was my relationship to this primordial consciousness like that of a helper T cell to a human body, for instance? Were soldiers hunter-killer cells?

When I died, others just like me would replace me and do exactly what I did. There would always be writers, telling the same basic stories over and over. There would always be policemen and teachers, too; were there ever years where no policemen were born? Every one of the ten billion skin scales that flake away each day was once filled with life and industry, but who mourns those tireless workers who live and die in staggering numbers just to maintain a human existence over eighty years? The only thing that made me, or any of us, special was that no one in the whole of history would ever see the universe exactly the same way any other of us saw it.

Like a caterpillar munching its merry mindless way through a leaf, the global entity, the biota beast of which we were part appeared to be devastating its environment, but something else was occurring on a different scale. The creature was consuming to fuel its metamorphosis. Even global warming could be seen as part of the incubation period, a sign of larval development reaching its crescendo, forcing us all to wake up, get moving, and leave the planet to its recovery.

Whatever it was—however you, the reader, choose to interpret this information—the experience completely rewrote me. It was a life-changing, game-changing moment that altered the trajectory of my life and work. It even gave me a kind of unshakable faith in a private religion that satisfactorily explained everything about how things work.

I'd been cursed or blessed with superhero vision, a science fiction revelation that seemed to draw to a center all the strands of my life so that everything made sense. My interest in higher dimensions, my obsession with UFOs and aliens, my job creating stories for pocket universes—it all finally added up.

In the immanent blue world, all of this had already occurred. The baby was already being born, fully grown like a fly from a maggot. Some of what they tried to show me was simply too fantastic, too reliant on higher-dimensional topographies for a 3-D mind to contain. They kept telling me to remember as much as I could as best as I could because so many of their concepts were quite simply beyond my comprehension and would not survive a return to human consciousness. "They" being distinct over-my-shoulder voices that came from inside and from somewhere else.

Television talks about the "fourth wall" of the set as being the screen itself. If so, this was a glimpse beyond the fifth wall of our shared reality. Five-dimensional intelligences could, as a condition of their geometrically elevated positions, get into our skulls quite easily, and we might expect their voices to seem to come from inside. They, in turn, could hear our thoughts as easily as we can read Batman's private inner monologues on a 2-D page. The interior of our skulls contains a portal to infinity. If my experience was not metaphor, might there be things *living* there, in that gargantuan ecological niche? Could fertile wet planets like our Earth really be nurseries where omni-anemones fed and grew to become quicksilver angels in a timeless AllNow?

This whole interlude, I can only repeat, was far more "real" than any other I have known before or since. Its colors were more resplendent, as if glowing on a celestial HD monitor. Its emotions were finer, its words expressed as huge, perfect, orchestral aggregates of symbol, emotion, and metaphor. The definition of things, especially feelings, was sharper, and the sense of being safely and finally *home* was devastating, haunting. Imagine the laser-edged precision and liquid crystalline hyperreality of computer graphics taken to powers of ten, and you will still be nowhere near this other *place*. The vast, star-spackled quantum dream room in which I sit and write as the warships parade up and down the sparkling sunlit blue of the loch might as well be a grainy black-and-white TV signal from the 1950s compared to the purity of Kathmandu's dazzling science fiction Elysium.

Understanding that boundary-shattering experience became fundamental to what I was doing, and I began to lose myself, to blur the limits between what was real and what was conceivable.

What happened to me can be interpreted in any number of ways. To some, it's sure to read as just one more trip story with no relevance to the material world. Occultists of a certain persuasion will recognize the knowledge and conversation of the holy guardian angel. My experience comfortably fit the profile for alien abduction reports, angelic contact, and temporal lobe epilepsy. None of these "explanations" for what I saw, coming as they did from a lower-resolution, flatter universe, could truly do the experience justice. Where higher dimensions are implicated, it's wise to remember the story of the blind men and the elephant and assume that all attempts to frame Kathmandu in 3-D terms are in some way absolutely true. But if it makes it easier to dismiss, feel free to assume I hallucinated the whole thing and went completely, gloriously, and very lucratively mad.

In the end, I stopped piling up rationalizations and dealt with what could be proven about this event, which was its undeniably positive effect on my life. Kathmandu fundamentally reprogrammed me and left me with a certainty stronger than faith that everything, even that which was sad and painful, was happening exactly the way it was supposed to.

All will be well, all will be well, and all manner of things will be well.

Years of living in a materialistic culture and of outwardly giving in to a kind of culturally enforced pessimism have left me with a more twenty-first-century, grounded view of that day in the Vajra.

Let's say there's a developmental level of human consciousness that was once almost mythical—Jesus, Buddha, and Allah experienced it—but which is now more freely available to a much larger percentage of the general human population, thanks to the easy bookstore and online availability of "magical" recipes and formulas, and of consciousness-altering methods.

Five-year-old children are developmentally unable to see perspective, while children of seven can. Twelfth-century artists were unable to render vanishing points on two dimensions, while fifteenth-century painters had mastered the trick to create convincing simulations of reality. Do civilizations follow the same growth and decline curve as human organisms with the same holographic imprint reiterating through all scales?

I can see how the sudden shock of accessing a natural holistic five-dimensional perspective might strike an unprepared human nervous system as contact with an alien intelligence; a "higher"-order entelechy. As far as the brain is concerned, that's exactly what it is. New neural pathways are being seared into the cortex by the demands of this way of seeing. I think the rational mind tries to make sense of its new perspective—as a child makes sense of the inner voice of dawning self-awareness by theorizing an imaginary playmate—by framing it in images of the alien, the uncanny, or the demonic. The fact that some people who've had this wake-up call report having seen aliens, while others saw Jesus, or the Devil or dead relatives, fairies or angels, suggests that the details are culturally determined.

What's important about this experience is not whether there are "real" aliens from a fifth-dimension heaven where everything is great and we're all friends. There may well be, but I have no real proof. Much of what I went through even makes sense within the current framework of string theory, with its talk of enclosed infinite vaults, its hyperdimensional panoramas of baby universes budding in hyperspace. The aliens are the least of it.

My Kathmandu vision of planet Earth's singular living form, that cosmic only child whose brain cells we are, on the other hand, requires no belief in the supernatural. Simply add the time dimension to your contemplation of life, look backward down your own history and family tree, all the way to the original mother cell three and a half billion years over your shoulder from here, and tell me if you can find one single join, or a seam, or any break.

This for me was bigger than any ultradimensional or quasi-religious afterlife, which I wouldn't be able to confirm until I died and either woke up back among the blobs or didn't. I couldn't deny that I was a tiny, short-lived temporary cell in something very, very big and very old. I even saw how that brute connection to every living thing might explain away the "supernatural" mysteries of things like telepathy or reincarnation as simple, direct connections between distant branches of the same majestic tree, like the tingle in your toe that sends a message to your brain, which launches your hand to scratch the itch.

I was deep inside my own story, further than I could have imagined. My sister covered my bedroom wardrobe with a collage of comics pages so that every time I faced my reflection, I appeared as one more panel in a tarot spread of scattered pages and images, part human, part fiction, a Gnostic superhero in PVC, shades, and shaved head.

As for drugs, I sampled various psychedelic compounds in the waning years of the nineties, hoping to re-create the Kathmandu connection. I was willing to write off the whole thing as some very enjoyable drug trip, but I never found a substance capable of reproducing that place, and I eventually gave up.

I was left with a stubborn conviction that when I died, my consciousness would start awake there, with the same shock of the utterly familiar, the same thrill-ride buzz of a job well done.

The initial shock of all this was replaced by a period of voices in the head, uncanny synchronicities, signs and dreams and remarkable new insights. I was haunted, inspired, possessed. I could lie on my bed, intone a homemade spell or evocation, and be transported to a convincing wraparound representation of a higher-conscious vibration where an infinite circle of golden Buddha beings solemnly overlook a white abyss into which the entire universe is funneling like water down a drain. It was even better than an issue of *Warlock*.

Each and every experience, even the ego-destroying blind terrors, went into the work, enriching *The Invisibles* and *JLA* a thousandfold. It was proof of the old saying "Where there's muck, there's brass." In an imagination economy, where ideas, trademarks, and intellectual properties held incalculable value, the coruscating quarry face of the interior world was the place to be. There was gold in them thar ghost mines.

I even tried to consider Kathmandu in terms of the fashionable idea that temporal lobe seizures could trigger authentic "religious" experiences. This sounded even better than 5-D angels. If science had identified a purely physical brain trigger for holistic god consciousness, would it not be in our own best interests to start pressing this button immediately and as often as we can? What would happen to the murderers and rapists in our prisons if we could stimulate a temporal lobe god-contact experience that caused them to empathize with everything in the universe? If electrical spasms in the temporal lobe are indeed capable of such remarkable world-transforming effects, let's see them become more than just another stick with which to beat an absent God to death. Push the button!

The 1990s was also the time of the ubiquitous alien head symbol, some of you may recall, a nineties freak version of the smiley face, in the era of TV's *X-Files*. In my imperial delirium, I was ready to believe that something from the future was trying to break through the walls of the world, using images of superheroes and aliens as a carrier signal.

As you might imagine, it was hard to sustain this level of controlled breakdown while running a business. My cometary rise was equaled by a fall; a plunge into dissolution. The more perverse and inhuman the enemies of the Invisibles became, the sicker I got. By the time I realized I'd become semifictional, it was too late to defend myself.

The downward spiral expressed itself in darker magic as the Invisibles faced bacterial gods from a diseased twin universe. After trying out a Voudon ritual in 1993, I found myself facing down an immense scorpion creature that tried to teach me how to psychically assassinate people by destroying their "auras." When the ritual was done, I switched on the TV to decompress and caught the last fifteen minutes of *Howard the Duck*, in which nightmarish extradimensional scorpion sorcerers attempted to clamber their way into eighties America. These spooky coincidences were commonplace, but I had no idea what I was letting myself in for when I wrote King Mob into the hands of his enemies. Tortured and drugged, he was made to believe his face was being disfigured by a necrotizing fasciitis bug.

Within three months, bacteria of a different kind had nibbled a hole in my cheek. My beautiful big house had degenerated into creepy, lightless squalor, with a duvet hung up in the bedroom window instead of curtains. I came out in boils, traditional signs of demon contact. Fortunately for me, I was physically fitter than I'd ever been, although it only delayed the inevitable for a few more months.

I'd been granted superpowers. I'd danced with monster gods and shaken souls with angels, but my end-of-act-2 reverse could no longer be denied. The Achilles' heel revealed! The death trap sprung!

On the night before I was hustled into the hospital, with what I later found out was probably less than forty-eight hours to live, I hallucinated something I recognized immediately as "Christ."

A column of light phased through the door, clear as day, then a powerful sermon seemed to download into my mind. I understood that this power I was facing was some kind of Gnostic Christ. A Christ of the Apocrypha. An almost pagan figure that I'd found at the bottom, at the last gasp. Here at the end, there was this light. Christ was suffering right there with us and promising salvation. This living radiance was nothing like the morbid fever visions of hearses and twisted window frames I'd been having. This was the force that turned dead-end junkies and alcoholics into born-again Christians, but of the whole heart-melting experience, I remember only the first resonant words:

"I am not the god of your fathers, I am the hidden stone that breaks all hearts. We have to break your heart to let the light out." These words sounded through my head, but they were bigger and more complete than any thoughts I was familiar with; more like a broadcast. The loving voice and its powerful words seemed not to be mine and offered me a stark choice there in the living room: I could die now of this disease or stay and "serve the light." I might as well have been recruited into the Green Lantern Corps, in what was for me a very genuine "cosmic" moment. I did as most of us would and elected to live. Like Captain Marvel, I wanted to go back to Earth armed with Eon's knowledge. I felt I'd lived my own *Arkham Asylum* dark night of the soul, and without the understanding that I was on a well-trod and signposted "magical" path, I'm not sure if I could have handled my illness or recovery process quite as well.

I'd reached that point in the story where I'd survived the crisis and still had a chance to be reborn with a new costume and better powers, but it was touch and go; every passing second was the ticking clock to the ultimate life-and-death cliff-hanger.

How the fuck would I get out of this one?

As it happened, as in the best serials, it was some kind of dumb luck that saved me. The day after Jesus popped by, something odd occurred. My sister was in London, and her boyfriend Gordon was on his way down for a visit. He'd just missed catching up with my mum, who'd been look-ing in on me, with increasing apprehension. She'd correctly diagnosed my appendicitis when I was twelve and now she was sure that the doc-tor's flu remedy was not what my damaged lungs really needed. She made it to her living room, looked out the window, and saw Gordon at the crossroads hailing a cab to take him to the station. She willed him to turn around, as she tells it, and he did.

Gordon came upstairs to collect a bundle of clothes for my sis. Mum told him about me, and he promised to mention it to his mate Graham, who had a good local doctor, apparently, a GP whose own bohemian temperament led him to specialize in the treatment of football stars, mu-sicians, and artists.

When he got to London, Gordon was as good as his word. Graham immediately called his miracle doc, who agreed to visit me on short no-tice. To my shame, I'm not sure that I would have acted so promptly (or at all) in the same circumstances. Graham didn't know me. He was five hundred miles away and had no idea how seriously ill I was. And yet.

The doctor checked my temperature and listened to my chest with grow-ing alarm before contacting the hospital. I felt safe at last, as if a true guard-ian angel had arrived to rescue me from the mire of disease where I could no longer function. There were no beds at the Tropical Diseases Ward (my travel history made this the obvious first port of call), but with so many coincidences already flying around, another one was attracted to all the com-motion: It just so happened that the receptionist had gone out with the doc-tor's friend. Charm and nepotism swung me a room. Within hours, I was in a private ward in Glasgow's Ruchill Hospital with a drip in my arm, while frantic doctors held me down as if I were devil possessed. They had to get the needle in when the tremors were at their most intense, so I lay shuddering, freezing, barely able to breathe as my arm was secured and blood drawn.

I was quickly diagnosed with a tempestuous *Staphylococcus aureus* in-fection in my lungs, collapsing one of them. I was septicemic and severely lacking in salts and minerals, but the good doctors pulled me back, with a warning that I could not have survived another forty-eight hours at home.

Two days later, I had a painful tube in my arm, the vein was hard as wood, but I was alive, and I could feel the venom of the scorpion *loa* succumbing to the mighty medicine of antibiotics.

Staph aureus, or golden staph, derives its distinctive color from carotene, and when the bugs had been flushed from my system, I succumbed to an epic lust for raw carrots that could be satisfied only by a daily three-pound bag from the greengrocer. Depleted, I had to consume my weight in the power elixir, the golden superfood.

Not even the junkies outside the window prowling the hospital grounds for used or discarded needles could intrude on my sense of having been rescued from the brink. I settled back to recuperate, imagining ocean sets, distant beaches, and health.

I counted the days between episodes of *Father Ted* and *Fist of Fun*, enduring a battery of painful tests to discover if the staph infection had spread to my heart, and reading comic books my friend Jim brought me from the Forbidden Planet store he owns on Buchanan Street. It was one of a growing chain of pop culture emporia that rewrote the comic shop idea for the High Street consumer. For a few days, there was even an AIDS scare, followed by a test and then the obvious relief.

My dad visited every night and told me stories from the war, his presence a calm rock. He insisted that he was trying to bore me to sleep, but it never worked that way. I could have listened to him all night.

While the doctors got on with their work, I also decided to take matters into my own hands and elected to treat the living bacteria inside me as totem animals. If, I speculated, they had a physical existence and purpose, surely they could be endowed with a mythic or magical intent by a human intelligence. In the wee small hours, with the alcoholic night nurse on duty, I spoke to the germs and promised them a starring role as the baddies in my current magnum opus, *The Invisibles*, if they left me alone. This, I explained to them, would give them a far longer life and greater symbolic significance than any mere physical overthrow of my body could offer. I gave *Staph aureus* the chance to become fiction. It was a good deal, and they seemed to go for it.

As I waited nervously for test results, I wrote King Mob's recovery into *The Invisibles*, spelling myself out of my own predicament by restoring the fiction suit to full health. If he could survive this and be stronger, so, naturally, would I. I'd made a magical model of the world, and by tweaking the model, I could seem to be able to effect actual changes in the real world.

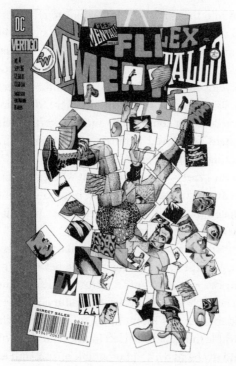

© DC COMICS

I came home, a stone and a half lighter, and promptly shaved my head for good. I wrote the final issue of *Flex Mentallo, Man of Muscle Mystery* shortly afterward on a balcony in Portugal, as the sun set, three years after writing the first one. The Frank Quitely cover showed the hero falling through space in a scattered collage where dozens of tiny images like Polaroid photos spilled, strobing and almost animated. Entitled "We Are All UFOs," it was my look ahead to the superheroes of the coming Renaissance, pouring down out of the sky in their hundreds on the final page.

My girlfriend sat in the room behind me, working on an online counterculture magazine. Suspicion, boredom, lack of commitment—our long-distance relationship couldn't take another aimless year, but it broke my flowery atomic heart when she sent me the letter that ended it all. I'd never been dumped before, and it really was about time. Now I had some idea of how Judy must have felt.

All of it went into the comics. Every breakthrough, every breakdown, became art and dollars. My diary had become my story.

The dark tunnel of the breakup year opened into sunshine when my beloved ginger cat Vinegar Tom, who'd appeared on the cover of *Animal Man* no. 26, developed a bone growth on his chin. Cancer was the immediate diagnosis, and other suspect lumps were found in his stomach. The cats were my constant companions and a powerful lifeline to responsibility. I saw them as beloved familiars who'd been with me faithfully since the beginning of my career. Although I loved them all, Tom had a special place in my heart—a tiny rescue runt who'd grown up cool, confident, and friendly. I wasn't prepared to let him go without trying every angle, so I revisited the Spiritualist Church to ask them if they knew of anyone who specialized in healing animals.

I left my number, and a very nice, very normal Glasgow woman named Lettie Moodie called the next evening with the news that it was all down to me to heal my cat. Her spirit guides were very clear about that, and she felt sure that I'd been chosen as a healer. She outlined the basic Spiritualist healing method for me, and I went home to give it a try, feeling slightly bitter that the whole thing had been left in my hands but willing to follow it through. I held my hand over a photograph of Tom and fervently asked the "healers and helpers on the Other Side" to work their magic through me. My diary records—and I'll still swear to this day—that I saw foggy white mist around my fingertips that came with a surge of emotion that brought tears to my eyes. The next day, I took my scrawny pal in a taxi from the vet surgery to the vet school, where a biopsy was expected to reveal cancer. I tried the technique again in the taxi and was again overwhelmed by tidal surges of love that seemed to be channeled directly into Tom's basket.

When the biopsy results came in, he was fine. There was, inexplicably, no trace of the alleged cancerous lumps in his stomach, and the bone growth in his jaw was benign.

I carried him home in his basket through the burnt-out winter afternoon, overjoyed. More than overjoyed, I was buzzing on some kind of euphoric frequency, like a guitar still ringing on its stand after being played by a genius. I experienced what I assumed to be inflation, in the psychological sense; I was filled to bursting with radiance, in touch, alive, and happy. I was sparking and streaming with an immense messianic sunshine energy. I woke up every day feeling like I'd necked two tabs of E, except this was a prolonged, unprecedented, and wholly natural high-altitude state of consciousness with no grungy comedown.

After passing on the healing technique to Jill Thompson, who also used it successfully on her own cat, I felt ready to embark on a new career as a savior of pets, just as Mrs. Moodie had predicted for me. But no one ever asked me to try again, and my belief in my own access to these powers faded when I was unable to prevent Tom's sweet-natured tortoise-shell sister B.B. from dying of kidney failure a year later.

After a year that was the longest I'd spent on my own since the teenage wasteland days, I was eager to join civilization. I'd taken up swimming to go with the weight training, martial arts, and yoga classes once a week. I ate only the best food, stir-fried in first-cold-pressing virgin olive oil. I wore PVC jackets and Frankensteinian Bunker boots, and I'd even become so slim during my illness that I could fit back into the ultranarrow snakeskin pattern ladies' shirts I'd worn in the band when I was nineteen. I'd seen beyond the last fading glow of irresponsible rave-era hedonism to the New Dark that was coming. I could almost smell the approach of *The Matrix*. I felt like a prophet.

I looked in the mirror, and there was King Mob grinning back. My life and his fed together in a stranger loop: Where at first I'd followed his steps, now he was following me, relying on my biography to breathe life into his backstory. Space-age bachelor pad music and the latest CDs from Paris and Tokyo DJs played in my house of magic, swirling lights, and designer chairs. The band was back together, making music and making one another laugh. I had become invisible. I was King Mob, International Man of Mystery, the James Bond of the counterculture, hanging out with sleek girls in vinyl, backstage with indie bands, footloose. My world and his drawn universe had blurred at the edges, and blended together, and now that the whole death-and-rebirth thing was safely out of the way, I was really able to enjoy myself.

It seemed as though anything was possible. Money was flowing, and nothing was too odd or out of bounds to be tried. I wrote the kind of girls I wanted to meet into *The Invisibles*, and they'd turn up a few weeks later to defy all my expectations. Using sympathetic magic to attract partners has unexpected and often unpleasant consequences, but I felt it was my duty to experiment with this hypersigil I'd built; it had brought me to death's door, I wanted to see what it could do that was more positive and life enhancing.

For a few years, the lovely things of the world synchronized into place all around me like fish in a shiny shoal. The world seemed made just for my tastes because I was writing it that way, somehow making it happen, like a cave painter drawing the hunt, or a god, or a wheel, and making it happen.

The King Mob experiment came to a close in 2000 with the concluding issue of *The Invisibles*, by which time I was more than ready to "kill Ziggy," as David Bowie had once put it. It felt like some extended art installation was finally over. I could get up off the gallery floor and go home for my tea.

CHAPTER 19

WHAT'S SO FUNNY ABOUT TRUTH, JUSTICE, AND THE AMERICAN WAY?

FLEX MENTALLO MADE me think about new ways of writing American superhero stories that didn't rely on British cynicism and self-conscious cool. The fourth issue of *Flex* hinted at the age beyond the Dark period. The signs were good. The new comics would be populated by relaxed, unashamed, confident superheroes, purged of Dark Age neuroses. There was also the small matter of my bank account. The money in comic books was in superhero comic books, and if I hoped to sustain the lifestyle to which I'd become accustomed, they were the future.

Still, I was single, newly confident, and wealthy. I was a globe-trotting freelance writer who specialized in a kind of neosurrealism that allowed me to get away with pretty much anything. I already had an articulate, enthusiastic readership, and I wanted to reach the widest possible audience, while avoiding the absurd arbitrary rewrites and malign editorial interference that often characterized my contacts with other media. Even in a bust period, comics could still be a lucrative and self-expressive business if you knew how to keep ahead of the trends.

I'd written the celebrity superhero, the outsider hero, and the freak team. I'd mined childhood nightmares and adolescent lonely nights. I was writing *The Invisibles*, which satisfied my desire to create the kind of progressive highbrow action-philosophy sex comics I loved most, and I wanted to remind prospective employers that I could still do something more mainstream. I wanted to do intelligent superhero comics that didn't rely on sexualizing cartoons, excessive violence, or nihilistic gloom. It felt like time to plunge the desiccated, overanalyzed superheroes back into the molten four-color tar pit where they could stew for a while in their own incandescent juices and reclaim their collective mojo. I drew inspiration from the cosmic comics I'd loved as a teenager and determined to write henceforth for an imagined demographic of bright and inquisitive fourteen-year-olds.

I'd heard that the sidekick comic *Teen Titans* was about to become available at DC. The book had grown in popularity to rival *X-Men* in the eighties, only to sink back into a post-*Watchmen* oblivion with sales figures that were slowly settling into the sediment at the lower end of the charts. I made a pitch for it, convinced that I could use *Teen Titans* as a vehicle for my new way forward—only to find out it had already been assigned to another creative team. However, my desire to explore the DC universe came to the attention of another editor who was by sheer coincidence looking to revitalize the ailing *Justice League* title.

The Justice League of America had been assembled in 1960 to feature all of DC's best and most popular superheroes in epic battles against foes that no single superhero, not even Superman, could hope to face alone. By 1995, the epic battle was against reader apathy, and in response DC had marshaled a team of Z-list heroes so defiantly useless that they often wasted entire issues doing nothing but eating and going to the toilet. This book seemed to be aimed at an audience embarrassed by superheroes who wouldn't be buying it anyway, leaving a regular readership of somewhere around twenty thousand a month. The last time the once mighty *Justice League* title had dominated the bestseller charts was in the eighties. That league had been played as a witty soap opera, filled with dysfunctional, bickering superheroes. But it could easily switch gears to reflect cosmic horror and deadly seriousness, which kept its twists fresh and unanticipated. Its cowriter with Keith Giffen was J. M. DeMatteis, a smart and literate Brooklynite who nursed a mean streak but was also a devotee of Indian mystic Meher Baba. His dialogue played a dense and relentless sitcom call-and-response game that often obscured the art-work, and alternated between exhilarating and exhausting in the space of a few pages. It didn't take long before the emphasis on humor caused the Justice League books to devolve into a series of increasingly unfunny, played-out shticks that snapped along like a slick, self-satisfied television hit on its final season prior to cancellation.

By 1994, the year Jack Kirby died of a heart attack, the book was crawling on all fours with kryptonite around its neck, and in spite of writer Christopher Priest's best efforts, the characters were creepy preforgotten no-hopers with names like Mystek and Bloodwynd. (And, no, it's not just you: He *does* appear to have based his superidentity on some alarming rectal trauma.) DC's flagship had simply lost its way, as the cataclysmic drop in sales confirmed. The Justice League title had been created to showcase the incredible adventures of the World's Greatest Superheroes, so, as with *Doom Patrol*, I did the straightforward thing and went back to first principles. But this time I couldn't get away with my own creations or characters based on my madcap, sometimes troubled, Bohemian friends. This time I was working with DC Comics' biggest and longest-running franchise characters, with faces on lunch boxes and duvet covers.

The 1960 Justice League comprised Superman, Batman, Wonder Woman, Aquaman, Green Lantern, and Flash, a pantheon of Pop Art divinities. Together with the 1950s stalwart, the green-skinned and noble superalien J'onn J'onzz, the Martian Manhunter, this was the roster of champions to which I immediately returned.

I had to fight to restore this original lineup and then put them front and center in a superhero title that sought to restore a mythic dimension to the DC universe. My quite reasonable demands were supported by my editor Ruben Diaz, a human fusillade of passion and positivity who teamed me with artist Howard Porter and the best inker in comics at the time, John Dell, whose thick, creamy black line could render incredible focal depth and create an illusion of 3-D. Porter combined the stocky solidity of the Image artists with a snarling gigantism that came from Jack Kirby and was well suited to tales of contemporary gods. Ruben even fought for us to bring Batman into the team against the wishes of Denny O'Neil, now in charge of the Bat-office and determined to make the Dark Knight's adventures as real and convincing as possible. This meant no fighting aliens or visiting the moon. Diaz kept his creative team safe from the madness and made sure that we could do exactly what we wanted, and *JLA* no. 1 hit the racks as an instant success story.

There would be no obtrusive postmodern meta-tricks in *JLA*, just unadulterated, gee-whiz, unadorned sci-fi myths in comic form, giving back to the superheroes the respect and dignity a decade of "realism" and harsh critique had stripped away. We awarded the team a modern Mount Olympus in the form of the new "Watchtower" on the moon, Earth's first line of defense against invasions from beyond. What's more, we added a few new members to adhere more closely to the lineup of Greek gods: Superman was Zeus; Wonder Woman, Hera; Batman, Hades; the Flash, Hermes; Green Lantern, Apollo; Aquaman, Neptune; Plastic Man, Dionysus; and so on.

The wounded, sneering reject heroes of *Doom Patrol* had been easy for me to write, but the JLA crowbarred me into the mind-set of the traditional DC American superhero, where I had to bend my head to think on their level. It turned out to be powerful fun. By taking the characters and their world at face value, I hoped to show how the superheroes pointed to something great and inevitable in us all. We've always known we'd eventually be called upon to open our shirts and save the day, and the superhero was a crude, hopeful attempt to talk about how we all might feel on that day of great power, and great responsibility.

I carefully constructed adventures to allow the JLA to display its powers in clever combinations, and I was happy to draw inspiration from time-honored tales: for instance, *JLA* no. 5's story about two mad scientists competing to create an artificial woman so complex that she developed a soul and betrayed them both was derived from "Blodeuwedd," the eleventh-century *Mabinogion* tale of the sorcerers Math and Gwydion, who created a woman out of flowers to deceive and destroy the Welsh mythic superhero Lleu Llaw Gyffes. Set free from the leaden constraints of realism, *JLA* allowed me to perfect my own glowing, buzzing mutant strain of the superhero germ. If Weisinger represented Freud, it was about time for some Jung comics, I reasoned.

It occurred to me that these characters, representing as they do specific human personality defaults, could function in a wider therapeutic context. The JLA were designed to solve any problem. Together there was no challenge, no matter how monumental or frightening, how unutterably nihilistic or ridiculous, that they could not overcome. In the realm of symbol, these, our imagined superselves, were indestructible. No god or devil could beat Superman and his pals in a fight. Ever. No heaven or hell could restrain them. Knock them down, blow them up, freeze them, lose them in time, brainwash them—and they came back stronger. So many ideas—fascism, pantisocracy, the mullet—fall apart under scrutiny, but the superhero meme refuses to die. Few flesh-and-blood heroes can stand up to the corroding effects of public scrutiny or simple age, but Superman, Batman, and their kin were conceived, designed, and unleashed to be unstoppable warriors on behalf of the best that the human spirit has to offer.

"ARE WE DOING TOO MUCH OR TOO **LITTLE**?" Wonder Woman asked, cradling a dying bird in a dust-bowl landscape. "WHEN DOES INTERVENTION BECOME **DOMINATION**?"

"I CAN ONLY TELL YOU WHAT I BELIEVE, DIANA," Superman replied. "HUMANKIND HAS TO BE ALLOWED TO CLIMB TO ITS **OWN** DESTINY. WE CAN'T **CARRY THEM** THERE."

Then the Flash countered with: "BUT THAT'S WHAT SHE'S **SAYING**. WHAT'S THE POINT? WHY SHOULD THEY NEED **US** AT ALL?"

"TO CATCH THEM IF THEY **FALL**," said Superman, gazing nobly at the sky. Issue no. 1 of the relaunched *Justice League of America* in 1987 had depicted its characters from an overhead perspective, giving the reader an elevated position that allowed us to look down on a newly humanized and relatable group of individuals.

At my request, Howard Porter drew our first cover shot of the JLA from *below*, endowing them with the majesty of towering statues on Mount Olympus, putting readers at the level of children gazing up at adults. *JLA* was a superhero title kids could read to feel grown-up and adults could read to feel young again.

I asked Howard to open the book with an image that I felt summed up its themes, of a vast flying saucer hovering above the White House. Quite independently, the same image appeared on the promo for Roland Emmerich's 1996 alien invasion film *Independence Day*, advertised, coincidentally, on the back cover of *JLA* no. 1.

We launched that same year. Sales went immediately from 20,000 to 120,000, and *JLA* stayed as DC's top-selling book for the rest of the decade. We had a genuine mainstream comic-book hit on our hands.

Readers responded to the optimism of the book, as I suspected they might. We'd seen superheroes sobbing and rending their capes in anguish, and it wasn't really what they did best. It was time to watch them wrestling with angels and tugging worlds on chains.

It was time they got their act together and gave us something to live up to.

It's not so much that history is simply cyclical, it seems to progress via recursive, repeated fractal patterns with minute variations. Early Renaissance comics' vogue for pastiche and the knowing reappropriation of kitsch objects to serve a deadly ironic purpose went hand in hand with the aesthetic of artist Jeff Koons, the young British artists, and writers like Mark (*Et Tu, Babe*) Leyner.

Like the reassembling liquid robot Terminator, the superhero concept had endured and survived total disintegration. Now that we truly understood the engine and how it ran, there was nothing left to do but reconnect the pieces to make something faster and better.

A new question would soon emerge: Was the superhero truly a Man of Tomorrow—a progressive image of futurity—or a nostalgic fantasy with nothing to offer beyond a sad, tired muscle show?

I'd been visiting my *Doom Patrol* editor Mark Waid's office on the day he was fired by Karen Berger for allowing a particularly tasteless joke to slip into the background of one of his comics. It seemed excessive, but Waid's career was one of pivotal moments. Mark came across as an almost stereotypical owlish geek from Hueytown, Alabama. He could have been Jupiter Jones of the Three Investigators grown up. At his best, he brought to his work a burning, compassionate humanity, a literate voice, an edgy humor honed in stand-up, and an honest sense of justice that helped define the Renaissance superhero, born of Waid's humility, fierce intelligence, and a childhood spent, like so many of us, osmosing Superman's moral code.

Now, six years later, he'd returned to DC as a writer, bent on restoring a sense of joyous, inventive acceleration to the adventures of the Flash. His

© DC COMICS

stories were never less than ingenious, with old-school heart-stopping climaxes, genuine romance, and a dozen never-before-seen tricks in every issue. They were the inheritors of the Julius Schwartz tradition, heartfelt bulletins from a southern geek with the steel-trap mind of a lawyer and the faraway eyes of a Silver Age boyhood never quite out-grown. Superheroes had been Waid's best friends, and there was no way he would allow them to become grizzled antiheroes, reduced to snapping spines or endlessly justifying themselves. He gave Wally West, the one-time kid Flash, a piece of his own soul that turned a B-list sidekick into a rounded, sympathetic young protagonist who you could root for easily. As the Flash had rescued superhero comics from the dead darkness of the fifties, he was here again to jump-start a new age of recapitulation, restoration, and Renaissance.

Waid's defining nineties blockbuster was *Kingdom Come*, an epochal, stress-filled collaboration with Alex Ross, the artistic sensation of the decade who had just completed *Marvels*. Ross was a staunch Silver Age traditionalist, and in spite of his early attempts to create an unhinged public persona—wild hair, shaggy beard, bulging eyes—he was a minis-ter's son with a ferocious discipline that showed itself in an attention to detail that forced his readers to slow down and reach for their scanning tunneling microscopes just to catch every carefully considered, mean-ingfully placed item of minutiae. Ross cast models, built props, and cre-ated costumes for his comics, posing his friends as Spider-Man or the Human Torch to create images that went beyond merely naturalistic into realms of the superreal. Closer contact with the undying heroes of Marvel and DC brought out the real Ross, who began to appear with neatly clipped hair as a star at conventions, dressed in a Clark Kent fedora, trench coat, and suit combination that suited his tall Baptist frame.

The Silver Age hero redux could assume a new guise as guardian of vanishing values. The superheroes as conformists had returned. They were representatives of a dream, a fantasy, that was losing more and more ground as each day passed without a manned mission to Mars, and now they knew it.

Ross's lush watercolors were the nearest that comics had come to film stills. His breakthrough project, with writer Kurt Busiek, was entitled *Marvels* and offered street-level, worm's-eye images of a towering Giant Man stepping almost delicately across the tops of skyscrapers overhead, which became instantly iconic and put familiar characters at a remove that paradoxically reconnected readers to the wonder, the marvel of these creations. First contact with an Alex Ross painting was genuinely astounding, as if someone had found a way to broadcast color TV from a real Marvel universe spinning somewhere in hypertime. The first pictures showed well-known superheroes as they might actually look from a human POV—suddenly, mind-bogglingly given the blurred veracity of Bigfoot or the Loch Ness Monster. The Marvel way had always been to drag the reader into the heart of the action, but decades of repetitive poses and setups had given the old meaty punch-ups a groaning familiarity that was taken for granted until Ross reminded readers how it was supposed to feel. He composed superhuman struggles not in the Kirby manner but as distant flashes in the sky, with tiny green figures facing towering tidal waves. Ross showed superheroes the way ordinary people might see them—briefly, and in all their strangeness—as meteoric streaks, distant explosions, and rainbows. Everything was lit for mood, and for the first time, the reflections across the Silver Surfer's chrome face and body were convincingly recreated, showing accurately distorted cityscapes. Or, for added excitement, an oncoming Human Torch.

Kurt Busiek, too, described the Marvel heroes as if we'd never seen them before, as here, when a character named Phil Sheldon encounters the first of them, the android Human Torch from 1940:

"IT LOOKED ALIVE—AS **HUMAN** AS YOU OR I—BUT IT WAS **ON FIRE**. AND I SWEAR—IT LOOKED **STRAIGHT AT ME**."

Or here, summing up the glory days of Marvel over sunlit shots of old-school Thor and Iron Man drawn as if from life.

"IT WAS **LIFE OR DEATH**—IT WAS **GRAND OPERA**—IT WAS THE **GREATEST SHOW ON EARTH**—AND WE—EVERY SINGLE ONE OF US—WE HAD THE **BEST SEAT** IN THE **HOUSE**."

The lead in *Marvels* was a typical Busiek witness to wonder: an ordinary Joe named Phil Sheldon, a *Daily Bugle* press photographer who'd been on hand to capture with his camera all the significant moments of Marvel's fictional history—from the elemental wars between the Human Torch and Prince Namor in the 1940s, to the discovery of Captain America frozen in Antarctic ice, to the arrival of Galactus and the death of Gwen Stacy at the hands of the Green Goblin at the beginning of the seventies. As his photo album grew, we experienced Sheldon's own life with his family across three tumultuous decades, a conceit that played well to Ross's great strengths.

Marvels had been so stuffed with startling, paradigm-shifting images of familiar characters that readers were eager to see what Ross could do with the DC lineup next. They didn't have long to wait. Ross had a driving work ethic, an all-consuming devotion to intricacy and tradition. By creating images that made it possible to believe in the reality of flying, burning men, Ross was perfect for a generation losing its strength to dream. Crude sketchy drawings would no longer cut it. Image Comics cartooning was out, and literalism had returned.

And in the manner of conquerors recasting the old gods as new devils, many of the early Renaissance-era books blamed the Image superhero for everything, especially the drastic plunge in sales that had all the usual pundits and pessimists predicting yet again the death of comics. So the villains of this period were caricatures of the savage, testosterone-driven heroes who'd slashed or gunned their way through the post-*Watchmen* story lines of a few years previously. This was the dynamic that informed Ross and Waid's epic *Kingdom Come*.

Kingdom Come was all a-trumpet with signs and portents from page 1, with a bold expressionistic painting showing a bat and an eagle at war in a symbolic sky. The opening captions only multiplied the sense of dread with Bible quotes that had been reliably terrifying the shit out of people for centuries:

"THERE WERE VOICES...AND THUNDERINGS AND LIGHTNINGS...AND AN EARTHQUAKE..."

Pages 2 and 3 offered a single ominous spread, upon which a terrible battle was already under way or over. Red lightning, green flame, a vast broken cup, and half-glimpsed, potent images of hands grasping Zeus-like bolts of electricity were the only clues to what might have occurred. It was elemental, doom laden, like a blind date with Saint John the Divine.

"AND THERE FOLLOWED HAIL AND FIRE MINGLED WITH BLOOD. THERE FELL A GREAT STAR FROM HEAVEN BURNING AS IT WERE A LAMP...AND I BEHELD AND HEARD AN ANGEL...SAWING WITH A LOUD VOICE...WOE, WOE, WOE TO THE INHABITERS OF THE EARTH."

Opening with these, the doomsday prophecies of a dying Golden Age Sandman and set in the DC universe twenty years from now, Waid and Ross introduced us to the next-gen superhumans of *Kingdom Come*. They were cast as violent, unprincipled superhooligans, Image-style heroes who didn't always care who got hurt in battles that left whole city blocks pulverized and, in issue no. 1's inciting incident, obliterated the entire state of Kansas when Captain Atom got into trouble and went off like a bomb. The core premise was expressed on page 10 by Norman McCay, the troubled elderly minister who narrated the story from the perspective of an ordinary man bearing witness to the end of the age of superheroes and the transfiguration of history:

ACCORDING TO THE **WORD** OF **GOD**, THE **MEEK** WOULD SOMEDAY **INHERIT** THE **EARTH**. SOMEDAY. BUT GOD NEVER **ACCOUNTED** FOR THE **MIGHTY**. THEY NUMBER IN THE **NAMELESS THOUSANDS**...PROGENY OF THE **PAST**, INSPIRED BY THE **LEGENDS** OF THOSE WHO CAME **BEFORE**...IF NOT THE **MORALS**. THEY NO LONGER FIGHT FOR THE RIGHT. THEY FIGHT SIMPLY TO **FIGHT**, THEIR ONLY FOES **EACH OTHER**. THE SUPERHUMANS **BOAST** THAT THEY'VE ALL BUT **ELIMINATED** THE SUPER-**VILLAINS** OF YESTERYEAR. COLD **COM-**

FORT. THEY MOVE **FREELY** THROUGH THE **STREETS** . . . THROUGH THE **WORLD**. THEY ARE **CHAL-LENGED** . . . BUT **UNOPPOSED**. THEY ARE AFTER **ALL** . . . OUR **PROTECTORS**.

Older heroes, like a retired Superman, still clung to their no-killing creed in a world where murder and mayhem in the name of "good" was no contradiction, but the irradiation of Kansas brought back the Man of Steel with one last mission to bring this rowdy horde under control. His decision split the superhero community down the middle, with one side supporting Superman's and his new Justice League's strict enforcement of law and order, and the others siding with Batman to resist the imposition of a superhuman global police state.

As Waid deftly laid out the steps on the road to planetary catastrophe and beyond, Ross's art came packed with new levels of detail and meaning. Everything was significant, even more so than in *Marvels*, which now seemed a mere warm-up for this tour de force. Every fraction of the background referenced some prior comics history, or introduced a new character concept or item of obscure trivia, like the glass case in the Planet Krypton restaurant containing in perfect miniature background detail, a photographic and shockingly convincing "Hero Dial" from a charming sixties wish-fulfillment strip entitled "Dial 'H' for Hero." This was story as museum, with Ross preserving the trophies and totems of the Big Two Universe forever in one place, capturing in uncanny trompe l'oeil clarity the flotsam and jetsam of his childhood reading.

The Alex Ross hero was both monumental and somehow vulnerable, poignantly mortal, as if Leni Riefenstahl had filmed her proud fascist athletes ten years after their Olympic triumphs of the will. Ross liked to show heroes with bald patches, paunches, and different types of physiques, and *Kingdom Come* offered a rare peek at DC's middle age. He used models to give each of the famous heroes a distinctive and realistic face, but as his models aged, his superheroes too grew more solid around the middle, more jowly of jaw. For all their Wagnerian lighting and megalithic posturing, these images of slightly out-of-shape, ordinary-looking men and women in ridiculous costumes came closest to how superheroes might look in "real life," and the results were oddly moving. It was often as if we'd been given the power to watch the face of the Mona Lisa sag with wrinkles. After the first shock of the new, some felt that Ross brought realism at the cost of wonder. Did we really need to see out-of-shape superheroes with comb-overs? Perhaps. *Kingdom Come* showed that superhero comics could be unobtrusively "meta" with their combination of adventure, political satire, and cultural commentary.

Kingdom Come climaxed with a grandiose Superman–Captain Marvel fight, the outcome of which reduced 90 percent of the world's superhuman population to skeletons and ash. Relinquishing his red and blue suit for the last time, an older and wiser Superman put his Clark Kent glasses back on and returned to his roots as a superfarmer dedicated to the restoration of the glowing Kansas wheat fields. The story ended with him and Wonder Woman announcing her pregnancy, while an aging Batman agreed to be the child's godfather—all in plainclothes. It was a farewell not to superheroes but to costumes and to posturing, and to the never-ending Dreamtime that recycled their stories with no hope of lasting change. Clark Kent, Diana Prince, and Bruce Wayne were set free of their trademarks, the signs of their divinity, but the price they paid was immortality. Perhaps, like Bowie's tormented gods in his song "The Supermen," all they really wanted was to change, and age, and die.

By the end of the nineties, I felt weary. My approach to *JLA*, which I'd imagined to be progressive, had instigated a wave of nostalgic "Dad comics," as I came to call them, that thrillingly fought to turn back the tide to the days of Julius Schwartz or Roy Thomas. A cloying yearning for the "fun" and moral simplicity of the Silver Age was rife.

In film and in music, James Bond and Oasis, respectively, were industriously ransacking memories of the sixties too. This was what happened when a generation of punks reached middle age, grabbed the reins of culture, and remade it in the rosy, glowing likeness of childhood. Pamela Anderson, a collagen- and silicon-implanted improvement on the Bardot look for the plastic age, personified the new supergirl android ideal. She was the "babe" goddess, the template for a fembot who was up for it with the lads emerged as a kind of ironic recapitulation of the sixties pinup girl: tousled, intoxicated, and up for anything. It was cool to admit that you liked pornography and football and dirty jokes, even when you didn't. It was normal. In fact, it was almost compulsory, especially if you were a girl. The homophobia, racism, and sexism of the seventies male was reinstated with a tongue-in-cheek distance.

I wondered what came next, and I felt certain that it would be something quite different from the happy-clappy idiot's fag-end of dance and ecstasy culture.

Then I found a guidebook that turned my aptitude for predicting pop culture trends into a martial art.

Iain Spence published *Sekhmet Hypothesis: The Signals of the Beginning of a New Identity* as a book in 1995, but it wasn't until two years later that I came across his ideas in an article he'd written for the magazine *Towards 2012*. As an illuminating way of reconsidering the familiar, I'm particularly fond of the Sekhmet Hypothesis, which never fails to get people talking at parties. As usual, please remember that this is just a framework; a way of ordering information into meaningful patterns in the service of creative lateral thinking, if you like. You may be able to find all kinds of examples to refute this data, but first bear in mind that I've used this predictive model to great effect and no small financial reward, and trust me when I say I'm passing it on as a tip, not as a belief system. If this book has made any point clear, I hope it's that things don't have to be real to be true. Or vice versa.

Soon you'll notice how many advertisers and trend makers are aware of this theory and have been applying it to product placement, design, and the seasonal shifts of the rag trade since Spence published it. The more people know about it and react against it, or try to preempt it, the more the effect is likely to dissipate or find different ways to express itself. That may already be happening in the windblown halls of popular culture, although as I write, in 2010, Spence's broad predictions are accurate still.

Sunspot activity follows a twenty-two-year cyclical pattern, building to a period of furious activity known as the solar maximum, then calming down for the solar minimum. Every eleven years, the solar magnetic field also undergoes a polarity reversal. It's a little like a huge switch that toggles on or off, or the volume slider on a mixing desk, with loud at one end and silent at the other, and each period is given an identifying number. Cycle 23, for instance, had its maximum in 1999.

Spence suggests that these regular rewirings of the solar magnetic field naturally have an effect on the human nervous system, which leaves its traces most clearly in our cultural record—like a desert wind carving the shape of its passage into the dunes of fashion, art, and music. As a shorthand toward understanding the two maximum states we flip between, we can regard one pole as having a "punk" character, while its opposite may be thought of as "hippie."

In Spence's lexicon, at least as I understand it (his own website will set you straight if I get it wrong), punk maxima can be identified in a fashion vogue for short hair, tight clothes, short, punchy popular music, aggression, speedy drugs, and materialism. Hippie, as I'm sure you'll have guessed, is associated with signifiers from the converse end of the spectrum, like long hair, loose or baggy clothes, longer-form popular music, psychedelic or mind-expanding drugs, peace, and a renewed interest in the spiritual or transcendental. He focused on youth culture trends on the basis that young nervous systems registered the magnetic reversals most profoundly and reflected them back in the lineaments of the art and music they made or consumed. So far, so good.

In 1955, when our planet was bombarded by cycle 19 solar magnetic waves, young people in the West responded like needles in a groove with rock 'n' roll's tight jeans, short hair, biker JD aggression, short, fast songs, and widespread use of stimulant drugs like speed and coffee.

Silver Age comic-book punk was embodied by crew-cut Barry Allen in his speed suit. "Chemicals and Lighting" could have been a song or a band. The tight suits, establishment men, and emphasis on science and rationality are all typical, as are Stan Lee's realistic superheroes such as the Fantastic Four and Spider-Man.

Eleven years later, cycle 20 reversed the polarity. By 1966, hair had become longer, clothes were looser and more flamboyant, music became more involved and sophisticated, and the drugs were mind expanders like LSD.

In 1966 the cosmic wave entered the comics, to bring with it the gods of Thor, villains like the Anti-Matter Man, and John Broome's psychedelic Flash stories. The new heroes were antiestablishment "freaks" and mutants.

Nineteen seventy-seven brought a shift back to punk, as expressed in

Malcolm McLaren and Vivienne Westwood's fifties-influenced clothes and music, bondage and restriction, amphetamine sulfate use, and angry, confrontational politics.

The comics boom of that cycle gave us *Judge Dredd*, Frank Miller's gritty noir, Alan Moore's harsh logical realism.

Nineteen eighty-eight saw ecstasy, or MDMA, as the favored drug, accompanying long-form trance, ambient and dance music, Manchester "baggy" fitness wear as street wear, grunge beards, and a return to long hair. In comic books, this was the time of *Deadline, Doom Patrol, Shade,* and *Sandman*.

Spence didn't get as far as 1999 in his *Towards 2012* essay, but he imagined the rise of a "Stormer" generation of what he called "imperial youth." As it happened, his predictions were more or less accurate. In 1999, we had nu-metal, *The Matrix*, tight clothes, short hair, *No Logo* anticorporate demos, the emergence of bondage styles, and the Goth underground moving into the mainstream, a revival of popularity for cocaine, and, more significantly, perhaps, the jittery rise of Red Bull, Starbucks and coffee society. Comics gave us proactive world-changing superheroes and villains in *Authority, Marvel Boy,* and *Wanted*.

This book will be published in 2011, when the fruits of the next wave will be hard to avoid. As I write, the word *psychedelic* is being used so often on TV and in magazines that it's barely funny. *Avatar*'s hippy eco-vision of an interconnected natural world and the massive success of *Alice in Wonderland* (always popular during hippie periods) exemplify this current, as do the vampire heroes who have occupied the imaginative place once taken by sixties Pre-Raphaelite fairies and Edwardian dandies. In comics, the "realism" boom has been quietly left behind like an unfashionable pair of trousers. The new superhero books are becoming more fantastic, colorful, and self-consciously "mythic."

Spence's article does not, nor will I, attempt to track the alleged effects of these undeniably real solar magnetic events on non-Western cultures. Neither does he extend his argument backward to consider the ways in which the popular arts scene of 1944 could be described in "hippie" terms (LSD, however, was synthesized in 1945), or that of 1933 as "punk" (although perhaps Weimar decadence and the art of George Grosz could build a case there). And so on. I leave that contemplation to skeptics who choose to debunk the idea or to zealots who want to believe it.

Unless Terence McKenna's "Timewave Zero" theories are correct, and we collapse into an atemporal singularity on December 21, 2012, 2021 will bring the cycle back around to "punk," and if this seesaw sounds horribly predictable and repetitive, be assured that it will all seem fresh to the young people who take their own inspiration from the solar trade winds.

As for me, I intended to bring my run on *JLA* to an end along with the century. *The Invisibles*, too, was scheduled to wrap in 2000, and I planned to re-create myself again to complement the change in the weather. I was almost forty, had never felt better, and wanted to be ready for the harsher spirit I'd decided was on its way in the wake of the Labour election win, the death of the former Princess Diana, and the commencement of cycle 23.

I'd also just met my future wife, Kristan, a stunning, brainy blonde who dressed like Barbarella to go to the pub, worked as a corporate insurance broker, and read Philip K. Dick. It would be another three years before our paths crossed again and we were able to get together, but that die was already cast.

On a trip to Venice, Italy, I bought my first real suit—Donna Karan—and was encouraged to go corporate. Smart tailoring and the jargon of advertising, motivational speaking, instead of fractal-patterned shirts and druggy psychedelia, seemed the way to go in cycle 23. At heart, I'd always been an uptight Presbyterian Scot anyway. I'd never been able to get back to the radiant world I'd reached in Kathmandu, and I'd begun to suspect it was because in some way I was already there. I had very little doubt that I'd "wake up" in that place at the moment of death, like a game player looking up from the screen where his avatar lies bleeding, only to realize he's home and safe and always was.

"The drugs don't work, they just make you worse," sang the Verve, and after eight years of experimentation, ruthless self-examination, ego infla-tion, and ego loss, I had to admit they were probably onto something. The shallow hedonistic spirit of the nineties was too fragile to endure the cold of the vast twin shadows cast backward by an onrushing age of terror. Darker times were on their way, demanding a new clarity and rigor of thought.

I tried to articulate the outlines of the next trend by introducing to the pages of *JLA* a military-funded superteam called the Ultramarines, whipped up by Uncle Sam to keep the Justice League in check should their internationalist stance ever compromise US military security. By the end of the story, the Ultramarines had split from their paymasters and joined with a group of like-minded DC heroes in a hovering city-sized headquarters named Superbia, there to announce a bold new manifesto for change:

SUPERBIA HEREBY DECLARES INDEPENDENCE FROM ALL NATIONS AND OPENS ITS GATES TO SUPER-CHAMPIONS FROM THE FOUR CORNERS OF THE EARTH. WE INTEND TO SERVE AS A FIRST-STRIKE **GLOBAL PEACEKEEPING FORCE**. WE WILL KILL IF WE HAVE TO. IF WE HAVE TO, WE'LL LET YOU **KNOW**. TERRORISTS, DESPOTS, CORRUPT BUSINESS-MEN . . . THE INTERNATIONAL ULTRAMARINE CORPS IS HERE. **THERE'S NOWHERE TO HIDE**.

As it happened, I'd almost exactly described what the next big development of the superhero concept would look like.

Meanwhile, I prepared myself for the oncoming zeitgeist by listening to Chris Morris's bleak, brilliant, bad-trippy *Blue Jam* on Radio 1 every Thursday after John Peel. Oddly enough, I was beginning to find humor in all the things that had once frightened me. The prying eye of Big Brother, the aging process, loneliness, failure, and death were all just punch lines to the joke. I loved to listen over and over again to HAL 9000's death scene from the soundtrack of *2001: A Space Odyssey*, and when Jarvis Cocker and Pulp released their masterpiece comedown album, *This Is Hardcore*, its unflinching evocation of middle age, stale waterbeds, and tinny bachelor pad music made me rethink my own lifestyle.

I was about as alien as I'd ever wanted to be, but I'd grown tired of one-night stands, drink, drugs, and the dating game.

It was time to get serious.

CHAPTER 20

RESPECTING AUTHORITY

SO CHARMED WAS I by the Sekhmet idea that I planned to put it to the test by creating a superhero especially for Iain Spence's projected Stormer generation of "imperial" youth: a punk, puritan, teen superhero who would rewire me to my roots. While I was thinking about it, history continued to march, and my friend Warren Ellis captured lightning in a bottle with the launch of the first and best of the Stormer books, entitled—imperially—*The Authority*, which pointed the way forward for the next decade, with a stripped-down filmic style and a cleverly calculated update on the Justice League team archetype, retooled and refitted for our *Matrix* millennium. Its members included Apollo and the Midnighter, obvious analogues of Superman and Batman, who also happened to be gay lovers.

LET ME MAKE THIS SITUATION CLEAR FOR YOU. I KNOW WHAT SPECIAL ABILITIES YOU HAVE. I CAN SEE THE ENHANCEMENTS. I CAN DETECT THE ELECTRICAL ACTIV-ITY IN YOUR BRAIN. I KNOW WHAT MOVES YOU'RE PRE-PARING TO MAKE. I'VE FOUGHT OUR FIGHT ALREADY, IN

MY HEAD, IN A MILLION DIFFERENT WAYS. I CAN HIT YOU
WITHOUT YOU EVEN SEEING ME. I'M WHAT SOLDIERS
DREAM OF GROWING INTO. I'M WHAT CHILDREN SEE
WHEN THEY FIRST IMAGINE WHAT DEATH IS LIKE. I'M
THE MIDNIGHTER. PUT THE CHILD DOWN . . .

That's the Midnighter, addressing a superhuman terrorist in *The Authority*
no. 2. In real life, any adversary would have started yawning in the middle
of the Midnighter's third sentence before opening fire in his fourth, if only
to try to shut him up. In a superhero comic, this cocky statement of powers and intent was immensely satisfying, a staccato, macho lyric. This was
comics as pop music, with just enough realism in the drawings, the characterizations, and the situations to make it seem contemporary, knowing,
and tough.

When I met Warren Ellis in 1984, he was a fusewire-thin, eager, and
brainy teenager who never missed a chance to mingle in the bar after the
Westminster Hall comics mart. I had few friends among that crowd and
always appreciated Warren's willingness to acknowledge my spectral
presence by the pillar. His early strips like *Doctor Death the Life Man* were
vibrant oddities, but by the late eighties, he was making a name for himself as a dissolute Nick-Kent-meets-Hunter-Thompson-style commentator, interviewer, and journalist via the lively comics fanzine network that
had sprung up to critique, chronicle, and document the new British
movement. Warren had opinions about everything and a wicked turn of
phrase, but most important, his fiction was as good, if not better than, his
opinion writing.

In many ways, Ellis could be seen as an obvious spiritual heir to
Michael Moorcock and Harlan Ellison, or to Norman Spinrad, M. John
Harrison, and the writers of the *New Worlds* generation of British speculative fiction. Ellis specialized in science fiction with a Goth edge, and his
work was enlivened by the scabrous wit and misanthropic turn of phrase
he'd perfected in his critical writings.

I lost sight of him in the nineties, when he was working with Marvel,
which had tapped him as Kurt Busiek's ideological opposite and invited

him to create *Marvels*' reflex, the venomous *Ruins*. Where *Marvels* had celebrated the dawn of a heroic legacy, *Ruins* offered an alternate world take on the Marvel universe where everything had gone completely and horribly wrong, and pretty much everyone was dying of cancer or selling their rotted bodies for food.

"God Found Dead in Space" was the headline alongside a painting of a newspaper photograph showing Kirby's majestic space god Galactus adrift in the outer reaches of nowhere.

Ruins, like Darren Aronofsky film of *Requiem for a Dream*, was so bleak it was funny, but at the time of its release, I was thoroughly sick of this brand of fancy-pants pessimism and wrote Ellis off as the kind of professional misery guts I no longer had any time for in my life of drugs, dancing, and jet-setting hedonism. I ignored the rest of his work in the nineties and missed the moment where he shrugged off the gloom and carefully assembled a working model of a new age of comics.

Before the Big Two recognized his talents, Ellis's specialty was the complete overhaul of Image Comics' hulks, rusting in what Alan Moore had taken to calling Ideaspace. It began when he took control of the directionless WildStorm universe that Jim Lee had established. Here Ellis streamlined Lee's black-ops heroes into UN-sanctioned operatives with a mandate to monitor superhuman activity and to police violations of the various protocols and sanctions governing the use of extranormal abilities. Costumes became functional field outfits, designed for espionage and black-ops work.

Ellis suggested a new take on the T.H.U.N.D.E.R. Agents–S.H.I.E.L.D. model, combining spy thrills with grimy, violent superheroics in a world of genetic manipulation, weaponized flesh, and budget restrictions. The JLA did what it wanted; Stormwatch was subject to red tape and the limits of physics. *Stormwatch* was perfectly tailored to make the best of Ellis's increasingly tight, hard, science fiction take on even the most fantastic material, mixing Nietzschean drama with savage, uncompromising global surveillance state politics. No one was safe in a Warren Ellis story, and he routinely killed as many superheroes as he created, each one offering a vicious twist on some comic-book archetype, like the High, a modern take on the original idea of the socialist superman, who was destroyed when his noble dream of a better world came into conflict with the hard facts of human nature. Ellis's stories often relied so heavily on the latest pop-science discoveries from the pages of *New Scientist* or *Scientific American* that a subscription to either of those magazines could be counted upon to provide conceptual trailers for Ellis comics published six months later. The nineties vogue for science jargon that I'd used to poetic effect in *JLA* became, in Ellis's hands, impeccably researched captions or scientific explanations that made even the most outlandish powers seem plausible. It was a winning formula.

When he and Hitch, another Englishman, combined this elegant, streamlined storytelling style with the expansive canvas of *JLA* and *Kingdom Come*, fusing the underground counterculture heroes of *The Invisibles* with the cosmic scope of *JLA*, the shamelessly filmic *The Authority* was born, fully grown and firing on all cylinders, an instant game changer.

The cover of *The Authority* no. 1 showed a poster shot of the team posed as if for a CD sleeve. Aside from the title, the names of the creators and the customary price and date information, there was no copy. The loud and vulgar starburst come-ons of Marvel detergent box covers had no place on this cool designer superhero book. An artful typeface with the title running horizontally along the top and vertically up the left like *Watchmen* made these comics look like hipster magazines. Following the *Stormwatch* model, Hitch took the idea of the superhero costume and realigned it with a twenty-first-century aesthetic more consistent with the way a band of strutting imperial warrior superhumans might dress. Hitch's were rock star superheroes, movie star champions, handsome, tough, and sexy. Batman's long black cape was updated to become the Midnighter's long black leather coat. The Engineer looked like a naked supermodel dipped in chrome. Hawksmoor wore a suit but had rugged tire treads on the soles of his bare feet, a touch Ellis had borrowed from a Pirelli advert. The Doctor was an ex-junkie "shaman of the global village" who dressed in a combination of medical scrubs and a hippie coat of many colors. Jenny Sparks had her Union Jack vests and white trouser suits. Swift wore aerobics gear. Only Apollo flew the flag with anything resembling a traditional muscle hugger, but as the team's resident solar-powered superhunk, he could afford to work a more traditional look. Unlike Alan Moore's troubled heroes, the members of the Authority were comfortable with their powers, using them sensibly to fight "bastards" and improve the lot of everyone on planet Earth. It was the utopian vision of Siegel and Shuster strained through British cynicism and delivered on the end of a spiked leather glove. It took the accusations of fascism that had haunted Superman and suggested a new kind of superfascist, one who was on our side.

The opening page of *The Authority* no. 1 showed Earth as seen from space accompanied by a single caption.

"They think there's no one left to save the world."

The story announced its intentions to operate in the big-budget *Independence Day* idiom, with a three-page sequence set in a Moscow convincingly re-created from photographic reference. The freeze-frame skeletons detonating to ash and cinders were straight from *Terminator 2*'s swing park apocalypse scene. The regular letterbox-shaped panels with black borders instead of white gave the impression of an auditorium with the lights down. These clever visual quotes reminded us that this comic was meant to be read as a movie. The storyboard style became the standard layout for twenty-first-century comics as they tried to emulate the look and feel of $200 million movies, even copying filmic narrative structures that didn't always suit the serial nature of comics and were already looking old hat in the face of the new immersive narrative forms that computer games had trained audiences to expect.

The villain of the first Authority story was Kaizen Gamorra, a terrorist who explained his devotion to violence with a speech that had a cold, prophetic ring:

"BECAUSE I AM A WOLF IN A WORLD OF SHEEP. BECAUSE TERROR IS THE BLOOD OF LIFE AND ITS GUIDING PRINCIPLE. I HAVE NO POLITICS TO ESPOUSE THROUGH MY TERROR, NO IDEALS TO FORCE THROUGH. TERROR IS ITS OWN REWARD. YOUR MISSILES AND BOMBERS MEAN NOTHING TO ME."

Fortunately for the world, Gamorra was up against the coolest, hardest new superheroes available, and it was obvious from issue no. 1 that he didn't stand a chance.

The Justice League never resorted to lethal force, but Ellis's heroes would happily cut off your head and beat you to death with it if that's what it took to stop you from being a dictator or a "bastard." These hombres meant business, and the bad guys could no longer rely on that handy code against killing, which had kept superheroes in check for so long.

These bolshy new superheroes spoke for all of us in the counterculture; on the outside at the moment, it became the inside. It felt like we'd won. When I took to the stage with a drunken victory yell as a speaker at New York's Disinformation Convention, organized and presented by culture commentator, publisher, and TV host Richard Metzger in 2000, it was to make that point.

For just a moment, there on the hinge of the millennium, it seemed as though the whole world wanted what we'd got. They'd seen how much fun we were having with our aliens, our Tantric sex, superhuman dreams, and glossy vinyl clothes, and they all wanted to join in.

Especially Warren's "bastards." They'd caught the glint of gold in a quiet corner they'd always shunned and laughed at. In the quirky, enchanted, self-absorbed, collector underworlds of geek fandom, fetish, and fantasy, there lay a picture of the human future. One day, someone thought, consumers will all be geeks, chained to computer screens, entangled with enthralling game worlds, surfing porn or squirreling through eBay as the seasons turn outside. One day soon, we would all be cyborgized by a rapidly evolving communications network of iPhones and iPads and their descendants, these portable exo-minds bonding like prostheses to more and more of us at a younger and younger age. Soon they'll be implanting phones and cameras in the womb, to get us addicted to the ads early on. In a world-to-come like that one, we might all be persuaded to buy into the fantasies of geeks. A growing population of "kidults" could be sold on boys' toys and the new, improved on-screen adventures of Batman, Spider-Man, the Hulk, and Green Lantern, helped along by books like this one—which would suggest some hidden value in the smeary power fantasies of the disenfranchised. And so it was.

But there on the brink, drunk on the victory wine of '99, it looked like a big win. I'd reconnected with Kristan, and life was fine. The twenty-first century would surely see the triumph of our sci-fi ideals along with the death of grim, old, outmoded conservative power structures, and *The Authority* spoke for that dream. We'd all be recognized as pioneers, imaginauts, weaving the bright myths of a brand-new day.

I knew the Justice League of America was suddenly obsolete. This was the future, and it was time to move on. The superhero story had grown through its stormy Dark Age adolescence into a kind of assured twenty-something confidence at last. There was a grown-up, nonexploitative sexuality and a healthy dose of smart humor too. The whole package seemed designed to make superheroes palatable to a nonfan audience once more, although sales on *The Authority* never quite reflected its mass-market potential.

If *The Authority* was the child of a *Stormwatch, Independence Day*, and *JLA* liaison, then Ellis's *Planetary* had traces somewhere in its complex ancestry of a type of superhero metacomic about comics in the vein of *Flex Mentallo* and Alan Moore's Superman pastiche *Supreme*. *Planetary* was an action lecture, a living, plot-driven treatise on pop culture that worked as well as an adventure story as it did as an ode to imagination and the odd. Typically, these comics offered insights into the creator's (usually the writer's) personal philosophies and ideas about time and space, comics, and myth. In a sequence of minimalist, mostly single-issue tales, Ellis and John Cassaday reworked and recombined the raw material of the pulps, fifties sci-fi movies, Japanese monster films, and superhero comics into a cohesive long-form complete story of "good" imagination—the Planetary team—versus "bad" imagination in the form of the Fantastic Four analogue the Four, who played the part of amoral corporate interests strip-mining the world of its extraordinary hidden wonders and secret artifacts. Analogues of Thor's hammer and Green Lantern's power battery were used as totemic icons to explore the power and persistence of pulp dreams, treated as if they were Arks of the Covenant, Holy Grails, or Shrouds of Turin—forgotten artifacts of a lost commonwealth of wonder and hope.

With the tagline "It's a strange world. Let's keep it that way," *Planetary* sought to create a single all-encompassing map of the territory of the fantastic, weaving together its every strand into a single vision of the entire field of superhuman literature.

It had a timeless quality. The three principal characters—"mystery archaeologists" who mapped the secret, fantastic history of the twentieth century—were barely drawn plot drivers, but Ellis knew when to play out just enough backstory, enough texture, to keep them somehow human and relatable without burdening any of the three (one-hundred-year-old hard man Elijah Snow, superstrong Wonder Woman–manqué Jakita Wagner, and a communications savant known only as "the Drummer") with the problems or issues of ordinary people. They were superhumans in the noncostumed, hard-as-nails Brit-com tradition that Ellis had honed to a knife edge, dressed in white suits, leather catsuits, and hoodies.

In Cassaday, Ellis had another pitch-perfect collaborator. He knew how to freeze and compose the intricate snap and tag of dialogue and double-page image. Cassaday, a handsome Texas film school graduate, brought a director's eye to his perfectly composed frame-ups. Like his peers, he favored long, horizontal panels that re-created how the cinema screen looks from the audience's point of view. The artists who were able to adapt to this new trend were masters of scale and perspective, and they framed their shots like the directors of Hollywood spectaculars and science fiction blockbusters. Comics muscled up to compete with the effects-driven action movies of the nineties, adding their own brand of deft characterization to the eye-popping action and multibillion-dollar visions realized with pencils on paper. The artists became a new royalty: Ross, Cassaday, Hitch, Quitely.

A major contributing factor to the tailored excellence of the Ellis brand product was the color artistry of Laura Martin (DePuy in 1999, before her marriage). She brought an unprecedented naturalism to her color palette, rendering subtle lighting conditions and regional skylines with a fidelity to the real that made Hitch's mind-boggling *Independence Day*–style battles between air force jets and alien fighters look even more like production stills.

My own desire was to see stories about how it felt to be the man who *never* failed and never gave up. What new perspectives might superhumanity bring that I hadn't considered before? I knew what it was like to be human, but I was determined to live up to my role models and was fascinated by how it would feel to think like a superhuman. Not the inhuman, neurotic, flawed, detached characters my peers seemed so attached to but *super*humans: emotionally healthy mature beings who came complete with all the reasoning abilities, compassion, inventiveness, and humor that made us special and lovable but added to that the new faculties, new philosophies, and fresh perspectives that would surely characterize Human Plus. I couldn't help noticing how embarrassed Brits were by optimism and decided to make it a feature of my new work.

I was taken to see *The Matrix* by my new friends, the Day-Glo-crested "Pleazure Terrorists" of Melbourne, Australia, and saw what seemed to me my own combination of ideas enacted on the screen: fetish clothes, bald heads, kung fu, and magic, witnessing the Gnostic invasion of the Hollywood mainstream.

The time of the punk superhero had come. Artists Joe Quesada and Jimmy Palmiotti had been given charge of the Marvel Knights imprint and steered it to great success with more grown-up takes on Marvel superheroes like Daredevil and the Punisher. When Joe asked me to join in, my idea was to create something I'd never tried: a quintessential Marvel superhero who would arrive with clockwork timing to embody the antiestablishment, anti-corporate movement and the spirit of Naomi Klein's *No Logo*. The young hero was Noh-Varr, a diplomatic envoy of the Kree supercivilization, and the book had the ironic title *Marvel Boy*, named for an obscure Bill Everett character. I reached back to the original Marvel hero—Everett's wild, teen-age Prince Namor—and found the template for the antiestablishment su-perman. Kal-El of Krypton's rocket had been found by a kindly couple, representatives of the best midwestern values could offer. What if he'd been found instead by a representative of America's corporate dinosauric military-industrial nightmare, as personified by the monstrous armored Doctor Midas and his zipped-up bondage babe daughter, Oubliette the Terminatrix, representing the entertainment media?

After enduring torture at Midas's hands, the young alien superhero chose not to fight for America or even for human values but to wage a one-man war on planet Earth from his underground lair in Times Square. It was the superhero as terrorist, and its hero was an idealistic boy from a better place who had seen firsthand the results of human cruelty and stupidity and could take no more.

"I'LL SHOW YOU PEOPLE WHAT PARADISE LOOKS LIKE IF I HAVE TO LEVEL EVERY CITY ON EARTH AND REBUILD IT STONE BY STONE."

Artist I. G. Jones and I positioned him too as an embodiment of the Egyptian god Horus, in his ferocious aspect as the Lord of Force and Fire. Horus was considered by Aleister Crowley to represent a youthful, ruth-less, and revolutionary current that would sweep through human affairs when the two-thousand-year Aeon of the Lawgiver, the Father God of the

Book, the Middle Eastern desert boss Jehovahallah himself, that inner voice, that imaginary playmate that whole cultures had mistaken for a giant, invisible overlord, was overturned by the unstoppable forces of the Aeon of the Conquering Child. According to occult author Ramsey Dukes's interpretation of this doctrine, any fool who prayed to "God" in the twenty-first century without realizing that He'd been replaced by a capricious divine brat would be assured of receiving no longer wise instructions for living but violent manifestoes for change. I like to think any Conquering Child would be fond of superhero stories, and perhaps the rapid growth of a superhero movie industry in the first decade of the twenty-first century can be understood as some attempt to entertain or divert this turbulent new child-of-zeitgeist with spectacle.

Noh-Varr's power was expressed not in the service of the status quo but as insurrection and anarchy. More frightening than his destructive capabilities were his beliefs.

We imagined our hero's creed as a strange, unthinkable, untranslatable mix of seeming opposites, described in the text as "Zen Fascism." We'd all seen what ray guns and flying saucers could do, but what if the alien had a belief system so seductive, so powerful and ultimately corrosive that it could destroy our own social structures? In a move that seems prescient, Jones and I had him attack Manhattan, burning the words FUCK YOU into the street grid, big enough to be read from space.

The third issue introduced Hexus the Living Corporation, an alien entity that arrived on our planet in the form of a mysterious logo. Hexus would root itself in a small office space somewhere and start spawning recruitment flyers—"DO YOU SINCERELY WANT TO GET RICH?"— to attract employees, who would then be swiftly assimilated into its workforce. Hexus traded up to bigger and bigger headquarters as it proceeded through its lifecycle. It was a naturally occurring "wild" corporate intelligence, a superpredator that began to gobble up the market territory of our own synthetic corporations, like Fox and AOL, on its way to devouring our planet's entire resources before sending out its spores in the form of spaceships carrying Hexus flyers. In the end, Noh-Varr defeated the creature by leaking its secrets to its competitors, who then tore the pretender apart on the international stock exchange.

With her beloved Noh-Varr banged up in an inescapable superpenitentiary, which he'd vowed with a smile to transform into the "CAPITAL CITY OF THE NEW KREE EMPIRE," Oubliette was pictured in the bombed ruins of Disneyland with Donald Duck lying facedown behind her, while the voice of Horus echoed loud and clear:

"THIS IS THE **END OF THE WAY THAT WAS**. COSMIC JIHAD HAS BEGUN. **YOU ASKED FOR THIS**."

A horrified President Bill Clinton stroked his chin, perhaps suspecting he wasn't long for office:

". . . IT WAS THE WAY SHE KEPT SHOOTING THE POOR DUCK GUY IN THE BACK LIKE THAT. I DON'T BELIEVE I'LL EVER FORGET THAT IMAGE."

And in hindsight, *Marvel Boy*, like *The Authority*, seems almost to be a transmission from a very different world that was waiting for us all across the millennial barricade.

Ellis and Hitch ended their run on *The Authority* after twelve issues. It was enough. They'd said what had to be said and showed the way, but the book was too good to waste, as Warren Ellis and I discussed when we met in New Zealand. It was agreed that the book should be handed to Mark Millar. I'd been showing Ellis some of Frank Quitely's pages from *JLA: Earth 2*, which I'd written the previous year as a ninety-six-page original graphic novel intended as a bridge between the work I'd been doing with *JLA* and the work I intended to do in the new century. Then and there we had our new team on *The Authority*.

I suggested to Mark that he play to his strengths with a punkier, funnier, and more shocking take on *The Authority* to really take advantage of the cycle 23 zeitgeist, and that's exactly what he did, making the title even more controversial and popular. Millar played down Ellis's utopian science fiction and dialed up the tabloid shock and controversy when he took the reins on the title's second volume. The gay subtext was made explicit, culminating in a white wedding between the superpowered hunks that even made it to the tabloids.

I met Mark Millar when he was eighteen years old in 1988. He turned up at the door to interview me for the comics fanzine *Fantasy Advertiser*. Unlike Warren, Mark truly loved superheroes, and we got on immediately, sharing a surreal and gruesome sense of humor.

Soon we were speaking on the phone every day, usually for four-hour stretches, in hysterics. I suppose I was flattered by his attention and his ability to find everything I said funny, so I overlooked the potential for disaster in our unequal partnership.

Through Mark, I reconnected with my roots in the working-class West of Scotland, embracing black humor, intoxication, and an unlikely end as the birthright of our people. We had such fun working together on the satirical *Big Dave* strip for *2000 AD* that we decided to do it again. As it all worked out, that was probably a mistake; *Big Dave* was two like-minded friends having a laugh, but as soon as we were working together on American superhero dramas, the division of labor became lopsided.

When I was offered the *Swamp Thing* series, I took the assignment on the condition that I would cowrite the first four with Mark to establish a new direction that he would continue under my supervision. I worked out a large-scale thematic structure based on a journey through the four elements and talked him through individual story arcs, even supplying dialogue and caption suggestions, which he applied diligently. Millar-Quitely's *The Authority* was a big hit with the cool kids, which led to Mark being hired, on my recommendation, to spearhead Marvel's new "Ultimate Universe" initiative, along with another new boy with attitude named Brian Michael Bendis.

I worked with him on the plots of the first five issues of the book and even ghostwrote one when Mark was ill and behind. As Mark's star began to rise, however, our collaboration fell by the wayside and he went his own way.

What Ellis had begun and Millar had completed was to make the Justice League and Avengers look out of date and out of touch. The threats in *The Authority* were enormous: insane tyrants commanding armies of genetically modified suicide supermen, a parallel world expansionist empire of courtly cannibals, and God itself. Millar's run brought in analogues of Marvel's Avengers, recast as baby killers and homosexual rapists before introducing an omnipotent pedophile sadist who caused the sky to rain dead pets and abortions. In the hands of a Dark Age writer, or in the pages of *Spawn*, this kind of thing might have been unbearably gruesome. Millar played it all for laughs.

His last four-part story line, however, went too far when big business concerns contrived to overpower and replace the Authority with a team of superpowered right-wing puppets. Brainwashed and degraded, the female members of the team were plunged into humiliating scenarios inspired by the online pornography that was now becoming a feature of most men's lives as the Internet got its hooks in deep.

When Millar's script called for a spot of necrophilia involving the corpse of ex–Authority team leader Jenny Sparks and a British superhero called the General—drawn by Quitely to look like a debauched David Beckham, the soccer legend—publisher Paul Levitz pulled the plug. The strip was heavily influenced by the dark comedy of Chris Morris and *The League of Gentlemen*, but that strain of macabre horror farce was still an unfamiliar flavor that lacked context in the upper echelons at DC and seemed merely, indefensibly sensational.

The Authority was castrated, reduced to a pallid shadow of its confrontational, hip, and cheeky glory. The comic hobbled along, sustained by a loyal audience who remembered the wonder years but knew deep inside they'd never come again. The fire was out. The Authority were finally no more, no less than the inhabitants of Earth-50 in a new DC Multiversal scale that came into being in 2007.

For a while, it was exciting. In *The Authority*, the no-nonsense army toughs were on our side for a change, but it was a particular kind of power fantasy: that of impotent liberals, who feared deep down that it was really only force and violence that got things done and not patient diplomacy, and that only soldiers and very rich people had the world figured out. Gifted Irish writer Garth Ennis had occupied this territory for years; his soldier-hardman heroes influenced the new generation of supermen and women. These books were a capitulation to a kind of thinking that would come to dominate the approaching first decade of the new millennium.

Soon the no-compromise bomb and "cripple what you don't agree with" approach of the Authority would be put to practice in the real world with horrific results. And it wouldn't be liberals doing the damage.

The quirky Joe Casey (later part of the team that created the popular kids' cartoon *Ben 10*), who'd contributed a thoughtful pacifist take on Superman and would join me on the spearhead of the next big shake-up at Marvel, reversed the dynamic with artist Sean Phillips, turning the evil-corporation theme on its head with a radical reinvention of Jim Lee's *WildC.A.T.S.* as a progressive, world-changing corporation with a super-CEO and board of directors who re-created the world with one simple product: a battery that never ran out.

CHAPTER 21

HOLLYWOOD SNIFFS BLOOD

ASIDE FROM THE ailing *Batman* franchise, superhero movies were few and far between in the nineties, giving no indication of what was to come.

On one side were the "dark" or Gothic offerings like Sam Raimi's manically inventive, pulp-infused *Darkman, The Crow,* and Todd McFarlane's disappointing *Spawn*, which failed to capture the goblin screech of the comic book. On the other side were the bloated *Dick Tracy*–style living cartoons and period pieces that completely lacked a discernible audience, such as *The Rocketeer, The Shadow,* and *The Phantom*, or interesting awkward oddities such as 1999's *Mystery Men,* which featured a cast of misfits culled from Bob Burden's *Flaming Carrot* series, as portrayed by talented comedy and character actors like Ben Stiller, Janeane Garofalo, William Macy, and voice actor in *The Simpsons,* Hank Azaria, who played the film's best character, the turbaned Blue Raja, who could "do things" with cutlery.

As the name perhaps suggests, *Flaming Carrot* was an indie black-and-white book starring a hero whose head was an enormous carrot, with a flame on top where the leaves would be. Burden's Dadaist take on Golden

Age superhero stories was genuinely inspired, and the book had enjoyed a season of faddish popularity during the first flush of the post-*Watchmen* wave of psychedelic superheroes. The Mystery Men from the back pages of *Flaming Carrot* were a disturbing bunch of redneck hobo loser supermen, and the movie failed to do them justice in spite of brave attempts by a cast that seemed uncertain as to the tone, which was never weird enough to truly honor its source or straight enough to keep the attention of a mainstream audience, who always felt cheated by "funny" superhero movies. The *Batman* franchise floundered in the same atmosphere of mockery and burlesque. No one had yet found a way to make superheroes convincing on-screen, but it was only a matter of time.

X-Men led the cavalry charge in the summer of 2000. Technology had caught up with the comics and believing a man could fly was as easy as believing a giant could be a midget. Despite being at least a foot taller than the pint-sized scrapper of the comics, Hugh Jackman's Wolverine was a defining role to which the actor brought exactly the right balance of toughness and sensitivity. Patrick Stewart, *Star Trek: The Next Generation*'s Captain Jean-Luc Picard, cornering the market in "bald white men" roles, was born to play Professor Charles Xavier, and if Sir Ian McKellen was a little older than the comic-book Magneto, he brought a strength and a nasty twinkle to the role that pretty much stole the show.

The story wisely dumped Claremontian soap gymnastics, opting instead for a taut science fiction plot about the next stage in evolution trying to find a place in a fearful, threatening human world. Here was a superhero film that didn't rely on powers and trademark costumes. In fact, X-Men uniforms had changed radically over the years, and here they were overhauled again as black leather flight suits unlike anything seen in the comics. It was about characters we could identify with and a theme that resonated particularly well on the cusp of the new century: old versus new. Tradition versus tomorrow.

Director Bryan Singer's *X-Men* was the film that made everyone in the comics business sit up and take notice, but comics were still the only place to find serious, well-made, and realistic superhero stories on a regular basis.

That too was to change a few months after *X-Men*, when the release of the masterly *Unbreakable* provided the first real hint of what was possible and what was to come. Writer-director M. Night Shyamalan had seemed to materialize fully formed with 1999's powerful twist-ending ghost story *The Sixth Sense*. In *Unbreakable* he cast a lugubrious Bruce Willis as David Dunn, whose alliterative name immediately fingered him as a potential comic-book hero. Dunn began his journey as the sole survivor of a horrific train wreck. He was unable to understand how he'd managed to survive until the measured unwinding of plot compelled him to face the impossible truth that he'd never been hurt, never been injured in his life. David Dunn, the ordinary Joe, married with a kid and a mortgage, was the world's first superhuman, and he'd lived to be forty without ever noticing.

Shyamalan gave the superman the full indie-auteur treatment. Piece by patient piece, he reassembled the building blocks of hero fiction to create what remains, in my opinion, the high-water mark of the cinema's treatment of the superhero theme.

The pivotal scene where Willis pumped more and more weights, testing his limits to find there were none, seemed to reach into the beating, golden core of what the superhero represented. Willis gave us a muscular, sweating Everyman hero, but it was Dunn's intense stillness, his self-doubt turning to conviction, and his character depth that made him feel like a Dark Age hero written by a Renaissance writer.

Even Dunn's tormented relationship with his young son—whose soul became the movie's battleground between forces of good and evil—was beautifully resolved in a compact, touching, and completely silent scene that set up a whole series of potential "Security Man" and sidekick movies—then judiciously left the sequels to our imagination. One hopeful rumor suggested a trilogy, continuing with *Breakable* and *Broken*. A scene in which he carried his wife upstairs was shot to look as if they were flying in a romantic, real-world echo of Lois Lane's "Can you read my mind?" scene from 1978's *Superman*.

Subtle, satisfyingly grounded in the commonplace, Willis, with his Security rain cape and hood, even had his own secret identity, costume, and logo. But it was only if we recognized the tropes, or watched a second time, that we saw how matter-of-factly they'd been deployed in the expert construction of a definitive superhero origin story that was faithful to the form in a way we'd never seen before on-screen or in comics.

There was the ultimate exquisite death trap, which used three simple ingredients—a flexible plastic sheet stretched across a swimming pool, body weight, and deep water—to encapsulate the suffocating, no-way-out, black-hole horror of the most thrilling comic-book cliff-hangers.

There was a monster: in this case, the sociopathic inhuman beast with no name who turned up in an orange boilersuit on the doorsteps of nice middle-class family folks with the words "I like your house. Can I come in?"

Cue screams.

There was Dunn's climactic fight with the psycho, which managed somehow to re-create the explosive high-stakes impact of a Kirby cosmic slugfest using a bedroom, a terrified hostage, and two men whose explosive releases of breath took the place of sound effects. And then there was Mr. Glass, the mastermind, pulling the strings since day one. The transformation of Dunn's friend and adviser Elijah Price into the supervillain Mr. Glass was accomplished in plain sight, but only in those last moments did it all make as much sense to us as it did to the horrified hero. Elijah's stylish purple suits and long leather coat, his wheelchair and spiked leg brace, and his private office with its multiple computer screens and memorabilia all assumed a grotesque new significance: He had become a cyborg master fiend in his secret lair. He needed someone to fight, to give his broken life meaning, and so he made big, strong David Dunn into his own personal superhero nemesis.

Samuel L. Jackson, himself a celebrity comic-book fan, was expertly cast as the troubled Price, a comic-book enthusiast with a disease that had left his bones brittle and easily broken—hence the cruel "Mr. Glass" nickname he'd been given at school. Price, who owned an art gallery with framed superhero originals on the walls, was the nerd pal of the hero: At first Jimmy Olsen, he became Lex Luthor, as admiration turned to hatred.

There was no pompous, triumphal march soundtrack, no striking of poses or corny melodrama. Willis was a world-weary, blue-collar Atlas with the weight of the world on his shoulders, setting the standard for a new decade of realistic superfiction with a stylish, original, and intelligent re-creation of the form.

———————

Superman died in 1993 in the pages of *Superman* no. 75, beaten and bludgeoned to death by a giant alien engine of destruction called Doomsday, who resembled the unfortunate collision of Marvel's Hulk with a truckload of slate, dinosaur bones, and broken tusks. Over twenty-four full-page shots of unrelenting punch-up combat, the last son of Krypton finally succumbed to the sheer battering brainless thuggery of his bestial opponent. It was bare and uncomplicated, and it left readers in no doubt: Superman had died saving the world.

There was very little about Superman's latest death that could be described as elegant or lyrical, but the response was phenomenal. A gullible media, happy to believe that DC Comics might actually kill off a lucrative trademark, created an intense buzz around the story of Superman's death, which resulted in record-breaking sales.

When he inevitably erupted from the grave eight months later, Superman came complete with a mullet, which presumably he'd picked up in hell. For several years after, the battle to restore Superman's traditional short back and sides caused fierce and ridiculous arguments in the halls at DC. But the Fabio do hung on grimly until 2000, by which time Superman had been turned into a blue electrical energy Superman for a year before splitting into a red and blue electric Superman in a thin-blooded, over-stretched homage to 1963's classic utopian fantasy "Superman Red/Superman Blue," which had inspired book 3 of *Marvelman* to much greater effect. The run of increasingly desperate stunts—the death, the replacements, the comeback, the marriage, the new powers and costume—had begun to give an impression that no one really knew how to write a straightforward, contemporary Superman story anymore. The best Superman comics were all special projects: limited-run series such as Jeph Loeb and Tim Sale's pastoral *Superman for All Seasons*, Mark Waid and Leinil Yu's passionate early-years tale *Superman: Birthright*; and Mark Millar's *Superman: Red Son*, a neatly constructed alternate history in which Superman's rocket landed twelve hours later, in Communist Russia instead of the Kansas wheat fields. Superman sales went into a slow decline, as if gliding in to land on the runway of oblivion. Superman's best hope for survival as a concept now lay with other media.

Nineteen eighty-eight's *Superboy*, by Alexander and Ilya Salkind, the producers of the Superman movies starring Christopher Reeve, was the first of a run of television series that kept the character if not in the public eye, then at least in the back of its mind. A Screen Writers Guild strike meant that a group of DC writers, including Denny O'Neil and J. M. DeMatteis, were given a chance to contribute stories with a more authentic comic-book feel. When John Haymes Newton, who played the Boy of Steel, asked for more money, he was unceremoniously replaced with Gerard Christopher, a Superman enthusiast and fan who took the show to greater heights of popularity. Effects improved over time, and the show, later retitled *The Adventures of Superboy*, was able to bring in characters like Bizarro, Mr. Mxyzptlk, and even the Golden Age Earth-2 Superman, as portrayed by Ron Eli.

In 1993 Superman scored an even bigger television hit with *Lois and Clark,* which translated the well-to-do urban professionals of the Byrne remake into a network-friendly romantic adventure show that followed the classic Superman-on-TV formula by keeping him on the ground until the last ten minutes. Unlike *Superboy*, it steered away from comic-book stories, and the dabblings in sci-fi were of a lightweight, uncomplicated nature, with themes designed to appeal to a general couples audience. Like most of the Superman shows, it did very well. Stars Dean Cain and Teri Hatcher became instant heartthrobs, and at a time when Superman was dead in the comics—replaced by four substitutes—he was more alive than ever in the public consciousness. It ran for four seasons, faltering when producers decided it was time for Clark and Lois to tie the knot. Immediately, the sexual tension that had given the stories their edge just bled out, and the audience evaporated.

Running from 2001, the most successful of all the small-screen Superman series was *Smallville*. This look back at a teenage Superman's formative years before he chose to wear the familiar suit and move to the big city introduced the character to a whole new audience, and proved that his brand of boy-next-door-handsome heroism never went out of fashion. And even that he could work just as well without the costume. This young Superman wrestled with tough decisions and wore ordinary clothes.

The persistent notion that Superman is an unpopular or dated character comes mostly from comic-book fans, who, pointing to the poor reception for *Superman Returns* in 2007, tended to overlook his appearance in hit TV shows since the eighties.

The film series that really kicked down the doors and brought superheroes into the mainstream began with *Spider-Man* in 2002. Until *The Dark Knight* swooped into town, the Spider-Man movies were the top three highest-grossing superhero films of all time, and they're still in the first four. What was it about Lee and Ditko's Friendly Neighborhood Spider-Man that allowed him to connect with the new global audience that Hollywood was eager to cultivate?

Parker was no badass motherfucker, he was a nice guy; gentle, shy, misunderstood, self-deprecating, and neurotic but funny, and brave, too. Parker was the nerd hero in excelsis, as he'd been when he was created in 1962 to connect with awkward, bookish high school students. Now we were all geeks, torn between duty and desire, freedom and responsibility, and Peter Parker, wrestling with his conscience on a daily basis, had become one of us again, a twenty-first-century Everyman.

Perhaps it was the mask, too; Spider-Man's face, completely hidden, allowed us to project ourselves onto its blank surface. Fully costumed, he had no nationality, no color, making him as popular in Bangalore, India, as he was in Boise, Idaho.

Taking a few cues from the Superman and Batman movies, Sam Raimi and his team also followed Brian Bendis's lead on the *Ultimate Spider-Man* series by slowing Peter Parker's origin story down a little and building up his rich supporting cast so that Peter's civilian life was at least as interesting as if not more so than his exploits in the Spidey costume. The scenes with Peter and Mary Jane Watson, his obscure object of desire, had a gawky adolescent tenderness and poetry that was refreshingly honest and youthful. Played by Tobey Maguire and Kirsten Dunst, the two leads shared a fragile, hopeful, high-pitched relationship that made us want to hug them, except that they both looked as if they'd break into pieces on contact.

Spider-Man's tumbling, weightless loops and falls through the spires and glass-walled ravines of Manhattan had an agreeably dreamlike rhythm that was even more fun than flying. First-person chase scenes down Fifth Avenue gave the films a rolling, kinetic energy that left the comics in the dirt, but there was something unconvincing about the normally dependable Willem Dafoe's hunched, by-the-numbers mental case portrayal of Norman Osborn's Green Goblin, and the set-piece fight during the Macy's Thanksgiving Day Parade was too reminiscent of an almost identical scene from Tim Burton's *Batman*. The setup was so good that the villain plot seemed almost an afterthought and was developed to far greater effect in the third installment of the series, when Peter's best friend Harry Osborn (actor James Franco) assumed his own villain disguise to avenge his father's death, without realizing that his attempts to kill Spider-Man were assaults on his own pal's life.

Spider-Man 2 brought the trilogy to its peak with nail-biting soap-operatic twists and action-fight scenes of a kind that had never been attempted before. The bright-eyed, enthusiastic Alfred Molina's tragic, roller-coaster breakdown on his way to becoming Doctor Octopus was a tour de force of villain acting that never lost its affecting human core, never pitched into scene-chewing pantomime.

By the time of the third film, the energy was dissipating. Peter, possessed by an alien, turned into a black-clad joke Goth version of himself in a move that was reminiscent of *Superman 3*'s evil doppelgänger fight sequences. *Spider-Man 3* felt like too many films at once and offered little that was new, except for an astonishing CGI re-creation of the shape-shifting human beach known as the Sandman (not DC's Sandman, the Lord of Dreams, but a man who actually turns into sand). Nevertheless, it too was a box office juggernaut, and the superheroes were here to stay.

Oddly enough, and only three years after the Raimi series, Marvel started work on yet another retelling of Spider-Man's origin, this time with a younger actor and a high school setting, perhaps to capture some of the *Twilight* dollars. Whether audiences are ready for a reboot with the original still fresh in their memories has yet to be determined, but the attempt to skew the new Spider-Man and X-Men tent poles in the direction of younger viewers might indicate a probably unfounded fear that the mass-market fad for superheroes on-screen is over.

As *Spider-Man* ignited the hero boom, the green lights flashed on a dozen Hollywood projects.

Seven actors have played Batman on the big screen, and if you can name all seven without reading any further, your youth has been wasted. Each man has approached the character differently, and each has worn his own distinctive adaptation of Batman's basic costume, with different colors, ear shapes, cape lengths, and choice of fabrics.

You may think you recognize the Batman costume and assume that it hasn't changed much since 1939, but you'd be wrong.

In 1939 Batman was drawn as a slim, young-looking man wearing a jet-black cape and cowl. The cowl had stylized vane-like ears, and the ankle-length, scalloped cape appeared to be reinforced with umbrella struts, picked out as thin blue highlights on black. He wore little purple Mickey Mouse gloves and knee-high black riding boots with a pointed cuff. The bat symbol on his chest was a tiny black silhouette, making the yellow utility belt the only touch of bright color.

Ten years later, Batman was a sturdier, more fatherly figure. The highlights on the black cape had taken over, turning the cape and cowl a bright blue. The dark vest and tights became dove gray. Smiling daytime Batman appeared as a friend to children everywhere. This was Batman as Santa Claus. The costume was no longer designed to frighten but to reassure. The only remnant of his past was the permanent shadow around his eyes, which, even at his most kid friendly, never lost their spooky pupil-less demonic glow. You may have noticed, of course, how all the screen Batmen have visible eyes. Obviously, this helps an actor work more effectively behind the mask, but Batman in the comics has always had white slits for eyes, explained by the presence of blank reflecting lenses that protect his eyes and enhance his vision.

As we know from the Silver Age chapters, the Batman concept has been stretched and distorted and taken to places from which it might seem impossible to return or recover, and the magnificent seven movie Batmen have each presented a very different take on how the adventures of the Caped Crusader might look in a world beyond the comics.

Simply entitled *Batman*, the live-action serial of 1943 starred Lewis Wilson, a conventional low-budget action lead with firm jaw and oil-slick hair. Wilson's groundbreaking turn offered an exhausting fifteen-chapter glimpse into what life might be like if Bruce Wayne's war on crime relied on the bare modicum of commitment and an allocated budget of $3.50 a week.

The first actor to play Batman on-screen crept around in a horribly convincing homemade Bat suit, muttering vile racist sentiments under his breath. With episode titles like "A Nipponese Trap," "Slaves of the Rising Sun," and "The Doom of the Rising Sun," it was plain to see what was on the collective mind of America's entertainment industry. Batman's comic-book foes had been street hoodlums, gangsters, and madmen. Now America's enemies were Batman's enemies too. On first impression, they didn't have much to fear from Lewis Wilson and his Robin, Douglas Croft, sporting such a distinctive and recognizable haircut that Robin was indistinguishable from his alter ego Dick Grayson.

Wilson's unimpressive "Bat's Cave" resembled a serial killer's converted basement, with an assemblage of high-tech crime-fighting equipment that amounted to a "shabby chic" wooden table and chair of the kind you'd hurry past at a flea market, a telephone, and some artfully placed, thoroughly unconvincing rubber bats on strings. Far from dedicating all of his vast wealth and resources to the fight against crime, Wilson's Batman seemed to have reluctantly forked out a few quid. His Batmobile was an ordinary convertible with a little trailer attached, while Douglas Croft turned Robin into a spunky twit with an Art Garfunkel do. Everything about this Batman's mission seemed half-assed, second rate, and ill considered. Barely able to muster the energy to tackle crime, this less than Dynamic Duo waited two days and three serial chapters before responding languidly and with zero conviction to a desperate emergency call. The scenes where they wriggled out of obligations and repeatedly let down Wayne's long-suffering girlfriend Linda Page were the best parts of an overextended propaganda workout.

At best, this was the Dynamic Duo as a pair of bored fops indulging in a spot of the latest dress-up-and-fight-crime lark. If only they'd been able to take it all the way and given us a serial based around the lunatic antics of a feckless playboy and his cockeyed work-shy ward. There's something to be said for a portrayal of Batman and Robin as thrill-crazy dilettante vigilantes, sipping cocktails and tooting cocaine before stretching into the tights and roughing up some Japanese ne'er-do-wells. *Batman* is a bold step in the direction of a hero for whom crime is less a scourge on society and more a frightful nuisance.

Somewhere during chapter 3, there came the nauseating realization that this was how it would look if Batman was real in 1943: a mad millionaire dressed like a Halloween Mephistopheles, crouched in a leaking cave with a wooden chair, a table, and a ham radio kit to broadcast his anti-Axis propaganda.

Wilson's awkward clambering gymnastics, miles away from Batman's effortless comic-book swings and leaps, seemed, as a result, more agonizingly real. His ponderous attempts to haul his bulk up a rope were exhausting to watch and more horribly convincing than any other "realistic" portrayal of Batman to date.

What worked in the comics seemed less convincing through the cruel Cyclops eye of the lens. If Lewis Wilson's bizarre appearance inspired any terror at all in the criminal classes, it was surely that instinctual dread engendered by the close proximity of the mentally ill, immensely rich, and unstoppably violent. Bruce Wayne was wealthier than any of us could ever dream of being. Who were we to say what was right and wrong in his world?

He even threatened one gullible criminal idiot with his bats. "My little friends," the Batman hissed as tiny plastic pipistrelles fluttered about his shrieking victim's head. "They might get hungry" was all the perp needed to hear before he started singing like a canary. Anything could happen.

Lewis Wilson's cape fastened around the neck over a cloth balaclava hood with curved devil horns and the tunic barely containing his impressive man boobs. This Batman costume was certainly not the result of trial and error and refinement: It was something he found in a party store bargain bucket. In one scene, his gloves disappeared for several minutes with no explanation for their absence—or for the prominent wedding ring on his finger.

Wilson's chest emblem lacked the distinctive yellow oval that first appeared as part of Carmine Infantino's New Look redesign for the comics in 1964. Taking its cue from Bob Kane's simple bat silhouette on gray, Wilson's costume added white border detailing to the graphic to suggest the skeletal structure of a bat's wings. This particular touch has never been used again and may be ready for a comeback.

The 1949 serial *Batman and Robin*, cheaper and seedier yet, featured a remarkably dissolute performance by actor Robert Lowery. Both he and Robin have a thuggish, sozzled, and aggressive air. There was something of late-period Dean Martin in Lowery's languid routine. With his tousled hair and hooded eyes, his was a grown-up, manly, and possibly alcoholic Batman in early middle age, while Johnny Duncan's Robin evoked a broken-down rent boy long past his best, delivering each of his lines in a frightening, lobotomized monotone. Bruce Wayne was played as a constantly enervated lush, drifting in and out of scenes so startlingly pedestrian they seemed to share that specific interest in the day-to-day and particular that characterized the cinema of the underground.

This one is notable for bringing in Commissioner Gordon (who was Chief Arnold in 1943) and introducing to the mythos the famous Bat signal atop police headquarters, known as the Batman signal in this early incarnation but otherwise undistinguished.

The serial opened unhelpfully with a title sequence that featured Batman and Robin running around in the dark as if both were completely and unutterably lost. It featured interminable tedious car chase sequences through the Warner lots and a recognizably Californian countryside that suggested the forced relocation of Gotham City to the West Coast. Demonstrating some remote-control toys of the kind that can be bought in any High Street toy store, Batman could only look on in horrified wonder. "The possibilities of this thing in criminal hands are appalling," he snarled as he piloted a toy car around with a joystick. Who dared disagree?

They were described as glamorous figures—"known to his neighbors as a wealthy playboy"—but the evidence of our own eyes forced us into an instantly combative position with the script. There was nothing glamorous about this pair of sinister sleazebags who appeared to have made any money they still had left from exploiting the poor and ignorant.

The Batmobile was a cheesy convertible—this one appeared to be bright red in black-and-white—where Batman changed in the backseat as the canvas roof folded into place, and *presto!* The easily identifiable roadster Bruce and Dick just arrived in became, in the blink of an eye, the wondrous Batmobile! When Batman awkwardly wrestled his clothes off and his bat drag on, the alleged Boy Wonder took the wheel illegally, and when it was the dissolute Robin's turn to squirm and twist into his togs in the backseat, Batman did the honors up front. This was a legendary partnership, after all.

The villain was the Wizard, a kind of anti-Batman in an executioner's hood and cape who could have been interesting if they'd paid enough money for anything interesting to happen in the script. But they hadn't, it didn't, and he wasn't.

The second Batman sported an interesting combination of bat and devil motifs, which never seemed to catch on again. Lowery's horns were sharp and pointed, vicious inverted cones that thrust belligerently from a beaky cloth executioner's hood. The eye holes were slanted at a curious angle, which gave him the untrustworthy look of Richard Nixon in a gargoyle mask.

His thick belt, lacking the utility pouches that made it functional in an urban combat context, seemed to be there for one reason only, and that was to hold up the heavy woolen underpants he wore to terrify criminals. The belt's heroic failure to control a rolling gut that Batman's years of devoted training in martial arts and tai chi had somehow failed to erase became a cruel feature of every scene.

This wrinkled costume he wore would be unable to stop a lit cigarette let alone a slug from a .45. With his pitiful fighting skills, which relied on clumsy haymaker punches and off-balance lunges, Lowery's Batman could expect a crime-fighting life span of three weeks, with a career ending abruptly the moment any half-trained yellow belt tae kwon do novice punched him in the head.

There was the sense that for Lowery the whole Batman thing had been assembled from a tramp's jumble, and he was simply doing his not very best with what he had. He was like a man waking from a wonderful dream to find that his incredible technology amounted to a tin can with string, his glorious mansion a wet cardboard box in an alley.

These serials provided the inspiration for the next and most successful iteration of Batman so far when thirty-eight-year-old Adam West was cast as the new-look Batman with twenty-one-year-old Burt Ward as his sidekick, and the Batman concept stretched accommodatingly to include self-mocking burlesque as if to prove it was somehow invulnerable to interpretation.

West wore his costume like Salvador Dalí rocked his mustache. His predecessors had no context for what they were doing, but West had worked it all out and distilled the quintessence of the serials into a thin-lipped, clipped, and stylized performance that was funny for adults to watch and utterly convincing, quintessentially heroic to children. The show was made for color TV, so out went the natural shadows of Batman's world, and in came the bright palette of a Roy Lichtenstein canvas or an Infantino cover. The blue was bright blue, the gray was light, the yellows were acidic, lysergic sun colors.

The ears on West's cowl were short and discreet, owing more to comic artist Dick Sprang's 1950s Batman than to the devil-horned serial heroes and even looking ahead to the Frank Miller Batman. The highlights sometimes seen on the eyebrows of Batman's hood were drawn as two gull wing arches, giving him a permanently surprised yet severe look. The emblem on his chest, a yellow cardboard oval with a jaunty little black bat, was stuck to his gray spandex tunic with what could have been model glue, as if a ten-year-old boy who was good with his hands had fashioned the outfit for Halloween. He wore a chunky 3-D cartoon of a belt, with useless pouches that opened upside down and were too thin to contain anything bigger than an after-dinner mint, all in blinding yellow.

This Batman's costume was for display, not for combat. No one had yet thought of making it appear functional. Again, the approach seemed based on a need to create living cartoons, which was the accepted approach to comic-book adaptations and lasted until the superhero movie boom of the twenty-first century.

The fighting hadn't changed much since the war. West's and Ward's Batman and Robin relied on a jump and tussle, rock 'em, sock 'em melee style that was based less on the techniques of ninja shadow assassins than on bar-fighting cowboy action. When the magnificent Bruce Lee appeared in a crossover episode with *The Green Hornet*, as sidekick Kato, he outclassed everyone on set. It was Lee, of course, who popularized Eastern martial arts and rewrote the rule book for what audiences expected from Hollywood fight scenes.

The last new episode of *Batman* went out on March 14, 1968, and guest-starred Zsa Zsa Gabor as an evil beautician. American boys were dying in Vietnam and on TV, students were rioting in Paris, and high camp just wasn't funny anymore. Even the introduction of Yvonne Craig as the shapely motorbike-riding Batgirl couldn't keep a fickle audience interested.

When the first intense flush of Batmania was revealed to be little more than a passing craze, audiences lost interest. Sales of the comic books, which had spiked at the height of the show's popularity, slumped once more, causing editor Julius Schwartz to change tack and commission a series of more somber character-based stories from writer Gardner Fox. The TV Batgirl was added to the DC universe too, then crippled by Alan Moore and Dave Gibbons in *The Killing Joke*. Today she's still in a wheelchair and, in the guise of Oracle, works with Batman as an online information broker. A character born to camp in one medium was transplanted to richer soil where she grew into a fascinating and complex living fiction.

So indelibly was Adam West's deadpan comedic Batman embedded in popular consciousness, it would take another twenty-two years—a whole generation—before audiences were ready to accept a different, darker take on the character that brought him closer to his roots.

Tim Burton's film *Batman* came as a revelation to audiences trained to expect the BIFF! BANG! POW! of the TV show. The idea of a grim, Gothic Batman was hardly new to fans of his comic-book adventures but it came as a pleasant revelation to an audience whose memories of the character were rooted in the sixties series. Suddenly it was okay to like Batman without buying into kitsch.

West was a knowing cartoon, accepting with the same poker-faced assurance everything that came his way, from the "Batusi" dance to Bat-Shark Repellent Gas. Sixties iconoclasm saw the crime fighter as an establishment joke from an era of kitsch and self-deceit. In antiauthoritarian times, the superhero was one more uptight Republican patsy to be mocked, but by 1989, he was the only thing that stood between us and chaos. The Batman of 1989 could at last be returned to the vice-haunted alleys and rooftops where he belonged, handed back to the shadows as an outlaw, an antiestablishment self-made hero.

The foundation of Tim Burton's *Batman* was sunk in Jack Nicholson's Joker. Nicholson had made a career playing extreme character roles, and his Joker was a study in excess, combining his turn as Ken Kesey's gaggle-eyed revolutionary Randall McMurphy from the film *One Flew Over the Cuckoo's Nest* with his performance as Jack Torrance in *The Shining* and his "horny Devil" in *The Witches of Eastwick*.

Nicholson's Joker makeup vied with that of female lead Kim Basinger for garishness and seemed made for remorseless HDTV scrutiny in later decades. As snoopy reporter Vicki Vale, Batman's very own Lois Lane, the undeniably attractive Basinger became another tragic victim of late-eighties cosmetic artistry and was painted to look like she'd followed the Joker's dip into the chemical vat with a matte orange neon lipstick and foundation so thick you could bury your dead in her face.

Burton's wisdom in casting Michael Keaton, an actor more renowned for his comedy roles, as Batman was soon apparent when he played the part absolutely straight, while adding to Bruce Wayne a quirky and offbeat vulnerability expressed as a distracted childlike engagement with the world. This otherworldly Bruce came across as a genuine trauma survivor and drew sympathy for a character hitherto portrayed as a one-dimensional playboy.

For the first time, the familiar costume was designed with at least one eye on its appropriateness in the area of urban vigilantism. Keaton's Bat suit replaced the flimsy cloth of old with molded black rubber that showed the new influence of punk and the S/M clubs on Tim Burton's brand of Goth fairy tale. The overpants were gone, and black dominated the look rather than the gray and blue of the comics. Barely able to move in the heavily protective suit, Keaton resorted to quick turns, snapping his entire body around to bring to the fight scenes a staccato rhythm that more closely approximated real martial arts kicks and blocks. The rough-and-tumble of Adam West, the have-a-go playground brawling of the serials, was replaced by more convincing nods toward the precision moves of Jeet Kune Do and karate. By 1990, audiences were familiar with Bruce Lee and Jackie Chan movies, and Batman's fighting style had to move with the times.

The taut muscles that stretched the fabric of superhero costumes in the comics pages to such unfeasibly unwrinkled extremes that it looked as if the costume had been painted on were never possible with cloth or spandex. But the costume designers solved that problem by creating fake muscles, sculpted into a durable breastplate reminiscent of a Roman centurion. Whatever his build or athletic ability, Batman could now sport impressive pecs and a washboard stomach. Screen Batman was at last the Dark Knight, and *knight* meant armor.

The chest shield was now a sculpted medallion. Infantino's oval frame remained, but here it contained a black bat bas relief, redesigned especially for the movie, that pushed and stretched the wings out to the curved edge, so that black negative space dominated and prepared to eclipse the last of the cheerful yellow. Reversing figure and ground had the effect of turning the sign into a gaping mouth, a maw hungry for consumer dollars, which gave the logo a new and more subliminally threatening appeal. His belt was once again wholly decorative, but now vaguely futuristic, with solid pods instead of pouches.

The second Burton film, *Batman Returns,* was even better than the first, although seen now, the Burton films have a claustrophobic, airless quality that is the result of the director's penchant for enclosed sets rather than location work. All the action occurred on small street corner sets, making Gotham City feel like a compact, sealed interior space rather than a sprawling, living city. Having said that, designer Anton Furst took inspiration from the etchings of the eighteenth-century Italian painter and engraver Giambattista Piranesi, so perhaps the stifling sense of an enclosed space, an "imaginary prison," was exactly what the filmmakers intended us to experience.

The standout character in the sequel was Michelle Pfeiffer's alluring and definitive Catwoman, who like Burton's Batman took her inspiration from punk and bondage clothing, with a shiny vinyl catsuit and spiked heels that in no way hindered her rooftop kung fu workouts and somersaults. As the mousy secretary Selina Kyle, who transformed into a seductive villainess after an attempt on her life, this version owed more to *Rose and the Thorn* than it did to any of Catwoman's previous origin stories. (Originally a daring cat burglar, she'd been recast as a wily prostitute with a taste for robbery in *Batman: Year One.*)

When Burton left Gotham to pursue his personal visions, the Batman franchise was handed to Joel Schumacher, who talked of creating a comic on-screen but who had not, one was forced to assume, bothered to consult any comic published since his own childhood. His additions to the Bat franchise owed nothing to the adult look and feel of the Batman stories that were being published or attracting media attention in 1995.

Moviemakers soon learned not to imitate comics or to try to reproduce specifically comic book–style storytelling and formal techniques onscreen. Comics are what they are, and a good comic page can do things that even great movies can't, just as a movie can achieve effects even the best comics are incapable of equaling. Trying to make comics more like movies is a dead end; trying to make movies that look like comics is generally box office disaster.

Val Kilmer, not long after his eerily accurate turn as Jim Morrison, made for a handsome and inward-turning Bruce Wayne, in a performance no less an authority than Bob Kane himself decreed the closest to his original vision for the character. Tommy Lee Jones's Two-Face turned up with a shrieking, cackling caricature that took Nicholson's Joker as its starting point before carefully removing any nuance or subtlety and screaming the result out through a megaphone. Comedian du jour Jim Carrey's take on the Riddler was slightly better, channeling his "Cable Guy" character by way of Frank Gorshin, but it was clear that Burton's wisely considered revamp was giving way to the "living cartoon" approach once again. As the failure of 1990's *Dick Tracy* (Warren Beatty's primary-colored big-budget folly and love letter to his main squeeze at the time, Madonna) had proven without doubt, moviegoers had no appetite for such artifice.

Val Kilmer's Bat suit retained the molded torso look but added a new detail in the form of nipples. His costume took on a display aspect that would be foregrounded in the next Batman film.

When Michael Gough's Alfred produced Robin's new costume from his sewing box with the words "I took the liberty, sir . . ." he spoke for a nation of perverts. The elderly butler had, in fact, taken the liberty of adding molded nipple cups to Robin's breastplate. Rubber tailoring is, of course, a highly specialized art kept alive by the tastes of the fetish underground, pop stars, and the fringes of catwalk fashion, but dear old Alfred appeared to have mastered it in his spare time, along with everything else. Accompanied by a fruity raised eyebrow, the moment skated around an abyss that Schumacher would jump into feetfirst with his next Batman picture.

The final Batman film of the nineties, and the one that transformed a money-spinning film franchise into a radioactive turkey cat dinner, was 1997's *Batman and Robin*, widely regarded as the worst Batman film ever made and indeed reviled by some commentators as the most indefensible artifact ever created by a so-called civilization.

Batman actors changed more often than the guard at Buckingham Palace, and now it was George Clooney's turn to star. His prematurely graying Hollywood-handsome face made for a different kind of Bruce Wayne, one that was more paternal and at the same time more vulnerable, a grieving son to Alfred's expiring surrogate father.

"I love you, old man," he all but wept.

The homosexual subtext that Dr. Fredric Wertham discerned in the blueprint for the Batman story was thrust aboveground. *Batman and Robin* was as gay as it got.

Clooney's Batman proudly embraced the disco aesthetic as no other before him had dared to do. This was Batman as peacock. The chest symbol had broken out of its confining oval to become huge, stretching its wings from shoulder to shoulder and cast in silver. There were inexplicable argent flashes and decorative panels that cried out for attention. It made little sense for Batman to look like this. He belonged not in the shadows but under the strobe lights dancing the Batusi with the Village People. It was pure design; nineties aesthetic with no substance.

Alicia Silverstone's baby-fattish Batgirl was an utterly unconvincing addition to the cast. The skills that had made Silverstone the perfect lead in *Clueless,* the comedy of Bel Air manners, were lost in this overcrowded, underwritten movie, which appeared to have been concocted principally to serve as the dictionary definition of *farrago.*

Arnold Schwarzenegger lumbered through the film, delivering his charmless turn as Mr. Freeze with all the enthusiasm of a postman dispensing dull circulars. His entire role was constructed around a two-page concordance of predictable one-liners— *"Freeze!" "Chill out!"* and so on— that even the mighty Arnold failed to sell with any authority. To make matters worse, he'd been recently outclassed by a cartoon. The Mr. Freeze episode "Heart of Ice," from *Batman the Animated Series* by Paul Dini and Bruce Timm (which *Batman and Robin* had the audacity to quote in the form of Mr. Freeze's sentimental snow globe memento of his dead wife), had broken new ground for a show allegedly aimed at kids, with its layered and emotive study of loss and madness. It spoke volumes about Schumacher's approach that the animated Mr. Freeze was a tragic creature of depth and pathos, while the real man on-screen was a cipher in plastic and tinfoil, a lumbering, sleepwalking cliché emitter, the seeming result of some drunken pool party bet that the future governor of California could be persuaded to spray paint his bollocks silver for enough cash.

It was left to girl of the moment Uma Thurman, fresh from her career-defining appearance as Mia Wallace in *Pulp Fiction*, to save the day. She looked great but hammed it up as a ridiculously over-the-top villainess, like Mae West as the evil fairy queen in a school play, hollering every line to the back row.

The idea of a psychedelic Batman was not entirely objectionable, and the colors and costumes were eye-catching, but the performances were simply too arch, or the lines were tired and hackneyed, delivered with a weary detachment that suggested the onset of coma.

At the end of act 2, Alicia Silverstone let slip the single line that seemed to sum up Schumacher's entire message:

"Suit me up, Uncle Alfred!"

Her chirpy call to arms was followed by fast-cut, hard-core dungeon-club close-ups of the teenager's hard thighs and toned ass sleeking into spray-on black leather. High heels, dominatrix corset, and molded plastic nipple cups that turned her breasts into advertisements came next. It was hard to escape the conclusion that dear old Uncle Alfred may have been choosing to die in order to avoid his inevitable arrest and conviction.

The popular brooding Batman had lasted all of two movies. The emphasis was back on camp and color with a complete disregard for the kind of Batman audiences wanted. *Batman Forever* and *Batman and Robin* played out like Broadway musicals without the tunes and effectively eradicated mainstream interest in Batman by ignoring Frank Miller and Tim Burton's restorative work and dumping the character straight back into a desperately dated Mardi Gras milieu that refused to take changing tastes into account.

The set design was the best thing about the movie: The vivid ultraviolets and neons that were the result of Schumacher's attempts to re-create a comic-book palette deserved to be in a much better film, and one day they will be. There was an overreliance on computer-generated imagery, the decade's new special-effects toy, but at least Gotham seemed bigger in the establishing shots, as though it had finally broken out of Burton's airless spaces and grown into a sprawling dream city built around soaring, improbable verticals and monumental statuary. And by this time, the fights had taken on a new gymnastic, acrobatic dimension as the result of softer and more yielding Bat fabrics.

Clooney, unfortunately, looked smug and self-satisfied, as if he knew only his career would survive this debacle. Michael Gough's Alfred, on the other hand, had to be replaced by a computer program following one mawkish deathbed scene after another in which the monstrous old pervert cheated the Grim Reaper yet again. Obviously, almost touchingly, these filmmakers imagined they'd be brought on for future sequels in the Batman series, and the frightening new *Max Headroom*–influenced CGI butler "Uncle Alfred" was nothing less than a death warrant for the frail Gough; his matte-complexioned, pre-embalmed digital counterpart had been designed to outlive the actor in the unlikely event of a follow-up.

George Clooney's jazzy metal Batman stands as the high-water mark of an approach that had reached its conclusion. The camp crusader was well past his sell-by date, as Schumacher might have realized had he paid any attention to what was going on in the comics and the popular animated show, where Batman was being played straight to great effect by Kevin Conroy. The voice actor perfected the self-assured, trustworthy cadence of a sane, truly adult Batman that didn't give kids the creeps or adults the excuse to go see another movie.

It took another eight years before Batman could be rehabilitated sufficiently for a return to the big screen, as a troubled hero for anxious times.

My own movie agent at Creative Artists Agency submitted a treatment I'd entitled *Batman: Year Zero*, which had a young Batman traveling around the world, slowly assembling the familiar components of his outfit and disguise in the year before returning to Gotham as its protector. As a change from the Joker or the Penguin, the villains were Ra's al-Ghul and Man-Bat from the Denny O'Neil seventies stories. Screenwriter David Goyer and director Christopher Nolan, who were assigned to the restoration of the bat franchise, obviously felt the same way I did, electing to return to Batman's roots as part of their reconstruction effort.

Goyer and Nolan's new Batman had learned its lessons from the Alan Moore years and the "Ultimization" of Marvel characters, which had refreshed tired Cold War franchises with a new post-9/11 immediacy and opened up the possibility that every stale trademark could be similarly enlivened. Everything about *Batman Begins* was as carefully worked out as Batman's crusade to be "believable." Every item of the new Batman's costume had to justify its place there.

With *Begins,* Christopher Nolan created a Batman more in tune with the nervous tenor of the times. His Batman, re-creating many scenes and themes from Miller and Mazzucchelli's *Batman: Year One,* was a soldier, pure and simple, adapting military equipment and tactics to suit a vigilante terror war on crime. For the first time on-screen, Batman's uniform was functional, and every single piece of it told the story, like a set of tattoos, of who he was, where he'd been, and what he'd done. His costume was armor, no doubt about it. It was for protection, not display, not for fun, and definitely not because that's how a drawing would look.

Batman Begins was simply, tightly wound around the concept of fear: facing fear, overcoming fear, and succumbing to fear. It tried to ground Bruce Wayne by showing, step by step, the journey that a rich, bereaved, otherwise ordinary boy would have to take to become Batman. The script held to its missile-like course and had in Christian Bale an actor who not only had the piercing eyes, high cheekbones, and brooding Romantic quotient of a Neal Adams drawing but also a personal intensity that matched the role. This was the Batman fans had waited to see, the one that most closely approximated the character we all knew in our heads.

The success of this believable Batman, and his willingness to engage in symbolic form with the hardcore issues of the day, allowed Nolan and his collaborators to aim higher with their second Batman feature. *The Dark Knight* would set a new standard for superhero films by talking directly to a mainstream global audience about the way the shadows had seemed to creep in while we were all watching TV.

Box office records proved that Batman was back doing the business. This time he appealed to the same aspirational dream culture that made Iron Man's Tony Stark such a popular character, but where Tony was ebullient and cocky, Bruce was a brooding Gothic hero of the old school. That made Batman ultimately a more potent figure. Iron Man pounded his evil doubles into the concrete to resolve the plot and restore the status quo, but Batman was twisted through the moral wringer only to wind up a fugitive in a world grown appreciably darker and more familiar.

At the heart of *The Dark Knight* was a reputation-assuring performance that seemed to burn and fizz off the screen; it was hard to recognize the face of handsome young Heath Ledger under the scars and smeared makeup of the Joker, but he owned the screen from the moment he first appeared and slammed a pencil through a man's head until his final dangling turn as the hanged man of the tarot, condemning Batman to an upside-down world of darkness and madness. The Bondi Beach hunk had transformed himself into a twitching, tongue-chewing agent of chaos. Where Cesar Romero's Joker had been a gibbering, essentially harmless mental patient and Nicholson's a twisted Pop Artist, Ledger's Joker was a force of dark nature, a personification of chaos and anarchy, or so he wanted us all to believe. In fact, Ledger's Joker lied constantly, insisting he had no plan when the whole movie bore witness to his grand and awful designs.

And it was hard not to compare Aaron Eckhart's sensitive, heartbreaking performance as the doomed district attorney Harvey Dent with the cackling over-the-top circus turn of Tommy Lee Jones in *Batman Forever*. Jones's Two-Face had no real name, no backstory, nothing but schizo shtick in the form of his divided HQ (one side clean, one side shabby) and his devil and angel girl assistants, Sugar and Spice. *The Dark Knight*'s Harvey Dent offered instead a complex portrayal of the same character as a man maneuvered into hell by the Joker to prove his point. Dent was the White Knight destined to fall—so that even the title was a double, an echo applying to two men, not one.

To match its theme, the movie's structure was divided in two clear halves that overshadowed the traditional Hollywood three-act structure embedded within. This dominating diptych effect gave the odd sensation of watching two movies, and it neatly echoed the turn of the decision-making silver dollar Two-Face used: bright on one side, scarred and blackened on the other, like the story itself and especially the arc of the Dent character.

The sprawling, expansive opening section took Batman from Gotham City to Hong Kong. With crime in Gotham City on the run, he could afford to extend his influence internationally. Then at the midpoint, where the Joker was captured and it all seemed to be over, everything changed. Where a conventional superhero movie would have ended with the apprehension of the villain, *The Dark Knight* had another game to play. Would the silver dollar fall on its "good," unmarked face or on its "bad," scarred face, compelling Dent to do evil? The coin flipped, and the dark side landed uppermost. The second half of *The Dark Knight* undid the expectations of the first, as the story narrowed focus from the international to the painfully intimate and stifling. It ended with both the crusading DA and the film's heroine dead, the Joker still alive, and the Dark Knight on his steed, accused of all the crimes in this darkest night of all. Nolan's Batman roared into the end credits hunted by policemen and dogs for crimes he did not commit. An outcast hero in a corrupt nighttime city.

A hero for a world in darkness.

CHAPTER 22

NU MARVEL 9/11

IN TRADITIONAL WESTERN occult symbolism, the gateway to the lunar realm of imagination is flanked by twin pylons, or towers. If you look at most versions of the tarot trump number 18, the Moon, you will see these towers. They represent the door that separates the world of fantasy from material reality.

The descent of the kabbalistic thirty-second path of the tree of life describes an apocalyptic event involving the merging of two distinct spheres: the earthly and the lunar. The lunar sphere is the imagination, the world of thoughts and dreams. The earthly sphere is of the mundane, solid and heavy. In short, not only does real life become more like a story, stories must pay the price of this exchange by becoming more real and allowing the rules of the material world to impinge upon their insubstantial territories.

I can think of no more potent image of this union of real and imaginary than the terrorist attacks on the World Trade Center on September 11, 2001.

How many times had we seen those towers fall? How many times had this soul-wrenching vision been rehearsed in our imaginations, and repeated in our fictions, almost as if we were willing it to happen, and dreaming of the day?

From the moment the towers were completed in 1973, they became a target for a sequence of imaginary demolitions.

King Kong was the first to climb them in Dino DeLaurentis's pointless 1976 remake of the giant gorilla classic. They'd been smashed by tidal waves, blasted by aliens, shattered by meteor strikes, and pulverized by rogue asteroids. The terrible fall of the World Trade Center towers on September 11 had the curious inevitability of an answered prayer or the successful result of a black magic ritual.

Adding to the aura of the uncanny surrounding that day and its aftermath were the creepy clairvoyant comic books published in the weeks and months prior to September 11, all of them haunted by eerie images of planes and ruined towers. Garth Ennis's *Punisher* depicted a hijacked 747 on a suicide dive into twin silos. *Adventures of Superman* no. 596, a book written by Joe Casey several months earlier but published on September 12, began with a scene showing Lex Luthor's twin LexTowers in the aftermath of an alien attack. It mirrored, almost exactly, the photographs on the front pages of the same day's newspapers. So accurately did the pictures match that DC made the book returnable in the event of any inadvertent offense. My own *New X-Men* no. 115 with Frank Quitely, published in August 2001, ended with a scene in which an airliner, fashioned into the shape of a giant fist, was flown through the side of a skyscraper. The cover of the following issue, released on September 19, 2001, but written and drawn months before, had X-Men character the Beast in close-up, weeping, with an opening sequence of rescue workers searching through the dusty rubble of fallen buildings for bodies.

Who knows? In a universe where time is fundamentally simultaneous, the idea that events that have already occurred in the future might influence the past may not be entirely far-fetched.

Marvel Comics responded to the tragedy in its hometown with a genuinely heartfelt tale in which the superheroes aimlessly assembled at Ground Zero. They were compelled to acknowledge the event as if it had occurred in their own simulated universe, but they hadn't been there to prevent it, which negated their entire raison d'être. If al-Qaeda could do to Marvel Universe New York what Doctor Doom, Magneto, and Kang the Conqueror had failed to do, surely that meant the Marvel heroes were ineffectual. September 11 was the biggest challenge yet to the relevance of superhero comics.

The disorientation of the time was captured by a single giddy moment wherein Marvel's ultimate evil dictator cum terrorist supervillain Doctor Doom arrived on the scene at Ground Zero only to be moved to tears by the devastation. This was the "World's Greatest Super-Villain" who had himself attacked New York on numerous occasions. Doctor Doom was exactly the sort of bastard who would have armed al-Qaeda with death rays and killer robots if he thought for one second it would piss off the hated Reed Richards and the rest of his mortal enemies in the Fantastic Four, but here he was sobbing with the best of them, as representative not of evil but of Marvel Comics' collective shock, struck dumb and moved to hand-drawn tears by the thought that anyone could hate America and its people enough to do this.

As the events of 9/11 demonstrated, heroes were real human beings doing the right thing for the best reasons. Next to policemen, firemen, doctors, nurses, and selfless civilians, the superheroes were silly, impotent daydreams, and for a moment, they seemed to falter, aghast. They hadn't been prepared for this and had nothing useful to offer. It was, again, the darkness before a triumphant dawn. In the ontological confusion sur-rounding the descent of the thirty-second path, superheroes had tried very hard to be "realistic," and reality had bitten back. They couldn't cope with an event so raw that it seemed to lie beyond the reach of the kind of metaphors in which they usually traded.

It would take the superheroes a few more years to sort out their priorities. They would come to realize that they were a different kind of real and best served the needs of the inner world. They would soon grow stronger and more ubiquitous, but for a moment at the end of 2001, they were knocked from the sky and left wounded.

What was real had slipped and become uncertain, fantastic. It would surely serve symmetry if the fantastic could become more real in response. In the confused mingling of two normally contradictory modes of being, comics fans were demanding *more* realism from their fantasy books. Writers like Warren Ellis attempted to "explain," using scientific language and sound contemporary theory, how preposterous powers like Cyclops's devastating eye beams or Iron Man's "repulsor rays" might actually work, as if that could help to restore our belief in the superheroes, like some collective clapping of hands for the fading Tinker Bell in *Peter Pan*. With no way to control the growing unreality of the wider world, writers and artists attempted to tame it in fictions that became more and more "grounded," down-to-earth, and rooted in the self-consciously plausible.

And so was born Ultimate Marvel.

The idea was simple: Retell the great stories of the Marvel universe with a contemporary twist. Brian Bendis brought movie and TV storytelling to *Ultimate Spider-Man*. Bendis came from the independent comics scene and, influenced by playwright David Mamet rather than Stan Lee, he made alarmingly convincing dialogue the focus of his style and broke the rules of comic-book storytelling by having characters exchange multiple balloons in a single panel. His dialogue had a call-and-response rhythm that captured each voice perfectly, like the strains in a chorus, and soon he was Marvel Comics's premier writer, dominating the sales charts for the next decade with no sign yet of slowing down. When Bendis committed to a title, it was like swans mating, with ten-year-plus runs on his pet books.

Marvel stepped into the post-9/11 breach with global-political thrillers that acknowledged contemporary events without dwelling on them. *The Ultimates*, re-created with Mark Millar's gleefully right-leaning heroes, gave a voice to Bush's America's posturing, superheroic fantasies of global law enforcement in a posttraumatic world. It was both a glorification and a satire of those attitudes, and Millar was savvy enough to maintain the ambiguity to the end.

The Justice League was a pantheon, the X-Men was a school, but the Avengers were a football team. I advised Mark to take an opposite tack from his work in *The Authority*, suggesting he look instead at the Roy Thomas–John Buscema *Avengers* where the superheroes often convened in Tony Stark's kitchen, sometimes wearing raincoats over their costumes. I suggested that he do *The Ultimates* "real," as a convincingly paced story of what might actually happen in a world with superheroes but no villains. What would be the result if America created supersoldiers with no one to fight but one another? What if Thor couldn't prove he was from Asgard and was seen as a David Icke–style New Age guru? What if the Hulk became not only enraged but also sex crazed on hyperdoses of testosterone, and a Bride of Frankenstein–style reluctant She-Hulk was engineered to keep him under control? Even Giant Man was forced to contend with the real world's square-cube law, which capped his growing ability at sixty feet, after which his thighbones would snap under his own weight (something I'd remembered from a Flash Fact page).

The Ultimates was stuffed with articulate pop culture references, which dated the books instantly but made them seem intimate and knowing at the time (e.g., the double-page splash "HULK SMASH FREDDIE PRINZE JNR!").

President George W. Bush himself turned up to welcome Captain America to the new millennium with the words "WELL, WHAT'S YOUR VERDICT ON THE 21ST CENTURY, CAPTAIN AMERICA? COOL OR UNCOOL?," to which the Captain replied, "COOL, MISTER PRESIDENT. DEFINITELY COOL." With photorealistic renderings of George W. Bush embracing an equally believable Captain America, there could be no mistaking the dizzying, stifling collapse of fact into fantasy.

Life became art became life when Nick Fury, agent of S.H.I.E.L.D., was recast in the image of Samuel L. Jackson, followed by a scene in *The Ultimates* in which the character of Fury himself suggested Jackson as the ideal actor to play him, in a Möbius-loop of such self-referential, cross-dimensional complexity, my powers of description fail me. The circuit was closed and the current sparked from page to screen to life when comics fan Samuel L. Jackson was asked to play Ultimate Nick Fury in *Iron Man*.

Millar and Hitch neatly encapsulated the mood in America when a shape-shifting alien Nazi demanded the surrender of Captain America, whereupon the undaunted hero pointed to the initial on his blue helmet and snarled, "YOU THINK THIS 'A' ON MY HEAD STANDS FOR FRANCE???" His bluster gave heart to an injured nation.

Then came *Civil War*, which gave Millar a chance to develop his knowing update on the relevant approach within the playground of the Marvel universe itself. *Civil War*'s release was expertly timed. It had, in its writer, the perfect man for the job, and artist Steve McNiven was Bryan Hitch with the last of the rough echoes of Neal Adams smoothed away to a liquid finish.

Readers in the first decade of the twenty-first century were raised on

DVD high-definition CGI, HDTV, and airbrushed glamour and they wanted to see that familiar aesthetic reflected in their comics: less cartoony, more illustrative, less graphic, more photographic. Flawless skin, lit as if from within. The new school aimed for a luminous photorealism, a beyond-natural 3-D simulated style where faces were Botoxed to a masklike sheen. At the extremes of this approach, every female Marvel character appeared drawn in poses derived from original photographic images of swimsuit or porn models. Sometimes the same unfortunate superheroine could resemble four or five completely different, completely lifelike women in a single issue, depending on how many different pictures of pouting odalisques the artist had light boxed from *Maxim* or *FHM*.

Civil War began with a skillfully drawn, immediately involving scene in which rookie superteam the New Warriors was shown converging for a covert raid on a supervillain safe house in Stamford, Connecticut. The teenage heroes had a film crew on their tail, and we soon learned that they were taking part in a reality-TV fly-on-the-wall series about their exploits. In terse exchanges, the young heroes worried about how they'd come across on-screen, fretting about zits, repeating cool one-liners for the cameras, and making sure they'd got their good side during fight scenes. The dialogue was witty, naturalistic, and lulling.

The raid, which should have been routine, went tits up when obscure *Captain Marvel* villain Nitro exploded and killed 612 civilians, mostly schoolchildren, leading to pointing fingers and a reassessment of the wisdom of allowing superhero vigilantes to run around flouting the law wherever they pleased.

The only survivor of the Stamford incident was the happy-go-lucky Speedball. Originally developed by Steve Ditko as his last original creation for Marvel, he was teenage Robert Baldwin, mysterious other-dimensional energy source blah blah accident at research lab blah blah ability to bounce off walls like a rubber ball, and so on. Of all the possible superhuman powers you might have received in the Marvel universe, you'd be entitled to feel quite disappointed with this one, but Baldwin did his best with a chipper and upbeat personality.

Never quite in line with the times, Speedball came to serve as Marvel's central casting version of the breezy, goofy, likable teenager, the Ringo of any team he joined, a cartoon stereotype of youth that was no longer in vogue.

By the time of *Civil War*, Speedball, whose very name evoked drug culture, could be understood as representative of the previous pop generation's experience of smiley rave, ecstasy, and shallow, hedonistic self-interest. But as the only survivor of the Stamford school disaster, Speedball became stricken with the guilt of a generation, a shame so profound it could only be assuaged when he donned the all-in-one agony-gimp suit of his new superhero persona, Penance. Fortunately for him, his superpowers could now be activated only when he felt pain, so the suffering, haunted, hated Robbie created a new costume that would hide his identity, activate his powers, and, most important, punish him mercilessly. Sewn onto the inside fabric were 612 spikes, one for each of the Stamford victims, to cut and score his flesh.

As Penance, the formerly lighthearted hero embodied the rise to mainstream of Goth and alternative-culture strands. The suffering Penance became the twenty-first-century teenager monstrous, pierced, tattooed, armored, and expressionless on the outside, bleeding and lost on the inside.

At the time, I found this character laughably "on the nose," as they say, but reading the stories again, he seems a poignant, distressing embodiment of those times and those young people. Penance stood for the cutters we kept hearing about in the news, the emo kids, the outsider vampires squirming in the pop culture klieg lights as they acted out the remorse of their culture in wartime. They'd been told that outsiders were cool now, geeks were heroes, and there was money to be made prizing them out of their cobwebby, culty corners and stealing their arcane shit, while pretending to attend to their obsessive trivial chatter. They were final proof that even death, despair, and loneliness could be commodified and repackaged as an overpriced Hot Topic satchel. There were online chat rooms now to herd, socialize, and normalize the weird kids, to smooth out their eccentricities among conformity-enforcing groups of the like-minded. Porn sites specializing in rebel girls, Goth girls, and punk sluts began to proliferate, while young men and women were bleeding and dying in Afghanistan and Iraq. The bloodletting, the sacrifice of youth to some dark ideal, seemed to repeat itself across scales.

The result was to increasingly fetishize children and young people as if we were—all of us—adults colluding in some mass corruption and deformation of youthful idealism until there could be nothing left but curdled cynicism. The kids were force-fed images of fear, torture, pain, and madness, along with assurances that their lives were essentially meaningless unless they made the Pop Idol Final and embraced the Church of Showbiz. They were being sold a powerful vision of tomorrow in which the planet itself was doomed to die choking on waste, its fate to be a spinning, godless cinder eternally haunted by the screaming ghosts of nations of pedophiles.

Back in the pages of *Civil War,* the Stamford incident precipitated a rapid and unprecedented reaction against Marvel's superhero community, which was when things began to get exciting.

At the beginning of act 1, Millar asked the obvious real-world question: Why were superheroes, essentially deadly living weapons, allowed to run around outside the law in these types of stories? If cops had to carry badges and go through training programs, shouldn't superheroes? It was the first major challenge to their outlaw-outsider status and had to be addressed. The series' central premise, then, was built around a leading question that was being asked more and more often in the media: How much freedom were we willing to give up in return for security?

America's rugged libertarian superheroes said, *"No way!"* to any state interference in their vigilante moral crusades. Led by an increasingly militant Captain America, who personified gung ho laissez-faire patriotism of the old school, one faction of heroes became divided from the rest over the question of a superhero registration bill that would require them to reveal their secret identities and answer to a central governing body.

The idea was not entirely original. Paul Levitz explained the last days of the Golden Age Justice Society with a similar story in which the "McCarthy Commission" forced the mystery men to unmask or retire. They agreed to disband rather than reveal their personal lives and secrets. *Watchmen* had its "Keane Act" banning superhero activity, and *Zenith* had the International Superhuman Test Ban Treaty forbidding the creation of new superpeople. However, Millar's reframing of a superhero registration bill in the context of post-9/11 paranoia chimed with the headlines and made superheroes "relevant" once more.

With Captain America on the side of the dissenters, the conformist lobby was led by his longtime Avengers buddy and teammate, Tony Stark, aka Iron Man, as the military-industrial complex given sleek armored form. The opening scene showed these two facing each other as comrades across the rubble of Stamford: Iron Man on the left and Captain America on the right.

Billionaire tech genius Stark represented the twenty-first-century model of success in an America whose wartime symbol Captain America was an essentially outmoded picture of self-reliant rugged individualism, a pioneer spirit no longer welcome in a globally connected world. The first issue of *Civil War* concluded with Captain America on the run—a wanted outlaw in his own country—and it signaled the end of the vigilante hero.

Covers were designed to resemble book jackets, featuring a single central image framed by tasteful black borders with the words "A Marvel Comics Event" lending a further epoch-inducing gravitas to the sales pitch.

Civil War's plot mechanics all served to initiate, in the penultimate issue, no. 6, a gigantic fight in the mighty Marvel tradition, which ended with the (by this point) highly anticipated, completely expected payoff. Cap's masked dissidents faced off against Iron Man and the conformist registered heroes across a double-page spread—the Captain on the left, Iron Man on the right this time—and between them a wasteland of misunderstanding.

The whole series, and with it a fraught moment in American history, was condensed into one supercharged image demonstrating once again that the best way to tackle contemporary political issues in a superhero story was with bold metaphor and a good punch-up. This was political cartooning, using the trademarked characters of the Marvel universe to make its point, however broad. It may have borrowed liberally from *Kingdom Come*'s plotline: the exploding superhuman killing civilians as inciting incident, the internecine warfare between heroes, and the way both stories centered around the construction of a super-Gulag. But that book's struggle between morally compromised, swaggering new heroes and the upright fictional role models of a previous generation was at heart a fan's tale of good old comics versus bad new comics. *Civil War*'s conflict served its appointed purpose as an excuse for a money-making Marvel superhero dustup, but it had its living roots in questions that were being asked of our own lives in the real world.

In the end, old-school Captain America won the fight but gave up in disgust and turned himself in.

When the mother of one of the Stamford victims was drawn in the final page scene so that her eye line all but challenged the viewer directly, it was hard not to feel the tension of the satiric venom coiled in every line:

"YOU'RE A GOOD MAN, TONY STARK. YOU RISKED **EVERYTHING** TO GET US TO THIS PLACE, BUT I TRULY BELIEVE YOU'VE GIVEN PEOPLE HEROES WE CAN **BELIEVE** IN AGAIN."

A haunted, conflicted Tony Stark inherited a nation's burden of pain and self-recrimination with a wry glint and a patronizing assurance that rang hollow. The final affectless image of the book showed two tiny anonymous silhouettes in an observation blister beneath the S.H.I.E.L.D. helicarrier as the sun went down dutifully:

"OH, THE BEST IS YET TO COME SWEETHEART . . . THAT'S A **PROMISE.**"

Shortly afterward, Cap, that now impotent symbol of twentieth-century US frontier spirit, was shot, assassinated on the stone stairs of history like John, Bobby, Martin, and Bonny Jock Lennon. In 2007 *Captain America* vol. 5, no. 25 was Steve Rogers's last tour of duty—until his inevitable return, better than ever, with a new costume and a new role as world cop in 2010's *Steve Rogers: Super Soldier.*

Another result of 9/11 meant that the wanton destruction of fictional representations of real cities that had made *The Authority* so much fun was no longer acceptable. Stories had to stay with the survivors, examine the repercussions, and treat formerly gratuitous scenes of carnage with some sensitivity.

The return of realism was under way, a change that, as I hope to have convinced readers by now, can be seen to be purely seasonal and predictable. A generation of writers who'd come of age reading Alan Moore in the 1980s began combing the headlines for material. The fear of a sinister military-industrial underworld that haunted Moore's *Marvelman* was inverted to become a joyous embrace of Republican America's undeniable access to the best guns, the best soldiers, and the best super-heroes in the world. For Mark Millar, it was a given that any real-world superhero would be co-opted by the powers that be and recruited as a soldier. The Moore-Miller Superman of the eighties, that helpless, unreconstructed tool of the ruling class, became the template for a new generation of reengineered characters. In *The Ultimates*, everyone worked for the government, but it was all cool. In the first decade of the twenty-first century, superheroes strove to preserve and embody the values of a defiant military-industrial corporate complex or they didn't work at all. The brief era of *The Authority* had passed and left the "bastards" in charge as usual.

Stories had to be about "real" things. As a result, more and more Marvel comics, including some of my own, had scenes set in the Middle East or on board hijacked aircraft. The emphasis veered away from escapist cosmic fantasy, nostalgia, and surrealism toward social critique, satire, and filmic vérité wrapped in the flag of shameless patriotism and the rise of the badass-motherfucker hero. The formal experimentation of the eighties and nineties had bred out a powerful strain of streamlined Hollywood-friendly product that came road tested and shorn of rough edges.

In this decade, craft improved in immense, unprecedented leaps, but creativity could be lost. It was often far easier and much more lucrative to steal an established character idea and rename it than to make up a completely new one. Everyone strove to learn the rules of Hollywood screenwriting and apply them with due care and diligence to perfectly built stories, while the opportunities for mistakes, fortunate accidents, and self-indulgent experimentation had diminished almost to zero, except for some of us, the "superstars." The last pirate art form had swapped its Jolly Roger for the Stars and Stripes once again, and this time it looked as if there was no turning back. Superheroes were big business as geek dreams became movies, TV, and games—and a license to print money until the ink ran out.

New X-Men began life in my notebooks as a direct follow-on from the joyful utopianism of *The Invisibles* and the more militant futurism of *Marvel Boy*. It was a three-year stint on a set of popular characters, detailing the rise and fall of mutant culture by treating it like any other minority struggling toward recognition. I felt awkward and angular again in this new decade, and although I'm still proud of my work, *New X-Men* became more like a prison than a playground.

I chose to cast the X-Men not as the victims "feared and hated" by a world that refused to understand them but as out-and-proud mutant representatives of the inevitable next stage of evolution. We hated them for the same reason we secretly hated our children: because they were here to replace us. The plot premise was that a newly discovered "extinction gene" was activated, dooming the human species to obliteration within several generations, and for the first time, the mutants were on the rise, poised to inherit the earth.

I imagined mutant culture not as a single monolithic ideal or the warring ideologies of "evil mutants" and "good ones," but as a spectrum of conflicting viewpoints, self-images, and ideas about the future. Artist Frank Quitely and I tried to imagine the emergence into our midst of a weird new culture, with mutant clothes designers creating six-armed shirts or invisible couture, mutant musicians releasing records that could by heard only on infra- or ultrasonic frequencies, art that used colors only mutant eyes could see. Instead of just a team, or even a tribe, we imagined a fully formed *Homo superior* society finally emerging into the light of emancipation. *New X-Men* would be about the dawning of a future with new music, new dreams, new ways to see and live. The Xavier Institute would be an outpost of tomorrow in the here and now, as well as a head-quarters and a school. I thought I could use the comic to talk about the positive and negative aspects of geek culture hitting the mainstream.

To undercut the confrontational paramilitarism that haunted previous portrayals, we chose to recast the X-Men themselves as a Gerry Anderson–style volunteer rescue and emergency task force, pledged to use their mutant powers to help both mutants and humans at a difficult time of transition. Then, shortly into the project, came the artistic reverberations of 9/11.

The story became about the lengths to which people might go to annihilate their own children, the beautiful and strange new Midwich Cuckoos who had come to replace them, redecorate the walls, and move around all the furniture. Over its forty-issue run, *New X-Men* turned into a diary of my own growing distrust of a post-9/11 conformity culture that appeared to be in the process of greedily consuming the unusual and different.

In "Riot at Xavier's," a mutant mash-up of personally formative narratives from *If . . .*, *The Prime of Miss Jean Brodie*, and *A Clockwork Orange*, Quitely and I depicted nerds as fascist thugs, chugging back power-enhancing drugs that came in the form of asthma inhalers. It was the dark side of Spence's imperial youth Stormer generation: sickly, vengeful, ignorant, and dully predictable in its demands.

"Planet X," my penultimate story arc, was a step too far for both me and long-term X-fans when I "ruined" Magneto (leader of the Brother-hood of Evil Mutants, as played in the movie versions by Sir Ian McKellen). The Master of Magnetism's high standing in an organization unafraid to use the word *Evil* on its business cards notwithstanding, Chris Claremont had spent some considerable time developing the archvillain from his origins as a one-note terror merchant in 1963 to a sensitive romantic an-tihero. Claremont's Magneto was a tragic, essentially noble survivor of the death camps, a man who had witnessed more than his fair share of sorrow and hardship and knew how to make tough choices. He had depth and dignity, so I turned him into a demented drug addict, unable to connect with a younger generation of mutants who wanted only his face on their Magneto Was Right T-shirts, like a latter-day Che Guevara.

By this time, I was coming into regular conflict with Marvel's new fire-brand publisher Bill Jemas over the direction and execution of my stories. He'd been brought in to modernize along with Joe Quesada as EIC, and we'd all started out on the same page. But slowly I began to feel that Bill misunderstood the fashion aspect of mainstream hero books and their need to constantly change with the times.

The old war between groovy Marvel and stuffy Brand Echh intensified into playground name calling. Jemas expertly manipulated the Internet crowd, stirring up controversy to draw attention to his books. He referred publicly and disparagingly to "AOLComics" and called his DC rival Paul Levitz "Lol Pevitz" over and over in interviews and inflammatory press statements, as if repetition could eventually make it funny. Mark Millar, now embedded at Marvel and still smarting over the censorship of *Authority*, posted on his website a photograph of Levitz next to a passport shot of a then notorious Euro pedophile and asked browsers if they could tell the difference. Levitz, who had elected, in old-DC style, to play the role of gray-templed gentleman, resolutely ignored the ruffians hurling their excreta at his drawing room window, but quietly placed his tormentors on a DC blacklist. For a while, the new nastier, sleazier version of the old rivalry made Marvel seem even cooler. DC was Dad Comics, and Nu-Marvel stood for all kinds of awesome. It was working, too; Marvel sales were up, Spider-Man was huge in the cinemas, and the muttering specter of bankruptcy began to recede, bringing a new braggadocio to the geek squad.

Since 2002, I'd been building up material for a potential new DC series entitled *Seven Soldiers*, and starring some of DC's least popular characters. I wanted to do a huge "team" comic where none of the heroes actually met up with one another but still managed to save the world. I'd written entire issues on my own time, fueled by sheer enthusiasm and the need to escape—if just for a little while—the increasingly mundane Marvel universe of 2002. It was like water piling behind a dam, accumulating new ideas of a kind I would never be allowed to do under the rapidly solidifying regime at Marvel.

Dan DiDio had been recruited as DC's new vice president executive editor from the groundbreaking computer animated series *ReBoot*, which featured Brendan McCarthy production designs and sharp comic-book-style story arcs. Dan was the same age as I, but bearlike and gregarious, with a Brooklyn tenor I loved to imitate when he wasn't around. I liked Dan immediately and appreciated the respect he was showing my work, after Bill Jemas's growing disinterest.

Dan asked me to come work for him immediately, offering to publish *Seven Soldiers* as well as a twelve-part Superman project with Jim Lee.

I still had six miserable months of my Marvel contract to play out, which meant that I missed out on working with Lee, although the Superman project went ahead with Frank Quitely. I tried to keep my head down, with the minimum of fuss, rounding out my X-Men epic on a collaboration with superartist and media mogul Marc Silvestri, which kept the book at the top of the charts for the duration of the entire farewell arc.

Somewhere near the end of those six months, Marvel decided to re-reboot the X-Men franchise by bringing back the familiar superhero costumes and stories that were a little more faithful to the canon. Toy manufacturers had decided they didn't like the rugged municipal worker outfits with fluorescent *X* logos that Frank Quitely and I had come up with for the 2001 relaunch. Trad was back, and the future had been quietly canceled like a date we'd all realized we couldn't actually afford.

It was announced at a DC panel at the San Diego Comic-Con—the industry equivalent of writing it on the moon in hundred-mile-high letters—that I would be returning to the bosom of DC Comics to accept a lucrative exclusive contract and a position as "revamp guy" in charge of rebooting dormant DC concepts. My notebooks had impressed Dan enough to throw in that last clause. As notice was given, one attendee sprang up from his chair like a Ping-Pong ball fired across a crowded Bangkok nightclub and ran out of the room, all the way to the Marvel booth with his news.

Somehow Kristan and I tried to convince ourselves that we could skip away from this declaration of hostilities without a backward glance. The one backward glance I did risk had a sinking, Orphean inevitability and revealed Joe Quesada charging toward us down the hall. We kept walking, slower now, preparing for the heavy hand on the shoulder.

I felt bad. I liked Joe a lot and told him so, blaming his boss for any breakdown in my brief relationship with Marvel Comics. I felt bad, but more than that I was excited. The dam was about to burst. I couldn't wait to leave the febrile soap opera theater of the X-Men behind. I couldn't wait to show what was possible with a handful of barely sellable DC archive characters, including some of King Kirby's own C-list like the Guardian and Klarion the Witch Boy. To make the challenge even more exhilarating, I'd make a point of working with new and unknown artists. Some of the first words I wrote were these, in the voice of the doomed narrator of the story cycle *Seven Soldiers*, comprising seven interlinked four-issue miniseries, which was the cornerstone of my return to DC:

"I DON'T WANT TO TELL HIM YET THAT IT'S ALL BECAUSE THE HIGHS AREN'T HIGH ENOUGH ANY MORE. BECAUSE THE BUILDINGS I JUMP FROM JUST AREN'T TALL ENOUGH. BECAUSE I'VE TAKEN THIS WHOLE MORALLY AMBIGUOUS URBAN VIGILANTE THING ABOUT AS FAR AS I CAN. AND NOW, GOD HELP ME NOW I WANT TO VISIT OTHER PLANETS AND DIMENSIONS AND FIGHT ROGUE GODS."

It was, I suppose, what I'd tried to explain to Bill Jemas, but it took Marvel another seven years to finally agree with me and inaugurate what editorial called the "Heroic Age," and by that time Bill had moved on.

I became the first weapon in the exclusive wars that followed as DC and Marvel struggled to tie down the services of the best writers and artists in the field. The barriers were up and sales were down. New blood was discouraged along with experimentation.

Screenwriters, tried-and-tested storytellers from a more glamorous medium, were the only strangers admitted into the comics field during this time of withdrawal and consolidation. They were fawned over like good-looking girls who'd finally noticed us and who might attract other better-looking girls to our shabby party or invite us home to join theirs. Unsurprisingly they didn't write comics quite as well or with the same freewheeling abandon as the people who did it for a living, and few lingered beyond their first few unimpressive checks. (To make good money in comics, it was necessary to write an awful lot of pages every month.) Joss Whedon, the creator of the long-running *Buffy the Vampire Slayer* TV series, stuck at it longer than most, with an emotive, extended run on *Astonishing X-Men*. Allan Heinberg's short but effervescent burst on 2006's nineteen-millionth *Wonder Woman* revamp was another rare exception, but the writer, who'd worked on the youth drama *The O.C.*, couldn't stand the poisonous atmosphere of comics fandom and made a swift, quiet exit after a promising start, leaving the field once more to the diehards.

CHAPTER 23

THE DAY EVIL WON

THE BIG TREND in the superhero comics of the twenty-first century was for the dystopian scenario, played out not as a moment of defeat for the heroes but as a moment of triumph for the villains and their embodiment of easily understood human vices.

The first comic-book bad guys were enemies of the workingman: the corrupt bosses, machine men, and domestic tyrants of the early Superman and Batman adventures, or hoodlums, street thugs, and bullies. The 1940s brought a parade of goose-stepping maniacs like the Red Skull, Captain Nazi, and Baron Gestapo, along with leering Japanese killers like Captain Nippon. The fifties dealt with the menace of communism in the form of space aliens or shadowy, unshaven secret policemen from grim Eastern European countries with names like Slobovia. Silver Age DC superheroes preserved the safety of the sunlit sidewalks of fifties suburbia against an onslaught of flamboyant bank robbers with gimmick weapons. It was rare for even the most diabolical of Silver Age supercrooks to kill anyone. These bad guys were antisocial schemers, slightly disturbed troublemakers constantly working to keep busy superhuman beings who would otherwise have no outlet for their show-offy superpowers and small ambitions. In the sixties, Marvel comics added a pro wrestling dimension to superheroes, having them fight one another, on the slightest pretext, with the same verve and enthusiasm they brought to their showdowns with Marvel's stable of science fiends, space gods, and towering, mindless monsters.

Criminals in the seventies were often killers, muggers, polluters, junkies, and deceivers of youth. On the other end of the spectrum, they were Ernst Stavro Blofeld types with their own two-hundred-bedroom luxury headquarters in orbit or under the sea, and an immense retinue of security and science staff, along with catering and cleaning personnel, the upkeep and maintenance of which were rarely factored in.

The eighties saw the rise of the sleazy, amoral corporate predator, the bastard in a suit and ponytail, clutching his FiloFax as he glared down on the lesser mortals crawling in the mud of morality below. This Wall Street tiger was an Ozymandias, dividing with his gaze the world and everything and everybody in it, a dead ham dressed for a butcher's chart.

Doom Patrol and *Shade* gave us walking nightmares, like the Scissormen, the American Scream, the Truth, and the Pale Police: living, crawling complexes and neuroses, incoherent, broken-backed abominations from the id. "DISCARDED CHILDHOOD TOYS GROWN BITTER AND DEFORMED AND HUNGRY FOR REVENGE!" as one of the "Archons of Nurnheim"—a Mr. Punch glove puppet on the hand of a lifeless marionette—put it.

Midnineties villains were Image louts and boneheaded Frank Miller knockoffs, violent unscrupulous remnants of the eighties adolescent rush that were now rounded up and brought to account.

It wasn't until the turn of the century that a new approach to comic-book villainy crystallized around a single terrible idea that seemed to resonate with the exhausted resignation of the Western imagination: What if the villains had *already* won? What if the battle between good and evil was now over, with good bleeding and broken in the corner while evil pissed in its old rival's sobbing face? In a world of catastrophic, knee-jerk war politics, typified by moronic medieval terrorists, the apish antics of George W. Bush, and the spinning of his eager-to-please sidekick Tony Blair, it was easy to get on board with this gloomy new paradigm. Better yet, it was a scenario that reinvigorated the superheroes by giving them a real challenge to face. Stories could begin at what was traditionally the end of act 2, with the hero on his knees while a cackling adversary seized his moment to launch the missiles, waken the dead, or threaten the girl. What would we learn by pitting our supermen against the day after the day they let us all down?

Wanted by Mark Millar and J. G. Jones was Millar's breakthrough work. He and Jones evoked a world that looked just like our own, but its familiar sidewalks and shopping façades hid a big secret that made horrible sense: Twenty years ago, all the supervillains had decided to gang up on the heroes once and for all. Overcoming their natural hatred and suspicion of one another for just long enough, they pooled mega-brains, billionaire resources, deadly technology, and a dozen foolproof plans for world domination. Thus armed, they overwhelmed the good guys before finishing the job with the help of diabolical superscience and evil five-dimensional magic, rewriting history so no one remembered that superheroes had ever been real. All that remained were their echoes in our comics and movies, mocking reminders of a world lost forever to corruption and greed. *Wanted*'s gleefully tawdry depiction of the world at its worst asked of its young media-literate audience some pertinent moral questions: If you were given a license that put you beyond the reach of all law and turned the everyday world into a Grand Theft Auto playground where any monstrous, violent, or depraved crime you committed would be covered up, as long as you surrendered to a quasi-Masonic "fraternity" of supervillains with VIP access to the best clubs, the coolest weapons, and the dirtiest birds . . . How far would you go, fan boy?

Wanted showed an abyss of horror beneath the comforting lies of our everyday world, where a successful coup by comic-book villains explained every rotten politician, every smirking gangster and puffed-up tyrant on the nightly news. For all his growing reputation as a shallow sensationalist, Millar was an altar boy at heart; he used the language of the lowest common denominator to preach hellfire. *Wanted* was an epic attempted exorcism, but its raw admission of Millar's own dark-side dreams and its flirtation with a genuinely nihilistic endorsement of every antivalue as the way to "make it" in this world suggested a demon big enough to leave sizable bite marks in any Augustine cassock.

Wanted articulated a new myth for the hordes of suddenly cool under-achievers who'd been lionized by the rise of "nerd culture." Big business, media, and fashion were, it seemed, so starved of inspiration, they'd reached down to the very bottom of the social barrel in an attempt to commodify even the most stubborn nonparticipants, the suicide Goths and antiestablishment nerds. The geeks were in the spotlight now, proudly accepting a derogatory label that directly compared them to freak-show acts. Bullied young men with asthma and shy, bitter virgins with adult-onset diabetes could now gang up like the playground toughs they secretly longed to be and anonymously abuse and threaten professional writers, artists, musicians, and actors with bills to pay.

Soon film studios were afraid to move without the approval of the raging Internet masses. They represented only the most minuscule fraction of a percentage of the popular audience that gave a shit, but they were very remarkably, superhumanly angry, like the great head of Oz, and so very persistent that they could easily appear in the imagination as an all-conquering army of mean-spirited, judgmental fogies.

In the shadow of *The Tipping Point*, Malcolm Gladwell's immensely influential book on social networks and marketing, nobody wanted to risk bad word of mouth, little realizing that they were reacting, in many cases, to the opinions of a few troublemakers who knew nothing but contempt for the universe and all its contents and could hardly be relied upon to put a positive spin on anything that wasn't the misery and misfortune of others. Too many businesspeople who should have known better began to take seriously the ravings of misinformed, often barely literate malcontents who took revenge on the cruel world by dismissing everything that came their way with the same jaded, geriatric "Meh."

The rise of the geeks, with their "SHORT ATTENTION SPANS AND HIGH EXPECTATIONS," as one New X-Men character put it, was an unstoppable tidal return of the repressed. *Wanted* took upon itself to coldly lay bare the desires of the new elite—which far from being revolutionary were sleazy, self-serving, and viciously cynical. Reduced to numbers and screen names, souls stood out in stark relief, revealing an audience that seemed determined to portray itself as hostile, ignorantly self-assured, conformist, and forever unsatisfied in a world of staggering consumer excess. It is, of course, telling that I've never met any reader at a comic convention who behaved the way many do online, suggesting that the Internet monster is a defensive configuration, like the fan of spikes a tiny fish erects when it feels threatened.

Wanted's lead was Wesley Gibson, drawn by J. G. Jones to resemble handsome rapper Eminem with an eye on the movie potential, but who stood for every shy, overweight, underweight, misunderstood kid reveling in the power to trash, denigrate, and insult his imagined enemies—who were just about everybody, especially the creators of the comic books, music, games, and movies that brought to these miserable lives the only meaning they would ever know. Geek royalty. Meet the new boss, same as the old boss.

Wesley acted out the new porn-fueled fantasies of dumping the fat girlfriend, hooking up with hot sex-mad assassin chicks, raping pretty newsreaders, and Getting Away with It All. At its best, reminiscent of the cool, amused cruelty of a Joe Orton play, the bludgeoning effect of *Wanted*'s uneasy satire exposed the horrible truth: The fragile, asocial, and different really just wanted to do coke, fuck bimbos, and bully people. The revolution had arrived.

When Millar and Jones concluded *Wanted* with a full-page close-up of the leering, triumphant Wesley Gibson screaming "THIS IS ME FUCKING YOU IN THE ASS!," his was the grotesque, swollen face of an outsider culture given the keys to the kingdom and revenge access to all our asses, as endorsed by the same old brute hierarchies. This was a face that any self-respecting boot might wish to stamp down upon eternally, but it was too late. Wesley was instead what we would bow down to. *Wanted* was a searing hymn to the death of integrity and morality, and Wesley's the victorious face of the New God.

I left the sweary adult superbooks to Mark and Warren and countered with a sugar-coated nightmare called *Seaguy*. In *Seaguy*, Cameron Stewart (an especially talented young Canadian artist I'd met through *The Invisibles*) and I created a dystopian not-too-distant future that was painted over with candy colors and storybook surrealism. Following an unspecified apocalyptic event at the climax of a final superheroic showdown between good and evil, the world was at peace. Repetitive isolated lives were played out under constant surveillance in designated "Comfort Zones": retro-nostalgic model marina villages arranged around sinister theme parks, in which everyone was a self-proclaimed superhero but no one had any real purpose other than to consume the new wonder food XOO!, watch endless reruns of disturbingly violent *Mickey Eye* TV cartoons, and visit scary Mickey Eye theme parks. "Pacified, safe and supervised," the inhabitants of Seaguy's world were trauma survivors in deep denial. Alienated, lonely, confused, and self-important, they confided these fears to an anonymous voice in "Diary Rooms," inspired by "Big Brother," while pretending an outward happiness to the other self-absorbed people they encountered on their trips to the shops or the park.

The Romantic idea of the special person, the genius, the "superhero," was dying before our very eyes. Our most successful movies starred children's cartoon characters as we cocooned ourselves with nostalgia and repetition against the howling, incoherent darkness of ecological disaster, paranoid surveillance culture, terror, and financial collapse.

Ex-supervillain turned bureaucrat Captain Lotharius Lee offered this proposal for a future where the family unit would be replaced with more manageable module living in "Big Brother"–style compounds:

"EACH HOUSE WILL PROVIDE A COMMUNAL LIFESPACE FOR SIXTEEN **INFANTILOIDS**. THESE BICKERING PACKS WILL STAY AT HOME UNDER 24-HOUR SURVEILLANCE WATCHING **ONE ANOTHER** ON TELEVISION. THE RESULTING **BEHAVIORAL FEEDBACK** WILL ACT TO RAPIDLY STANDARDIZE HUMAN BEHAVIOR."

Reacting against the realist approach for our own pet project at least, Cameron Stewart and I were digging out influences like Sinbad, *Parsifal*, and *Don Quixote*. We liked the idea of re-creating the superhero in terms of medieval quest allegories, Celtic wonder tales, and picaresques, combining the aesthetic of *1984* and *The Prisoner* with Saturday morning cartoons, talking animals, and LSD bubblegum colors.

Seaguy asked how it felt to be a hero in a world with no more need for heroes and was, I felt, my first truly modern and inspired re-creation of the Siegel and Shuster formula since *Flex Mentallo*. But I had to recognize that it was a little out of time and doomed to appeal to only a small but much-appreciated cult audience of forward-thinking, early-adopting hipsters!

Nevertheless, I'd become fascinated by the power and the existence of the evil-has-won narrative and resolved to explore it further in a major DC universe crossover event. I was asked to complete what Dan DiDio was now calling his *Crisis* trilogy with a wrap-up book to be called *Final Crisis*. Dan wanted to use this series as a showcase for Kirby's New Gods characters, and if I was excited by the idea of having to improvise on that theme, I was even more overjoyed to know that I had access to Darkseid himself, the ultimate supertyrant with his Anti-Life Equation. As far as I was concerned, the Anti-Life Equation was being rammed down my gullet every day in the papers and on TV, and I was sick of it; sick of being told the world was dying, and it was all because I'd forgot to turn off the bathroom light; sick of Fina(ncia)l Crisis, the War, and the teenage suicide bombers willing to die for the promise of a cheesy afterlife that sounded like a night out with the lap dance girls at Spearmint Rhino.

With J. G. Jones and later Doug Mahnke on art, we set about dramatizing the breakdown of the rational enlightenment story of progress and development as it succumbed to a horror tale of failure, guilt, and submission to blind authority.

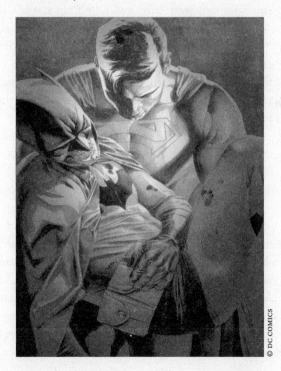

I brushed up on the cheerful literature of apocalypse and doomsday, refamiliarizing myself with the various revelations, Ragnaroks, and myths of the end times to construct a thoroughly modern Armageddon in which half the human race was possessed by an evil god who announced his arrival in the form of Anti-Life Equation e-mails and small acts of cruelty that grow to consume the world. What would it look like if a comic-book universe died, and what could it tell us about what we were doing to ourselves?

The "final crisis," as I saw it for a paper universe like DC's, would be the terminal war between is and isn't, between the story and the blank page. What would happen if the void of the page took issue with the quality of material imposed upon it and decided to fight back by spontaneously generating a living concept capable of devouring narrative itself? A nihilistic cosmic vampire whose only dream was to drain the multiverse dry of story material, then lie bloated beneath a dead sun, dying.

I tried to show the DC universe breaking down into signature gestures, last-gasp strategies that were tried and tested but would this time fail, until finally even the characterizations would fade and the plot become rambling, meaningless, disconnected. Although I lost my nerve a little, I must confess, and it never became disconnected enough.

This, I was trying to say, is what happens when you let bad stories eat good ones. This is what it looked like when you allow the Anti-Life Equation to turn all your dreams to nightmares.

In the end, there was nothing left but darkness and the first superhero, Superman, with a crude wishing machine, the deus ex machina itself, and a single wish powered by the last of his own life force.

He wished for a happy ending, of course.

Final Crisis was a bestseller, but it divided the Internet crowd like Alexander's sword. One outraged reader even confidently predicted that I would, someday soon, be brought to account for the "evil" I had done. For a comics fan scorned, it seemed, the measure of evil lay not in genocide or child abuse but in continuity details deliberately overlooked by self-important writers, of plot points insufficiently telegraphed, and themes made opaque or ambiguous.

If only one-tenth of the righteous, sputtering wrath of these anonymous zealots could be mustered against the horrors of bigotry or poverty, we might find ourselves overnight in a finer world.

That'll catch on.

As a popular writer, I was often invited to signings and got to see the inside of more comic shops than anyone would care to. They ranged from chain store emporia like Forbidden Planet to mom-and-pop stores or head shops run by creepy stoners and eccentrics.

Once the location was Sheffield, a postindustrial, heavy metal Goth town in the north of England. It was 1989, and I was one of five or six comics professionals arranged along a trestle table like a panel of judges at a young offenders court hearing. The only people who'd come to see us were five outlandish individuals, each with his own eccentric dress and appearance, each more freakish than the last. There was a painfully shy, long-haired, and wild-bearded giant. Another man was a tiny, furtive character with the twinkling jet-black eyes of a water vole. The others are shapeless in my memory; an identikit lineup that's part Wallace from *Wallace and Gromit*, part Punch and Judy, arranged along the wall like a parade of suspects for a fairy-tale crime, the witnessing of which would make unlikely any cordial relationship with sanity.

And there they stood silently, waiting, allowing the awkwardness to build into a mute, motionless pressure that soon became intolerable. I could see the now sweating giant's mind calculating furiously behind his gentle, frightened eyes. I could see that he felt personally responsible for the embarrassed, dumbstruck silence of the others. I could see the tension in his body as he built toward some kind of primordial release so that when his outburst came, it was in the form of a high-pitched yelp. "I'm so sorry! I don't have a question!" He had done what none of the others seemed capable of and overcome a lifetime's worth of introversion to make his mark, and now the whole thing was over in a kind of grunt and spew—the noise you'd get from the last of its kind finally giving in to the future and extinction's call. Then, as if on a visit from another world in a Ditko cupboard, the smallest man looked around as if to let us know that he was in on some immense joke and had nothing to do with these others whom he seemed only now to be aware of. He was one of us, an understanding that the brute boundary of the trestle table between us could never truly grasp or define. He was, he explained, a professional writer of comedy. Then, with a knowing glint, he presented his credentials in the form of a tiny wrap of paper, pushed with one finger across the table toward me.

"Here's one for you," he said, then retreated, backward—a special effect in a Cocteau film—to assume his previous position against the wall. His eyes twinkled, a micro-nod of encouragement anticipating my response. And while the corners of his mouth flirted with the wry knowing smile of Mr. Mxyzptlk, the fifth-dimensional imp, I defolded the paper again and again and again and again until infinitesimal pencil marks, small as the inscription on a fairy knight's tombstone, could be read:

"The Campaign for Surreal Ale."

I didn't know whether to laugh or cry. After an hour and a half of being stared at, the baffled, embarrassed proprietor led our mildly traumatized group out to a waiting car, anxious to be rid of the embarrassment.

As we huddled outside the shop, like last night's curry leftovers, with our dreams of fame and groupies cast into callous relief by an unforgiving Sheffield afternoon, a tiny, fierce, bald man wearing platform shoes, flared trousers, an open-necked shirt, and a leonine chest medallion strode past like an engine on a track, then stopped, froze, turned, and snarled in our faces.

"You fucking Tory bastards! *I've* been to Barbados, I have!"

Superhero comic-book fans often struggled with the unflattering stereotype of the unloved, awkward, and ugly, and while there was and still is some element of truth there, it should be remembered that the same accusations can be just as easily leveled against film fans, music fans, or football fans—with examples to prove it. Zealous fans of anything, as well as hobbyist types and collectors of all kinds of memorabilia, often share traits with comics fans. But I have to say that I only ever encountered Sheffield-class levels of physical and behavioral freakishness once again in Auckland, New Zealand, but there it came with a dull aggression, and only one young and bloodlessly pale yokel from miles away in sheep farming country came close to matching his English counterparts for Lewis Carroll levels of tomfoolery. With rolling eyes behind lenses that

Sherlock Holmes could use to solve crimes on the cellular level, his hair was oddly whipped up into the exact shape of an inverted ice-cream cone and left behind the haunting, disconcerting impression that it was made all of one awful, congealed synthi-substance the texture and color of mashed potato. His rapid-fire, high-pitched questions and abrupt body language suggested some missing link between man and an ostrich, and I have never seen any living thing that resembled him again. I can only pray that country boy who fell to Earth had a kind word for us when he testified to his machine-ostrich alien masters.

Even the loud and crazy, sex-starved fan boys of snowbound New Jersey, with their confused cries of "She-Males! Best of both worlds!" and the voluminous Goth girls, victims of some unspeakable abuse, were unable to compete. These physical marvels tended to heave into view like stricken Zeppelins cradling grotesque homemade Sandman dolls—imagine a cutout of Neil Gaiman's face pinned to a boxing nun hand puppet or adorned with a crown of pressed black roses. But they were essentially kind souls and more or less harmless, like news reports of disasters on the other side of the world.

I crossed the globe as a guest at conventions in San Diego, Lucca, Paris, Barcelona, Melbourne, Oslo, Reykjavík, Bristol, Aberdeen, London, Philadelphia—and as far as I could see, my readership was made up of mostly clever, earnest, and studenty or alternative young men and their generally even more clever girlfriends. They were, as I say, readers, not fans, for whom a good comic book was just one more item on their regular pop culture diet.

Stranger to me than the fans were the professional veterans of the convention circuit; former science fiction "babes," ex-starship captains and Imperial Stormtroopers, cult-show survivors who spent their lives traveling from one event to the next, living off appearance fees as they endlessly circled the world signing old photographs and DVD boxed sets.

One sci-fi show stalwart, still stunning in her rubber dress, traveled with a twelve-year-old son who quietly, politely, and dutifully made sure that her makeup was ready for her on the tour bus after her riotous nights out on the tiles of another convention city, on a tab that never ran dry. It's not all that difficult to mine this potential sitcom scenario for easy laughs, but I often think of that dedicated, uncomplaining boy with his world-weary look of resignation and his beautiful mum, squeezing the last of the juice from her time as a party girl space fleet pinup, on her way to the dark side of the MILF, staggering home drunk in her highest heels, immaculately wasted.

Another cult-TV regular who was hard as nails, witty, and cynical had this piece of advice to offer the budding sci-fi starlet: If you need to speed up a line of hovering fan boys, you must slowly open up the top button of your blouse, as if the whole thing was getting too much, too hot. To accelerate the flow of punters, pop a few more buttons, as many as necessary to achieve the desired turnover. Apparently, and this is from the mouth of an expert, shy fans become embarrassed by exposed cleavage and tend not to linger any longer than is necessary. This woman had achieved such precise control over the technique that it was like working a sluice gate.

My time on the merry-go-round rarely amounted to much more than a weekend of signings and panel discussions, but the diehards were heading on to Argentina, then Mexico, Singapore, Oslo, or Birmingham. A nomadic tribe of Flying Dutchmen and -women, committed to a potentially lifelong schedule of personal appearances. "Cult" TV and film audiences were all forgiving; no matter how many decades had passed since your last voyage to Arcturus, they still used your chain mail swimsuit shots as aids to masturbation. They created an atmosphere of ambiguous transaction, where it seemed somehow normal and not grotesque to present photographs of handsome musclemen to be shakily autographed by the geriatric actors they'd become, as if enacting *The Picture of Dorian Gray* in reverse.

Then there's San Diego Comic-Con International, which is Rabelais and Fellini all rolled into one and fuel-injected into a twenty-first-century theme park where everyone will be a superhero forever. This particular taste of the future requires an entire book to itself, and it's not going to be this one.

Suffice it to say that San Diego, as we call it, is the world's largest pop media culture marketplace fringe madness festival, and every year it grows larger as more people come to experience an entire city peel off its civvies and transform into a science fiction/horror/sex simulation of Oz.

On my first visit as a convention guest, twenty years ago, I saw a young man dressed as Green Lantern being harassed down Main Street by hostile marines. This year it was as if the pages of the comics and fantasy novels, and the glass of TV screens had shattered, burst, and filled three aircraft hangar–sized halls, spilling out to invade and surrealize every hotel bar, every motel lobby, every city block for miles around with monsters, femmes fatales, and self-made superheroes. The San Diego Comic-Con is an event that everyone should experience at least once. It's a big rehearsal for tomorrow, where Second Life becomes real.

I have to say that wherever I went, the audience was young, enthusiastic, polite, and intelligent. The people who connected with my stories were the sort of people I hoped would enjoy them, and I got on with pretty much all of them. I didn't find them creepy, or nerdy, or geeky, or whatever the marketing labels became, but I suppose that's what they were and what we all were.

And that's why the gold medal will always go to Sheffield.

CHAPTER 24

IRON MEN
AND INCREDIBLES

THERE WERE MORE and more superheroes now, roosting on the billboards at the local Cineplex, straddling buildings, bigger than Ultimate Giant Man. Marvel made the most of it, unleashing a conga line of titles that translated their appeal from the page to the screen and fed a growing hunger. Scary times and superhero movies go together like dirt and soap.

Daredevil in 2003 successfully captured the atmosphere of Catholic suffering and guilt that had enlivened Frank Miller's *Born Again*, the book on which it was loosely based, but the wire work was tired, giving every character the same high-jumping fight style. Miller's pulp vision would be better served by later adaptations of his graphic novels like *Sin City* and *300*. Although *Daredevil* offered a bold stab at developing Miller's stained-glass noir into a convincing street-level neighborhood superhero franchise, the underlying tone of the movie was whiny and petulant. In our first introduction to the hero, he wrecked a dive bar and beats to a pulp almost all of the seemingly innocent regulars on his way to the real crook, with no explanation or apology for the severity of his behavior.

The League of Extraordinary Gentlemen was next on the production line. Unlike Daredevil or Spider-Man, who were from the sixties, this was a new title, an Alan Moore and Kevin O'Neil coproduction. But although published in 1999, it was set in 1898 and starred several famous characters of late Victorian adventure fiction—many of them archetypes for later heroes of the Marvel Comics universe, in particular, and banded together as a kind of gaslit society of champions with the opening epigram:

"The British Empire has always had difficulty in distinguishing between its heroes and its monsters."

The League of Extraordinary Gentlemen assembled H. G. Wells's Invisible Man with H. Rider Haggard's Allan Quatermain, Mina Harker, the heroine of *Dracula*, Doctor Jekyll and Mr. Hyde (done here as a proto-Hulk), and Captain Nemo, under the guiding mitt of Campion Bond, grandfather of James, and his boss, M, for Moriarty, to stand against the enemies of Empire.

Like the awe-inspiring zoological grotesques fashioned from stray beaks and lemur tails by Victorian taxidermists, *The League of Extraordinary Gentlemen* was a delightful, outrageous platypus of many parts. The series is still running, gobbling up the entire continuum of fiction and knitting it all into one seamless canvas where *The Story of O* is an unrevealed chapter in the life of Virginia Woolf's Orlando and where Billy Bunter went to spy school with Emma Peel's dad and Orwell's O'Brien. The most recent League adventure, *Century*, brought characters from Brecht's *Threepenny Opera* together with Raffles the Gentleman Thief, Carnacki the Ghost Finder, and Iain Sinclair's time-displaced Norton.

The movie, unsurprisingly, was far less ambitious than Moore's book and its fin de siècle steampunk trappings were at odds with a vogue for the down-to-earth and contemporary. It was scripted by the English comic-book author James Robinson and produced by Don Murphy (husband of my friend Susan Montford, who had directed me as Roman Polanski in her short film *Strangers*). Better books than mine will be written about Don (they already have been, in fact, and I recommend *Killer Instinct*, Jane Hamsher's account of the filming of Oliver Stone's wonderful *Natural Born Killers*), but suffice it to say that not for nothing is his production company known as Angry Films. The Murphy I know has a tender side too, but I'd hate to put a dent in his fearsome reputation with any tales of his kindness and humor. The afterparty for *League* brought me within feet of Sir Sean

Connery, Scotland's own absent father, but I didn't say more than hello to him.

Ang Lee's *Hulk* was an ambitious attempt to do something adult with Lee and Kirby's anger-management metaphor. Distinguished by its beautiful and inventive CGI scene transitions, it lacked a strong story, sympathetic characters, and, most important, the Hulk-style tank-tossing mayhem that audiences, especially those weaned on the comic-book adventures of "Ol' Greenskin," had come to expect. By the time *The Incredible Hulk* was released a mere five years later, in 2008, Marvel Entertainment had perfected a formula for introducing its characters on-screen, in which the lead would invariably encounter some bigger, more numerous, or meaner version of himself in the last reel, which meant, in this case, act 3: Hulk versus Abomination.

As superheroes regained their popularity, some filmmakers cottoned on to the fact that there was nothing stopping them from launching their own new creations without relying on the DC and Marvel standbys.

The Incredibles was Pixar animator Brad Bird's foray into the costumed hero arena, with a typically slick, witty, and accomplished piece that swiftly established a whole new universe of characters and possibilities and remains the most successful of cinema's original superhero creations. For longtime comics fans, however, there was nothing new: *The Incredibles* borrowed from *Fantastic Four*, as well as *Superfolks* and *Marvelman*'s vision of an out-of-shape, middle-aged superhero, and even quoted *Watchmen*'s hero ban, but its intended all-ages audience and high standards of writing and animation gave it a refreshing Silver Age exuberance. The film's color and charm hid a lack of originality, but it was hard not to enjoy the effortless character work and the adrenaline-powered fight scenes that played out like childhood memories made real (although why Mrs. Incredible never used her stretching power to tighten the spreading butt she complained about was never adequately explained).

As for Marvel's First Family, they had their own live-action shot at the big time with *Fantastic Four*, a shallow, uncool, family-oriented crack at updating the quintessentially Cold War hero team. Its sequel, *Fantastic Four: Rise of the Silver Surfer*, maintained the kiddie tone and unforgivably copped out of showing Galactus, but its eerily realized

CGI Silver Surfer, particularly as seen during a breathtaking aerial chase sequence through the skyscrapers of midtown Manhattan, was a genuine triumph that, for the first time, came close to the purity of Jack Kirby's vision, and offered a foretaste of what might be possible when the moviemakers finally caught up to the King's best work.

The year 2005 also served up the most interesting new approach to the superhero movie formula since *Unbreakable*, with Christopher Nolan's *Batman Begins*, while 2006 brought the much-anticipated but unsatisfactory *Superman Returns*, the last installment of the *X-Men* trilogy, and another Fox Studios original, which made the most of Uma Thurman's leggy Hollywood glamour for *My Super Ex-Girlfriend*. Unfortunately, this uneasy romantic comedy about a superwoman scorned, which might have been hailed as a breakthrough graphic novel, made little impression and was memorable only for one genuinely nightmarish and alarming scene in which Thurman as G-Girl tossed a live shark into her boyfriend's bedroom.

Hancock had the most startling flying effects since the first *Superman*, and the eye-popping opening sequence with Will Smith whizzing between moving traffic as a scuzzy alcoholic superman was satisfyingly big-budget. But after that, it was all downhill; the big origin reveal, with its near-incomprehensible tale of angels and reincarnation, killed what should have been a tent pole, a potential franchise, and a groundbreaking black superhero series, collapsing the premise under the weight of its own ludicrous mythology.

But it was *Iron Man*—a B-list Marvel star—who gave notice of a new kind of superhero film, one that could reach a bigger audience than ever before, without a big brand name; no longer genre bound but universal in its appeal and held in place by great supporting actors and a bravura central performance by the remarkable Robert Downey Jr. There may have been a certain self-satisfaction to the Downey Jr. smile since his stint in rehab, but no one could have summoned to life the Tony Stark of *The Ultimates* with the flair and insight that he brought to the role. *Iron Man* was the perfect breakthrough superhero for the blankly aspirational first decade of the twenty-first century. He was the millionaire man-and-machine cyborg we were all becoming, grafted to our phones and VDUs, our poker faces like locked and polished doors.

Iron Man reminded us that our man-machine future was more than a simple triumph of soulless technology but involved an exchange, an eroticization and softening of metal's contours. Iron Man was no robot, as he may have appeared at first; the impenetrable armor concealed a soft center and those melting puppy dog eyes. The man of metal had a shattered heart of shrapnel. Tony Stark became the tender center, the wounded soul in the military machine that helped to sell a war and humanize its warriors.

At an advance screening in Los Angeles of Christopher Nolan's *The Dark Knight*, I found myself sitting next to Jim Lee and David and Victoria Beckham, along with their sons. Halfway through the movie, Christian Bale's Bruce Wayne took his brand-new Lamborghini Murcielago for a spin through the streets of Gotham.

"Batman's got your car, Dad!" yelped the elder Beckham boy over the blissful sound of illusion crashing headlong into reality.

The day after, I was invited to the Warners office of Zack Snyder to watch some *Watchmen* footage. High-definition CGI technology had caught up with Dave Gibbons's hyperreal freeze-frames, his profusion of tiny meaningful details and infinite depth of field. Doctor Manhattan, in all his cock-out glory, could now be rendered completely digitally, as Alan Moore himself had suggested many years before. The film was released to a lukewarm reception, but I suspect its reputation will grow.

A fist-shaking Moore disowned this loving tribute to his most famous book and gave his share of the movie money to Gibbons. His experience on *The League of Extraordinary Gentlemen* had been a step too far, after a lawyer working for Universal Pictures dragged him into a plagiarism case that saw him accused of basing his first volume of *League* stories on a prior screenplay entitled *Cast of Characters*. Moore was not above borrowing ideas, as the very concept of the League proved, but the indictments were as ludicrous as they were convoluted, eliciting another grand exit, which saw him sever all remaining ties with Hollywood and mainstream comics and return to his roots in music, small-press publishing, and the underground arts scene.

Watchmen, the book, which had become DC's single most lucrative publishing venture ever, sold one million copies in 2008–9 alone, which must at least have kept the writer in cigarettes and scorpion rings.

Mark Millar's *Wanted*, directed by the Russian action stylist Timur Bekmambetov, barely survived its translation to the screen (the writers boasted how they'd only bothered to read the first issue of the comic book), but despite the loss of its central premise, the film did remarkably well at the box office and opened the doors for Millar's subsequent page-to-screen translation, *Kick-Ass*. *Wanted* began its journey as a proposal for DC's *Secret Society of Super-Villains* title, and every character was a variant on a DC stalwart, so the Joker became the diabolical Mister Rictus. Clayface was reborn as Shit-Head, Two-Face was Johnny Two-Dicks, and—you get the picture. With its roots in DC history and superhero revisionism, *Wanted* may have seemed an unlikely choice for Hollywood, but its core story—of the nerd who seizes his chance to be the big man at all costs—had mass appeal. And the addition of Angelina Jolie to the cast list gave it a cachet beyond its humble beginnings.

Wanted the movie bore only the slightest relation to the comic book, but there was enough. The engaging superhero plot was replaced by a bizarre "secret society" angle. Millar's supervillains became a shadowy and barely comprehensible league of assassins, or "Weavers," who worked apparently for the "Loom of Fate" to remove undesirable elements from society. It had taken forty years to get Spider-Man off the page, but the new superheroes were hitting the cinemas barely months after their comic-book adventures came hot from the presses. The comic book was just a pitch now, a stepping-stone to celluloid validation.

TV jumped back on the superhero bandwagon with *Heroes*. The first season was tight and engaging, although every single plot element appeared to have been lifted from some familiar comic-book story, but the show lost its way rapidly. The highlight was the origin reveal of the villain Sylar with a script as elegant, satisfying, and involved as the *Watchmen* episodes it so fondly quoted and drew upon for its inspiration. *Heroes* combined the innovations of the Dark Age and Renaissance into a TV-friendly stew with an ensemble cast of noncostumed superhumans.

The United Kingdom's *No-Heroics* took a lo-fi look at the pointless lives of Z-list superhumans, who congregated in a London bar with pictures of Warren Ellis and me on the walls. It was played for laughs, but there was an attention to detail, a world-building that showed the influence of the best "serious" superhero titles.

The Cape, Misfits, No Ordinary Family, and *Alphas* joined the growing gallery of hero shows and, although all but one met cancellation, are unlikely to be the last of their kind. Superheroes add an extra level of spice to any genre they touch, and we can expect to see their presence enliven all kinds of otherwise ordinary scenarios.

Even Edgar Wright's film of Bryan Lee O'Malley's comic-book series *Scott Pilgrim vs. the World* played a shallow teenage relationship as a series of titanic superhero battles, on the understanding that this was how it *felt* to be in love: It felt like being a superhero. These days everything felt like being a superhero. They were everywhere now. They walked among us.

CHAPTER 25

OVER THE EVENT HORIZON

A NEW TYPE of story began to dominate the comic-book universes, as if in response to the challenge from film and games. "Event comics," as they were called, had existed since Marvel's *Secret Wars* and DC's *Crisis on Infinite Earths*. They were an excuse to feature every company character in panoramic summer stories that could be hyped like Hollywood blockbusters.

The first of these twenty-first-century event series to be a defining milestone in the development of the superhero narrative was 2004's *Identity Crisis*. Readers were assured of a story so shocking that it would change everything we knew about the DC universe, including our memories of the comics we'd loved as children.

Identity Crisis was a mystery that began with a brutal rape and murder, and one could hardly think of a single DC character less deserving of the victim role than the one chosen. One image will be branded into my brain folds forever: of the formerly breezy Sue Dibny sobbing in her husband's wraparound arms on the reflective floor of the Justice League satellite headquarters—a beloved childhood locus of excitement and opportunity—with the arse ripped out of her tights after what looked like forced back-door entry by Doctor Light.

Crooked physicist Arthur Light, famed for his manipulation of lenses and photons, had launched his career as an enemy of the Atom, who also played a major role in the story. Light was a typical Science 101–based villain of the Julius Schwartz Silver Age, devised to teach kids some basic physics in the sly guise of gimmick villainy. He'd gained a little extra depth and personality from his stint as a bumbling Teen Titans antagonist, but nothing in his previous record—including several counts of botched luminosity-related larceny—suggested an aptitude for forced sodomy until *Identity Crisis* chose to make this previously neglected facet of his appeal into its driving engine. Soon all the stalwarts of the DC hero community were living in fear for the rectal security of their own loved ones as Doctor Light's behavior spiraled out of control. He became more lascivious in every subsequent appearance, culminating in his rise from the dead as a lewd zombie.

As for Sue Dibny, you may remember Sue and her husband, Ralph, the Elongated Man, from the Silver Age as wisecracking mainstays of the lighter fringe of the DC universe. Drawn to resemble Dick Van Dyke and Mary Tyler Moore, Ralph and Sue Dibny were DC's answer to Nick and Nora Charles, the mystery-solving couple played by Dick Powell and Myrna Loy in *The Thin Man* movie series. (The Elongated Man, see?) A charming nonslapstick take on the Plastic Man stretchable-hero concept, *The Elongated Man* ran as a backup feature in *The Flash* with tidy eight-page puzzle and solution stories of the kind that Julius Schwartz favored. Ralph and Sue traveled the world as a happy couple, solving Ellery Queen–flavored science fiction parlor mysteries with very little fuss and typically smoochy endings that made married life seem like an endless honeymoon. They were young, they were in love, they were happy.

And then came Brad Meltzer.

Meltzer, a published novelist and longtime comics fan, knew his stuff, and it was clear he'd waited a long time to get his hands on these characters. Articulate, unassuming, and bookish, he seemed the boy least likely to immerse DC's stable of heroes in a queasy world of dubious ethics, paranoia, ultraviolence, and sexual assault, but he did. The effect was astonishing; it was like hearing "All You Need Is Love" performed by a satanic death-metal band from Norway.

Its opening was a challenging, bravura statement of intent that brought Meltzer's novelistic intentions to the foreground before showing his mastery of the comic format:

> DR. FATE ONCE TOLD ME, "LIFE IS A MYSTERY." BUT IT ISN'T. EVERYONE KNOWS HOW IT ENDS. IT'S JUST A QUESTION OF WHEN. IN A NOVEL, IT'S DIFFERENT. THERE YOU START WORRYING ABOUT THE MAIN CHARACTER'S SAFETY ALMOST IMMEDIATELY. OF COURSE, IT'S A FALSE WORRY. NOTHING BAD EVER HAPPENS TO THE MAIN CHARACTER IN A NOVEL. BUT IF THE STORY OPENS WITH A MINOR CHARACTER OR TWO—

Which, of course, *Identity Crisis* did, with Elongated Man and Firehawk perched on a rooftop stakeout. The captions were measured out across the whole sequence, set in exquisite counterpoint to the visuals and dialogue between the two characters.

On page 4, the scene moved to a kitchen in Smallville, with Clark Kent and his adopted parents and a new narrator we instantly recognized to be Superman.

These and further Joycean shifts of POV were accomplished by the use of multiple color-coded captions. A two-page sequence of green boxes, indicating Green Arrow's interior monologue, might be followed by a string of light-blue captions for the Atom, gray for Batman, or yellow for Robin, and yet, remarkably, Meltzer's story was never confusing. Every voice was so distinct and memorable that even with fifteen separate monologue strands in addition to dialogue and an authorial scene-setting voice, the colors were scarcely needed, even when taut, heart-stopping editing of scenes meant that sometimes four or five voices were in counterpoint across a single scene—the nearest anyone had come in years to the orchestral "sound" of Roy Thomas.

Issue 1 ended with Ralph's discovery of Sue's corpse, shown in no uncertain terms. The breezy detective was pictured kneeling, his ridiculously extended arms wrapped *several times* around the violated, burned remains of his beloved wife, while thick comic-book rain cataracted down on his anguished face. His head thrown back, his mouth stretched open like a freshly dug grave for a pet guinea pig, tears rivered down his rubbery cheeks. It was a far cry from the anniversary cruise to Cairo, where he and Sue had solved the riddle of the Sphinx and Ralph almost put his back out. The death of innocence had a new face, a new iconic image. This was the hideous promise of *Watchmen*'s bloodstained smiley-face badge made manifest as a rubber detective cradling a murdered rape victim, his wife. For the Dibnys, the Silver Age was well and truly over. The death of dreams was becoming a defining myth of post–Trade Towers America. Writers like Meltzer saw in the champions of their untroubled youth a bold metaphor for American innocence, and they savagely expressed the death of that hopeful naivety in a blast-radial discharge of explosive venom and expert cruelty. This was punk superheroics, American style.

The art was by up-and-comer Rags Morales, who cunningly orchestrated his compositions for maximum emotional symbolic impact and ramped up the pliable expressiveness of his characters' faces, pushing them to the new extremes of suffering that suited the story's pedal-to-the-metal disregard for propriety. Morales's specialty was superheroes at the absolute end of their tethers. He drew them sweating, sobbing, unmanned, bereaved, and paranoid—sometimes all at the same time if the story's roller-coaster acceleration demanded it.

The solution to Meltzer's murder mystery when it finally came was bizarre and a little anticlimactic, but it scarcely mattered and even had more impact on the third reading. What was important was the texture, the believable human voices, the sense of absolute danger and outrage that made *Identity Crisis* riveting. The cumulative effect of the series was to bring a new intimacy and vulnerability to the DC heroes. If they could cope with this and emerge intact, they could handle anything. The sales were spectacular, the buzz was electric, bringing DC to a middecade peak, as Marvel reconsidered its approach. One of the first reactions was a series entitled *Identity Disc*. Nu-Marvel was nothing if not shameless.

The final issue even quoted playwright Arthur Miller—"An era can be said to end when its basic illusions are exhausted"—as it laid to rest the assumptions of the Silver Age.

A rejuvenated DC followed the controversial success of *Identity Crisis* with a crowd-pleasing celebration entitled *Infinite Crisis*, a twentieth-anniversary sequel to the first great event comic, *Crisis on Infinite Earths*. Written by Geoff Johns, with a frightening eye for detail, the comic was an arcane encyclopedia of dense data, where decades of plot twists might be explained in a single panel, or histories of entire universes and countless characters condensed into walls of tiny text. All the while, the action never let up, as Johns and his artists orchestrated a literal cast of thousands of heroes and villains, with emotional moments, soap opera beats, and character development that seemed to streamline the entire DC style into a single voice. Johns often seemed possessed by the animating spirit of the DC Comics universe and had a facility for compressing years of continuity into a single telling line, such as in Batman's bitter dismissal of his old ally:

"LET'S FACE IT, **'SUPERMAN'** . . . THE LAST TIME YOU REALLY INSPIRED **ANYONE**—WAS WHEN YOU WERE **DEAD**."

Infinite Crisis was dense and arcane, a combination of guidebook and comic book that both thrilled and comforted DC's core audience.

Geoff Johns's work was always perfectly tuned to the exact sensibilities of the DC fan-boy demographic, and he knew when to roll out characterizations they were familiar with and when to add shock or novelty. But it was hard to imagine this concordance appealing to a wider audience. Its raisons d'être were specialist concerns, lacking mainstream appeal, although as an introduction to the expansive, bewildering DC virtual reality, it was hard to beat.

Alongside *Infinite Crisis*, DC was publishing my *Seven Soldiers* project. This was the mega-series I'd been building like some madman's matchstick cathedral while I was still at Marvel, and it was all about exploring the underbelly of the DC universe: the therapy groups for superheroes with low esteem; the wannabes who'd bought their magic rings off eBay; the men who watched superporn where girls poured steaming sulfuric acid over perfect, invulnerable breasts.

I wanted these disillusioned, half-trained supernobodies to have to face the kind of epic villainy that tended to be the preserve of big-time superheroes in the Justice League. It was one thing to watch a powerless mystery man go into action against a few thugs, but another to watch him take on an alien empire armed only with a shield and a nightstick. My villains in this were called the Sheeda (after the Celtic *Sidhe*, or fairy folk of the Otherworld, those mysterious "others" who turn up in the folk tales of most cultures), a rapacious carrion race of pointy-eared spindly goblins, riding huge, genetically engineered flies and spiders, like some eruption from a Richard Dadd canvas into the modern world. The Sheeda were revealed to be humanity's last descendants from one billion years in the future, evolved to become the final ferocious survivors on a doomed earth under a dying sun and using stolen time machines to keep themselves alive by eating their own history.

"WE ARE THE **END RESULT** OF **NATURAL SELECTION,** THE **WINNERS** OF A SAVAGE AND BLOODY STRUGGLE FOR PLANETARY **DOMINION.**"

Led by Gloriana Tenebrae, the apple-chomping Queen of the Fairies, the ultimate Wicked Witch, the Sheeda periodically sent their multitudinous armies back through time to "harvest" ripe civilizations by stealing their cultural, scientific, and environmental treasures, leaving whole centuries fallow only to return en masse when the next high culture had bloomed.

HERE THEY CLING TO A SPECTACULAR HALF-LIFE IN A
GROSS AND CLAUSTROPHOBIC IMITATION OF CULTURE
AT THE END OF ALL THINGS. THE CREEPLE-PEOPLE—THE
UNHOLY SHEEDA. HERE HAS ERUPTED, LIKE A JEWELLED
ABSCESS, THE ULTIMATE EARTHLY EMPIRE—STEAMING IN
THE SQUALID, LUSCIOUS DECAY OF THE REFUSE-LITTERED
SLOPES AT SUMMER'S END WHEREIN ARE NOURISHED THE
FAIRY HARVESTERS OF UNWHEN.

Another bold format experiment, *52* (2007), was a yearlong mega-story published in fifty-two real-time weekly installments, cowritten, TV-show style, by DC's big four writers at the time—Geoff Johns, Greg Rucka, Mark Waid, and me—with layouts and story breakdowns by artist Keith Giffen and finished art by a cast of up-and-coming DC talent.

It was a huge hit, and despite the difficult and demanding schedule, we all bonded quickly and were able to go into far greater depth than was usual with our core cast of C-list DC heroes and villains. We celebrated the completion of *52* with a trip to Las Vegas, where Greg Rucka suggested a visit to the shooting range. He was keen to sample a semiautomatic rifle, but as a confirmed pacifist, I'd never even held a real gun, let alone fired one. I found the pistol's thudding kick of pressure unexpected but not unappealing, and soon both Kristan and I were coldly pumping bullets into the sneering paper face of Osama bin Laden. The strange allure of cold-blooded murder seemed a little clearer in that roomful of whooping rednecks and nervously tittering first-timers.

Marvel parried with its own events. *Civil War*, as I've already discussed, was the best of them. But Brian Bendis also contributed the lukewarm *House of M*, and *Secret Invasion*—his sequel to the Kree-Skrull war in which the aliens won, Earth was conquered, and some slightly hamfisted attempts to compare Skrulls to radical Islamists were made, borrowed wholesale from TV's *Battlestar Galactica*.

Next came *Dark Reign*, in which the deranged, medicated Norman Osborn, aka Spider-Man archfoe Green Goblin, replaced Tony Stark as director of S.H.I.E.L.D. before assuming a new armored identity as the

Iron Patriot and drafting members of the supervillain community to serve as violent substitutes—"Dark Avengers"—for the Marvel superheroes. The series was notable for its subtle, multifaceted character study of Osborn as a bad man doing his best to live up to his onerous new role as a good guy, even as it fell apart all around him. Anyone who'd ever suffered the stress of too much work, too many hard decisions, and the cruelty of crushing deadlines could feel Osborn's pain as he struggled to hold together his unruly team and his country. This led directly into *Siege*, another epic chapter in the same enormous, ongoing story that proved, if nothing else, that Bendis was a one-man event machine and quite indispensable to the smooth running of the modern Marvel universe.

Then it was my turn to bat for DC on 2008's *Final Crisis*. I'd considered *Infinite Crisis* to be the quintessential event book and felt slightly intimidated. Geoff had left no stone unturned and effortlessly woven hundreds of characters into a story that gave them all something meaningful to do or say while setting up new plotlines and characters for other creators to explore. In his hands, the DC universe actually felt like a unified, if crowded, place. He'd even managed to introduce some notes of genuine emotion, such as the moment where the Lois Lane of the Golden Age dies in the arms of the original "pre-*Crisis*" Superman of 1939. On Earth-2, they'd married and grown into touchingly romantic late middle age together. I would have to do a very different kind of sequel to *Crisis*, and I hoped I could add something new and say something worthwhile.

During *Final Crisis*, I was on double duty with another big, controversial title spinning out of my productive and lucrative death psychedelia phase. In *Batman R.I.P.*, the Black Glove, a group of mega-wealthy international gamblers led by a sinister Dr. Hurt—who could have been the Devil or perhaps Bruce Wayne's presumed dead father—set about breaking the Dark Knight's will in every way, using his own mind and memories against him:

"NOTHING LESS THAN THE COMPLETE AND UTTER **RUINATION** OF A NOBLE SPIRIT."

I had fun doing a vulnerable Batman, stumbling homeless through the streets on heroin, deranged and betrayed. The comeback when it came was sweet but short-lived fruition, removing Bruce Wayne from the Batman trunks and launching him through time.

Batman R.I.P. even made headlines on the BBC, and the collected edition was a big hit in the mainstream bookstores, where handsome "graphic novels" or comic-book collections were slowly filling more and more shelf space. Some people seemed to take *R.I.P.* very seriously, and I was accused of murdering one furious correspondent's childhood—which, had it only been true, would surely have prevented that person from being around to make his complaint in the first place. It was almost funny, but when the *death threats* started to appear, we walked away from our website again and left the lunatics to their asylum.

Batman R.I.P. was no sooner cold in its casket than Frank Quitely and I launched our next title, *Batman and Robin*—an acid-tinged modernization of the sixties TV show as if directed by David Lynch, which became DC's biggest Batman book of 2009. Dick Grayson, the original Robin, was now a younger, more laid-back, and optimistic Batman, while the part of Robin was played by Bruce Wayne's long-lost son, Damian, who'd been raised by assassins as a scowling, privileged chip off the old block. The reversed dynamic duo—grim Robin, cheerful Batman—went down so well that many readers were actually deeply disappointed when Bruce Wayne came back to reclaim his cape. *Batman and Robin* flowed naturally into the equally successful *The Return of Bruce Wayne, Batman: The Return,* and *Batman Incorporated,* event after event after event. Some readers protested, and the term "event fatigue" became common, conjuring images of frail fans shuddering in darkened rooms as they attempted to recover from the exhaustion of reading stories where too much went on. But even when they complained, they couldn't stop buying, addicted to a narrative equivalent of crack cocaine that made old-fashioned non-event books taste like baby powder.

Hoping to drive the old nag so hard its heart burst, I decreed a new escalation of freelancer hostilities by condensing more and more story into fewer pages, declaring each arc, each issue, each panel an event!

Marvel closed the book on the last decade with the *Heroic Age.* The lights had come on again. The villains had been given their chance to rule the day, and it was over. All along the watchtower, all was well. The deliberate inversions of *Earth 2* and *Wanted* notwithstanding, the superheroes always won in the end. The fears of 9/11 had been processed, exhausted, and left behind, or so it seemed.

Our Worlds at War, DC's funereal turn-of-the-century alien war epic, which had shown two towers burning behind an anguished figure of Superman, set the dystopian tone for the decade. In this despairing image of a Superman who'd arrived too late to save the day, a new energy was found. He'd failed. Now what? Incredible new story potential!

DC ended the events decade with Geoff Johns's magisterial, morbid *Blackest Night*, in which a cosmic villain resurrected DC's dead superheroes and deceased supporting cast members as zombie "Black Lanterns," then *Brightest Day*, which deepened the contrast and announced a new chapter in the long-running DC universe saga. Johns applied a child's logic to his deft and engrossing expansion of the Green Lantern mythos, creating an entire spectrum of Yellow Lanterns, Blue Lanterns, Red Lanterns, and so on. This inevitably gave rise to the horrific notion of zombie Black Lanterns.

After a headline buyout by Disney in 2009, Marvel's dark-trending "realistic" phase was brought to a deliberate conclusion in Brian Bendis's *Siege*, where Asgard, the supercity of the Norse gods, as envisaged by Jack Kirby, was brought crashing to Earth, made solid, and then broken. From the rainbow ruins of the old mythology, a new myth could arise.

The following month brought *Heroic Age*, which was branded across the line and promoted with 2008 buzzwords like *mythic* and *iconic* in a hasty attempt to adapt and improve upon the big science fiction formula of the DC books. Whether or not Marvel's *Heroic Age* about-face also represented a simple capitulation to more family-friendly market forces driven by mouse diktat remained to be seen. The result for the superhero inhabitants of the Big Two comic-book universes was the same.

The long night was over.

Had the brief, angry, sex-mad, and individualistic adolescence of superhero comics come to a close at last? Comics were no longer some last-chance hotel for fantasy-prone mavericks who found other entertainment outlets too tame or too restrictive for their visions. They were now a respectable stepping-stone to Hollywood and big money. Cleaned up, hair cut, prepped for a settled life in the suburbs. No more noise, no more corrupting the kids or making them think about stuff they shouldn't.

At least for now. Nothing stays the same and everything stays the same for the superheroes of DC and Marvel. They won long ago.

Perhaps the final shock is this, the terrifying lesson of 2010's gleaming new superhero story:

The bad guys didn't win after all. We did.

Now what?

STAR, LEGEND, SUPERHERO, SUPERGOD?

THE SINGER ROBBIE Williams had, in his spare time, developed an interest in magic and the occult and, in 2005, he got in touch with me in my capacity as a "chaos magician" to ask if I could walk him through some of the basics.

He was a textbook forward-thinking dissatisfied Aquarian, and he knew—years ahead of everyone else in his business—that superheroes were the next big thing. He asked if we could turn him into a superhero for his next tour, so Frank Quitely drew up some Super-Rob sketches before we all decided he'd look ridiculous in a cape and circus suit and went to work devising a more twenty-first-century Elizabethan "occult" approach for the record sleeve, which would be packed with secrets and hidden meanings in the *Magical Mystery Tour* puzzle tradition. He would become a British superhero in a coat and scarf, a time-traveling shaman, the "Good Doctor."

Quitely and I created a sequence of "alien abduction" tarot cards for the album *Intensive Care*, but far from provoking the hoped-for tabloid screamers—"Robbie in Black Magic Shock!"—the talismanic images and witchy hieroglyphs were completely overlooked by a usually prurient media.

Not a single "What's he gotten himself into now?" story. Even when I wrote my own article for the *Sun* newspaper, it was rejected on the grounds that no one would be interested in Robbie Williams's dalliances with the powers of the pit! I planted a sigil on the cover, which can be activated by finding the CD in the shops or pulling the cover up on-screen and pressing Rob's finger. If enough of us do this the world will most certainly enter a new Golden Age of peace, creativity, and prosperity! . . .

Gerard Way, the lead singer of the band My Chemical Romance, was a very different kind of entertainer, a New Jersey art-punk rocker who'd been an intern at Vertigo back in the days of *The Invisibles* and a fan of my *Doom Patrol* run, although we'd never crossed paths.

In mid-2006, with *Final Crisis* on my mind, I caught the video for his band's song "Welcome to the Black Parade," a searing slice of punk psychedelia I was primed to like anyway. What really made me sit up were the outfits the band was wearing.

Dressed in black-and-white marching band uniforms as they led a procession of sexy walking dead through a bombed-out city, My Chemical Romance looked like a glamorous postmortem Sgt. Pepper's Lonely Hearts Club Band. They had fused the images of two opposites—the tough soldier and the frail emo kid—to create an image of what was to come. Nor was the sound morbid or dark; it was triumphal, chiming, imperial rock. The new psychedelia would learn to make friends with darkness. It would come from the Goth and alternative frontiers of the last twenty years into the mainstream, laughing at cancer as it put a beat to the Dance of the Dead and began to have fun again, however dark that fun might seem to grown-ups.

That fall, I listened to *The Black Parade* over and over and over again, to inspire cosmic mortuary scenes for *Final Crisis* and Batman's mental breakdown. MCR had shown me a picture of the new superhero, post-traumatic, postwar, the hero with nothing left to believe in. The supersoldier was home from the front, jumping every time a car backfired, staring at his hands.

Neil Gaiman put me in touch with Gerard, and we met in Glasgow before a gig, forming an instant connection. He led a new young generation of musicians who had grown up with superhero comics and had no qualms about saying so. He walked the walk too, with *Umbrella Academy*, his own award-winning re-creation of the superhero formula with artist Gabriel Ba. It was a kaleidoscopic tour de force. There was no shaky start, no cramming of balloons with words (a common tyro error), and none of the familiar missteps that dogged so many other celebrity-fan forays into the comics biz. *Umbrella Academy* was the end result of years of reading and thinking about superheroes and science fiction: Funny, scary, cerebral, arty, and violent all at the same time, it harvested all the fruits of Gerard's own "iconography tree." The heroes of *Umbrella Academy* were a group of outsider kids who grew up to be the world's greatest superheroes. It was the story of his band. It was my story too. It was a premonition of where we were all headed.

These days, it's no longer enough to be a star or even a superstar. Today even the most slender and ephemeral talents are routinely described as "legends." There's no need to slay ten-story sea beasts, endure complex and life-threatening quests or epic military campaigns: Simply release a couple of dodgy records or do some stand-up, and you too will be elevated to the ranks of the mythical King Arthur, heroic Lemminkainen, or mighty Odysseus. You too will become legend.

With our superlatives and honorifics devalued so that *star*, *legend*, and *genius* will suffice as descriptors for any old cod with half a good idea he stole from someone else, what lies next on the upward trajectory of human self-regard from star to superstar to legend? Once upon a time, a star was an individual of exceptional sporting, musical, or acting talent. Then it became every child who could grip a crayon and scrawl a daisy for Mother's Day. When we all became stars, stars became superstars to keep things straight, but they were swimming against the tide. In a time of Facebook and Twitter, where everyone has a fan page, when the concept of "genius" has been extended to include anyone who can produce a half-competent piece of art or writing, where is there left to go but all the way? We may as well crown ourselves kings of creation. Why not become superheroes? Supergods, in fact. Isn't it what we've always known we'd have to do in the end? Nobody was ever going to come from the sky to save us. No Justice League; Just Us League.

Back in 1940, Ma Hunkel, the Red Tornado, was the first attempt to depict a "real-life" superhero in comics. Not a spaceman from Krypton, not a billionaire playboy with a grudge, Ma had no powers except for her formidable washerwoman build. She wore a homemade costume to dish out local justice in the stairwells and alleyways of the Lower East Side in some aboriginal memory of the early DC universe.

She was joined by characters like Wildcat, the Black Canary, the Mighty Atom, the Sandman, and other tough but good-hearted vigilante crime fighters who took to the mean streets in nothing but their underwear. They had no special powers, just fists, and an attitude—at best, a gun that shot darts or gas or bees.

Seventy years after Ma Hunkel, sixteen-year-old Dave Lizewski, the hero of Mark Millar and John Romita Jr.'s *Kick-Ass*, asked the question "WHY DOES EVERYONE WANT TO BE PARIS HILTON BUT NO-BODY WANTS TO BE A SUPERHERO?" Leaving aside the cynical response that nobody in their right minds wanted to be Paris Hilton, Dave's question had already been answered by a handful of brave souls, real people in the real world who dress up in capes and masks to patrol the streets and keep people safe. You can read all about them online if you type "real world superheroes" into a search engine. They even have their own registry, like *Civil War* veterans who fought on Iron Man's side.

The TV and film hopefuls, the half-baked actors, are easy to spot. But to the others, fierce behind homemade masks and hoods and helmets, the superhero's calling is as important as religion, or at least as important as the youth cult demographic you conformed to at school. They are the future.

Who are these valiant harbingers, concealing their identities behind colorful masks and costumes to serve their communities as best they can? There's Portland's Zetaman, who patrols the city with gifts of food and clothing for the homeless. Atlanta's Crimson Fist hits the sidewalk of his city twice a month "to help those in need." There's Geist, "the Real Kick-Ass." Thanatos, Phantom Zero, the Death's Head Moth, and the Black Monday Society, a team of activists including Insignia, Ghost, and Silver Dragon. Captain Prospect. The list echoes the mesmerizing lullaby of Golden Age character names except for a lightning-stroke realization that these are real people, with curtains and light switches. This is what it's like to be a superhero with no plot, no Aristotelean thematically interconnected story arcs, no cliff-hangers, no tidy resolutions. Only raw motivation.

Many of them, like Entomo, the Insect Man, construct their own personal continuities on elaborate websites with animated graphics and voice-overs that hint of adventures we will never know or comprehend. These are florid private worlds glimpsed to best effect—like Phil Sheldon's photographs of Marvel heroes—from a distance, and fleetingly, but they speak of the power of pretend to ennoble ordinary lives. These real-life superheroes are waiting for a world that's not quite here, but one day soon they might be recognized as pioneering neonauts, part human, part story.

We allow people to tattoo themselves and even change sex: Can we deny these supervestites the opportunity to take it all the way and physically become the lunar-dwelling, light-speed-racing amphibians they've always wanted to be? Like a flock of wingless, fabulous missing links on a hostile shoreline, they seem to await the day when the skies will be filled with their kind, when they'll be able to hurdle tall buildings (one-eighth of a mile will do for a start) or stick to sheer glass the way nature intended. Ask real-life superhero Angle Grinder Man from England if he awaits the holy day as he goes about his business breaking council wheel clamps on behalf of grateful motorists. Does he dream that one day he'll be called upon to shatter the restraints on Batmobiles and Fantasticars?

In one notable respect, the real-life superhero fraternity differs from its Justice Society predecessors: The majority of our embryonic champions have so far avoided any rash assaults on the entrenched might of organized crime, international terrorism, or even the most rudimentary of deranged master-fiend behavior. With the exception of one or two hard men like Seattle's Phoenix Jones, who uses his martial-arts skills and Taser weaponry on drug dealers and other street criminals, most of today's early-adopting real-life superheroes prefer to keep an eye on the homeless or prowl around deserted warehouses looking for "clues."

"Every man and every woman is a star," wrote Aleister Crowley, little suspecting how literal those words might become in his prophesied new Aeon of Horus. With cameras everywhere, even on our personal computers and phones, we may as well be actors, performers, and stars in some filmic archive of the microscopically commonplace—every gesture, every frown recorded, filed away in some CCTV surveillance central AI that might as well be Brainiac, recording us down to the last byte and love bite before he shrinks Las Vegas into a jar and routinely demolishes Earth on December 21, 2012. Anything's possible on the thirty-second path where the real and the imaginary convene and collide in a sex club atmosphere of danger and masquerade.

If the superheroes come too soon from the 3-D screen to our material world, might they lose the privileges of fiction and run the risk of growing old and useless like the rest of us?

In his fascinating book *Becoming Batman*, E. Paul Zehr worked out exactly what kind of real-life training, diet, and exercise regime would be required to produce a physical specimen in the Batman mold and how long it would take to become a superhero, calculating that a real-world Batman might prepare his entire young-adult life for a window of physical and mental effectiveness that was barely five years long. Consider then the active life of Citizen Prime, the Watch Man, or Metro Woman, brave recension of Ma Hunkel and Pat Parker, who hands out mass transit information in Washington, DC. What white-hot collector's item award-winning six-issue prestige series will re-create her for a new generation of fans when the cartilage goes in her knee?

> I KNEW THE **IMAGE** WAS RIGHT. PEOPLE **LOVE** SUPER-HERO MOVIES. I **KNEW** ALL THAT BUT YOU KNOW THE RIDICULOUS THING WAS THAT EVEN **AFTER** ALL MY SURGERY AND TRAINING, EVEN AFTER THE **THERAPY,** I STILL . . . I JUST DIDN'T **LOOK** RIGHT. MY BODY NEVER SEEMED TO GET BIG ENOUGH OR IMPRESSIVE ENOUGH TO MAKE MY MESSAGE CONVINCING. IT WAS FUN TO POSE IN MY OUTFITS IN FRONT OF THE **MIRROR** BUT THE IDEA OF ACTUALLY GOING **OUTSIDE** BECAME MORE AND MORE TERRIFYING. I KEPT MAKING **PLANS** TO LEAVE THE APARTMENT . . . BUT CAN YOU IMAGINE SOME WEIRD GUY WITH MUSCLE DYSMORPHIA PROCLAIMING HIMSELF THE WORLD'S FIRST SUPER-HERO? THEY'D ALL JUST LAUGH. THAT'S THE REAL TRUTH.

That was Max Thunderstone—the self-styled "Man-Made God" from *The Filth,* my sci-fi series with artist Chris Weston—the world's first superhero. Thunderstone was a geek who'd spent a massive lottery win improving his body and mind. Filled with big marketable ideas about how to save the world, Thunderstone succumbed to self-image problems and an obsession with the unlikely shape of his penis.

By the end of the twenty-first century's first decade, the entertainment industry had become increasingly democratized, the renaissance concept of genius had been expanded to include everyone, and the idea of the star had been worn flat by reality TV. It was inevitable that superheroes would be subjected to the same process. Suddenly they were real again, ordinary people like the rest of us. The comic-book superheroes who'd begun the decade as soldiers and celebrities, VIPs, ended it as everyday people dressing in the colors of their dreams to defy the mundane. We real-life organisms began the new century as ordinary, frightened people and ended as potential superheroes, inspired by our fictions to surpass our limits. To get close enough for contact to happen, like Michelangelo's God assuming the form of a man to better touch Adam's extended finger, the superheroes gave up even their special powers and their wealth. They became ordinary boys like Kick-Ass or fucked-up delusional losers like the Crimson Bolt, the "hero" of James Gunn's *Super*. They had deep, emotional histories, opinions, sexuality. They became real enough for us to rise to meet them, stretching out to receive the spark, the lightning bolt that signaled contact.

That divine electricity connects lowest to highest, the real to the fantastic, and fuses the streets and the sky together as one seamless whole. We've seen what happens when superheroes become us. What happens when we become them?

New technologies allow people to move remote-controlled cars just by thinking about it, a precursor of the Green Lantern ring. The Chinese government has just endorsed the use of genetic-engineering technologies still considered dubious in the West to "improve" the Chinese people in the direction of a superhuman ideal. We can divide atoms, track particles so small and so ghostlike they can scarcely be said to exist at all. We can fly across the Atlantic in hours, access any information instantaneously, see the world from space or zoom in our own rooftops, like Superman home from a mission. We have online secret identities, other lives, missions. Everyone is special, everyone is a superhero now. Even the president of the United States.

At the end of 2008, Barack Obama, the president-in-waiting, courted the geek vote by joking about his birth on planet Krypton. Even Alex Ross, who'd painted a controversial *Rolling Stone* cover with George Bush as a vampire feasting on the exposed jugular of the Statue of the Liberty, depicted Obama in classic Clark Kent pose, tearing open his shirt to reveal an *O* insignia on his chest. It was too early to tell if this was pop politics disguised as a millennial promise of superhuman salvation or simply an invitation to fill the cipher on his chest with hopes and dreams to give it meaning.

The "real-world" approach to superhero movies that spawned the likes of *Kick-Ass* began to reverse itself in 2010, when the cycle was ready to move from realism back toward the phantasmagorical. Unsurprisingly, expansive, fantastical films like James Cameron's eco-tribal hippie extravaganza *Avatar,* Tim Burton's *Alice in Wonderland,* or Chris Nolan's cryptic, elliptical *Inception* were all immensely popular that year, and it will be interesting to see how well the cosmic *Green Lantern* will fare with audiences in 2011. If Ryan Reynolds proves popular in the role of Hal Jordan—test pilot inducted into an intergalactic police force—we may see further evidence that a decade of uniformed, militant psychedelia has arrived. Marvel characters appear in three movies planned for summer 2011, and two of those—*Thor* and *Captain America: The First Avenger*—are based around some of Jack Kirby's outré concepts, like the reality-warping Cosmic Cube and his Asgardian techno-deities.

From the heads of artists and writers, to print, then to moving images, and slowly off the screen into our real lives, the men and women of tomorrow marched closer, racing toward us out of the future.

Mark Millar, Tom Peyer, Mark Waid, and I had approached DC in 1999 with the idea of relaunching Superman for a new generation in a series to be entitled *Superman Now* or *Superman 2000,* depending on which version of the story synopsis you read. We'd spent many enjoyable hours in conversation, working out how to restore our beloved Superman to his preeminent place as the world's first and best superhero. Following the lead of the *Lois and Clark* TV show, the comic-book Superman had, at long last, put a ring on his long-suffering girlfriend's finger and carried her across the threshold to holy matrimony after six decades of dodging the issue—although it was Clark Kent whom Lois married in public, while Superman had to conceal his wedding band every time he switched from his sober suit and tie. This newly domesticated Superman was a somehow diminished figure, all but sleepwalking through a sequence of increasingly contrived "event" story lines, which tried in vain to hit the heights of "The Death of Superman" seven years previously. *Superman Now* was to be a reaction against this often overemotional and ineffectual Man of Steel, reuniting him with his mythic potential, his archetypal purpose, but there was one fix we couldn't seem to wrap our collective imagination around: the marriage. The Clark-Lois-Superman triangle—"Clark loves Lois. Lois loves Superman. Superman loves Clark," as Elliot S. Maggin put it in his intelligent, charming Superman novel *Miracle Monday*—seemed intrinsic to the appeal of the stories, but none of us wanted to simply undo the relationship using sorcery, or "memory wipes," or any other of the hundreds of cheap and unlikely magic-wand plot devices we could have dredged up from the bottom of the barrel.

Stuck with the problem, I found myself chewing it over with my JLA editor Dan Raspler at one in the morning in an airless hotel room overlooking the naval yards of San Diego harbor. We were there for 1999's Comic-Con. To clear our heads, we went downstairs and crossed the street, an oddly landscaped liminal zone between the rail tracks and the city. We were deep in discussion, debating earnestly the merits and demerits of a married Superman when we both spotted a couple of men crossing the tracks into town. One was an ordinary-looking bearded dude, at first sight like any of a hundred thousand comics fans. But the other was Superman. He was dressed in a perfectly tailored red, blue, and yellow costume; his hair was slicked back with a kiss curl; and unlike the often weedy or paunchy Supermen who paraded through the convention halls, he was trim, buff, and handsome. He was the most convincing Superman I've ever seen, looking somewhat like a cross between Christopher Reeve and the actor Billy Zane. I knew a visitation when I saw one.

Racing to intercept the pair, Dan and I explained who we were, what we were doing, and asked "Superman" if he wouldn't mind answering a few questions. He didn't, and sat on a concrete bollard with one knee to his chest shield, completely relaxed. It occurred to me that this was exactly how Superman would sit. A man who was invulnerable to all harm would be always relaxed and at ease. He'd have no need for the kind of physically aggressive postures superheroes tended to go in for. I suddenly began to understand Superman in a new way. We asked questions, "How do you feel about Lois?," "What about Batman?," and received answers in the voice and persona of Superman—"I don't think Lois will ever really understand me or why I do what I do" or "Batman sees only the darkness in people's hearts. I wish he could see the best"—that seemed utterly convincing.

The whole encounter lasted an hour and a half, then he left, graciously, and on foot I'm sad to say. Dan and I stared at each other in the fuzzy sodium glare of the streetlamps then quietly returned to our rooms. Enflamed, I stayed awake the whole night, writing about Superman until the fuming August sun rose above the warships, the hangars, and the Pacific. I was now certain we could keep the marriage to Lois and simply make it work to our advantage.

Bumping into someone dressed as Superman at the San Diego Comic Convention may sound about as wondrous and unlikely as meeting an alcoholic at an AA meeting, of course, but it rarely happens at night, and of the dozens of Men of Steel I've witnessed marching up and down the aisles at Comic-Con, or posing with tourists outside Mann's Chinese on Hollywood Boulevard, not one was ever as convincing as the Superman who appeared at the precise moment I needed him most. This is what I mean when I talk about magic: By choosing to frame my encounter as a pop-shamanic vision quest yielding pure contact with embodied archetypal forces, I got much more out of it than if I'd simply sat there with Dan sniggering at the delusional fool in tights. By telling myself a very specific story about what was occurring, I was able to benefit artistically, financially, and I like to think spiritually, in a way that perhaps might not have been possible had I simply assumed that our Superman was a convention "cosplayer." *Superman Now* never happened, but I'd come to envisage a Superman project that would serve as the pinnacle of my work on hero comics, and a way to put all of my thoughts about superheroes into a single piece.

There is, you'll be heartened to discover, a cruel, ironic counter to the tale of glory and grace I relate above. Coincidences came with fangs in the 9/11 decade. During the 2002 Comic-Con, artist Chris Weston was in full enthusiastic flow, telling me just how much he wanted to draw a story featuring Bizarro, Superman's deranged "imperfect duplicate." At that very moment, as they say, a convention goer, dressed as the deformed, backward-talking Bizarro, appeared in the street ahead of us. Chris, sensing an opportunity for a spirit encounter of his own, dragged the green-painted stranger along to a party but unlike the courteous Superman of 1999, Bizarro refused to leave Chris's side, becoming ever drunker and more belligerent, raucous and true to character. The more drunk he became, the more authentically possessed he was by the Dionysian spirit of Bizarro. Clearly distressed, Chris wailed, "I can't get rid of him! What am I going to do?"

In the end, much as Superman often found himself doing, we had to trick Bizarro into going home by using his own code of "uz do opposite" against him. On the topsy-turvy Bizarro world, we explained, a party was when you were alone, not with other people. Other people, in fact, ruined a party. He was forced to admit this made perfect Bizarro sense and marched backward up the stairs, blind drunk, while we all waved and yelled, "Hello, Bizarro!"

I imagined him being pulled over by the highway patrol an hour later, pissed at the wheel in his baggy costume, and flaking gray-green face paint. Running this fantasy to its inevitable conclusion, I couldn't help but picture him on CCTV curled in a fetal position whimpering "Yes! Yes! Hit Bizarro again!" as his tormentors pummelled him back to sanity with rubber truncheons.

From the ashes of *Superman Now,* I started work on what became *All-Star Superman* after my return to DC in 2003. The story I had planned was to deal with Superman's mortality, depicting his final days, and the twelve heroic labors he would perform for the benefit of all humankind. When my dad died the following year, he gave a part of his spirit to the book. Walter Morrison's exit was a long and hard battle of the kind he'd loved best when he knew such battles were winnable; first came a stroke that disorganized his vision so that he saw restless moving figures flickering in the corner of his eye; "the passing show" as he called it. Then the cancer struck, and left him unable to walk, unable to fight, unable to speak. During the early period of that final sequence of events, he composed a short book about his beloved Corkerhill community, his own achievements there, and how best the needs of its people might be served by local government. I edited the result, correcting his lapses in spelling and grammar, with the understanding that I was collaborating with him on his final statement. We fought when he didn't think my first attempt was good enough, and I blamed him for not doing it properly in the first place, but he was right and we made it better. By the time I brought the bound and finished books—made up by a local printer—in a box to his bed, he was barely capable of acknowledging their existence. By then he was robbed of the ability to speak, to write, or to read. His last, barely there, yet still defiant scrawl appeared in my forty-third birthday card: "I'LL BE BACK."

My sister maintained an almost twenty-four-hour, seven-day vigil at his bedside, but by the time we finally got him out of the hospital and into a calm hospice on the banks of the Clyde, Dad had only a day left to live. His face looked strange and somehow raw, and we finally realized the hospital had shaved off the moustache he'd had since the age of sixteen as a soldier in India, his badge of pride. My dad would never have wanted this, could never have deserved it, and yet here was this grinding, epic deconstruction. Cancer didn't give a flying fuck for the warrior socialist; the principled, honest fighter for justice; the funny, insightful, out-of-the-box thinker; the activist; the soldier; the dad. There was no one in charge; there could be no appeal, no reward or censure. As we sat holding his hands in what felt like some anteroom of the afterlife, his breathing changed tempo, then ceased, and Walter was gone.

Just in case the Tibetans were onto something, I'd made up my mind to follow Dad into the *bardo* in the hope of helping out if I could. In the event that Walter's disembodied consciousness really was still hanging around like a slowly evaporating thought balloon, I didn't want him to drift out there alone. I read up on, then performed the *tonglen* meditations for the dead, and experienced vivid visions of Indian jungles and a voice telling me that my dad was having an adventure among "snakes that walk and trees that talk." When I slept, I saw him young, in the steaming Burmese rain forest of dreams.

On the day of the funeral, a troop of drummers turned up like warriors, in kilts, carrying bodhrán drums emblazoned with Celtic knot work. It was the funeral of a chieftain, a fighter, and as the coffin descended, the bodhráns started up a defiant storm. I tried to follow instructions by visualizing a glowing miniature sun above the descending coffin. I saw my dad, young, reaching the top of a flight of overgrown stairs and the wide-open doors of a temple, where he turned and waved once before disappearing into the darkness under the arch, and we all filed out of the crematorium through a blurred-glass haze of tears, a cannonade of drums.

In the Tibetan Buddhist tradition, it's said that only a rainbow remains when an illuminated master dies. True to form, I went outside after the service, and there in the fragile blue sky above the chimney was a perfect rainbow.

Later that year, Kristan and I got married in Mauritius and honeymooned among the soaring World of Krypton star-scrapers of deeply sinister Dubai. That felt like something from a Superman annual, too. The Death. The Wedding. It could have been an "80-page Giant" special edition featuring "Superman's Red-Letter Moments!" All we needed was our own Fortress, and that came along in its turn, quite unexpectedly, in the form of the house we found to live in together. Things felt epic, ordered, possessed of an architectural quality that suggested, at least to the crazy-ass mind of the superhero writer, the careful hand of some higher-dimensional storyteller working his pet themes and images into a mandala made of my life. The structure of *All-Star Superman* was intended to have a foursquare solidity, a kind of mystical Masonic architecture, and our new home seemed to concretize the same principles. The house even had a tall stained-glass window depicting the history of life on earth, with a central, zodiacal tree-of-life panel surmounted by the blazing sunshine-yellow face of a young, beardless God with a streaming solar corona for hair. Just below him were the words "*Deus Pater Omnium.*" Even without my determination to find meaningful resonances in everything, it was hard to ignore the confrontational nature of the way the house so perfectly crystallized the themes and structure of *All-Star Superman,* and so much else about that time, into quarried stone, timber, and glass, a spell made so manifest you could trip down its stairs and break your neck.

I wrote my personal best story of the world's greatest superhero, for my favorite artist to draw, overlooking a loch where Trident submarines still sailed in all their stately satanic splendor, with black bellies full of hellfire sufficient to blind and vaporize me in a fraction of a heartbeat, even as it liquefied the ancient stones of my walls, cracked Scotland in half, and turned the world into a refrigerated postnuclear litter tray. I wrote it scant miles from the former American navy base, where my parents had protested, where Dad had been arrested, and where American comics had arrived in Scotland with the sailors and submariners. It felt like ground zero, the center of a web of coincidence and personal mythology that was as ordered and symmetrical, as self-referential, as an issue of *Watchmen*.

The writer Alvin Schwartz worked on Superman and Batman strips for eight years during the Golden Age. Like so many of the writers who found a welcome in the comic books, Schwartz had close ties to the underground radical scene of his time and moved in a circle with Jackson Pollock and Saul Bellow.

Schwartz, who wrote libretti for two Superman operas, went on to write *An Unlikely Prophet,* a book about his own spiritual experience, in which he claims to have encountered Superman in the form of a *tulpa*. *Tulpa* is a Tibetan description for a solid object, or person, created from thought alone; i.e., literally and deliberately willed into tangible form from nothing. His Superman, he reported, was all made of one substance: hair, skin, costume, molded from a single material; like a creature formed of resplendent talking clay. Alvin Schwartz insisted that Superman was an idea that had become strong enough to manifest itself as a material entity, and after my experience with the real Man of Steel in 1999, I found myself inclined to agree with at least a portion of what he had to say, although I didn't have to meet Superman in the flesh to believe in him. He was already real for me, in glorious 2-D continuity, in the DC universe. A comic book, like any object created by human minds and hands, is already a *tulpa*: What else is it but a thought so perfectly condensed from brain electricity onto paper and ink that someone can hold it in their hands?

It's surmised that many, if not all, of the cave paintings dating back to our remote prehistory, and to the beginnings of human self-awareness, were created not simply as Paleolithic wallpaper but with magical intent.

The comics share some of the primitive vitality of early art and often a sense of the same deliberate spell-casting at work. Sympathetic magic involves making a scale model, a simulation, or isomorphic mapping, of the real world, and by causing changes in the model—whether by sticking pins through the heart of a voodoo doll or painting spears in the hides of a herd of cave-wall aurochs—real-world events can be persuaded into a synchronous relationship with the magician's will or intent. Will, as anyone who has ever tried to give up smoking or start exercising should know all too well, is the power humans have to act against our tendency toward inertia. Will motivates us to undertake hazardous journeys, build cathedrals and jet aircraft, and change our lives. With strong enough willpower, we can alter our behavior, our surroundings, our beliefs and ourselves.

Writers and artists build by hand little worlds that they hope might effect change in real minds, in the real world where stories are read. A story can make us cry and laugh, break our hearts, or make us angry enough to change the world. We know that medical placebos work when a trusted authority figure, in the form of a doctor, simply tells us they will. There is even a "nocebo" concept to explain why some people get sick or die when they are cursed by a witch doctor, wrongly diagnosed by a medical doctor, or otherwise have reason to believe that they might. We know that hypnosis works. There is observable evidence to suggest that what we believe to be true directly affects how we live. As the first few years of the twenty-first century wore on, I wondered just how badly people, especially young people, were being affected by the overwhelmingly alarmist, frightening, and nihilistic mass media narratives that seemed to boil with images of death, horror, war, humiliation, and pain to the exclusion of almost everything else, on the presumed grounds that these are the kinds of stories that excite the jaded sensibilities of the mindless drones who consume mass entertainment. Cozy at our screens in the all-consuming glare of Odin's eye, I wondered why we've chosen to develop in our children a taste for mediated prepackaged rape, degradation, violence, and "bad-ass" mass-murdering heroes.

And so *All-Star Superman:* our attempt at an antidote to all that, which dramatized some of the ideas in *Supergods* by positioning Superman as the Enlightenment ideal paragon of human physical, intellectual, and moral development that Siegel and Shuster had originally imagined. A Vitruvian Man in a cape, our restorative Superman would attempt to distill the pure essence of pop culture's finest creation: baring the soul of an indestructible hero so strong, so noble, so clever and resourceful, he had no need to kill to make his point. There was no problem Superman could not solve or overcome. He could not lose. He would never let us down because we made him that way. He dressed like Clark Kent and took the world's abuse to remind us that underneath our shirts, waiting, there is an always familiar blaze of color, a stylized lighting bolt, a burning heart.

With Frank Quitely on board to perfectly realize the stories and inspire me to my best efforts, the coloring job went to Frank's studio buddy Jamie Grant, another Scot, whose intense, saturated computer effects made Superman's world glow like a rose window. America's greatest hero had fallen into the hands of three Scotsmen as if, at last, we were being given a chance to pay back the debt of all those Yankee mags, harvesting the fruit of the wondrous seeds they'd left growing in our skulls, and sending it all back Stateside where *All-Star Superman* became the most successful Superman comic of the new century.

Dan DiDio's *All-Star* trademark harked back to the venerable showcase title of the 1940s and hoped to suggest the caliber of the writers and artists he planned to assign, but Quitely and I chose to take it literally. We put the blazing sun at the very center of our tale and made *All-Star Superman* the story of a solar hero, a man who quite literally becomes a star. The twelve-issue format allowed us to present Superman with a mythic twelve labors, following the sun's path across the day, as well as the changing seasons in a year. Each issue featured a complete story, and they all connected to make a twelve-part final adventure for Superman, facing his death, composing a last Will and Testament while settling his affairs and trying to ensure the world would prosper when he was gone. Halfway through, in issue no. 6, which was set at Christmas, in midwinter, we plunged Superman into the nightmare backward world of Bizarro, in a classic "night journey" of the kind mapped onto the mythology of every culture by Joseph Campbell.

We aimed for the pared-down clarity of folktales: stories of a world where intimate human dramas of love, jealousy, or grief were enacted upon a planetary scale by a group of characters whose decisions could shake worlds. In the grand arena of *All-Star Superman,* a broken heart, a tear, or a single good deed would inevitably unleash massive, cosmic consequences. *All-Star Superman* was a divine Everyman, Platonic man sweating out the drama of ordinary life on an extraordinary canvas.

The attempt to be true to the underlying spirit of Superman, as we saw it, had brought out the best in all of us. Like a monk contemplating the deeds of a saint, I was elevated by the time I spent imagining how Superman might feel. The whole world seemed fragile, infinitely precious, all-connected, and ultimately worthy of, if not a happy ending, at least a To Be Continued . . .

All-Star Superman was turned into an animated feature in 2011, as one of a series of comic-book adaptations from DC. The script by the talented Dwayne McDuffie—who died tragically on the weekend the DVD was released—captured the episodic, mythic countdown of the comic book and demonstrated how to do a Superman that was lyrical and Romantic, as well as stoic and tough. As Superman hugged the woman who'd been with him since the beginning and spoke his final words—"I LOVE YOU, LOIS LANE. UNTIL THE END OF TIME"—before hurtling into the sky to die, our best-ever friend, in the service of humanity, it was hard not to feel a pang.

Somewhere in the middle of all this I mysteriously turned forty-five, which meant I'd been working long enough to qualify and became the recipient of the highest honor it was possible for the UK Eagle Awards for comics to bestow, scoring the outsize Roll of Honor Lifetime Achievement version of their famous Eagle statuette. In the heart of all this perfect symmetry, a magnificent handcrafted bird of prey with my name on it arrived in its box on the doorstep. Inside I found the emblem and totem of my life's achievement in comics with one outstretched, gilded wing cleanly snapped off at the rib cage.

OUTRO: 'NUFF SAID

WE HAVE MADE YOU A CREATURE NEITHER OF HEAVEN NOR OF EARTH, NEITHER MORTAL NOR IMMORTAL IN ORDER THAT YOU MAY, AS THE FREE AND PROUD SHAPER OF YOUR OWN BEING, FASHION YOURSELF IN THE FORM YOU MAY PREFER. IT WILL BE IN YOUR POWER TO DESCEND TO THE LOWER BRUTISH FORMS OF LIFE; YOU WILL BE ABLE, THROUGH YOUR OWN DECISION, TO RISE AGAIN TO THE SUPERIOR ORDERS WHOSE LIFE IS DIVINE.

It's 1486, almost half a century into the new Western dawn, and that's one man's idea of "God" having a quiet word with man. We're at the beginning of the great European Renaissance of culture, the end of a long dark age, and here's Count Giovanni Pico della Mirandola, aged twenty-six, seizing his moment in the piazza. This is it; his big chance to impress posterity and an audience of hostile clerics with his observations on philosophy and human nature.

"Born to a high position we failed to appreciate it but fell instead to the estate of brutes and uncomprehending beasts of burden."

Pico's *Oration on the Dignity of Man* is still regarded as the foundation stone of the "humanist" movement that strove to cast off the manacles of Church dogma, locked in place since the founding of St. Peter's Basilica in AD 324, but for all its status as a humanist manifesto, the *Oratorio* is without a doubt urging us to go far beyond the human, into the realms of angels and gods. It asks us to accept the superhuman as an undeniable fact of our nature, and the goal of our future evolution as people.

As we draw close to the back cover, I'd like to think Pico's time has come around again, one reason why he was given a cameo role in *All-Star Superman*. What he's saying still makes sense, perhaps more than ever given the possibilities of our technology and medicine, because Pico is telling us about the power of stories and imagination to reshape our future. He's doing me a big favor by explaining what this book is all about, in fact. Although his metaphors are Biblical, suggesting Cherubs and Seraphs and Thrones as our role models and intermediaries on the road to "God" or "cosmic consciousness," we can just as easily call them superheroes.

Pico tells us that we have a tendency to reenact the stories we tell ourselves. We learn as much (and sometimes more that's useful) from our fictional role models as we do from the real people who share our lives. If we perpetually reinforce the notion that human beings are somehow unnatural aberrations adrift in the ever-encroaching Void, that story will take root in impressionable minds and inform the art, politics, and general discourse of our culture in anti-life, anti-creative, and potentially catastrophic ways. If we spin a tale of guilt and failure with an unhappy ending, we will live that story to its conclusion, and some benighted final generation not far down the line will pay the price.

If, on the other hand, we emphasize our glory, intelligence, grace, generosity, discrimination, honesty, capacity for love, creativity, and native genius, those qualities will be made manifest in our behavior and in our works. It should give us hope that superhero stories are flourishing everywhere because they are a bright flickering sign of our need to move on, to imagine the better, more just, and more proactive people we can be.

Here in the twenty-first century we're surrounded by proof that we tend to live our stories. As I brought this section to a close, one last synchronicity directed my attention to an article in *New Scientist*'s February 12, 2011, issue about the work of William Casebeer of the US Defense Advanced Research Projects Agency (DARPA), based in Arlington, Virginia. Casebeer, a neurobiologist, goes so far as to suggest that certain narratives are as addictive as cocaine, commenting on the effects a compelling yarn might have upon the minds of enemy soldiers or suicide bombers. He is convinced that we should be investigating the military potential of stories, by creating "counter-narrative strategies" engineered to undermine or oppose the religious or political storylines that inspire war, oppression, and greed. We may scoff and leave it to military experts to develop a technology whereby a cadet is told a story so convincing he believes he's superhuman before a battle, but I'd like to think that magic words and spells belong to the rest of us as well. If Pico is correct, we can write new lives and new futures, and, more important, live them. Stories can break hearts or foment revolutions. Words can electrify us or make our blood run cold. And the idea of Superman is every bit as real as the idea of God.

If our shallow, self-critical culture sometimes seems to lack a sense of the numinous or spiritual it's only in the same way a fish lacks a sense of the ocean. Because the numinous is everywhere, we need to be reminded of it. We live among wonders. Superhuman cyborgs, we plug into cell phones connecting us to one another and to a constantly updated planetary database, an exo-memory that allows us to fit our complete cultural archive into a jacket pocket. We have camera eyes that speed up, slow down, and even reverse the flow of time, allowing us to see what no one prior to the twentieth century had ever seen—the thermodynamic miracle of broken shards and a puddle gathering themselves up from the floor to assemble a half-full wineglass. We are the hands and eyes and ears, the sensitive probing feelers through which the emergent, intelligent universe comes to know its own form and purpose. We bring the thunderbolt of meaning and significance to unconscious matter, blank paper, the night sky. We are already divine magicians, already supergods. Why shouldn't we use all our brilliance to leap in as many single bounds as it takes to a world beyond ours, threatened by overpopulation, mass species extinction, environmental degradation, hunger, and exploitation? Superman and his pals would figure a way out of any stupid cul-de-sac we could find ourselves in—and we made Superman, after all. All it takes is that one magic word.

Somewhere, still, Pico is wrapping up his *Oratorio*. Somewhere right now Joe Shuster is putting pencil to paper and bringing Superman to life for the first time. If Superman stood on a hypothetical planet orbiting the ancient red star Antares in the constellation of Scorpio, he could watch the arrival of light from the cultural Renaissance and catch the *Oratorio* on its way past, going on forever. I can see 1489 just by looking up at the night sky where Antares is the fifteenth-brightest star. The photons traveling down my optic nerves into my brain were launched on their epic interstellar dash around the time Pico was clearing his throat, ending their journey in my eyes five hundred years later.

We love our superheroes because they refuse to give up on us. We can analyze them out of existence, kill them, ban them, mock them, and still they return, patiently reminding us of who we are and what we wish we could be. They are a powerful living idea—a meme, to use the terminology of Richard Dawkins that has propagated itself from paper universes into actuality, with unknown consequences. The Bomb, too, was only an idea that someone hammered into being.

But the superheroes showed me how to overcome the Bomb. Superhero stories woke me up to my own potential. They gave me the basis of a code of ethics I still live by. They inspired my creativity, brought me money, and made it possible for me to turn doing what I loved into a career. They helped me grasp and understand the geometry of higher dimensions and alerted me to the fact that everything is real, especially our fictions. By offering role models whose heroism and transcendent qualities would once have been haloed and clothed in floaty robes, they nurtured in me a sense of the cosmic and ineffable that the turgid, dogmatically stupid "dad" religions could never match. I had no need for faith. My gods were real, made of paper and light, and they rolled up into my pocket like a superstring dimension.

Superhero stories are sweated out at the imagined lowest levels of our culture, but like that shard off a hologram, they contain at their hearts all the dreams and fears of generations in vivid miniature. Created by a workforce that has in its time been marginalized, mocked, scapegoated, and exploited, they never failed to offer a direct line to the cultural subconscious and its convulsions. They tell us where we've been, what we feared, and what we desired, and today they are more popular, more all-pervasive than ever because they still speak to us about what we really want to be. Once again, the comics were right all along. When no one else cared, they took the idea of a superhuman future seriously, embraced it, exalted it, tested it to destruction and back, and found it intact, stronger, more defined, like steel in a refiner's fire. Indestructible. Unstoppable. The superheroes, who were champions of the oppressed when we needed them to be, patriots when we needed them to be, pioneers, rebels, conformists, or rock stars when we needed them to be, are now obligingly battering down the walls between reality and fiction before our very eyes.

There's only one way to find out what happens next . . .

SUPERGODS IS A subjective history, not an encyclopedic one, so while I tried to provide as broad an overview of the life of this idea as I could, there were necessary—and intentional—omissions.

Given the chance to atone for my authorial sins in this paperback, however, I've corrected a few factual errors and repetitions in the text, but there are two final additions here and one update that I'd like to make to this new edition of the book. One concerns the essential Superman movies of Christopher Reeve; the other, Kurt Busiek's *Astro City*, which features in the "Suggested Further Reading" section yet failed to make the hardback edit. I'd also like to take this opportunity to bring readers up to date on the spate of superhero films released just as the hardcover of *Supergods* was going to press. By the time you read this there will have been ten more, of course, but the completist in me had to try.

CHRISTOPHER REEVES AND THE REBIRTH OF THE MOVIE HERO

Father and son producers Alexander and Ilya Salkind, riding high on the success of *The Three Musketeers* and its sequel (surprisingly entitled *The*

Four Musketeers), now announced their intention to re-create Superman in a big-budget movie to be written by the *Godfather* author, Mario Puzo, and aimed at a general international audience. When *Superman* the movie showed up, with director Richard Donner at the wheel and a tagline that read "You'll believe a man can fly," it originated the blueprint for a very different approach to live-action superheroics. Blazing a trail as ever, the first and greatest of the superheroes was the test pilot for a new kind of straight-faced respectful approach to outlandish source material that would define an entire wave of successful comic book–to–movie adaptations twenty years later.

Although showcasing Hollywood royalty in the form of Marlon Brando, who played Superman's father, Jor-El, in the extended opening scenes set on a chilly, austere vision of the planet Krypton, and Oscar-winning Gene Hackman, whose comedy turn as Lex Luthor seemed out of synch with the movie's otherwise serious tone, *Superman* was given its true heart and an unlikely gravitas by the conviction of Christopher Reeve in the lead role.

Reeve was a twenty-eight-year-old stage actor, unsure about taking on the role of a world-famous comic book character. He had doubts about Superman's lack of depth that quickly vanished when he realized that the alien hero's human disguise as Clark Kent allowed him to play two complementary roles. His Kent was neither cowardly, nor oafish, but somewhat shy, diffident, human, and likable, while his portrayal of Superman brought to life the character's nobility, determination, and essential decency in a resolutely non-ironic manner that gave his performance its convincing sincerity. Purely on a physical level, Christopher Reeve *was* Superman; he'd bulked up for the role, of course, but there was something else, something about his otherworldly blue eyes, his dignity and poise, and the set of his chiselled jaw that seemed to embody the Platonic Superman and inspire immediate trust. Other actors, before and after him, might have played Superman, but Reeve somehow became the definitive embodiment of the character, possessed, enthused as it were, by his spirit and likeness. By prioritizing Clark Kent's pastoral youth and foregrounding his relationship with Margot Kidder's anorexic, coffee-fueled Lois Lane, the movie transformed the comic book superhero into an American folk story that could play to a grown-up mainstream film audience without mocking or alienating the enthusiasts.

The sequel, aptly entitled *Superman II,* managed to improve on the original when a gang of evil superpowered Kryptonian criminals led by Terence Stamp's Mephistophelean General Zod began their three-man invasion of Earth by targeting a small dirt-road dustbowl town. It was an oddly unambitious way to begin the conquest of the human race, but things livened up when the Kryptonian villains made their way to Metropolis, setting the stage for a battle of titans, which, for the first time onscreen, actually played like the kind of over-the-top property-pulverizing skirmishes Jack Kirby had popularized, and which comics had, until now, specialized in. As sneering superfascists tossed buses and cars around like snowballs, or were themselves hurled through exploding billboards, their pyrotechnic displays of superhuman might and majesty were a demonstration of just how close movie special effects might come to duplicating and surpassing the scope and spectacle of the comics.

The tendency toward gags and slapstick that diluted Hackman's portrayal of Luthor was pushed center stage in *Superman III,* which cast the incendiary comedian Richard Pryor as a blundering ingenue tricked by evil business interests into the near-murder of the Man of Steel. Casting a supercomputer as the story's climactic villain just prior to the dawn of the Information Age was an effective callback to Superman's Luddite roots, but it left him with very little to hit. The filmmakers dealt with the oversight by inserting a scene in which Superman is separated like Jekyll and Hyde into a good Clark Kent (still with his super powers, inexplicably) and an evil unshaven Superman for a pivotal but not entirely logical throw down in a junkyard setting—a prophetic glimpse at where this series would soon be headed.

By the time of *Superman IV: The Quest for Peace,* the reigns of production had been handed to the budget-conscious Menahem Golan and Yoram Globus who made sure all the wheels came off the trolley in a shoddy and mercifully forgettable symbolic punch-up pic that pit Superman against a sparkly, blond-maned Aryan superrobot called Nuclear Man, as an alleged show of support for the disarmament movement.

Contributing to its low-rent home-movie allure, much of *Superman IV* was filmed in England, specifically within the environs of the architec- turally planned "new town" Milton Keynes, which was, in somewhat demanding fashion, expected to understudy for the soaring midtown skyscrapers and teeming avenues of Metropolis. This was like asking a ladies handbag to pass for Macy's department store. With its broad empty thoroughfares and low-roofed pre-fab circuit-board perspectives, Milton Keynes looked more like a hastily assembled business park than the City of Tomorrow. The drab vistas of the British motorway system, with its polite hedgerows and austere median strips, were poor substitutes for the highways and turnpikes of the urban USA, and the attempts of the direc- tor to prove otherwise invited incredulous mockery. Only diehards were watching now anyway, but Reeve had already left an indelible mark and a classic performance. Cruelly, the actor was paralyzed from the neck down in a horse-riding accident in 1995. Reeve remained active as a campaigner and lobbyist for the rights of the disabled to new and sometimes contro- versial medical treatments until his untimely death in 2004. His image became the official contemporary look of the DC comics Superman when artist Gary Frank redesigned the character using the actor's distinc- tive build and features as a basis. The admirable Christopher Reeve may have left the building, but his clear, honest, and unsmirking portrayal of the archetypal, unconditionally "good" superhero is likely to remain an onscreen standard.

KURT BUSIEK AND ASTRO CITY

The postmodern appropriation and rebranding that characterized the relationship of many Image heroes to their predecessors was a notable aspect of Kurt Busiek's *Astro City* (Image Comics, 1995), a still-running experiment in growing and sustaining a long-term superhero universe. Set in and around a scrupulously imagined fictional city that's been home to generations of superheroes and other remarkable beings, *Astro City* is the perfect simulacrum of the simulacrum; a fully thought-out sand-box world born complete with its own detailed alternate histories, its ready- made continuities, artfully compiled to resemble the natural bricolage of

DC and Marvel. What makes *Astro City* even more exceptional is its creative team, which has remained the same since the title's launch almost twenty years ago. Imagine a beloved band, producing music of sustained and unvaryingly high quality, year after year, through sickness and in health, and you have some far-off flavor of this massive project's steadfast, dependable charm.

Writer Kurt Busiek processed the world-building experiments of the Image founders through his own famously systematic and thorough understanding of the mechanics of Marvel and DC continuity, before constructing an entire miniature universe with one mighty Big Bang in *Astro City* no. 1. In a world of his own, a kind of Image for well-adjusted grown-ups, he could ask questions no one else was tackling in the comics. His characters were, like Liefeld's, inspired by existing superhero trademark properties, but Busiek approached the task with an immense creativity and attention to minutiae that endowed creations like Superman stand-in Samaritan, or Fantastic Four substitutes the First Family, with such unique quirks, complex inner lives, and rounded personalities that they rapidly transcended their sources. Busiek's mastery of the single-issue complete short story form allowed him to build up the rich texture of his imaginary territory by shining the spotlight on a new protagonist, a new theme, each month. One issue might feature the bittersweet reminiscences of an elderly crime fighter, the next could lead with a queasy existential horror story worthy of Philip K. Dick, about a do-gooding android beauty with a memory reset button. Busiek and his collaborators assembled their universe as a collage, a jigsaw, a mosaic that accumulated span and connectivity with each new added facet, lending *Astro City* a sparky unpredictability to balance its calm, literate authorial voice and the comfort factor of the series' relentlessly reliable creative team.

Alongside his co-creators, artist Brent Anderson and cover painter/character designer Alex Ross, Busiek made his increasingly fine-grained virtual world a space in which to explore the energetic clash of the epic and mundane: what would life be like for a defence lawyer in a world where people could turn invisible or travel in time? How would it feel to be a superhero's girlfriend or to lose a loved one down the cracks of fractured space-time during a cosmic crisis? What was everyday lowlife like for a henchman in the pay of a flamboyant master-villain? The space wars, monster throw downs, and pulverizing team vs. team rumbles that took center stage in the typical superhero story, became noises off in *Astro City,* distant rumors of war glimpsed between clouds, TV reports playing out a chorus of wonder and *excelsis* behind the lives of the ordinary men and women, the citizens and visitors who remain at the heart of Astro City's unfolding history.

THE FUTURE OF SUPERHERO CINEMA

Green Lantern with its infinite intergalactic backdrop and expansive mythology had the potential to provide the superhero movie genre with its own *The Lord of the Rings,* but the stars failed to align with the tale of Hal Jordan, whose luminous brand of Silver Age science fiction tended to stress the credulity of audiences around the world beyond tolerable levels. Jordan, you may recall, was a test pilot inducted into an intergalactic police force by a dying alien. The chief weapon of the Green Lantern Corps of extraterrestrial lawmen is an emerald ring that converts the thoughts of its wearer into solid green objects of any size or shape. The ring is charged by holding it against the titular lantern and reciting a stirring oath in rhyming couplets. It's a lot for anyone to take in all at once.

Although both films were curiously similar in tone and general appearance, given the choice between DC's cocky space cop and a likably boneheaded rebel thunder god, audiences chose Marvel's cosmic-inflected *Thor* over *Green Lantern. Green Lantern* felt like too much of everything, all at once; a Roman banquet too overstuffed with the grotesque, too oblivious to its own childlike freakishness.

While DC's traditional second-tier heroes struggled to make an impact onscreen, Marvel characters continued to roll off the racks perfectly formed, with the engaging, old-school *Captain America: The First Avenger* and *X-Men: First Class,* which reunited the *Kick-Ass* team of screenwriter Jane Goldman and director Matthew Vaughan and relocated the X-Men to a chic fantasia of the Cold War/Bay of Pigs era of the early Marvel books. A lively contemporary energy and knowing humor neatly sidestepped the pitfalls that might have resulted in tedious and irrelevant period follies, and the Marvel movie machine rumbled on confidently, drawing the energy of the comics directly onto celluloid, and building bridges between franchises like the *Hulk*, *Thor*, *Iron Man*, and *Captain America* that were the first steps toward re-creating the entire Marvel universe onscreen as *The Avengers*. With a storyline indebted to some of Jack Kirby's outré concepts, like the reality-warping Cosmic Cube and his Asgardian technodeities, *The Avengers* may be the first summer blockbuster to accurately reconstruct the elevated hyperreality of a superhero team comic, paving the way for further excursions into even more outlandish territory.

A different approach to dressing the impossible in the rags of the real was suggested by Max Landis's unsettling "found footage" film *Chronicle*, which gave its teenage losers the powers of gods and trained an unflinching eye on the funny, then terrifying results. *The Dark Knight Rises* promises a bleak, operatic conclusion to Christopher Nolan's Batman trilogy. New Spider-Man and Wolverine movies are just around the corner, together with the long-awaited return of Superman, all striving for that sweet spot where the distinction between the things we know can't happen and the things that happen every day—just disappears.

ACKNOWLEDGMENTS

THANKS TO Jay Babcock, then editor of the counterculture magazine *Arthur* and a longtime friend, who got the ball rolling when he innocently suggested I should compile in a single book the interviews I'd done over the years on the subject of superheroes. It all sounded so easy until Peter McGuigan, my agent at Foundry Media, ventured that such a book might be enlivened by new and more biographical material, and I looked up one day to find myself writing a personal overview of the superhero concept from 1938 until the present day. Fifteen months into the book, which had, by that time, already doubled its original projected page count with no sign of stopping, and beset with a dozen other writing deadlines, I began to wonder why I'd ever agreed to this epic folly. Now that it's all over, I'm immensely grateful to Peter for talking me into it and selling the idea so effortlessly. Thanks also to Stephanié Abou, Hannah Gordon, and all at Foundry.

Thanks to Julie Grau and Cindy Spiegel at Spiegel and Grau for seeing the potential of *Supergods* and making me feel instantly welcome. My appreciation also goes out to my editors, Chris Jackson and Alex Bowler, and their teams, for such patient and sensitive sculpting of a sprawling, idiosyncratic text.

Thanks to DC Comics for the use of the images, and for decades of regular freelance work, too!

Big love to my wife, Kristan, who spent many days proofing the first edit, while thrashing out contracts and putting up with my hermitlike gloom during the lost summer of 2010. And to the cats, who kept me company all the way with their clever quips and dry repartee.

Thanks to my mum for the sci-fi and comic books, to my dad for providing me with the tools to express myself, and to both of them for their constant encouragement and the high value they placed on creativity and self-expression.

My deepest apologies to all the great comic-book writers and artists of yesterday and today whose contributions to the ongoing development of the superhero story would have made the final book three times as long if I'd included them all. I had to be selective with a few specific examples to illustrate each superhero "Age," and a great many of my favorite stories, characters, and creators were left out. If this book has done its job, however, I hope readers will be encouraged to make their own investigations into the secret history of the superheroes and their creators.

I suppose I should have suspected Superman hadn't quite finished with me. How could a book that set out to chart the journey of a solar superhero across a hundred years of sky fail to end on some profound image of circular symmetrical closure? It's not the sort of thing you can just manufacture. And yet, with only moments to spare before the deadline of the final edit, the Man of Tomorrow returned to my life with a wink.

In summer 2011, a newly invigorated regime at DC, spearheaded by Jim Lee, Dan Didio, and Geoff Johns, decided it was time to defy doom, gloom, and declining comic-book sales in a defiant flourish of bravado that would include the relaunch and reimagining of the company's most venerable titles and characters, including the Zeus, the Allfather, of superhero books, *Action Comics* itself.

The DC Comics makeover, with fifty-two new first issues and blank-slate restarts for almost all of the company's line successfully reinvigorated its fortunes as 2011 yielded to the ominous, apocalyptic 2012, the end of a cycle. With market share dominance for the first time in years over its old rivals at the House of Ideas, and DC titles dominating the top ten charts, seasonal shifts of creativity and canny marketing favor the older publisher for the time being, but Marvel is already gearing up to fight back with a juggernaut event entitled *Avengers versus X-Men*. Like their corporate custodians, the superheroes show no signs of giving up their skyscraping struggles. To survive, they are shedding once again their dried-out, inked-over skins to emerge as freshly silvered mirrors, repolished to reflect the dreams and fears of another new decade.

And so, along with other venerable titles like *Batman, Detective Comics,* and *Justice League, Action Comics* returned and began again in September 2011 with its first number one issue since 1938 and the debut of a new-look, T-shirt-and-jeans-wearing socialist Superman, redesigned and retooled for a contemporary audience. The artist was Rags Morales, of *Identity Crisis* fame, and the delighted writer of this once-in-a-lifetime opportunity to restart superhero history . . . would like to thank you all very much for reading *Supergods*.

SUGGESTED FURTHER READING

BOOKS ON COMICS

The Comic Book Heroes: The First History of Modern Comic Books—
From the Silver Age to the Present, *Gerard Jones and Will Jacobs*

Tales to Astonish: Jack Kirby, Stan Lee, and the American Book
Revolution, *Ronin Ro*

The Ten-Cent Plague: The Great Comic Book Scare and How It Changed
America, *David Hajdu*

Reading Comics: How Graphic Novels Work and What They Mean,
Douglas Wolk

The Silver Age of Comic Book Art, *Arlen Schumer*

Marvel: Five Fabulous Decades of the World's Greatest Comics, *Les Daniels*

DC Comics: Sixty Years of the World's Favorite Comic Book Heroes,
Les Daniels

Superman: The Complete History—The Life and Times of the Man of
Steel, *Les Daniels*

Batman: The Complete History, *Les Daniels*

Wonder Woman: The Complete History, *Les Daniels*

The Encyclopaedia of Superheroes, *Jeff Rovin*
The Encyclopaedia of Super Villains, *Jeff Rovin*
Encyclopedia of Comic Characters: Over 1200 Characters, *Dennis Gifford*
The World Encyclopedia of Comics, Volume 1, *Maurice Horn*

ESSENTIAL COLLECTED EDITIONS

This is by no means a comprehensive list of the best superhero comics available, but no one with any interest in the subject should miss these books. Each of them is an exemplar of its time. Modesty forbids me from adding any more of my own books, but obviously you should buy those first!

GOLDEN AGE

Superman Chronicles, Volumes 1–9, *various authors*
Batman Chronicles, Volumes 1–10, *various authors*
The Wonder Woman Chronicles, Volume 1, *William Moulton Marston and Charles Paris*
The Shazam! Archives, Volumes 1–4, *various authors*
Captain America: The Classic Years, Volumes 1 and 2, *Joe Simon and Jack Kirby*

SILVER AGE

Superman: Man of Tomorrow Archives, Volumes 1–2, *various authors*
The Flash Archives, Volumes 1–5, *John Broome and Carmine Infantino*
Marvel Masterworks: Fantastic Four, Volumes 1–12, *various authors*
Marvel Masterworks: The Amazing Spider-Man, *various authors*
Essential Avengers, Volumes 1–7, *Roy Thomas, John Buscema, and Neal Adams*
Jack Kirby's Fourth World Omnibus, Volumes 1–4, *Jack Kirby*
Jack Kirby's O.M.A.C.: One Man Army Corps, *Jack Kirby*
The Life of Captain Marvel, *Jim Starlin*

DARK AGE

Green Lantern/Green Arrow, Volumes 1–2, *Dennis O'Neil and Neal Adams*
Black Panther, *Don McGregor and Billy Graham*
Killraven, *Don McGregor and Craig Russell*
X-Men, *Chris Claremont and John Byrne*
Strange Days, *Peter Milligan, Brendan McCarthy, and Brett Ewins*
Marvelman, *Alan Moore*
Watchmen, *Alan Moore and Dave Gibbons*
Batman: The Dark Knight Returns, *Frank Miller*
Batman: Year One, *Frank Miller and David Mazzuchelli*
Daredevil: Born Again, *Frank Miller*
Zenith, *Grant Morrison and Steve Yeowell*
Batman: Arkham Asylum, *Grant Morrison and Dave McKean*
Rogan Gosh, *Peter Milligan and Brendan McCarthy*
Enigma, *Peter Milligan and Duncan Fegredo*
Marshal Law, *Pat Mills and Kevin O'Neill*
Astro City, *Kurt Busiek and Brent Anderson, with Alex Ross*
Spawn, *Todd McFarlane and various authors*

RENAISSANCE

Marvels, *Kurt Busiek and Alex Ross*
Kingdom Come, *Mark Waid and Alex Ross*
The Authority, *Warren Ellis and Bryan Hitch*
Planetary, *Warren Ellis and John Cassaday*
Marvel Boy, *Grant Morrison and J. G. Jones*
Wildcats Version 3.0, *Joe Casey and Sean Philips*
The League of Extraordinary Gentleman, *Alan Moore and Kevin O'Neill*
New X-Men, *Grant Morrison and various artists*
The Ultimates, *Mark Millar and Bryan Hitch*
Wanted, *Mark Millar and J. G. Jones*
Identity Crisis, *Brad Meltzer and Rags Morales*
Civil War, *Mark Millar and Steve McNiven*
All-Star Superman, *Grant Morrison and Frank Quitely*

ILLUSTRATION CREDITS

All interior images courtesy DC Comics.

INDEX

NOTE: Names of comic-book characters and superheroes are listed by their first names and/or titles. So you will find Clark Kent in the "C" section of the index, and Doctor Octopus in the "D's". Names of real humans follow the normal method of listing by their last names, so you will find Woody Allen in the "A" section.

PHOTO: © ALLAN AMATO

GRANT MORRISON is one of the most popular and acclaimed contemporary writers of any genre. His long list of credits as a comic-book writer include *JLA, New X-Men, Seven Soldiers, Animal Man, Doom Patrol, The Invisibles, We3, The Filth,* and *Batman: Arkham Asylum,* the bestselling original graphic novel of all time. He is also an award-winning playwright and screenwriter.